D0931102

THE CHINA MODEL

THE CHINA MODEL

Political Meritocracy and the Limits of Democracy

DANIEL A. BELL

Princeton University Press Princeton and Oxford

Published by Princeton University Press, 41 William Street,
Princeton, New Jersey 08540
In the United Kingdom: Princeton University Press, 6 Oxford Street,
Woodstock, Oxfordshire OX20 1TW

press.princeton.edu
Jacket photograph: A general view of the closing session of the
National People's Congress, at the Great Hall of the People on March 16, 2007.
Photograph © Andrew Wong/Getty Images.

Library of Congress Cataloging-in-Publication Data

Bell, Daniel (Daniel A.), 1964–
The China model : political meritocracy and the
limits of democracy / Daniel A. Bell.
pages cm
Includes bibliographical references and index.
ISBN 978-0-691-16645-2 (hardback)
1. Political culture—China. 2. Merit (Ethics)—Political aspects—China.
3. Political leadership—China. 4. Elite (Social sciences)—Political activity—
China. 5. Democracy—China. 6. China—Politics and government—
1976–2002. 7. China—Politics and government—2002– I. Title.
JQ1516.B45 2015
306.20951—dc23 2014044502

British Library Cataloging-in-Publication Data is available

This book has been composed in Electra LT Std

Printed on acid-free paper. ∞

Printed in the United States of America

1 3 5 7 9 10 8 6 4 2

To my Chinese mother and father

CONTENTS

ACKNOWLEDGMENTS

I should confess that there is not a single original idea in this book, except perhaps for the way ideas have been put together. I have relied on the kindness of both strangers and intimates to think through these ideas, and the product is a communal work (though I need to take final responsibility for what's written on the page). If I were to thank everyone who generously gave of their time, I'd have to add an additional page of notes on each page, thanking this or that person for nearly every idea in this book. Plus, I also need to confess that I've forgotten most of who said what. So let me offer thanks here, though I need to doubly apologize for my memory lapses because I'm sure I've forgotten some people.

Early drafts of chapters were presented and discussed in lectures, seminars, and workshops. I am grateful for the feedback of colleagues and students at the following institutions: Tsinghua University, Peking University, Shandong University, Renmin University, Wuhan University, National Taiwan University, Wesleyan University, Kenyon College, Harvard University, Stanford University, State University of New York at Buffalo, National University of Singapore, Nanyang Technological University, Sungkyunkwan University, the Seoul Institute, the Nordic Institute of Asian Studies (Copenhagen), University of Iceland, University of Greenland, University of Duisberg-Essen, Université de Montréal, and McGill University, as well as Unirule (Beijing), Intelligence Squared debate (Hong Kong), and annual meetings of Ideacity (Toronto), the World Economic Forum (Davos and Dalian), the Institute for New Economic Thinking (Hong Kong), the Asan forum (Seoul), and the American Political Science Association (Washington, D.C.).

Special thanks to Tan Sor-hoon and Terry Nardin for organizing sabbatical leave at the University of Singapore that allowed me to work on this book in an intellectually stimulating environment (and with unrestricted access to the Internet!). I am also grateful for the support of colleagues and friends at Tsinghua's Department of Philosophy and Schwarzman Scholars program. For (in)valuable research assistance, I thank Jia Peitao, Liu Yuhan, Sun Simeng, Wang Binfan, Wei Ran, Yuan Jingyan, and Zeng Rui. For meticulous copyediting, I thank Madeleine Adams, and for efficient help with production, Natalie Baan.

I thank the following friends and colleagues for helpful discussions and/or for providing material helpful to my research: Joseph Adler, Roger Ames, David Anderson, Yuen Ang, Steve Angle, Anthony Appiah, Timothy Garton Ash, Julien S. Bell, Thomas Bernstein, Ben Richard Kelsey Blumson, Cai Xianhui, James Caldwell, Mark Cameron, Gilles Campagnolo, Cao Feng, Ivan Cardillo, Kateri Carmola, Jennie Chen, Chen Lai, Chung-Ying Cheng, Siyao Cheng, Valerie Cher Goh May, Ja Ian Chong, Chien-min Chou, Chu Yun-han, Chua Beng-huat, Jon Chua, Jean-Marc Coicaud, Margaret Conley, Sam Crane, Cui Zhiyuan, Fred Dallmayr, Jørgen Delman, John Delury, Avner de-Shalit, Bruce Dickson, Doh Chull Shin, Els Van Dongen, Wolfgang Drechsler, Du Lun, Duan Demin, Prasenjit Duara, Peter Edwards, Yiran Elenaz, Mark Elliott, Amitai Etzioni, James Fallows, Fan Ruiping, Fang Fenglei, Fang Zhaohui, Paolo Farah, Allan Fels, Ann Florini, Edward Friedman, Francis Fukuyama, Gan Chunsong, Gan Yang, N. Ganesan, Mobo Gao, Nathan Gardels, Farah Godrej, A. Tom Grunfeld, Linyu Gu, Werner Gundel, Seref Ulug Guner, Hahm Chaibong, Ken Hammond, Han Sang-jin, Dag Hareide, He Baogang, Geir Helgesen, Tze-ki Hon, Huang Jing, Huang Yusheng, Michael Ignatieff, Bruce Jacobs, Martin Jacques, Kanishka Jayasuriya, Sivanathan Jheevanesh, Jiang Haibo, Jiang Qing, Kang Xiaoguang, Peter Katzenstein, John Keane, David Kelly, Parag Khanna, Sang-jun Kim, Sungmoon Kim, Leo Koguan, Kong Lindong, Kong Xinfeng, Chandran Kukathas, Kwa Chin Lum, Mean Luck Kwek, Martin Laflamme, Lee Chun-yi, Richard Levin, David Li Daokui, Li Qiang, Li Wanquan, Li

Yong, Liang Zhiping, Chong Ming Lim, Teng Leng Lim, Liu Chunrong, Liu Kang, Liu Wei, Susanne Lohr, Simon Long, Lu Feng, Lu Keli, Du Lun, Steve Macedo, Kishore Mahbubani, Philippe Major, Ian Malcolm, Margali Menant, Thaddeus Metz, Donald Moon, So Young Moon, Christopher Mosch, Guido Muehlemann, David Mulroney, Ng Han Wei, Van Hiep Nguyen, Joseph Nye, Leanne Ogasawara, Lynette Ong, Evan Osnos, Jeremy Paltiel, Pan Wei, Pasquale Pasquino, Randy Peerenboom, Peng Guoxiang, Jane Perlez, Philip Pettit, Ora-orn Poocharoen, Ethan Putterman, Qian Jiwei, Qin Hui, Gideon Rachman, M. Ramesh, Marie-Eve René, Sidney Rittenberg, Daan Roggeveen, Philippe C. Schmitter, Mark Schwartz, Orville Shell, Sheng Hong, Geir Sigurdsson, Neil Sinhababu, Billy So, Dorothy Solinger, Jaeyoon Song, Song Min, Kristin Stapleton, Andrew Stark, Su Jun, Anna Sun, Sun Hsiao-Li Shirley, Sun Zhe, Charles Brian Suresh, Michael Szonyi, Kevin Y. L. Tan, Tan Sek-loong, Fred Teng, Carsten Boyer Thøgersen, Tu Weiming, George E. Vaillant, Marius Vermaak, Michael Walzer, Wan Junren, Wang Hui, Juan Wang, Jun Wang, Kan Wang, Ken Wang, Wang Shaoguang, Wang Xuedian, Daniel Weinstock, Leif Wenar, Tang Wenming, Lynn White, Charles Wolf, Benjamin Wong, Reuben Wong, Wu Genyou, Wu Wanwei, Wu Yun, Xiao Geng, Hong Xiao, Xiao Wei, Xie Weihe, Xibai Xu, Alexander Yakobson, Yan Xuetong, David Yang, Yang Mu, Yang Ping, Yang Qianru, Yang Ruqin, Yang Xiao, Yao Xinzhong, George Yeo, Yvonne Ying, Yu Yongding, Yuan Yue, Zhang Feng, Lovis Zhang, Zhang Maoqi, Zhang Mei, Zhang Ming, Ning Zhang, Zhang Weiwei, Zhang Xudong, Zhang Yongle, Zheng Yongnian, and Qin Zhu. I should add that while I've learned from the views of the people named here, some will vehemently disagree with the normative orientation of the book.

I am particularly grateful to friends and colleagues who generously gave of their time to write comments on earlier drafts of chapters: Bai Tongdong, Gerald Chan, Joseph Chan, Chen Ruoyu, Cheng Xiaoxu, John Dryzek, Benjamin Elman, Émilie Frenkiel, Jean-Yves Heurtebise, P. J. Ivanhoe, Liu Yuhan, Richard William Miller, Paik Wooyeal, Graham Parkes, Qiu Feng, Sun Haiyan, Sun Yan, Kenneth Paul Tan, Melissa Williams, and Elena Ziliotti.

Last but not least, I am most grateful to: (1) my friends Ian Holliday, Robert Lawrence Kuhn, Li Chenyang, Yuri Pines, Qian Jiang, and

Matthias Risse, who wrote detailed comments on earlier drafts of the whole manuscript; (2) two referees for Princeton University Press, who wrote lengthy and constructive reports on an earlier draft; (3) my editor, Rob Tempio, for his support and insights (and for coming up with the title!); (4) Mo Yingchuan and Zhao Bingbing, for co-authoring the two online appendices to this book; (5) Nicolas Berggruen, for his commitment to the world of ideas; (6) Vice-Minister for the Environment Pan Yue, for inspiring discussions about Chinese culture and political reform; (7) Eric X. Li, for support of a workshop on political meritocracy and always stimulating conversation; (8) my family members in Canada, China, the United States, France, and Japan, who make the whole thing worthwhile; (9) my wife, Bing, who has shaped and refined my ideas more than anybody else; and (10) my Chinese mother Xue Yunjing and father Song Xiaolun, for their commitment to a beautiful family and a beautiful country. I dedicate this book to them.

THE CHINA MODEL

Introduction

In October 2013, a slick cartoon video of mysterious provenance went viral, with more than ten million viewings in two weeks.[1] The video, released at the time of the U.S federal government shutdown, contrasts the selection of leaders in different countries. It depicts the meteoric rise of President Barack Obama, aided by hundreds of millions of dollars in campaign financing, with victory coming in the form of a countrywide national election on the basis of one person, one vote. This process is labeled "democracy." It also depicts President Xi Jinping's decades-long ascent to the pinnacle of Chinese power: his promotions from leadership in a primary-level office to the township level, the county division, department levels, the province-ministry level, the Central Committee, the Politburo, and then the leading spot in the Standing Committee of the Politburo, with rigorous and ultra-competitive evaluations at each stage meant to test his political leadership abilities. This process is labeled "meritocracy." The clear implication of the video is that Chinese-style political meritocracy is a morally legitimate way of selecting top political leaders, perhaps even better than democratic elections.

The video was likely produced and distributed by a Chinese Communist Party (CCP) organ, but if political meritocracy is so good, why can't the CCP take responsibility for the video? More generally, why can't the CCP officially embrace political meritocracy and openly take pride in its meritocratic system? The main reason is that Chinese-style political meritocracy is imperfect in practice. But this leads to the question of what should be the moral standards for evaluating political progress (and regress) in a regime that aspires to be a political meritocracy? More questions come to mind. The video suggests that political meritocracy and electoral democracy are fundamentally incompatible political systems. But is it possible to reconcile the best of meritocratic and democratic practices, and if so, how? The video says nothing about China's harsh treatment of political opponents. If the system is so great, why is there a need to crack down on political dissent? Is it really possible to structure political meritocracy so that it is seen as legitimate by the people and avoids the abuses of authoritarian rule? My book is an attempt to answer such questions.

Political meritocracy is perhaps the most studied and the least studied topic in political theory. The idea that a political system should aim to select and promote leaders with superior ability and virtue is central to both Chinese and Western political theory and practice. The reason seems obvious: we demand trained and qualified persons in leadership positions in science, law, and corporations; why not also in the most important institution of all? As the distinguished American sociologist Daniel Bell (1919–2011) put it, "one wants men in political office who can govern well. The quality of life in any society is determined, in considerable measure, by the quality of leadership. A society that does not have its best men at the head of its leading institutions is a sociological and moral absurdity."[2] Hence, political thinkers—from Confucius, Plato, and Zhu Xi to John Stuart Mill, Sun Yat-sen, and Walter Lippmann—struggled to identify the ways of selecting the best possible leaders capable of making intelligent, morally informed political judgments on a wide range of issues.

But such debates largely stopped in the post–World War II era. In China, they stopped because Maoism valued the political contributions of warriors, workers, and farmers over those of intellectuals and educators. Whatever the top-down political reality, revolutionary leaders claimed they were building a new form of participatory socialist democracy from the ground up, and defenders of political elitism were nowhere to be seen (or publicly heard from) in mainland China. In the West, they stopped largely because of the intellectual hegemony of electoral democracy.[3] A democracy demands only that the people select their leaders; it is up to the voters to judge the merits of the candidates. If voters are rational and do a good job choosing leaders, there is no need to agonize too much over what ought to be the qualities of good leaders and which mechanisms can best select such leaders. Political theorists therefore shifted their interests to questions such as how to deepen democracy in politics and other spheres of social life and how to promote fair forms of wealth distribution in the nation and the world at large.

The debates over political meritocracy were revived in the tiny city-state of Singapore. Starting from the 1960s, the country's leaders advocated the institutionalization of mechanisms aimed at selecting leaders who were best qualified to lead, even if doing so meant imposing constraints on the democratic process. They argued that political leaders should take a long-term view rather than cater to electoral cycles, and the political system can and should be structured to prevent the exercise of power by short-term-minded "populist" political leaders. But Singapore's discourse on political meritocracy failed to gain much traction abroad, largely because it was not presented as a universal ideal. Rather, Singapore's leaders emphasized that the need to select and promote the most capable and upright people is particularly pressing in a tiny city-state with a small population, limited resource base, and potentially hostile neighbors. Hence, why debate the exportability of an ideal that is meant to fit only a highly unusual city-state?

But two recent developments put debates about political meritocracy back on the global map. For one thing, the crisis of governance in Western democracies has undermined blind faith in electoral democracy and opened the normative space for political alternatives. The problem is not just that democratic theorists came to realize the difficulties of implementing democratic practices outside the Western world; the deeper problem is that actually existing democracy in the Western world no longer sets a clear-cut positive model for other countries. In difficult economic times, for example, voters often select populist leaders who advocate policies inimical to the long-term good of the country, not to mention the rest of the world. Hence, innovative political thinkers argue that governance in Western democracies can be improved by incorporating more meritocratic institutions and practices.[4]

Equally important, the theory of political meritocracy has been reinvigorated by the rise of China. Since the early 1990s, China's political system has evolved a sophisticated and comprehensive system for selecting and promoting political talent that seems to have underpinned China's stunning economic success. Like earlier practices in imperial China, the political system aims to select and promote public servants by means of examinations and assessments of performance at lower levels of government. Chinese-style meritocracy is plagued with imperfections, but few would deny that the system has performed relatively well compared to democratic regimes of comparable size and level of economic development, not to mention family-run dictatorships in the Middle East and elsewhere. And the world is watching China's experiment with meritocracy. China, unlike Singapore, can "shake the world." In the early 1990s, nobody predicted that China's economy would rise so fast to become the world's second largest economy. In twenty years' time, perhaps we will be debating Chinese-style political meritocracy as an alternative model—and a challenge—to Western-style democracy.

Before saying more, let me clarify some terminology. My book is a defense of *political* meritocracy. Liberal democracies empower meritocratically selected experts in administrative and judicial positions, but they are accountable, if only indirectly, to democratically elected leaders.[5] They are meant to exercise power in a narrowly defined domain and should try to remain politically neutral to the extent possible. For example, British civil servants are meant to serve elected politicians and may need to set aside their own political views as they do so.[6] In contrast, political leaders in meritocracies such as China are meant to exercise political judgment in a wide range of domains. They hold the ultimate power in the political community (including control over the instruments of violence), like elected leaders in democracies. And there is no clear institutional distinction between civil servants and political leaders in a political meritocracy. In short, meritocratically selected public servants in democratic countries are not meant to be political, whereas meritocratically selected public servants in political meritocracies are meant to exercise political power.

It is also important to distinguish between political and economic meritocracy. In English, the term *meritocracy* can refer to a principle governing the distribution of economic resources:[7] meritocracy is a system that distributes wealth according to ability and effort rather than class or family background. Karl Marx criticized capitalism because it tends to distribute resources according to class background, notwithstanding the myth that people are rewarded mainly according to ability and effort. Communism aims to abolish class differences, and the distribution of resources in the immediate postcapitalist period ("lower communism") will translate capitalist rhetoric into reality: economic resources will be distributed according to the principle "from each according to his ability, to each according to his contribution." Although this seemingly meritocratic principle recognizes no class differences, it is still flawed because "it tacitly recognizes unequal individual endowment and thus productive capacity as natural privileges." That is, people should not benefit from unearned natural talent and it is unfair to penalize those who are less productive through no fault of their own. Hence, society should move on to "higher communism" so resources can be distributed according to the principle "from each according to his ability, to each according to his needs."[8]

John Rawls, the most influential political philosopher in the twentieth century, similarly recognized the danger that seemingly fair opportunity could lead to "a callous meritocratic society."[9] Being born with ability confers no moral right to wealth because what one is born with, or without, is not of one's own doing. Instead of distributing wealth on the basis of productive contribution, Rawls defends the "difference principle" that inequalities are allowed only if they benefit the least well-off. More surprisingly, perhaps, the world's most powerful central banker, then–Federal Reserve chairman Ben Bernanke, expressed a similar critique of meritocracy in a graduate address at Princeton University in 2013:

> A meritocracy is a system in which the people who are the luckiest in terms of their health and genetic endowment; luckiest in terms of family support, encouragement, and, probably, income; luckiest in terms of educational and career opportunities; and luckiest in so many ways difficult to enumerate: these are the people who reap the largest rewards. The only way for even a putative meritocracy to hope to pass ethical muster, to be considered fair, is if those who are the luckiest in all of those

> respects also have the greatest responsibility to work hard, to contribute to the betterment of the world, and to share their luck with others.[10]

I am sympathetic to these critiques of "meritocracy" as an economic system, but my aim here is not to defend a particular theory governing the distribution of material goods. My concern, to repeat, is to defend *political* meritocracy—the idea that political power should be distributed in accordance with ability and virtue—and I invoke arguments about the distribution of economic resources only insofar as they bear on the issue of how to establish a morally desirable and politically realistic form of political meritocracy (see chapter 1, section 2 and chapter 3, section 2).[11]

1. Outline of the Book

The idea that political leaders should be chosen according to one person, one vote is taken for granted in so many societies that any attempt to defend political meritocracy should begin with a critique of electoral democracy: most readers in Western societies won't even be willing to contemplate the possibility of morally justifiable alternatives to one person, one vote as a means of selecting political leaders, so a book arguing in favor of an alternative must at least raise some questions about democratic elections. Some philosophers have defended the rights to vote and run for office on the grounds that political liberties are intrinsically valuable for individuals whether or not they lead to collectively desirable consequences. These arguments, however, have been vigorously contested. And if the aim is to promote electoral democracy in China, arguments for democracy appealing to the intrinsic value of voting will not be very effective because political surveys consistently show that citizens in East Asian societies understand democracy in substantive rather than procedural terms: that is, they tend to value democracy because of its positive consequences rather than valuing democratic procedures per se. So the politically relevant question is whether democratic elections lead to good consequences. Democracy has had a good track record over the past few decades: rich, stable, and free countries are all democratic. But democracies also have key flaws that may spell political trouble in the future, and it is at least arguable that political meritocracies can minimize such problems.

Chapter 1 discusses four key flaws of democracy understood in the minimal sense of free and fair elections for the country's top rulers, and each flaw is followed by a discussion of theoretical and real meritocratic alternatives. The first flaw is "the tyranny of the majority": irrational and self-interested majorities acting through the democratic process can use their power to oppress minorities and enact bad policies. Examinations that test for voter competence can help to remedy this flaw in theory, and Singapore's political meritocracy is a practicable alternative. The second flaw is "the tyranny of the minority": small groups with economic power exert disproportionate influence on the political process, either blocking change that's in the common interest or lobbying for policies that benefit only their own interest. In theory, this flaw can be remedied by means of a citizen body that excludes wealthy elites, and China's political system is a practicable alternative. The third flaw is "the tyranny of the voting community": if there is a serious conflict of interest between the needs of voters and the needs of nonvoters affected by the policies of government such as future generations and foreigners, the former will almost always have priority. One theoretical remedy is a government office charged with the task of representing the interests of future generations, and Singapore's institution of a president with the power to veto attempts by politicians to enact policies that harm the interests of future generations is a practicable alternative. The fourth flaw is "the tyranny of competitive individualists": electoral democracy can exacerbate rather than alleviate social conflict and disadvantage those who prefer harmonious ways of resolving social conflict. A system based on consensus as a decision-making procedure can help to remedy this flaw, and China's political model has some practical advantages in terms of reducing social conflict.

In short, there may be morally desirable and political feasible alternatives to electoral democracy that help to remedy the major disadvantages of electoral democracy. If the aim is to argue for political meritocracy in a Chinese context, however, we do not need to defend the strong claim that political meritocracy consistently leads to better consequences than electoral democracy. We can simply assume that China's one-party political system is not about to collapse and argue for improvements on that basis.[12] Chapter 2 proceeds on the following assumptions: (1) it is good for a political community to be governed by high-quality rulers; (2) China's one (ruling) party political system is not about to collapse;[13] (3) the meritocratic aspect of the system is partly good; and (4) it can be improved. On the basis of these assumptions, I draw on social science, history, and philosophy to put forward suggestions about which qualities matter most for political leaders in the context of large, peaceful, and modernizing (nondemocratic) meritocratic states, followed by suggestions about mechanisms that increase the likelihood of selecting leaders with such qualities. My findings about which abilities, social skills, and virtues matter most for political leaders in the context of a large, peaceful, and modernizing political meritocracy are then used as a standard for evaluating China's actually existing meritocratic system. My conclusion is that China can and should improve its meritocratic system: it needs exams that more effectively test for politically relevant intellectual abilities, more women in leadership positions to increase the likelihood that leaders have the social skills required for effective policy making, and more systematic use of a peer-review system to promote political officials motivated by the desire to serve the public.

Any defense of political meritocracy needs to address not only the question of how to maximize the advantages of the system but also how to minimize its disadvantages. Chapter 3 discusses three key problems associated with any attempt to implement political meritocracy: (1) rulers chosen on the basis of their superior ability are likely to abuse their power; (2) political hierarchies may become frozen and undermine social mobility; and (3) it is difficult to legitimize the system to those outside the power structure. Given that electoral democracy at the top is not politically realistic in China, I ask if it is possible to address these problems without democratic elections. The problem of corruption can be addressed by mechanisms such as independent supervisory institutions, higher salaries, and improved moral education. The problem of ossification of hierarchies can be addressed by means of a humble political discourse, opening the ruling party to diverse social groups, and allowing for the possibility of different kinds of political leaders selected according to new ideas of political merit. The problem of legitimacy, however, can be addressed only by means of more opportunities for political participation, including some form of explicit consent by the people. The question, therefore, is how to reconcile political meritocracy and democracy. Can it be done in morally desirable ways without multiparty competition and free and fair elections for top leaders?

Chapter 4 discusses the pros and cons of different models of "democratic meritocracy": more specifically, models that aim to reconcile a meritocratic mechanism designed to select superior political leaders with a democratic mechanism designed to let the people choose their leaders. The first model combines democracy and meritocracy at the level of the voter (e.g., allocating extra votes to educated voters), but such proposals, whatever their philosophical merit, are not politically realistic. The second (horizontal) model aims to reconcile democracy and meritocracy at the level of central political institutions, but such a model will be almost impossible to implement and sustain even in a political culture (such as China's) that strongly values political meritocracy. The third (vertical) model aims to combine political meritocracy at the level of the central government and democracy at the local level. This model is not a radical departure from the political reality in China and it can also be defended on philosophical grounds.

The political model in China, however, is not simply democracy at the bottom and meritocracy at the top: it is also based on extensive and systematic experimentation in between the lowest and highest levels of government. The concluding chapter sketches out three basic planks of the China model and shows how political reform in the post-Mao era has been guided by the principles of "democracy at the bottom, experimentation in the middle, and meritocracy at the top." There remains a large gap between the ideal and the reality, however, and I suggest ways of closing that gap. The legitimacy problem is perhaps the most serious threat to the meritocratic system. At some point, the Chinese government may need to secure the people's consent to the Chinese adaptation of vertical democratic meritocracy by means such as a referendum. The chapter ends with remarks about the exportability of the China model: while the model as a whole cannot readily be adopted by countries with a different history and culture, different planks of the model can be selectively adopted and the Chinese government can play a more active role promoting its model abroad.

This book's central area of concern is the question of how to maximize the advantages and minimize the disadvantages of a political system that aims to select and promote political leaders of superior virtue and ability, particularly in the contemporary Chinese context. Other than arguing for the need to enact policies that benefit the people, I have been deliberately vague about what those leaders should do: China is a large, complex country with different needs and priorities in different times and places, and any informed answer needs to be partly based on what the Chinese people actually want. That said, some general guidance may be helpful and the book includes two appendixes published online at http://press.princeton.edu/titles/10418.html. The first appendix is a Harmony Index that ranks countries according to how well they do at promoting four different types of social relations characterized by peaceful order and respect for diversity. This kind of index, either in part or in whole, can be used to judge social progress (and regress) in China and elsewhere. Another possible use of the Harmony Index more specific to the Chinese context is that it can be considered as a standard to judge the performance of political officials for purposes of promotion (or demotion), especially given the widespread consensus that economic growth can no longer be used as the sole indicator of good performance.

The second appendix is a real political dialogue (carried out in person and via email) with a political official in the CCP. My own ethical commitments are largely inspired by Confucian values, but I do not think that Confucianism is the only way to justify political meritocracy, so I have not been too explicit about the empirical and normative relevance of Confucianism in this book. Still, Confucianism can influence how one thinks about political meritocracy, and the second appendix focuses more directly on the role of Confucianism in shaping China's political meritocracy. The dialogue is a rare window into the views of an erudite CCP official who is speaking in a private capacity. The appendix is titled "A Conversation between a Confucian and a Communist," but by the end of the dialogue it will not be clear who's who.

2. A Note on Method

Notwithstanding the importance of the topic, there is a dearth of contemporary political theorizing about political meritocracy (in contrast, there are thousands of books about democratic theory). So the main research for this book involved extensive reading in the social sciences, philosophy, and history (in English, Chinese, and French), and trying to put together a book out of material that does not always (or even usually) bear directly on the topic. Equally if not more important, I have benefitted from exchanges with people who helped me to make sense of the theory and practice of political meritocracy. In a (selfish?) effort to help further my own thinking, I coorganized two conferences with leading philosophers, historians, and social scientists that examined the rise (or revival) of political meritocracy and what it will mean for political developments in China and the rest of the world. The first (English-language) conference, coorganized with Chenyang Li, took place at Nanyang Technological University (Singapore) in January 2012 and led to the publication of an edited volume (coedited with Chenyang Li) titled *The East Asian Challenge for Democracy: Political Meritocracy in Comparative Perspective* (Cambridge: Cambridge University Press, 2013). The second (Chinese-language) conference, coorganized with the Department of Philosophy at Tsinghua University and the Equinox (*Chunqiu*) Institute in Shanghai, took place at Tsinghua University in October 2012 and led to the publication of a special issue of *Wenshizhe* in March 2013. I have benefitted tremendously from the intellectual exchanges at these two conferences. I have also benefitted from interviews with political leaders in China and Singapore. I am grateful to several academic friends who generously took time to comment on earlier drafts of this book. Last but not least, I have assigned readings on political meritocracy (including, I confess, my own half-worked-out ideas) to students at Tsinghua University (Beijing), Shanghai Jiaotong University, and the National University of Singapore over the past few years and have benefitted much from their criticisms and suggestions for improvement. I am particularly grateful to graduate students in the Department of Philosophy at the National University of Singapore who organized an informal reading group to comment on an earlier draft of this book: I hope you will judge this book to have been improved as a result of your critiques!

3. A Note on Motivation

Why do I care about this topic? I developed an interest in political meritocracy as a result of engagement with the Confucian tradition, and my earlier writings on political meritocracy tended to be inspired more by Confucian philosophy than by actual politics. Over the past few years, I came to realize that China's political system has meritocratic characteristics, if only because my own high-achieving students at Tsinghua University were being increasingly recruited in the CCP. Clearly it made sense to relate philosophizing about political meritocracy more directly to the political reality of China. I realized that I had stumbled onto something of political importance and wrote some op-eds in leading media outlets in China and the West. However, I was ruthlessly savaged by critics, accused of being everything from an apologist for the CCP to an agent for Goldman Sachs (my wife's employer).[14] Hence, I realized the need to write a book with more detailed and nuanced argumentation, filled with the usual academic qualifications and notes (all the while trying to write in as accessible a manner as possible). I'm not sure if I've succeeded, but I've done my best during the course of a self-imposed five-year plan.

It's also worth asking why I'm publishing a book that seems mainly about China with an American academic publisher. One reason is that I write in English.[15] But this book will likely be translated into Chinese and I hope that it will have an impact in China; the mechanics of how the political system works will be familiar to Chinese readers, but the book may contribute to more discussion of appropriate standards for judging political progress (and regress). I also hope the book can be read in English-speaking countries to promote better understanding of political meritocracy as an ideal and the Chinese political system as a reality, and perhaps even to inspire meritocratic reform in democratic countries.[16] At the very least, Western readers may benefit by being given Chinese perspectives on topics they usually take for granted: I would not have written this book without a decade's experience living and teaching in Beijing, and perhaps I would have been shocked by some of my own arguments had I read them two decades ago. But the truth is that my political views are quite middle-of-the-road among academics living and working in China.[17] This book is not meant to be provocative or contrarian, even if it may be viewed as such by Western readers. Notwithstanding more legally protected freedom of speech in Western countries, there is much better understanding of Western-style democracy in China than of Chinese-style meritocracy in the West, and my book is meant provide some symmetry. I look forward to the day when Westerners and Chinese can have informed debates about politics without deep ideological fissures or cultural misunderstandings, and if I can contribute a tiny bit to making that day a reality, I can go to bed a happy man.

CHAPTER 1
Is Democracy the Least Bad Political System?

It is a truism that modern Western societies are pluralistic. We argue about everything and agree, it seems, about nothing. Actually, we do agree about one thing: that we should choose our political leaders by means of one person, one vote.[1] Electoral democracy has assumed almost sacred status in modern Western societies. We can question faith in God without being accused of having lost our moral compass, but the same tolerance is not extended to those who question faith in one person, one vote; almost inevitably, they are tarred with the brush of being apologists for "bad" authoritarian regimes.

Plus, we agree that electoral democracy is a universal political good. It is good not only for us, but for the rest of the world. Hence, when "bad" authoritarian regimes fall, they are supposed to be replaced by a form of government chosen by means of one person, one vote. Hardly anyone contemplates an alternative. From a normative point of view, democracy is seen as the best possible political regime. More precisely, it is a necessary condition for the best possible regime. Free and fair elections for political leaders need to be supplemented by other political goods—and here there are endless disputes about what those goods should be (civil society, social justice, democracy in the workplace, forums for deliberation, additional ways of monitoring power,[2] etc.)—but we agree that those goods (whatever they are) should be implemented on a foundation of electoral democracy.

That said, political "realists" warn us that democracy cannot readily be established in poor, developing countries. In his 1968 work *Political Order in Changing Societies*,[3] Samuel Huntington controversially argued that political order was necessary for economic and social development. Premature increases in political participation—including early elections—could destabilize fragile political systems in the developing world. Hence, a modernizing dictatorship that provides political order, the rule of law, and the conditions for successful economic and social development may be necessary. Still, Huntington did not mean to justify dictatorship as a permanent arrangement. Once the building blocks are in place, then the time is ripe for democracy and further delays are not justified from a moral point of view.

In other words, the dispute between "idealists" and "realists" is primarily a dispute about timing; neither side means to question the ideal of electoral democracy. Ethnic warfare, crippling poverty, pervasive corruption, and lack of education may pose obstacles to the successful establishment and consolidation of democracy, but they are seen as unfortunate (we hope temporary) afflictions that delay what Francis Fukuyama (Huntington's student) called the "end of history," when democracy has finally triumphed over its rivals. It is widely assumed that democracy is something that all rational individuals would want if they could get it.

Surprisingly, perhaps, the view that electoral democracy is the best possible political regime is commonly (but far from unanimously) held in China as well. Whatever we hear about "civilizational differences" between China and the West, many Chinese political thinkers share the view that democracy is the best possible political system. It is dangerous to organize a movement for the implementation of multiparty competitive elections in China—that's what landed Liu Xiaobo in jail—but Chinese political thinkers can and do argue for electoral democracy as an ideal in academic publications. An often-heard argument among Chinese intellectuals is that democracy should not be implemented now because of the prevalence of "low-quality" Chinese farmers, but democracy will become more viable once Chinese people become more educated and urbanized.[4] The political reformer Yu Keping famously authored an essay titled *Democracy Is a Good Thing* and has called for more electoral competition at different levels of government.[5] Yu Chongqing argues that the fundamental building block of democracy is multicandidate competitive elections—whether at the local or the central level of government—and it is meaningless to talk about other forms of democracy (such as intraparty democracy, democratic deliberation, or local-level democracy) without this foundation.[6] More cautiously, Ma Ling argues that the immediate task in China is to implement "democratic supervision," but he goes on to say that it should be followed by democratic elections.[7] Here too, the dispute is less about the desirability than about the timing of electoral democracy.[8]

On the face of it, it is hard to understand why electoral democracy came to have such widespread appeal. For one thing, the practice of choosing a country's top leaders by means of free and fair competitive elections has had a relatively short history (less than a century in most countries, compared to, say, thirteen hundred years for China's examination system).[9] Like any other political system, it has advantages and disadvantages, and it seems too soon to affirm that it's the best system of all time for all time. More fundamentally, it seems peculiar to take an almost unquestioned stance in favor of a system that does not require experience (and expertise) for leadership. There are many ways of exercising power—in workplaces, schools, hospitals, prisons, and so on—and the natural assumption is that prior experience is necessary for the exercise of power by top leaders. No corporation or university would pick a top leader without substantial leadership experience of some sort, preferably in the same field.[10] Yet *political* power is an exception: it's fine to pick a leader with no prior political experience, so long as he or she has been chosen on the basis of one person, one vote.

So why exactly did we come to believe that electoral democracy is a necessary foundation for a morally desirable political system? Few people have the time and motivation to read the debates in political science journals,[11] so the key explanation cannot be the result of reflective endorsements of arguments in the academic literature.[12] The value placed on equal voting rights may be a result of prolonged political struggles by (formerly) marginalized sectors of the political community, such as women and minority groups.[13] Another reason may be the growing significance of national identities in the twentieth century: as more and more people think of their prime identities as tied to their nation, they come to value the equal right of participating in national politics as key to human dignity. Another reason may be the economic, political, and ideological hegemony of the United States in the post–World War II period, especially since the collapse of the Soviet bloc. The United States promotes electoral democracy as the "only game in town," and the rest of the world sits up and listens. To paraphrase Karl Marx, the ideas of the ruling country are the ruling ideas. Perhaps the idea that we are equal in the eyes of God became transmuted into the idea that we are political equals in the eyes of the government,[14] and the idea that we are political equals then became translated in the popular mind into the (mistaken) belief that political equality must take the form of one person, one vote.[15] There is something about the act of voting that confers an experience of psychological power: I come to feel that I have a say in choosing my ruler (even if my vote does not make any difference), and I come to treasure the right to vote, a sense of empowerment that may also extend to other areas of social life.[16] Any attempts to modify or abolish one person, one vote will be intensely controversial because those deprived of an equal vote will feel that they are "losers" and officially labeled as inferior in terms of the capacity to make informed political judgments.[17] Perhaps the idea of choosing leaders by means of competitive elections is easy to understand and implement. And maybe voting is a communal ritual that produces and reinforces a sense of civic solidarity for the people involved: we feel part of a community when we vote. Most likely, different combinations of these factors operate to different degrees in different contexts.[18]

Whatever the history and the psychological mechanisms that underpin support for voting, it is worth asking if the arguments for electoral democracy are morally defensible. Philosophers tend to distinguish between two sorts of arguments for democracy. Some philosophers argue that the rights to vote and run for political office are intrinsically valuable for individuals whether or not they lead to collectively desirable consequences: democratic procedures such as the equal right to vote and majority decision making express intrinsically valuable goods such as equality, fairness, dignity, autonomy, participation, solidarity, and mutual trust, which do not depend on desirable consequences for their moral power.[19] But such arguments have been vigorously contested,[20] and the leading Anglo-American philosophers from J. S. Mill to John Rawls and Ronald Dworkin tend to defend political equality in the form of one person, one vote on instrumental grounds.[21] And if the aim is to promote electoral democracy in China, arguments for democracy appealing to the intrinsic value of voting will not be very effective because political surveys show that citizens in East Asian societies typically understand democracy in substantive rather than procedural terms:[22] that is, they tend to value democracy because of its positive consequences rather than valuing democratic procedures per se.

So the politically relevant question is whether democratic elections lead to good consequences. The prodemocracy case in terms of consequences is perhaps best captured by Winston Churchill's famous quip: "Democracy is the worst form of government, except for all those other forms that have been tried from time to time." This quotation is endlessly trotted out as a defense of democracy, more often than not as a way of silencing debate about the pros and cons of democracy.[23] Whatever the flaws of democracy, other alternatives are even worse, so let's not push too hard to undermine our faith in democracy. Even the harshest contemporary philosophical critic of the right to vote in the Western world affirms (without any empirical evidence) that "democracy performs better, even with low voter participation, than its competitors (oligarchy, etc.) do."[24]

But is democracy really the least bad system? True, the two major political alternatives in Churchill's day—Nazism and Soviet-style communism—have been (rightly) consigned to the dustbin of history. But the case for democracy as the least bad regime is not so clear if the alternative is political meritocracy as it has been practiced in the modern world. Consider the two most seemingly iron-clad consequentialist arguments in favor of democracy: (1) Amartya Sen's argument that famines do not occur in democracies,[25] and (2) the argument that democracies do not go to war against one another.[26] Without questioning the validity of such arguments, it is worth noting that they also hold true in two nondemocratic countries—China and Singapore—since they have consciously implemented meritocratic reforms designed to improve the quality of political leadership (starting from the mid-1960s in Singapore and the early 1980s in China). Singapore has achieved a stunning

economic miracle and has not gone to war since independence in 1965. In the case of China, not only has it eradicated famine, it also has a much better record on malnutrition than, say, democratic India.[27] And China's last full-scale war was with Vietnam in 1979.[28] Still, I do not mean to question the point that democracies have the best record overall compared to other forms of government in the past. What I do mean to question is the idea that democracies will continue to perform better than political meritocracies on key indicators of good government in the foreseeable future.

Hence, in this chapter I will discuss some standards of good government that should not be too controversial—voters should do their best to select wise leaders, the government should try to structure the economy so that the benefits do not accrue only (or mainly) to a small group of rich people, leaders should not enact policies that wreck the environment for future generations, and the political system should not poison social relations and unduly penalize those who seek harmonious ways of resolving conflict—and ask if there are meritocratic alternatives, both in theory and practice, that produce better (or less bad) consequences than democracies. My aim here is simply to cast doubt on the idea that one person, one vote is the least bad way of choosing leaders to enact good policies, not to provide a comprehensive defense of political meritocracy as an alternative to electoral democracy. In other words, I seek only to establish that the consequentialist case for democracy is not so straightforward. Once we "desacralize" democracy, then we can proceed to discuss the advantages and disadvantages of political meritocracy with a more open mind.

To make my case harder, however, I want to emphasize that my target will be free and fair competitive elections (or the kinds of elections that would be endorsed by the Carter Center).[29] The political economist Paul Collier has written a grim book on democracy in poor, ethnically divided countries (the "bottom billion"). Over the past two decades or so, high-income countries have actively promoted democracy across the low-income world, with the result that democracy *increased* political violence. But elections in the poorest countries tend to be characterized by bribery, the intimidation of voters, exclusion of strong candidates, and miscounting votes; in other words, the elections are not free and fair.[30] It would be too easy (from a theoretical point of view) to criticize flawed elections, so I will criticize the main flaws of free and fair elections.

And to make my case even harder, I will draw most of my examples from the most powerful and influential democracy in modern times: the United States.[31] Given that my book is mainly written with the Chinese context in mind, it might make more sense to compare China with democratic countries such as India and Indonesia, which are closer to China in terms of GDP per capita and population (in the case of India). It would not be a big challenge to point to widespread malnutrition in India or corruption in Indonesia to show the superiority of the Chinese political system in terms of delivering benefits that the population cares about. But I draw most of my examples from the United States for the following reasons: (1) there is an extensive academic literature on the pros and cons of the American political system, and (2) most Chinese intellectuals and reformers typically compare their system to the American political system on the (implicit) assumption it should set the standard for evaluating China's political future.[32]

To make my case that there are desirable (or less bad) alternatives to democracy, I need to argue for alternatives that conflict with the practice of free and fair competitive elections. It will not suffice to argue for meritocratic institutions within an overall democratic context, such as the Supreme Court, the Federal Reserve, and the military in the United States or the civil service in the United Kingdom. These institutions can exercise power only in a restricted domain and are ultimately accountable and subordinate to democratically elected politicians; they are meant to supplement, rather than pose alternatives to, electoral democracy.[33] In other words, I need to argue for political proposals and institutions composed of leaders not chosen by means of free and fair elections (one person, one vote) with the power to debate and decide on a wide range of issues affecting the political community in ways that can override the decisions of democratically elected leaders.

In this chapter, I will discuss four key problems with electoral democracy: the tyranny of the majority, the tyranny of the minority, the tyranny of the voting community, and the tyranny of competitive individualists. Criticisms of democracy have a long history—from Plato onward—but I will focus mainly on key drawbacks of electoral democracies today.[34] Following a discussion of each drawback, I will argue for theoretical alternatives to electoral democracy that do better (or less badly) than actually existing democracies. However, it seems unfair to compare the flaws of actually existing democracies with as-yet-unrealized theoretical alternatives, so I will end each section by discussing examples of actually existing political meritocratic arrangements in China and/or Singapore that may minimize the flaws of electoral democracies.

1. The Tyranny of the Majority

In an electoral democracy, voting power translates into political power. Perhaps the most common criticism of democracy is that the majority of voters can use their power to oppress the rest. For Plato, rule of the "many" meant that simple-minded citizens can easily be swayed by the emotive arguments of demagogues (or Sophists), leading to injustices such as the death penalty for his teacher Socrates. In *The Republic*, Plato defended the idea that a minority of moral experts should rule. Just as a ship should be captained by a trained and competent expert, so the leaders of political communities should be trained in the philosophy of how to rule in a just way and serve at lower levels of government before they are put in command of the whole. Plato's student Aristotle held that since most men pursue the useful and not the good, citizens should be those with virtue and ability; hence citizenship should be restricted to elites with sufficient free time to seek the good life. The phrase *tyranny of the majority* was popularized by the nineteenth-century British philosopher J. S. Mill, who worried that irrational and self-interested majorities acting through the democratic process could use their power to oppress minorities and enact bad policies.

In the twentieth century, however, liberal democracies consolidated constitutional restraints on majority rule, and liberal democracies typically protect minority groups and unpopular individuals from gross abuses of human rights. The progress did not always (or even usually) come about as a result of enlightened views about the need for mutual respect between groups—Michael Mann argues that the idea of rule by the people has often defined "the people" as the dominant ethnic group, generating organic conceptions of the nation and the state that encouraged the murderous cleansing of minorities so as to produce many monoethnic citizen bodies in the present, a process that has finished passing through the North and is now engulfing parts of the South[35]—but it is hard to argue against the claim that wealthy, consolidated liberal democracies now better protect individuals and minority groups from gross abuses of human rights than other forms of government. The problem, however, is that the majority of voters in electoral democracies, including rich and wealthy liberal democracies, do not perform well in selecting political leaders with the motivation and ability to enact wise policies in areas such as economics and science. In Chinese terms, this means that voters in "advanced" democracies are also "low-quality"; lack of political competence is a feature not just of Chinese farmers. Let's review some evidence for this criticism, followed by suggestions for improvement and comparisons with political meritocracies.

The original democracy—ancient Athens—treated citizens as equals, but slaves and women (the majority) were excluded from citizenship. Aristotle put forward dubious arguments on behalf of their exclusion—women and slaves were said to be naturally inferior and thus presumably must be ruled despotically. Aristotle did, however, hold out the possibility that slaves could be freed, thus suggesting that slavery need not be a permanent state.[36] Even "natural inferiors" could be educated, with the exception of those with undeveloped mental capacities similar to mentally handicapped people in the modern world. Today, it is widely recognized that there are differences in innate intelligence; not everyone can be Einstein, and professors and human resource officers often compare the intelligence of others, assuming that differences will emerge even with similar family backgrounds and educational profiles. Still, for purposes of citizenship, none of this should matter; the large majority of people can and should be educated to be rational voters and twelve or thirteen years of compulsory schooling should suffice.

In short, modern-day democratic politics is founded on the idea that people generally act rationally in pursuit of their interests and preferences.[37] We know what we want and we will vote in ways that satisfy our wants.[38] A common critique of this view is that voters should not be too selfish. Voting is not like going to a movie; if I watch a bad movie, I waste my own time but do not impose costs on other people. In contrast, I vote for political leaders who exercise power not just over me but also over other members of the political community. Hence, I have a moral obligation to consider the legitimate interests of other people when I vote: in other words, I have a duty to vote for the common good.[39] But, the story goes, most people vote their pocketbooks. In fact, the empirical evidence suggests that voters tend to vote according to what they perceive to be the national common good rather than what they perceive to be in their self-interest.[40] The basic problem is not that most voters seek to maximize their self-interest, but rather that most voters lack the knowledge necessary to make informed political judgments. Even if the majority wanted to maximize their self-interest, they often lack the knowledge that would allow them to do so.

For one thing, most people lack the time to inform themselves about political events and vote accordingly. The problem may be even worse now than in the time of ancient Athens: as Bai Tongdong puts it, the use of slave labor

> freed Athenian citizens from daily work and made it possible for them to fully participate in political matters. But even by using slaves, the adequacy of the political competence of Athenian citizens was still challenged by classical writers such as Plato and Aristophanes. Then how likely is it that the common people in a modern democracy, who need to work hard to maintain their desired standard of living (this is a basic fact of capitalism and perhaps all modern societies that rid themselves of the guilty pleasure of slavery), can participate in politics to the extent of acquiring the political competence necessary for a desirable form of liberal and deliberative democracy?[41]

The problem is not just lack of time. Compared to ancient Greek city-states, modern-day democracies are large in scale, and individual votes are not likely to make any statistical difference in the outcome. Hence, it is rational for voters to spend time doing other things: as Jason Brennan puts it, "citizens are *rationally ignorant*. Individual citizens have almost no power over government, and individual votes have almost zero expected utility. Thus, political knowledge does voters little good. Acquiring knowledge is costly and difficult. If you knew that your vote were likely to be decisive, then you would invest time and effort into acquiring political knowledge. However, when you realize that your vote makes no difference, you probably decide not to bother."[42] In short, voters in modern-day democracies lack both the time and the motivation to improve their political competence.

Even if voters had the time and motivation to learn about politics, they would be subject to various cognitive biases—unconscious errors of reasoning that distort our judgment of the world. The Nobel prize winner Daniel Kahneman has summarized several decades of academic research showing that people place too much confidence in human judgment. An example of overconfidence is a "pervasive optimistic bias" that generates the belief that we are in control of things: "Psychologists have confirmed that most people genuinely believe that they are superior to most others on most desirable traits. . . . The observation that '90% of drivers believe that they are better than average' is a well-established psychological finding." Entrepreneurs suffer from such delusions too: "The chances that a small business will survive for five years in the United States are about 35%. But the individuals who open such businesses do not believe the statistics apply to them. . . . Fully 81% of the entrepreneurs put their personal odds of success at 7 out of 10 or higher, and 33% said their chance of failing was zero." Kahneman suggests that it is possible to improve our judgment and biases, but "little can be achieved without considerable effort." Moreover, it is easier to identify a cognitive minefield "when you observe others wandering into it than when you are about to do so." And "organizations are better than individuals when it comes to avoiding errors, because they naturally think more slowly and have the power to impose orderly procedures."[43] Kahneman doesn't say this, but the voting booth—where individuals express their political preferences without any obligation to inform themselves beforehand (i.e., no effort required) and without any feedback from other people or organizations that might be able to check cognitive biases—seems almost designed to maximize irrational decision making.

Given that most voters lack the time, motivation, and cognitive skills to acquire political knowledge, it should come as no surprise that most voters often seem ignorant on key issues: "For example, 79 percent of Americans cannot identify their state senators. During election years, most citizens cannot identify any congressional candidates in their district. Immediately before the 2004 presidential election, almost 70 percent of American citizens were unaware that Congress had added a prescription drug benefit to Medicare, though this was a giant increase to the federal budget and was the largest new entitlement program in decades. Generally, citizens in other democracies are no better informed than Americans."[44] Some voters "have patently stupid beliefs. For instance, a 2009 poll of likely voters in New Jersey found that 8 percent of them (including 5 percent of Democrats and 14 percent of Republicans) believe Barack Obama is the anti-Christ, while 19 percent of them (including 40 percent of self-identified left-liberals) believe George W. Bush had knowledge of the 9/11 attacks before 9/11."[45] A poll for the American Bar Association in 2005 found that 22 percent of respondents thought the three branches of government were "Republican, Democrat, and Independent," and in 1987—before the Soviet Union had collapsed—about half of Americans thought Karl Marx's dictum "from each according to his ability, to each according to his needs" was in the U.S. Constitution.[46]

Contemporary politics, of course, is not just about knowledge of political personalities and institutions. Economic policy is a primary activity of the modern state, yet Bryan Caplan has shown that beliefs about economics are riddled with severe systematic errors: "People do not understand the 'invisible hand' of the market. I call this *antimarket* bias. People underestimate the benefits of interaction with foreigners. I call this *antiforeign* bias. People equate prosperity not with production, but with employment. I call this *make-work* bias. Lastly, people are overly prone to think economic conditions are bad and getting worse. I call this *pessimistic* bias."[47] Science also matters for politics, and voters' beliefs about science are equally riddled with systematic errors. Defying a near-consensus among scientists, only 44 percent of Americans believe that global warming is caused mostly by human activities; in contrast, 77 percent of Americans believe there are signs that aliens have visited earth.[48] An overwhelming majority (97 percent) of the scientific community says that humans and other things have evolved over time due to natural processes, but only 21 percent of Americans believe in evolution.[49]

Perhaps voter ignorance is not really a challenge for democracy. Voting is simply a fair procedure that gives everyone an equal chance of influencing political outcomes, and we cannot expect democratic decisions to respect standards or truth, prudence, or justice. But fair proceduralism, taken alone, is a weak reason for endorsing democracy. As David Estlund explains, "Democratic procedures (some of them anyway) might indeed be fair, but this will turn out to be morally too small of a matter to support an account of authority and legitimacy. Procedural fairness alone cannot explain most of the features of democratic institutions that we are likely to feel are crucial. To anticipate my argument with a one-liner, if what we want is a procedure that is fair to all, why not flip a coin? That is, why not choose a law or policy randomly?"[50] In other words, we care about the voting process not just because it is a fair procedure (a coin toss is equally fair) but also because we think it will lead to fair outcomes.

Another reason not to worry about voter ignorance is the argument of "collective wisdom," first put forward by Aristotle himself. A large group has more wisdom and virtue than a small group: however imperfect individual knowledge might be, when the views of the "many" are added up, it makes for some form of collective wisdom. There is some evidence for this view: for example, a simple average of well-known economic forecasts is substantially more accurate than individual forecasts.[51] However, such beneficial outcomes will occur only when individual beliefs are already informed by substantial knowledge: for instance, the average American thinks that 18 percent of the federal budget is devoted to foreign aid (in fact, it's about 1 percent), and hence most Americans would prefer to see foreign aid reduced.[52] There is no "invisible hand" in politics that aggregates wrongheaded views into beneficial outcomes. As Brennan puts it, "Systematically biased crowds do not make good predictions. . . . When it comes to making accurate predictions, increasing the amount of cognitive diversity among decision makers is as important as increasing the predictive power of individuals within the group."[53] That is, the "collective wisdom" argument works only if the crowd is not wrongheaded in the first place—which is not the case with most voters.

Perhaps the most compelling reason not to worry about voter ignorance is that the politicians they elect are not so ignorant. Voters may lack knowledge about political institutions and policies, but what matters is that democratic citizens are good enough judges of character that they can choose leaders with sufficient virtue and expertise to guide the polity wisely. And when politicians do pander to voter irrationality during campaign season, they routinely break campaign promises that they know to be unrealistic or immoral after they are elected. For example, U.S. presidential challengers since the 1970s have tapped voters' antiforeign bias by accusing incumbents of "coddling" China, but then typically continue in the same moderate vein as their predecessors once they assume positions of power.[54] Even if politicians hold the wrongheaded views of the people who elected them, judicial and administrative agencies composed of meritocratically selected experts often serve to inject good sense in the policy-making process. In the most clear-cut case, the U.S. Supreme Court has the power to overturn laws that curb individual rights protected in the U.S. Constitution.

Unfortunately, such checks on voter irrationality are not sufficient to prevent (or minimize) bad policies. The best social scientific research shows that politicians generally attempt to give people what they ask for, with the result that "citizens have to live with racist and sexist laws, unnecessary wars, fewer and lower-quality opportunities, higher levels of crime and pollution, and lower levels of welfare."[55] The problem may be particularly acute in newly democratizing countries: in societies with intense levels of hatred and mutual mistrust, the majority group often decides to oppress minority groups democratically, which may be a special reason for pessimists (realists?) to worry about democratization in China.[56] As mentioned, ethnic conflict tends to be muted in established liberal democracies with constitutionally enshrined mechanisms such as federalism and minority rights.

But there are few checks against other forms of irrationality that can lead to disastrous political consequences. A study of CFOs showed that those who were most confident and optimistic about the S&P index before the 2007–2008 financial crisis (followed by the Great Recession) were also overconfident and optimistic about the prospects of their own firms, which went on to take more risk than others. As Kahneman notes, "optimism is highly valued, socially and in the market; people and firms reward the providers of dangerously misleading information more than they reward truth tellers."[57] Unfortunately, politicians and regulators had the same optimism bias (or at least did not feel the need to check the optimism bias of people in the business world). In California, ordinary voters repeatedly vote for lower taxes and higher public spending—an irrationality enshrined in 1979 by Proposition 13, which severely limited California counties' primary source of financing by freezing property taxes—leading to mountains of public debt and more public spending on prisons than on higher education.[58]

Poor knowledge of science in the voting community also has negative political consequences. Most obviously, the disjunction between expert opinion and voter ignorance makes it harder for U.S. policy makers to counteract climate change, which perhaps ought to be the biggest political issue of our day. Less obviously, science and democratic politics have fundamentally different cultures that make it hard to cross from one domain to another. Scientists value intellectual honesty: as Mark Henderson puts it, "There is no shame in having a bad idea that fails to survive contact with evidence, so long as it is not clung to in defiance of the data. Scientists are allowed—encouraged even—to change their minds." But successful democratically elected politicians often prefer to proclaim the unshakable truth of their convictions, and what ought to be seen as new thinking in response to new information is seen by voters as an indication of an untrustworthy and unprincipled political player who can't stick to his or her views. Hence, few scientists go into politics and even fewer are elected to high office, with the result that the value of science "is seldom grasped either by the ministers, advisers and officials who take the decisions that shape everybody's lives."[59]

In the United States, "too many policies fly in the face of empirical principle. Medicine remains driven far more by business concerns than by data. We still forbid needle exchanges for addicts despite overwhelming evidence that we should do otherwise. We let pharmaceutical companies push new, more expensive drugs, even though they work no better than cheaper drugs we already have."[60] Even China policy trades on voter irrationality, to the detriment of voters themselves: In 2009, the

Obama administration unilaterally imposed a duty on imports of Chinese tires, a move questioned by most economists. The tariffs protected twelve hundred American jobs but cost American consumers $1.1 billion in 2011 alone in higher-priced tires, or about $900,000 per job.[61] In short, the lack of political, economic, and scientific knowledge on the part of the electorate often translates into bad policy making.[62]

So what should be done? John Stuart Mill famously defended democracy on the grounds that political participation serves to educate the citizen.[63] Just as jury duty forces the participant to think beyond his or her narrow self-interest and to deliberate in a rational way about what's good for others, so the necessity of exercising power is valuable training for the people who have to do it. By allowing and encouraging people to stand up for their rights and by requiring a degree of public spirit, democratic participation leads to the moral and intellectual development of the people. We are exposed to other perspectives, refine our own views, and consider the interests of other people. In other words, the solution to voter ignorance is to provide more meaningful opportunities for political participation, from the village council to global Internet communities. Unfortunately, the evidence shows otherwise: the deliberative citizen who has frequent crosscutting political discussion, who can intelligently articulate arguments both on behalf of her own views and on behalf of contrary views, and who has a high level of objective political knowledge tends not to participate in politics, and the active political citizen tends not to deliberate much.[64]

So the solution to voter ignorance may be more straightforward: to educate voters. In a recent book, Jamie Terence Kelly discusses the impact of one cognitive bias—the framing effect—on political behavior. He shows that different but equivalent formulations of a problem result in substantively different political decisions. To remedy the problem, Kelly suggests programs of public education designed to overcome cognitive pathologies like framing effects. The problem, as he recognizes, is that there is no strong evidence that public education can eliminate all (or even most) biases. Moreover, such programs "can be financially expensive, and they do require some deference to expertise."[65] Given an anti–big government and anti-elitist political culture in the United States, it is hard to imagine such programs being implemented on a widespread basis.

More worrying, the people who most need education to overcome cognitive biases are the least likely to read articles and books designed to be helpful. In the afterword to his book *The Ethics of Voting*, Brennan suggests a few tips designed to help us overcome cognitive biases, such as "For a period of one year, don't read *anything* defending your current view."[66] But such tips are likely to lead to a period of political paralysis, leaving the political field to extremists and dogmatists. Brennan does argue that those inclined to vote wrongly (that is, in an immoral and/or irrational way) should abstain from voting, but how many irrational voters will contemplate his arguments and take his advice? Brennan writes: "a person who votes to ban gay marriage because she finds it disgusting would, except in extraordinary circumstances, be guilty of harmful voting."[67] Is this homophobe (or sincere Christian) likely to read Brennan's sentence and conclude, yes, he's right, I should refrain from voting? Is there any evidence that making ignorant voters conscious of their false political beliefs will cause them to abstain from voting? Economists are virtually unanimous in thinking that it is hard for an individual investor to beat stock market indexes, but only 55 percent of the American public agreed; the public actually grew more confident in its ability to pick stocks successfully after learning that economists think it is close to impossible.[68] In Thailand, "84.2% expressed confidence in their ability to participate in politics—and included among these were a striking 71.7% who said they could participate even though they could not understand politics."[69] The uncomfortable truth is that the best (perhaps only) way to reduce the political influence of ignorant voters is to deprive them of the vote.

In a more recent article, Brennan takes the plunge. He argues that citizens have a right that any political power held over them should be exercised by competent people in a competent way, and that universal suffrage violates this right. Hence, he argues that suffrage should be restricted to citizens of sufficient political competence and he suggests that a properly administered voting examination system could serve to implement this principle. But Brennan's argument is questionable. He appeals to the jury analogy to defend the competence principle: juries hold serious power over defendants, and hence potential jurors can and should be disqualified because they exhibit certain bias or certain kinds of incompetence. In the same vein, voters exercise power over others and should be disqualified for immorality or incompetence. But there is a key difference. If a jury is incompetent, the impact on a person's life is clear and immediate (e.g., the defendant will go to jail). If a voter is incompetent, however, the causal chain on policy outcomes is highly indirect at best. So an incompetent voter is not as much of a threat (or source of worry) as an incompetent juror. In any case, the key objections to Brennan's proposal are political. He suggests that "we [Americans] might experiment with voter examination systems on a relatively small scale at first. For instance, perhaps it would be best if one state in the US tried the system first. . . . If the experiment succeeds, then the rules could be scaled up."[70] But such experiments are not likely to be constitutional.

More serious, it seems hard to imagine voters ever agreeing to an "experiment" that takes away their right to vote, especially in the United States with its strong "anti-elitist" political culture.[71] In fact, I do not know of any single modern-day democracy where voters agree to qualify the practice of one person, one vote: the political pressure is always for fewer limits, such as reducing the voting age from eighteen to sixteen. Once electoral democracy is in place, the only way to change the political system is by the use of military force (as in Egypt). Arguments for "epistocracy" (rule by the "knowers") are more likely to be taken seriously in East Asian societies with a deeply rooted culture of political elitism and where democracy in the form of one person, one vote has yet to achieve almost sacred status.[72]

An Alternative to Electoral Democracy: Singapore-Style Political Meritocracy

Singapore has democratic elections, but they are severely constrained: ballots are numbered (hence, the voter may worry about being identified after the vote), the media is far from free, open, and balanced, there are strict constraints on the freedom of association, voters are threatened with retaliation (e.g., with slower upgrades of public housing in opposition districts), and opposition candidates have been subject to severe retaliation.[73] Singapore has improved (from a democratic point of view) over the past decade or so, but elections are still far from free and fair. It should come as no surprise that the same party—the People's Action Party (PAP)—has ruled Singapore since independence in 1965.

Westerners tend to divide the political world into "good" democracies and "bad" authoritarian regimes, but Singapore's leaders reject this dichotomy. Rather, they argue that the concept of meritocracy best describes Singapore's political system: given Singapore's small population and limited resource base, the country should be led by people with the greatest talent and best characters, chosen according to merit. As founding father Lee Kuan Yew put it:

> Singapore is a society based on effort and merit, not wealth or privilege depending on birth. [The elite provides] the direction, planning, and control of [state] power in the people's interest. . . . It is on this group that we expend our limited and slender resources in order that they will provide the yeast, that ferment, that catalyst in our society which alone will ensure that Singapore shall maintain . . . the social organization which enables us, with almost no natural resources, to provide the second highest standard of living in Asia. . . . The main burden of present planning and implementation rests on the shoulders of 300 key persons. . . . The people come from poor and middle-class homes. They come from different language schools. Singapore is a meritocracy. And these men have risen through their own merit, hard work, and high performance.[74]

The basic idea of political meritocracy is that everybody should have an equal opportunity to be educated and to contribute to politics, but not everybody will emerge from this process with an equal capacity to make morally informed political judgments. Hence, the task of politics is to identify those with above-average ability and to make them serve the political community. If the leaders perform well, the people will basically go along.

Such an approach resonates strongly with the Confucian ideals of Singapore's Chinese community. As Prime Minister Lee Hsien Loong explains, "Many Confucian ideals are still relevant to us. An example is the concept of government by honorable men (*junzi*), who have a duty to do right for the people, and who have the trust and respect of the population. This fits us better than the Western concept that a government should be given as limited powers as possible, and always be treated with suspicion, unless proven otherwise."[75]

Over the past few decades, Singapore has evolved a rigorous and sophisticated method for recruiting and promoting political leaders. The search for top talent begins in the school system, where promising students are identified and trained for future leadership roles in government. Major national examinations are conducted at key stages of students' school life. The high-performing students are then further tested for intellectual ability as well as integrity, commitment, leadership skills, and emotional intelligence. Those ranked highest are then awarded government scholarships to study at prestigious overseas universities (and they are contractually bound to return to Singapore). Upon graduation, a minority of scholars are then selected to join the elite Administrative Service. The process of selecting ministers is as systematic and even more rigorous, and once they are identified, they are expected to stay at least three to five terms in office because (according to Lee Kuan Yew) it takes about two terms in office for a minister to become good at his job. As a consequence, Singapore has a high percentage of trained political leaders with expertise in economics and science, and political leaders who can engage in long-term social and economic planning.[76]

What makes Singapore-style meritocracy attractive is its stunning economic success: the PAP has guided the country "from the Third World to First," as Lee Kuan Yew put it.[77] Hence, the PAP has won the large majority of the vote since the early 1960s, and even social critics contend that most citizens are relatively satisfied and support the system with good reason. So why doesn't Singapore become a "true" electoral democracy, with free and fair elections? The key reason is the contradiction between meritocracy and democracy. Singapore-style meritocracy is based on the assumption that political leaders have a better sense of the community's long-term interest than ordinary citizens do. For example, the PAP has attempted to combat all forms of ethnic parochialism by fostering the growth of a new Singaporean identity that would underpin security and prosperity. The government broke up ethnic enclaves by moving people into ethnically mixed public housing blocs and marginalized ethnic Chinese clan associations.[78] It also promoted the use of English, which involved overriding the wishes of all groups, including the majority Chinese. Lee is quite explicit that Singapore's nation-building exercise was incompatible with majority rule:

> Supposing we had chosen Chinese or tried to sponsor Chinese, how would we make a living? How would we fit ourselves into the region and into the world? We could not have made a living. But the Chinese then would have wanted it. And if we had taken the vote, we would have had to follow that policy. So when people say, "Oh, ask the people!", it's childish rubbish. We are leaders. We know the consequences. . . . They say people can think for themselves? Do you honestly believe that the chap who can't pass primacy six knows the consequences of his choice when he answers a question viscerally, on language, culture and religion? But we knew the consequences. We would starve, we would have race riots. We would disintegrate.[79]

Today, English is the lingua franca in Singapore and the race riots from the more democratic era of the 1960s are a distant memory.

Moreover, the need for training of leaders over several electoral cycles means that meritocracy is incompatible with multiparty rule and the possibility that it would lead to the alternation of political power. Given Singapore's small talent pool (it is a tiny city-state of five million citizens), Singapore's top talent would not put themselves through a decades-long training process if they felt that success would not be rewarded with political power, and they would refrain from throwing themselves into the political turmoil of a multiparty system without likely victors. Even if talented leaders were chosen, they would lack the motivation to engage in long-term planning if they worried about losing power every four or five years.

That said, further democratization may be necessary to make the government more responsive and sensitive to the needs of ordinary citizens. Meritocracy has served as a powerful ideological resource to maintain the PAP establishment's hegemony, particularly over the decades of national survival and rapid development. In recent years, however, the state's ideological hegemony has begun to crack. New social formations bearing alternative perspectives have come to be more audible and persuasive to a larger segment of Singaporeans with new media. As the problems that attend Singapore's commitment to economic globalization pervade the daily aspects of citizens' experience, popular belief in meritocracy has weakened, leaving a strong sense that in its place is now elitism of the kind that focuses on winning and maximizing rewards for the winners, while downplaying factors and reasons that limit opportunities for the disadvantaged. Meritocracy, as Kenneth Paul Tan puts it, has become a dirty word in Singapore.[80]

As meritocracy has lost moral authority, counterhegemonic leadership and alternative ideological formations have been energized in an expanded and politicized new media environment. The 2011 parliamentary elections proved to be a watershed moment in Singapore's political history: the PAP won "only" 60 percent of the popular vote, and it lost six parliamentary seats.[81] In response, the PAP establishment has taken steps to catch up with the new media environment, and Singapore has now become more politically open. Arguably, the PAP needs to expand its narrowly technical and academic notion of merit, in part to recognize the importance for political success in competitive elections of communicative talent and emotional intelligence. The question is whether it can do so before the energized and (relatively) unconstrained opposition forces really threaten PAP rule. What if the PAP fails to win a majority (or a plurality) of the vote in a future election? Will the PAP voluntarily give up (or even share) power? At that point, the contradiction between Singapore-style meritocracy and democracy will really show itself. Perhaps it was a mistake to try to build single-party meritocracy on the foundation (or form) of a democratic electoral system inherited from British colonial rulers.

China, of course, does not even pretend to select its top leaders via one person, one vote, and it has been looking to Singapore's political model for inspiration.[82] Since the early 1990s, Chinese officials have gone to Singapore for training and to learn from the Singapore experience.[83] Of course, Singapore's political values and institutions cannot readily be transferred to a huge country such as China, but aspects of the Singaporean political system may be transferable.[84] From Deng Xiaoping to Xi Jinping, China's leaders have repeatedly stressed the need to study aspects of Singapore's political model. Partly inspired by Singapore, China has evolved a sophisticated and comprehensive system for selecting and promoting political talent (see chapter 2). As a result, the Chinese government has a high proportion of economists and scientists willing to experiment on the basis of trial and error (most of whom could not have been elected in a democratic context), and several hundred million Chinese have been lifted out of poverty over the past three decades. The meritocratic ideal—the idea that government officials are selected and promoted on the basis of ability and morality rather than political connections, wealth, and family background—is still a long way from the political reality in China. But if China continues to "meritocratize" and avoids the bad policy making stemming from voter ignorance in democratic countries (especially the United States, the powerful and populous country it is usually compared to), it will set a model for others. At the moment, China is not good enough (in terms of governance), and the United States not bad enough, for China's political meritocracy to exercise much soft power abroad. But things can change and China may pose more of a normative challenge to electoral democracies in the future.[85]

2. The Tyranny of the Minority

In a democracy, according to Aristotle, the lower classes (the majority) will dominate, and the property of the rich will not be secure. He did recognize that the rich could exercise a corrupting power by tempting other citizens to embrace a life aimed at acquiring unlimited wealth (and the shallow pleasures to which wealth gives access) at the expense of living well—which helps to explain why he favored depriving traders of citizenship in the best possible regime[86]—but he didn't foresee the possibility that the rich minority could find ways of furthering its economic interests at the expense of the majority in democratic political systems where the poor (theoretically) have more political power.

America's founding fathers, whatever their political differences, agreed with Aristotle that commerce undermines the capacity for independent political judgment.[87] To minimize the power of private property, "the Constitution included what were, at the time, extremely limited property qualifications for voters and—in a dramatic break with most states' practices—no property qualifications for elected representatives."[88] But the founders feared mob rule by the poor more than the economic power of the rich, and they sought to check the tyranny of the majority with institutions like the electoral college, the deliberative Senate, and nonelected bodies like the Supreme Court. A free press would help to expose abuses of power by elites, and the founders may also have been heartened by what seemed to be a dawning pluralist age "when a wide spectrum of social groups, relatively equal in power and influence, might supplant the rich/poor citizen cleavage that prevailed in the republics of previous ages."[89] It seemed highly unlikely that the rich could exercise economic tyranny in a democratic system based on one person (or, more precisely, one white man), one vote; hence, the founders did not seek to minimize the power of the wealthy by designing institutions that acknowledged, addressed, or reflected socioeconomic distinctions. The chief danger of democracy, as Alexis de Tocqueville put it in his 1835 masterwork *Democracy in America*, is rather that the less affluent majority would use its political power to expropriate wealth: "In all the nations of the world, the greatest number has always been composed of those who did not have property, or those whose property was too restricted for them to live in ease without working. Therefore universal suffrage gives the government of society to the poor."[90]

What the founders didn't foresee (or fear) was the rapid development of industrial capitalism in the following two centuries, along with attendant concentrations of wealth and widening inequality. Today, well-funded and organized minority interests can and do get their way against relatively powerless majorities on issues such as environmental regulation, gun control, and the regulation of financial institutions. Because most people have little time or energy to devote to politics, small groups with a strong commercial or ideological motivation can exert disproportionate influence on the political process,[91] either blocking change that's in the common interest or lobbying for policies that benefit only their own interest. The problem is magnified when the wealthy class has both a clear sense of its economic interests and the motivation to defend them against the interests of the majority of voters.

The influence of money on politics is the scourge of most existing democracies, and the United States is perhaps the most extreme case. In contrast to the shared prosperity that defined the decades immediately after World War II, the vast majority of Americans have fallen further and further behind a tiny superrich segment of society over the past generation: "From 1979 until the eve of the Great Recession, the top one percent received 36 percent of all gains in household income—even after taking into account the value of employer-sponsored health insurance, all federal taxes, and all government benefits. . . . Economic growth was even more skewed between 2001 and 2006, during which the share of income gains going to the top one percent was over 53 percent."[92] This income split is often blamed on technological change and globalization, which handsomely reward winners but leave their many losers behind: as Charles A. Kupchan puts it, "the primary source of the declining fortunes of the American worker is global competition."[93] But inequality in the United States has grown consistently more quickly than in other affluent democracies, and an important cause, according to Jacob S. Hacker and Paul Pierson, is a long series of policy changes in government that overwhelmingly favored the rich: political lobbying by corporate and financial sectors led public officials to rewrite "the rules of American politics and the American economy in ways that have benefited the few at the expense of the many."[94] From tax laws to deregulation to corporate governance to safety net issues, business interests pressured government to enact policies to allow those who were already wealthy to amass an ever-increasing share of the nation's wealth. Even after the 2008 financial collapse, the most culpable banks were able to exert continued control over the decisions of policy makers and legislators, and the small group of individuals hauling in more than $50 million annually increased fivefold from 2008 to 2009.[95] As the economy recovered in 2009–2010, 93 percent of the income gains went to the top 1 percent of taxpayers.[96]

Perhaps a glaring income split, even if new wealth is concentrated at the very top, need not be cause for concern. From the point of view of justice, what matters is really the fate of the disadvantaged: according to John Rawls's theory of justice, income inequalities can be justified if they benefit the less well off. In the United States, however, the poor have gotten poorer: In November 2012, the U.S. Census Bureau reported that more than 16 percent of the U.S. population lived in poverty, including almost 20 percent of children (the highest level since 1993), up from 14.3 percent in 2009.[97] And the poorest of the poor are even worse off: In 2011, extreme poverty in the United States, meaning the number of households living on less than $2 per day before government benefits, was double 1996 levels at 1.5 million households, including 2.8 million children.[98] In short, the problem is not just that the superrich are getting richer but also that the poorest of the poor are getting poorer.

Another argument against egalitarian critics is that large income gaps are necessary for economic progress. The economist Daron Acemoglu argues that cutthroat capitalism in the United States allows for more innovation than welfare spending does in relatively egalitarian countries such as Sweden: "effort in innovative activities requires incentives which come as a result of differential rewards to this effort. As a consequence, a greater gap between successful and unsuccessful entrepreneurs increases entrepreneurial effort and thus a country's contribution to the world technology frontier."[99] Innovation increases the growth rate of the entire world economy, with the implication that "cuddly capitalists" free ride on the United States' cutthroat form of capitalism (one might add that the United States' outsized military expenditures provide security protection for allies and allow them to spend more on welfare). But much of the income growth has benefited the financial sector and it is at least arguable that complex financial innovations did more economic harm than good by concealing risks from traders, buyers, and regulators, ultimately contributing to the 2007–2008 financial crisis.[100] Moreover, the idea that Nordic societies are less innovative than the United States is contentious, and Acemoglu himself recognizes that the United States can provide more of a safety net at the bottom while allowing for outsized rewards at the top.[101]

In any case, income inequality is not worrisome to the point that it threatens the democratic political system. Voters in the United States still have faith that their country is rich in opportunities to move up the income ladder even if the reality is different:

> [The United States is] less mobile than nearly every other industrialized democracy in the world. . . . And yet, in one of the

> grand ironies of American public opinion, the United States is still the place where the meritocratic faith burns brightest. . . . Since 1983 an occasional CBS/New York Times poll has asked people: "Do you think it is still possible to start out poor in this country, work hard, and become rich?" In 1983, 57 percent answered yes, and by 2007 the number had risen to 81 percent. Even in 2009, after the worst financial crisis in recent memory, and epidemic levels of unemployment, the overwhelming majority of those surveyed (72 percent) still held on to this singular faith.[102]

Such (false) beliefs stabilize the political system because the "losers" do not blame the system as much as they ought to. The electoral system itself also provides an element of illusory control. Discussion of current politics—in the media and in everyday life—is dominated by the conventional narrative of election-driven change. As Hacker and Pierson put it, "Clashes between the 'red team' and the 'blue team' become no different from a game between the Celtics and the Lakers. This is no doubt why politics as electoral spectacle is so appealing to the media: It's exciting, and it's simple. Aficionados can memorize the stats of their favorite players or become experts on the great games of the past. Everyone, however, can enjoy the gripping spectacle of two highly motivated teams slugging it out."[103] In reality, policy making takes place between elections, largely outside the glare of media focus: that's when big business interests mobilize and pressure policy makers to influence the structure of "private" markets in their favor. To pursue the sports metaphor, it's as though baseball fans believe they influence outcomes in baseball because they can vote for the players in the All-Star Game, without realizing that outcomes are largely determined by the teams' wealth and the league's rules of ownership. An election, in other words, helps to divert attention from political problems by inducing the (often false) belief that changing the government is the most effective way to get political change,[104] and voter irrationality helps to limit the political damage of income inequality.

From a moral point of view, an economic and political system that is stabilized by false beliefs is not as desirable as it should be. More important, perhaps, income inequality is bad for society: the more unequal the society, the less the social mobility.[105] Drawing on extensive statistical evidence, the social scientist Richard Wilkinson argues that inequality leads to stress, stress creates sickness on the individual and the mass levels, and society overall suffers widespread unhappiness and high levels of violence, depression, and mistrust across the social spectrum. Even small reductions in inequality can lead to better health, less violence, and more harmonious relations with family members, society, and the environment.[106] In other words, there is a need to reduce high levels of income inequality, even if the worst off are not desperately poor, the economy is highly innovative, and inequality is supported by voter irrationality.

So what should be done? Timothy Noah puts forward solutions to the problem of income inequality that do not call into question electoral democracy: a more progressive tax system, putting more workers on the federal payroll, increasing importation of skilled labor, universal preschool, price controls on colleges and universities, regulation of Wall Street, and reviving the labor movement; he urges voters to support a Democratic president.[107] There may be reasons for optimism. Echoing the revival of progressive causes after the Great Depression, the financial crisis and its aftermath has focused more public concern on income inequality and its real causes. From President Obama's critique of financial institutions to publications and media reports that highlight the economic dominance of the 1 percent, "the many" may be waking up to reality and demanding change.

But perhaps the problem runs deeper and cannot be addressed merely by writing books that expose the causes of income inequality and urge voters to become more rational and to seek political change in the majority's economic interest. If the democratic system can be captured so easily by organized groups that promote the interests of the wealthy elite and if elections themselves focus people's attention away from the real problem (and if people seem more inclined to believe in Horatio Alger–type rags-to-riches fairytales than the hard evidence of social scientists), is it possible to take measures to reduce inequality without calling electoral democracy into question? An increasing number of critics argue that the primarily electoral model of popular government fails to keep political elites accountable and responsive to the general public and neglects to counteract the disproportionate influence of the wealthy on the workings of government.[108] Electoral politics can be supplemented by institutions such as deliberative polls meant to create more informed and reflective public opinion, but so long as elections are viewed as the only (or main) mechanism to choose "real" decision makers, it will be difficult, perhaps impossible, to counteract the "tyranny of the wealthy minority" in capitalist democracies.

An Alternative to Electoral Democracy: Curbing Capitalists

Perhaps there's a need for more strong-arm tactics to curb the power of capitalists. Most famously, Karl Marx called for expropriation of private property and a "dictatorship of the proletariat" as a temporary stage on the way to true communism, but "experiments" with Marxism in the twentieth century have (rightly) discredited that option. Still, there may be other possibilities. Niccolò Machiavelli is best known for his cynical advocacy of the use of cunning and duplicity in statecraft, but he despised rule by the rich and argued for republics in which the people vigorously contest and constrain the behavior of political and economic elites by extraelectoral votes. Inspired by Machiavelli, John P. McCormick proposes a citizen body for the American context that excludes socioeconomic elites and political elites and grants randomly selected common people significant veto, legislative, and censure authority within government and over public officials. In theory, this kind of powerful citizen body could counteract the disproportionate influence of the wealthy on the workings of government, but it is not politically realistic. For one thing, the wealthy are not likely to go down without a fight. McCormick does suggest one measure for "disenfranchising the magnates" with their consent: "we might consider whether individuals under present conditions earning more than, say, $150,000 in income, or belonging to households of more than $350,000 in net wealth (income, property, and assets), should be relieved of all tax burdens as compensation for giving up eligibility to vote, to stand for office, or to contribute funds to political campaigns." But even if the rich value wealth more than honors or office, as McCormick recognizes, they are not likely to "resist the temptation to convert their economic privilege into political power, especially in order to use the latter to inflate the former even further."[109] More fundamentally, the practice of one person, one vote (I repeat!) has assumed an almost sacred quality in modern democratic societies, and any calls for political institutions that formally exclude a class of people are likely to be viewed as beyond the moral pale (I leave aside the issue of whether such proposals would violate the U.S. Constitution). It's not just the rich who will object to proposals to deprive a class of equal citizenship rights: most people in democratic societies will object, even if it's not in their economic interest to do so.

So again, it's best to look to nondemocratic societies for realizable alternatives. Political meritocracies, unburdened by the need to choose political leaders by means of free and fair elections, might find it easier to rein in the political power of capital without sacrificing market mechanisms that underpin innovation and productive capability. Singapore's economic rise has been guided by meritocratically selected leaders who have consistently taken advantage of global upheavals. The government has kept a tight rein on domestic finance and done what it could to induce international firms to come, while keeping abreast of the social scientific research about the best means of regulating finance and retaining the ability to implement necessary measures unencumbered by the lobbying of special interests. As *The Economist* puts it, "The only people who have read all of America's gargantuan Dodd-Frank financial regulation act are American academics, who find it a mess, and the Singapore Monetary Authority, which is mulling the opportunities it might create."[110] China, for its part, has developed a model of state capitalism that keeps the principal levers of intervention within the hands of government. The model has allowed it to avoid major financial and economic crises that have plagued capitalist democracies in the past three decades, to orient development in vital sectors such as telecommunications, transportation, and energy, and to keep control over foreign investments and financial fluctuations.[111]

But China and Singapore are not doing much better than the United States in terms of income inequality, which has worsened over the past two decades.[112] Although both countries have high rates of homeownership and low rates of unemployment (especially Singapore), which reduce the toxic effects of income inequality, income inequality is nearly as great a social problem and political challenge as in the United States. So what can be done to bring soaring income inequality under control? In the case of China, Martin King Whyte argues that the leadership needs to enact strong and comprehensive reforms of taxation policy, investment patterns, state bank lending, educational access, and the *hukou* (household registration) system.[113]

No matter what the political system, however, reforms in highly unequal societies will be successful only if the rich are somehow made to care more about other members of society.[114] And the best way to make rich, powerful people care about the less fortunate is not by means of rational argumentation, but rather by creating a sense of community that emerges from common social interaction.[115] For example, it would not be too difficult for wealthy Japanese or Swedish citizens to avoid (or evade) high tax rates and other measures meant to redistribute wealth, but they largely comply with the rules not just because they have to but also because they feel a sense of solidarity with the rest of society. A key explanation for willing compliance is that the rich have not retreated into their own communities: well-off Japanese partake of common rituals and everyday activities that generate a sense of common identity. In the United States, however, a geographical shift "has occurred during the past three decades—one in which communities are increasingly segregated not only by race but by politics, culture, and income. Your likelihood of even *seeing*, much less exchanging views with, anyone who doesn't share your precise demographic identity is becoming more and more remote."[116] As a result, America's wealthy elite is strikingly indifferent to working-class concerns such as unemployment and is much more conservative than everyone else on a whole range of economic issues.[117] In China, the trends are similar (if not as extreme), with segregation of the rich in urban coastal cities, and within gated communities in those cities, with the result that there are fewer shared social activities and growing mutual alienation and incomprehension between social classes.

So how to promote more social interaction between classes? It is unrealistic to expect leaders of big business to develop a richer sense of solidarity; in an age of globalization, corporations develop interests separate from and in conflict with the interests of their "home" countries, be they democratic or otherwise.[118] But political leaders can try to implement policies that mix social classes, such as zoning laws that limit gated communities for the rich. Equally if not more important, leaders should ensure that school funding does not depend only on local income sources so as to avoid the result (more typical in the United States) that higher-quality schools in rich neighborhoods mainly serve the rich and lower-quality schools in poor neighborhoods mainly serve the poor. In the United States, arguably, the top leadership has the motivation to help reduce income inequality but lacks the ability to do so: President Obama's efforts are likely to be stymied by lobbying efforts that pressure members of Congress to enact measures that benefit the wealthy. In American politics, it is hard to get things done and easy to block them, and obstruction by special interests has increased over the years.[119] China, to oversimplify, has the opposite problem: the top leadership has greater ability to enact measures designed to reduce the income gap (including measures designed to mix social classes),[120] but lacks the motivation to do so. Top Chinese leaders, for one thing, tend to be either wealthy personally or linked to families with tremendous assets.

So which system is likely to improve? To my mind, it is less difficult to change the motivation of leaders in a system that generally allows leaders to implement policies once they make up their minds to do so than to change a dysfunctional political system that blocks well-intentioned leaders. The key to changing motivation is to encourage more direct experience with the less well off, so as to generate sympathy with their fate. In the United States, progressive political leaders such as President Obama can make a deliberate effort to engage with the underprivileged in deprived neighborhoods as part of a self-imposed program of political education. But most leaders will lack such foresight. In China, by contrast, there is growing awareness of the need to break down the social barriers between people. Over the past few years, CCP cadres have been sent to poor rural communities for extended periods (at least one year) as part of their political training, and these leaders will rise to the top over the next couple of decades.[121]

If it's true that the best way to sensitize powerful elites to the plight of the poor is to encourage mixing with different social classes as part of political education, then China is on the right side of history. The problem in the United States (and other democratic societies) is that political leaders are chosen by the people and need not have received training designed to extend class sympathies; no sort of political leadership training could be made compulsory in electoral democracies. Hence, a political meritocracy will find it easier to implement compulsory political training for leaders designed to make them understand and care for the interests of the less-well-off members of society. At the moment, the "tyranny of the minority" may be similarly problematic in China and the United States, but it may be more realistic to expect improvement in China.

3. The Tyranny of the Voting Community

Even if electoral democracy works as it's supposed to—voters are rational and public-spirited and policies generally benefit the large majority of the voting public, not just (or primarily) a wealthy elite—it is still a deeply flawed political system. Political equality ends at the boundaries of the political community: those outside are neglected. The national focus of the democratically elected political leaders is assumed; they are meant to serve only the community of voters. The problem is that a government's policies do not affect just the voting community: they also affect nonvoters such as future generations and foreigners, yet nobody represents the interests of nonvoters in a democratic political system.[122] Hence, if there is a serious conflict of interest between the needs of voters and the needs of nonvoters, the former will almost always have priority.

One problem is that democratization tends to strengthen the political salience of national identity, which can increase tension with neighboring countries.[123] But long-established democracies have an even longer track record of committing harm against nonvoters. Consider gross human rights violations, such as the systematic use of physical torture. We tend to think that such violations are primarily done by "outlaw" regimes such as North Korea that do not seem overly concerned with the need to adhere to a universal human rights regime. It is true that the worst of the worst—with Nazi Germany at the extreme end of the spectrum of immoral states—tend to be such outlaw regimes. But Darius Rejali has shown that "some democratic states have legalized torture, treated it as a quasi-legal investigative procedure, or practiced it routinely on the quiet, despite a formal ban." Democratic states developed a distinctive form of torture that leaves few bloody marks or visible traces in order to avoid public monitoring and accountability: "the modern democratic torturer knows how to beat a suspect senseless without leaving a mark." Rejali catalogues, in more than eight hundred pages, the various forms of "clean torture" that democracies have developed over the past two centuries or so, from the use of electric torture by French forces in Algeria and American forces in Vietnam to the use of positional torture and violent shaking by Israeli forces against Palestinians in the occupied territories. Another feature of "democratic torture" is that it tends to be carried out most systematically against noncitizens. In ancient republics, torture was more explicitly tied to citizenship, and torture was inflicted exclusively against slaves, foreigners, and "barbarians." In modern democracies such as France, torture typically begins in colonies or war zones and may then spread backward to the metropole. The victims of torture in democracies today are not spoken of as slaves, but as "street children, vagrants, loiterers, and illegal immigrants . . . [who] fall into a class of quasi-citizens that is perceived as vicious." In other words (and Rejali doesn't say this directly), torture by democratic states tends to be carried out against those deprived of the vote, with nobody to represent them, show outrage, and fight for their interests in the democratic system. And sometimes many (or even most) citizens cheer for, or silently endorse, what appears to be necessary dirty work to support their democratic way of life.[124]

More commonly, perhaps, nonvoters suffer less egregious violations at the hands of the voting community. Consider the phenomenon of foreign domestic workers (FDWs) in Hong Kong and Singapore. Both territories depend on several hundred thousand FDWs to do the dirty, dangerous, and demeaning work that locals won't do. FDWs have better rights and protections in nondemocratic Hong Kong than in Singapore.[125] One important reason is that FDWs in Hong Kong (like other residents) are free to organize self-help groups and public protests to secure their interests. But the relative lack of political rights in Hong Kong may be another factor that favors the interests of FDWs. In Singapore, as noted, there are substantial constraints on the democratic process, but elections are still competitive, and political parties must be seen to campaign for the interests of their constituents. Since employers are constituents, their interests are more likely to be taken seriously in the political process than the interests of disenfranchised FDWs (one Singaporean civil servant told me that the government feels constrained by a large constituency that opposes recommendations, such as more days off for FDWs, in a Human Rights Watch report issued in 2005). In other words, even well-intentioned and far-seeing political leaders are constrained by antiforeign populist sentiment in Singapore.

In Hong Kong, there is no pretense that the people choose their top leaders on the basis of one person, one vote, and it is quite likely that many political leaders (both before and after the handover to China) would not have been chosen by the people in free and fair competitive elections. Hong Kong decision makers, in other words, are less constrained by the interests of Hong Kong citizens (more precisely, permanent residents), and they can rely to a greater extent on their own sense of justice and decency to implement policies that favor FDWs (not surprisingly, prodemocracy parties in Hong Kong have been very cautious about articulating proposals that favor FDWs).

In the case of Taiwan, the development of a more democratic, responsive government has been bad for FDWs—under increasing pressure from specific domestic groups that (mistakenly?) blamed foreigners for growing unemployment of indigenes and blue-collar workers, in September 2000 then-President Chen Shui-bian promised to cut the number of foreign workers by fifteen thousand annually, the goal being to reduce the number by sixty thousand by 2004.[126] I do not mean to imply, needless to say, that the East Asian public is uniquely reactionary: episodes of rights expansions for immigrants in Germany, France, and the Netherlands "were conditional on keeping the public out and containing the issue behind the closed doors of bureaucracy and judiciary."[127] In short, there is a tension, both theoretical and real, between the interests of the voting community and the interests of foreigners and foreign residents, and the latter groups often pay the price.

That said, democracies can survive the fact that noncitizens are often subject to immoral policies at the hands of representatives who act first and foremost for the interests of voters who elect them. Perhaps the Achilles' heel of electoral democracy—what really may lead to its downfall—is the negative impact it has on children and future generations who are deprived of the vote. One problem is what Nicolas Berggruen and Nathan Gardels term "consumer culture" politics: voters constantly demand instant gratification and have no patience for long-term structural reform or for politicians who impose pain, with the result that entitlement spending and public debt explodes to unsustainable levels.[128] Greece is the poster child of how things can go wrong as "the result of the fatal alliance between politicians who gave the people everything they wanted in return for votes, and the people who voted for politicians who promised them the impossible, as if no one ever expected the bill to arrive."[129] But electoral democracies may really come under strain when the United States and Japan—the two most economically powerful democratic countries—need to rein in their soaring national debts (in the case of Japan, the national debt is more than twice the size of its economy) if it means imposing serious costs on the interests of the voting community.[130]

The most worrisome threat to future generations, arguably, is global warming. Dealing with it requires a decades-long horizon, and electoral democracies seem singularly ill-equipped to make the sacrifices that are necessary to benefit future generations several decades from now. The philosopher Tim Mulgan imagines an eerily plausible future world where resources are insufficient to meet everyone's basic needs and where a chaotic climate makes life precarious. In this world, people are not kept alive once they can no longer make a productive contribution or when they have little chance of survival even if they are fed. The reason such a world came about, Mulgan suggests, is that affluent democracies did not treat future people justly. In theory, democratic voters could have chosen future-friendly policies, but "once intergenerational conflict began to bite, and democratic citizens (raised to expect the state to pander to their whims) were called on to make significant personal sacrifices to save future lives, their intergenerational compassion proved inadequate."[131] Hence, it should not be surprising that policies meant to curb global warming such as Australia's carbon pricing scheme get repealed by populist governments as soon as they are seen to impose substantial economic costs on voters.[132]

So what can be done? If it seems recklessly optimistic to expect that voters will sacrifice their own interests to benefit people fifty years from now, how is it possible to protect the interests of future generations without challenging the idea that the country's most powerful decision makers should be chosen by means of one person, one vote? Political thinkers have put forward proposals to appoint representatives for future people, such as reserving a few seats in the legislature for future representatives or appointing special future-oriented officials with the task of issuing reports, warnings, or advice to voters and legislators regarding the likely future impact of policy proposals.[133] To date, however, no affluent democracy has seriously tried to enfranchise future people,[134] and there is no reason to expect much progress in the future.[135]

An Alternative to Electoral Democracy: Veto Power for Representatives of Future Generations

Once again, we need to look to nondemocracies for inspiration. In theory, it is not difficult to imagine political institutions that could represent interests beyond the community of voters. Consider Huang Zongxi's proposal for what Theodore de Bary terms a "Parliament of Scholars."[136] Huang, a seventeenth-century Confucian scholar, proposed strengthening the political role of the schools for the training of Confucian scholar-officials. Schools of all levels, in Huang's view, should serve as forums for open public discussion. He noted that during the Eastern Han (25–220 CE), scholars at the Imperial College, the top school for the training of scholar-officials, engaged in outspoken discussion of important issues without fear of those in power, and the highest officials were anxious to avoid their censure. Moreover, Huang proposed that the rector of the Imperial College, to be chosen from among the great scholars of the day, should be equal in importance to the prime minister, and that once a month the emperor should visit the Imperial College, along with the prime minister and other ministers. The emperor was to sit among the ranks of the students while the rector questioned him on the administration of the country.[137] The primary function of the system would be to hold rulers accountable, but

Huang also proposed revising the Confucian examination system for selecting scholar-officials. He condemned the examinations of his day for rewarding superficiality and plagiarism, thus failing to identify scholars of "real talent." Examinations, in his view, should test for both the capacity to memorize the classics and subsequent commentaries as well as the capacity for independent thought: "After listing one by one what is said by the various Han and Song scholars, the candidate should conclude with his own opinion, there being no necessity for blind acceptance of one authority's word."[138]

Even if Huang's proposal for a parliament of scholar-officials could empower scholars of "real talent," the main problem from a contemporary standpoint is that it still deprives ordinary people of any voice in politics. But his proposal can be modified to make it more appealing today. For example, a Huang-style meritocratic house composed of representatives selected on the basis of competitive examinations can be combined with a democratic house composed of representatives selected by competitive elections. The democratic house would have the task of representing the interests of voters, and the meritocratic house would have the task of representing the interests of nonvoters affected by the policies of government, such as foreigners and future generations. Deputies of the meritocratic house could be chosen on the basis of examinations that test not just for knowledge of the classics, but also for knowledge of international relations and environmental science. To ensure that the interests of nonvoters are not systematically marginalized in the political process, the meritocratic house could have veto power over any policies that it judges harm the interests of future generations.[139]

Whatever the theoretical appeal of this proposal, it is not realistic from a political point of view: a democratically elected legislature would never allow itself to be subject to the veto power of a house of government charged with the task of representing the interests of nonvoters. But there may be more hope in nondemocracies, or at least, political systems that allow a voice for the people but without free and fair elections for the country's most powerful leaders. Consider Singapore's "elected presidency." Since 1993, the president needs to be elected by the majority of the people, but a person who wishes to run for the office of president has to fulfill stringent qualifications, such as being a "person of integrity, good character, and reputation" who has served for a minimum of three years as minister, chief justice, or speaker, or "in any other similar or comparable position of seniority and responsibility."[140] The strictness of these qualifications led to the 1999 and 2005 elections being walkovers as S. R. Nathan was the only qualified candidate on nomination day. Critics rightly complain that the elected presidency serves as a constraint on democracy,[141] but that is the whole point. The president has the power to veto attempts by democratically elected politicians to enact policies that harm the interests of future generations, for example blocking attempts by the government to draw on reserves not accumulated by the government during its current term of office. It remains to be seen whether the president has sufficient powers to take necessary measures for Singapore to do its share to protect the world from the effects of catastrophic climate change, but perhaps the institution of the elected presidency is a step in the right direction.

In any case, the real player (among nondemocratic countries) in the climate-change debate is China, given its size and power. If we can't expect electoral democracies to take necessary measures to protect the interests of people several decades from now, is there any reason to be optimistic that China's unelected leaders can do better? From the planet's point of view, it is imperative that China set a good example. If China were to use as much energy per capita as the United States does, it would produce carbon emissions in such volume that our planet would be condemned to unmanageable climate change. So, clearly, China must embrace an outlook that puts resource management at the center of all policy making.[142]

Equally clearly, China's disastrous environmental record is cause for concern. Yet the Chinese government also seems to be taking steps in the right direction, if only because growing public concern over air pollution in China has made environmental sustainability a political issue. China has won praise for its efforts to boost energy efficiency and invest in green technologies;[143] it installed more solar power in 2013 than the United States has in its whole history.[144] The central government has built an infrastructure of high-speed rail that is more carbon efficient than air travel, and it has prioritized the development of electric vehicles.[145] It has launched experiments with carbon permit markets in seven pilot areas that cover areas accounting for nearly one-third of

China's GDP (in contrast, the United States has resisted such market-based schemes to reduce carbon emissions).[146] An important reason for China's pollution problem is that in the past cadres tended to be promoted almost exclusively based on standards that measured economic growth, but wider assessment criteria are being used now: targets for pollution control are being linked to cadre evaluation processes,[147] and the promotion of cadres in experimental low-carbon-emission cities such as Hangzhou is based on criteria that incorporate environmental, energy, and climate-change-related performance criteria.[148] China's powerful economic ministry is considering an outright cap on emissions for its next five-year plan (2016–2020), which could help to break the stalemate in global climate talks.[149] And the government has adopted an environmental protection law that gives authorities more power to crack down on polluting industries than they have in large electoral democracies such as India: as Stephen O. Andersen of the Institute for Governance and Sustainable Development in Washington puts it, "It's easier for them to put the national interest before the interest of one manufacturing sector."[150] In comparison to other large emerging economies, China has slowed the rate at which its greenhouse gas emissions have grown in the past decade, thanks partly to policies to improve efficiency and boost renewable energy.[151] Finally, the government recognizes that top-down approaches won't be sufficient, and it has tolerated and even encouraged a surge of bottom-up green initiatives over the past decade or so.[152]

Perhaps the best reason to be optimistic is that the same party will likely still be in power several decades from now. The CCP is likely to stick to its long-term commitments. In 2014, both President Xi and President Obama made pledges to curb net greenhouse gas emissions: in the case of the United States, to reduce net greenhouse gas emissions by 26–28 percent below 2005 levels by 2025, and in the case of China, to reach a peak year for its carbon emissions by 2030 and to increase the share of renewable energy to 20 percent by that year.[153] Who is more likely to stick to these pledges? The United States may set aside its pledge if the Republicans win the presidency.[154] No such worries in China, unless the whole political system collapses. In addition, the CCP derives much of its legitimacy from its capacity to perform well, including its ability to anticipate and respond to natural and social disasters. The idea that the government is responsible for disaster prevention, especially flood control due to the enormous scale of the project, goes far back in Chinese history and the same is true today (see chapter 3, section 3). In contrast, political rulers in democracies derive legitimacy by virtue of being chosen by voters, and if things go wrong several decades from now, the particular government at the time will take most of the blame. In other words, it is in China's rulers' self-interest to prepare for disasters both short-term and long-term, and if the CCP doesn't do so, it will lose much of its legitimacy. I do not know if China will be able to develop an environmentally sustainable way of life, but so long as it does not adopt a democratic system that privileges the interests of the voting community at the cost of future generations, that's where I'd place my bet.[155]

4. The Tyranny of Competitive Individualists

One feature of electoral democracy is the open competition for political power: a major election is typically a period of sustained and intense mobilization and engagement, in which contending sides reach out to and seek the support of every last voter. The problem is that electoral democracy can exacerbate rather than alleviate social conflict. "Negative campaigning" is a feature of most elections, with politicians and political parties tainting electoral competitors with false and unsubstantiated allegations in order to saddle them with the disapprobation of the voters. Such campaigning is both rampant and effective: as the American journalist Dan Rather put it, "Negative campaigning works!"[156] In the worst cases, political leaders representing the interests of majority groups appeal to ethnic and racial solidarity and tyrannize minority groups, both during the electoral campaign and after they win the vote (see section 2). Electoral political divisions generate "identity politics" in which voting for a certain party becomes something akin to a tribal identity, as in Thailand, polarizing society to the point of endangering the polity's survival. If the question of who counts as "we the people" has not been settled in democratic countries, the threat of civil war is omnipresent.

In more established liberal democracies basic civil and political rights cannot easily be abridged by a majority vote, but electoral campaigns can be so poisonous that reasonable accommodation of differences becomes almost impossible: in the U.S. case, the vitriolic hatred between Republicans and Democrats has made *compromise* a dirty word. Differences between political groups stem from genuine disagreements over ways of life and conceptions of the good, but elections can and do exacerbate differences,[157] in the same way that going to court as a first option for dealing with family conflict is likely to further disrupt harmony between family members.[158] And if the Tocquevillian argument that the power to participate in electoral politics also empowers individuals in other spheres of social life is correct, it is also true that divisive elections can set a bad model for resolving conflict outside of the political arena.[159]

In a society composed of competitive individualists, the disruption of social harmony is something to be expected: I fight for my interests or my interpretation of the common good, you fight for yours, and let the best person win. The problem is that many people prioritize social harmony, and they are disadvantaged in a political system that has the effect of exacerbating social conflict. Consider adherents of Confucian ethics. Confucians emphasize that a good life is characterized, first and foremost, by rich and diverse social relations. This is not just a descriptive banality about how our identities are shaped by our communities, but is rather a normative claim that human flourishing is constituted by social relations of certain kinds, so that we have an obligation to nourish those relations. More specifically, we should strive for harmonious social relations, whether in the family, society, or the world or with nature. Harmony, at a minimum, means peaceful order (or the absence of violence). Conflict is unavoidable, but it should be dealt with in a nonviolent way to establish a peaceful order. But peaceful order is not sufficient for a relationship to be characterized as "harmonious." The Confucian idea of harmony also values diversity. Partly, there are aesthetic reasons to value diversity: an ingredient, such as salt, that tastes bland on its own becomes flavorful when mixed in a soup with other ingredients. There are also moral reasons to value diversity: early Confucians emphasized that the ruler should be open to different political views so that mistakes can be exposed and corrected. In short, the Confucian-inspired ideal of harmony is that relations among family members, citizens, and countries, as well as between humans and nature, are key to human flourishing, both in the sense that they matter for well-being and in the moral sense that they generate social obligations. Those relations should all be characterized by peaceful order and respect for diversity.

One response might be to question the extent to which the ideal of harmony is still endorsed today. It may have been a dominant value of preindustrial Chinese society,[160] but today we are supposed to care more about individual freedom, including the right to vote, than about a society that seeks to maximize harmony. But social scientists in a wide array of fields maintain that Chinese characteristically value and strive for Confucian-style harmony in their everyday lives to a much greater degree than average Westerners do.[161] And there is widespread agreement that harmony should be an important goal of government policy: even in Hong Kong—supposedly the most individualist part of China—55.3 percent of people surveyed by the Chinese University of Hong Kong in 2012 agreed that harmony should be the goal of development, compared to 17.8 percent that saw democracy and freedom as goals.[162]

Moreover, the ideal of harmony is widely shared and prioritized outside of China. Confucianism spread beyond China to East Asian societies such as Japan, South Korea, and Vietnam, and today East Asian societies still tend to prioritize the value of harmony. Beyond East Asia, many other societies and cultures also value harmony, even if they have not been influenced by Confucianism in historical practice. Ubuntu, the main ethical tradition in sub-Saharan Africa, is strongly committed to harmony. *Buen vivir* (good living), an idea rooted in the worldview of the Quechua peoples of the Andes that has gained popularity throughout Latin America, emphasizes living in harmony with other people and nature. And so on. In fact, it could be argued that the value of harmony is more widely shared and prioritized in the world's cultures, ethical systems, and religions than supposedly universal values such as freedom. As in many other domains where the citizens of Western, educated, industrialized, rich, and democratic (WEIRD) societies are the international outliers,[163] the "Western" devaluation of the ideal of har-

mony is highly controversial in the rest of the world.[164] In any case, it doesn't take a lot of thought to realize the importance of harmony for human well-being: how many of us can thrive without families and societies characterized by peaceful order and respect for diversity, not to mention a peaceful international order and a nondestructive approach to the natural environment?[165]

Another response might be to question the value of harmony from the perspective of human nature. At the end of the day, we are competitive egoists, and any society that seeks to promote the value of social harmony goes against the grain of human nature. Xunzi, perhaps the third most influential Confucian thinker in the preimperial era, famously questioned Mencius's claim that we are born good. To show innate goodness, Mencius used the example of a child falling down a well: even if we have no personal relationship with that child, we immediately feel a sense of alarm and distress rooted in natural human sympathy. In contrast, Xunzi argued that we are born bad and concerned first and foremost with maximizing our own desires.[166] Contemporary studies in decision neuroscience show that Mencius may have been correct: the brain areas that are active when a person experiences pain firsthand are the same areas that are active when a normally developing child or adult sees someone else experience pain. Even six-month-old infants prefer helpers over neutral parties and neutral parties over competitive types.[167] The ability to feel concern and to respond with sympathy and imaginative perspective is a deep part of our evolutionary heritage, and it is shared with primates of many species.[168] That said, it is obvious that people can become ruthlessly competitive and egoistic if they are placed in a social context that inhibits or punishes the realization of goodness. Mencius himself said that the government must provide for common people's basic means of subsistence so that they won't go morally astray: "The people will not have dependable feelings if they are without dependable means of support. Lacking dependable means of support, they will go astray and fall into excesses, stopping at nothing."[169] Other than heroic figures such as Mahatma Gandhi or Jesus Christ, most people will not behave morally toward non–family members if they are in a situation that necessitates bad behavior in order to survive. More specifically, research suggests that people behave badly when they are not held personally accountable, when nobody raises a critical voice, and when human beings over whom they have power are dehumanized and deindividualized.[170] Here we can add that competitive elections, instead of allowing for the flourishing of human goodness that underpins social harmony, almost counteracts human nature by allowing for, if not encouraging, the demonization of political opponents. And the privacy of the voting booth encourages bad behavior by allowing people to act without being accountable for their actions and without anybody raising a critical voice.

So what can be done? Democratic optimists propose solutions to improve other-regarding behavior and social harmony without questioning the political institution of one person, one vote. Martha Nussbaum argues that moral education in the humanities can teach students to think critically and become knowledgeable and empathetic citizens.[171] Deliberative democrats argue that citizens can and should seek public-spirited perspectives on public issues and promote mutually respectful decision making rather than flattening the political landscape into a contest among interests and preferences.[172] The problem is that nothing prevents politicians from taking the low road on the way to electoral victory. And there is little evidence that the arguments of well-intentioned political theorists have succeeded in promoting a form of political discourse that stems the tide of competitive individualism. If anything, the advent of the Internet facilitates irresponsible and mean-spirited political speech that further (and needlessly) poisons social relations.[173]

An Alternative to Electoral Democracy: No Party Politics

Yet again, we need to turn to alternatives to competitive electoral democracy for inspiration. The philosopher Kwasi Wiredu argues that democracy should not be conceived only as multiparty competition for power. Given that democracy is government by consent, the question is how to devise a form of democracy that is less adversarial than the party system. Wiredu contends that a system based on consensus as a decision-making procedure is a better form of democracy. The kind of consensus need not be agreement regarding questions of truth and morality, but rather agreement about what needs to be done. A consensual system of this sort would be a nonparty arrangement.[174]

Wiredu's theory is inspired by the precolonial history of government by consensus in Africa, but early Anglo-American theorists of representative democracy were also skeptical of multiparty politics. America's founding fathers saw a no-party system as the best for the democracy they envisioned,[175] and the nineteenth-century British liberal theorist John Stuart Mill similarly argued against political parties as expressions of partial interests rather than the common good. The problem is that the system of one person, one vote necessarily slides into multiparty politics as people with different interests and values coalesce into different groups. Wiredu argues that multiparty politics can be prevented by institutionalizing formal representation for different groups in the legislature: "civil organizations might be assigned some agreed number of representatives in the governing body."[176] Wiredu's proposal is similar to Hegel's proposal for a lower house of corporations and social guilds. Hegel worried that individuals not tied to any groups or organizations would be, in his words, "elemental, irrational, barbarous, and terrifying."[177] According to Hegel, individuals come to take an interest in common enterprises and to develop a certain degree of political competence only by joining and participating in voluntary associations and community groups, with the political implication that the lower house should be composed of corporations and professional guilds (the upper house should be composed of the landed propertied class).

In the modern world, the closest approximation of the Hegel/Wiredu ideal is the Legislative Council of Hong Kong. In 1985, the British colonial government decided to institute elections for a number of seats in order to represent more authoritatively the views of Hong Kong people. But it disparaged the idea of introducing direct elections for universal suffrage on the grounds that this might lead to instability. So the government decided that a large number of seats should be allocated to functional constituencies based on various interest groups, a system that still exists, with the largest block of seats assigned to business groups and professional associations. But the functional system lacks legitimacy: most functional constituency representatives are perceived as serving the narrow interests of the richest groups and most privileged members of the community, and there are endless disputes over how to draw the lines within and between the various voting blocs. Not surprisingly, the large majority of Hong Kongers prefer to replace this system with directly elected seats based on multiparty competition and one person, one vote[178] (i.e., precisely the kind of democratic system that is rejected by Wiredu). To be fair, Wiredu argues for a democratic system that would be based on consensus, with policies being enacted only after agreement about what needs to be done by all groups in the legislature, so groups could not simply represent (or be seen to represent) the interests of a particular group. But appealing to the value of consensus solves one problem at the cost of creating an even bigger one: the expectation that everybody in a large, modern, and pluralistic political community can agree about what needs to be done is not realistic. Perhaps small, relatively homogenous communities can agree in a consensual way about what needs to be done, but the result of striving for a genuine, unforced consensus in a country like China is that nothing would get done.

In fact, there is no need to posit an entirely imaginary (and unrealistic) political ideal if the aim is to minimize adversarial politics and promote social harmony. China has many problems, but most citizens perceive China as a harmonious society and the country is more harmonious than large democratic countries such as India and the United States.[179] Here China's political model may be helpful. At the local village level, elections take place without competitive party politics on the assumption that there can be some sort of village-based consensus about what needs to be done. While there is a large gap between the ideal and the reality, it is not unrealistic to strive for more such "democracy by consensus" in villages where the issues are not complex, people know one another and their political leaders, and there may be a stronger sense of community (see chapter 4, section 3). At the central level of government in a country of 1.3 billion people, the best we can hope for (in terms of achieving consensus) is a common view that emerges from public-spirited deliberation among elites. Of course, China relies on force to prevent the open articulation of diverse interests and the formation of political parties that compete for political power, which may only serve to bottle up social conflict so that it explodes later. Social harmony in China may be (at least partly) the product of top-down campaigns that are not as effective at promoting other-regarding behavior (especially toward strangers) as citizen empowerment and community development.[180] Hence, political reformers in China argue for intraparty democracy that would allow for internal competition within the CCP, more independent organizations in civil society, and a freer media environment.[181] Such developments can and should help to bring about a more harmonious society. But full democratization in the form of one person, one vote and a competitive multiparty system is likely to aggravate social conflict and forever bury the ideal of a harmonious society.

This chapter was written primarily for Western readers brought up in a political culture that sanctifies electoral democracy as the best (or least bad) regime and for Chinese democrats with a blind faith in the benefits of electoral democracy.[182] I have argued that there are morally desirable and politically feasible alternatives to electoral democracy that can help to remedy major disadvantages of electoral democracy. I realize that the discussion of nondemocratic theories and real politics in Singapore and China is bound to be controversial, and I do not expect the reader to endorse the view that political meritocracy is superior to electoral democracy. But my aim thus far has been more modest: to "desacralize" the ideal of one person, one vote by showing that electoral democracies do not necessarily perform better than political meritocracies according to widely shared standards of good government. At the very least, Chinese-style political meritocracy can be viewed as a grand political experiment with the potential to remedy key defects of electoral democracy, and outsiders should encourage the experiment rather than hoping for its failure (not to mention promoting a "prodemocracy" foreign policy designed to increase the likelihood of failure).

So long as the reader is willing to question the view that democracy is the least bad system, then we can proceed to the next chapter. There is no point in arguing for political meritocracy with democratic fundamentalists. That said, it may not really matter what democratic fundamentalists think. If the aim is to propose suggestions for improving China's political system, we can simply assume that China's one-party system is not about to collapse and argue for improvements on that basis. Hence, I will not pursue the question of whether China should adopt one person, one vote and competitive multiparty politics to choose its top rulers because that question is not likely to be on the political agenda in the foreseeable future. It is a nonquestion, politically speaking.

CHAPTER 2

On the Selection of Good Leaders in a Political Meritocracy

In the early 1990s, several Asian officials and their supporters put forward the idea of "Asian values" to assert that Asian societies should not adopt liberal democratic political values and practices. As Singapore's former prime minister Lee Kuan Yew put it, "Asians have little doubt that a society where the interests of society take precedence over that of the individual suits them better than the individualism of America."[1] Such claims attracted international attention primarily because East Asian leaders seemed to be presiding over what a United Nations human development report called "the most sustained development miracle of the twentieth century, perhaps all history."[2]

The debate over "Asian values" was led by political leaders with questionable motives, but the views of Lee and his colleagues did have some traction in Asian societies: it prompted critical intellectuals in the East Asian region to reflect on how they can locate themselves in a debate on human rights in which they had not previously played a substantial part.[3] In the 1990s, the values debate focused mainly on human rights. How "universal" is a human rights regime that draws only (or mainly) on the moral aspirations and political practices found in Western liberal democratic societies? If Asian cultures are less individualistic than Western ones, then perhaps certain forms of governance and policies are more suitable to Asian societies that are different from the human rights standards typically endorsed by liberal theorists, Western governments, and international human rights documents formulated without substantial input from East Asia. How can "Asian values" and cultural traditions enrich the "international" human rights regime so that it truly becomes an international order based on universally accepted human rights? Asian critics of "Western-style" human rights criticized liberals both for not respecting nonliberal moralities in Asia that might justify deviations from a "Western" human rights regime, and for failing to do what must be done to make human rights a truly universal ideal.

In 1997–1998, however, the East Asian miracle seemed to have collapsed. And the debate over "Asian values" was one casualty of the crisis. For many, the end came not a minute too soon because the whole debate seemed to rest on faulty theoretical premises. Most obviously, Asia is a huge and exceptionally diverse landmass, encompassing much of the world's population. It hosts a number of religions, such as Islam, Hinduism, Confucianism, Christianity, and Buddhism, as well as myriad races, ethnicities, customs, and languages. The assumption that Asia has its own cultural essence fundamentally different from that of the West is, to say the least, dubious. And Asian politicians such as South Korea's former president Kim Dae Jung openly questioned the idea of "Asian values" defended by Lee Kuan Yew, arguing that liberal democratic political values and practices are both universal and appropriate for his country.[4] It would be only a slight exaggeration to say that "Asian values" were really "Singaporean values" as interpreted by that country's political leaders!

Ironically, few paid attention to the really innovative Singaporean contribution to the debate about political values: the official discourse from Singapore has theoretical and practical interest not so much because it challenges the universality of human rights but because it challenges the universality of democracy. Singapore's leaders reject the dichotomy between "good" democratic and "bad" authoritarian regimes. Rather, they argue that the concept of meritocracy best describes Singapore's political system: given Singapore's small population and limited resource base, the country should be led by people with the greatest talent and best characters, chosen according to merit. But what does it mean to select political leaders according to merit? Which abilities and which virtues matter for political leaders? For Singapore's leaders, intellectual ability matters most, as measured by su-

perior academic performance. In terms of political virtues, Singaporean leaders emphasize clean government, meaning lack of corruption. Leaders are not selected so much on the basis of positive virtues,[5] but they are deselected if they are shown to be corrupt.[6] In short, Singaporean leaders argue for the need to institutionalize selection and promotion mechanisms for choosing noncorrupt and highly intelligent leaders with the power to decide on a wide range of issues affecting the political community, even if it means constraints on the democratic process.

Since the country's independence in 1965, Singapore's leaders gained the trust of the population by presiding over stunning economic growth. Over the past few years, however, the Singapore government has struggled to retain the trust and respect of the population. Therefore it has changed its ways. In response to widespread aspirations for more political participation, the government has loosened controls on political speech and no longer relies on harsh retaliation against political opponents. In response to high income inequality and less social mobility, the government has provided more benefits for the disadvantaged and the middle class. The government still emphasizes that meritocratically selected leaders should take the long view beyond the next electoral cycle, but it recognizes the need for political leaders with a more caring outlook. The new outlook has been termed "compassionate meritocracy."[7]

Such debates over political merit have a long history in China. The idea of "elevating the worthy" emerged in the wake of the disintegration of the pedigree-based order of the Spring and Autumn period (770–453 BCE) and proliferated rapidly throughout the Warring States period (453–221 BCE), being shared by every major intellectual current. As Yuri Pines shows, there was wide disagreement over what counts as "worth" or "merit."[8] For Confucius and his followers, "worthiness" is primarily related to one's morality. For pragmatic statesmen known as Legalists, morality cannot be objectively measured and they warned that unless precisely defined, "worthiness" can be manipulated by hypocrites and one's partisans rather than used as a criterion for selecting truly capable public servants. Imperial China's great contribution to the debate on political meritocracy is the public service examination system: for more than thirteen hundred years, public officials were se-

lected largely by means of competitive examinations. Here too, political thinkers debated what constitutes political merit (and whether exams are appropriate mechanisms for selecting political leaders with merit), but the idea that political theorizing should be concerned with the question of how to select political leaders with superior abilities and virtues was rarely questioned.

The ideal of political meritocracy is not foreign to Western political theory and practice. Plato famously defended a meritocratic political ideal in *The Republic*: the best political regime is composed of political leaders selected on the basis of their superior ability to make morally informed political judgments, who have the power to rule the community. Meritocracy was influential throughout subsequent history, although thinkers from Aristotle on rarely defended a pure form of political meritocracy. The U.S. founding fathers were committed to some form of democracy, but they also agreed that the political system should be designed with the aim of selecting rulers with superior ability and virtue: as Thomas Jefferson wrote in a letter to John Adams in 1813,

> I agree with you that there is a natural aristocracy among men. The grounds of this are virtue and talents. . . . There is also an artificial aristocracy founded on wealth and birth, without either virtue or talents; for with these it would belong to the first class. The natural aristocracy I consider as the most precious gift of nature for the instruction, the trusts, and government of society. . . . May we not even say that that form of government is the best which provides the most effectually for a pure selection of these natural *aristoi* into the offices of government?"[9]

In the same vein, nineteenth-century "liberal elitists" such as John Stuart Mill and Alexis de Tocqueville put forward political ideas that tried to combine meritocracy and democracy. In the second half of the twentieth century, however, such debates in Western political theory (and in the discourse of political leaders) largely came to an end. The key reason is the almost universal consensus (in Western societies) that political leaders with the power to exercise political judgments in a wide range of domains should be selected by means of one person, one vote.[10] Liberal democracies do empower experts selected because of their abilities in administrative and judicial posts, but those experts must be accountable, if only in an indirect way, to democratically elected leaders. They are not meant to exercise power beyond the limited mandate endorsed and given to them by democratically elected leaders. It is fine to discuss, say, what ought to be the desirable character traits of democratically elected leaders with the aim of influencing voters, the leaders themselves, and/or the democratic process,[11] but those leaders should be chosen by the voters, not by an alternative mechanism explicitly designed to maximize the likelihood that leaders will have those character traits. The question of how to institutionalize nonelectoral mechanisms for choosing political leaders with superior abilities and virtues that have the power to decide on a wide range of issues affecting the political community has come to be regarded as irrelevant to political theorizing, if not beyond the moral pale.

In contemporary China, it's a different story. After the political chaos of the Cultural Revolution, Chinese leaders realized the need to implement a system for the selection and promotion of high-quality leaders appropriate for a period of peaceful economic development. Inspired by China's history of selecting officials by examination and recommendation[12] and (to a lesser extent) by the Singapore model (see chapter 1, section 1), they devised a sophisticated and comprehensive system for selecting and promoting political officials, involving decades of training and a battery of exams at different stages of their careers.[13] Yet the system is still in its early stages and plagued by imperfections: officials are selected and promoted not just on the basis of ability and morality, but also (if not more so) on the basis of political loyalty, social connections, and family background (see section 3). The political system is notoriously corrupt and the practice of buying and selling posts at lower levels of government in poor areas has yet to be completely eradicated.[14] More serious (from a theoretical point of view), the ideal itself is not so clear: which abilities and virtues should set the standard for the selection and promotion of government officials so that the Chinese political system can be improved? And what sorts of mechanisms and institutions can increase the likelihood that officials are selected and promoted on the basis of those abilities and virtues? Given the centrality of these questions to China's political future, the absence of systematic research is striking (and disappointing).

Hence, any answer is somewhat speculative and needs to be put to the test of social scientific research.

This chapter, I say without any false modesty, is the beginning of a sketch of an answer. The first section will discuss the context for the relevant kind of leadership: how does political leadership differ from other forms of leadership, and what does it mean to be a leader in a modernizing, relatively peaceful society such as China that aims to be governed by meritocratically selected leaders? The following three sections will put forward ideas of what ought to be the key qualities (intellectual abilities, social skills, and virtues) of political leaders and suggest mechanisms that increase the likelihood that leaders will be selected and promoted on the basis of those qualities. This chapter is written with the Chinese context in mind, but each section begins with more general considerations that may apply to considerations of political leadership in other societies.

1. Leadership in Context

According to one estimate, more than 250 English-language books on leadership are published every year.[15] I confess I haven't read them all, but the ones I did read often share a common trait: they describe the qualities of good leaders as though the same qualities apply regardless of context. Perhaps all leaders of large organizations in the modern world do share some qualities. But it is hard to describe those qualities without resorting to general platitudes—leaders should make sound decisions and implement them effectively, manage individuals as they move through the organization, appropriately disburse funds, meet certain outcomes, be responsive to the needs of the stakeholders, and so on—that do not really deepen understanding, not to mention serve as concrete guides for action. If the aim is to think about the qualities of political leaders and to specify mechanisms that can increase the likelihood of such leaders being recruited and promoted, it is important to be more sensitive to context. Surely different organizations have different requirements, meaning that they may need leaders with different abilities, skills, and virtues. And surely the same organization may have different requirements at different times, meaning that it may need different kinds of leaders at different times with different kinds of qualities. So what are the qualities required of political leaders? To be more specific, what are the qualities required of leaders in the upper echelons of the CCP?

In August 2013, Singapore's former foreign minister George Yeo published a thought-provoking article titled "China and the Catholic Church."[16] Yeo argues that the newly installed leaders of the Catholic Church and the CCP face similar challenges. Both head organizations responsible for about one-fifth of humanity. Neither was elected by the entire citizenry or congregation of the faithful, and in both cases "the idea of direct election to the top leadership would have been thought absurd." Despite centralized bureaucratic governance, there is much regional and local diversity in both organizations. With the social media revolution, the hierarchical structures of both organizations are coming under attack and leaders once protected by ritual and distance and sometimes hypocrisy and ignorance now seem more human. Corruption and sexual misdeeds have been widely reported in both organizations, not necessarily because they have become more common but because they are harder to cover up. And the leaders of both organizations have responded to the new challenges in similar ways. Both President Xi and Pope Francis have made efforts to seem more authentic and close to the people than their predecessors. Both leaders took symbolic actions signaling that leaders with power should be humble and lead modest lifestyles. In short, even organizations that seem strikingly different (the CCP is officially atheist!) require similar abilities and virtues in their top leaders.[17]

Still, it must be recognized that there are also organization-specific leadership skills. Consider the sixth-century *Book of Pastoral Rule* by St. Gregory the Great, a Christian classic that details the qualities required of those who come to a position of spiritual leadership. Some qualities seem applicable to leaders of different sorts of organizations—for example, "He must set such a positive example for others that he has nothing for which he should ever be ashamed." But other qualities seem specific to the Catholic Church—for example, "He must be dead to the passions of the flesh and live a spiritual life."[18] Ascetic experience may be a prerequisite for leadership in the Catholic Church, but a political leader need not be entirely dead to the passions in order to serve the public, nor should he or she spend too much time living a spiritual life if it interferes with, say, communicating with the public and reading up on current events. Moreover, it may be true that "the spiritual director in his zeal should not desire to please others, but should focus on what ought to please them,"[19] but a political leader should be at least partly concerned with pleasing others, not simply with trying to implement a vision of the common good that owes nothing to what people actually want. Clearly, leaders of religious organizations are concerned first and foremost with a spiritual mission that may require qualities different from those required of political leaders.[20]

Today, it is more common to compare leadership skills required in business and those required in politics. In January 2012, I was lucky enough to participate in the annual World Economic Forum meeting in Davos, Switzerland. At a luncheon meeting with CEOs of Fortune 500 companies, I asked the CEOs if they think the qualities required of leaders in large business organizations differed in any way from the qualities required of political leaders. To my surprise, the whole panel of CEOs agreed that there were no differences. To press the point, I then asked a CEO on the panel, "Is there anything that you do that you think leaders of government should NOT do?" Again, he responded, no, leadership is leadership.

In fact, such views are not uncommon. Most books on leadership are written for the business world and few distinguish between the qualities required of business leaders and the qualities required of political leaders. One particularly insightful (and entertaining) book on leadership is titled *The 100-Mile Walk*. A father-and-son team, separated by differences in generation and political outlook, discuss the qualities of leadership during the course of long walks over several days. Contrary to expectations, they settle on common ideas about leadership. Effective leaders must be able to inspire, not simply direct or compel followers. Other traits include having sufficient self-esteem to recruit and reward intelligent people and to accept criticism from them. Leaders also need a sense of purpose and passion. Leaders should continuously work at their craft. Such traits do indeed seem like general traits of all effective leaders. But some traits clearly seem confined to the business world. For example, the elder Flaum says that leaders should be paranoid (like fighter pilots) and do what is necessary to keep a competitive edge and not be copied by others. But for political leaders, paranoia may be a vice rather than a virtue (President Nixon is a famous case) and it is not necessarily a problem if good policies are being copied by other political leaders. The book also praises a former New York City fire commissioner for relating better to low-status people than to wealthy elites: a sound practice for a public servant, perhaps, but not necessarily a desirable trait for a CEO. Yet not once in the book is there any attempt to distinguish between the different requirements of leadership in politics and business. The leadership qualities of public officials such as John Glenn are praised along the same lines as the leadership qualities of senior leaders of PepsiCo and Johnson and Johnson, as though the same types of leaders are meant to serve different types of organizations.[21]

To the extent business leaders do recognize that there are differences between politics and business, the point is often that government can and should learn from business. Some of the world's business leaders, including Jack Welch, have suggested that government should be run more like a business.[22] Over the past few decades, government has become more businesslike in the management of its affairs: government reliance on advisors and services provided by the corporate sector has hastened the advance of businesslike approaches in government, with a substantial increase in the use of modern management tools and principles, such as business strategy, key performance indicators, professional procurement, and operational efficiency. Hence, it should not be surprising that aspirants to political leadership such as Mitt Romney and Donald Trump often tout their business experience as evidence of their ability to manage the affairs of their country.[23]

While some business leaders have made relatively successful transitions to the political world (Michael Bloomberg is a good example), the experience with bringing business models into government is not so positive: highly polarizing cases such as Thaksin Shinawatra in Thailand, and Silvio Berlusconi in Italy may be more typical than success. Similarly, political leaders often fail when they venture into business. The Chinese government has acknowledged the concern among many economists that China's state-owned enterprises (SOEs) are an unsustainable drag on the country's economy and that the government's overwhelming role in appointing the top leaders of SOEs promotes not just corruption but also inefficiency. Hence, China's leaders launched pilot schemes to improve corporate governance, including measures allowing SOEs' boards of directors to appoint senior management and set performance metrics regardless of the policy orientations of the state.[24] The aim of the reforms is to open recruitment at state firms for senior management jobs and increase the likelihood that key personnel are selected on commercial rather than political grounds.[25] Although there may be a good case to be made for the CCP's Organization Department (responsible for the selection and promotion of party cadres) to promote some form of "leadership training" in state firms,[26] given the importance of economic considerations in shaping political decisions,[27] the idea that the government should use purely political criteria to select leaders for top posts in SOEs is just as controversial as the idea that political leaders should govern the polity strictly according to the same criteria used to run a business.

An important reason that business models do not translate so well into politics, and vice versa, is that public and private organizations have different aims.[28] For better or worse, few business leaders would deny that the primary purpose of business is the maximization of profit. There are different views about whether it should be in the short term or the long term, but business leaders cannot lose sight of the fact that business is ultimately about making a profit. In contrast, the task of government is not so clear. Most political thinkers, whatever their orientation, agree that government leaders are supposed to serve the people. But what is the government supposed to do for the people? Provide security, combat poverty, protect individual liberty, increase happiness, reduce inequality, promote social harmony, protect a country's historical heritage, or all of the above in different proportions? What constitutes performance within government "is more complicated, pluralistic, value laden, and controversial than is true with the performance of private firms. . . . Unlike private firms for which profits and returns on investment provide widely accepted measures of success, for public organizations the criteria of success are many and controversial. . . . There is also a significant symbolic component to the actions of government, consisting of the language and the images to describe what is taking place and the public's reactions to those messages. Appearances matter almost as much as reality."[29]

Given the different aims of business and government, leaders often need different qualities. In business, the key stakeholders are relatively clear: the owners and (to a lesser extent) employees. In government, the stakeholders are more comprehensive and diverse. Who are political leaders supposed to serve? All those affected by the policies of government, the people in the country's territory, future generations, ancestors, or all of the above in different proportions? How to distribute desired goods among the relevant group of people and who is supposed to pay for them? Whatever the political leader's own views, she should be willing to revise her views in response to input from the diverse set of stakeholders. Hence, a government official should be willing to listen to diverse and often conflicting perspectives, to balance different goals, values, and interests, and to shape her aims at least partly in response to such widespread engagements. A business leader needs to incorporate the views of other people, but only insofar as it contributes to the bottom line. A CEO such as Jack Welch can use methods such as "criticizing, demeaning, ridiculing, humiliating"[30] that are unlikely to be effective in a political world that relies more on cooperation, praise, and strategic ambiguity to get things done.[31] And different sectors of society in a modern political community will evaluate and criticize the performance of political leaders; in business, there is less need for public scrutiny. Hence, political leaders need to be more willing to accept and respond to criticisms from diverse sectors of society.

The focus on profit also means that business leaders need to reward high performers, meaning those who contribute to the profitability of the firm. Regarding underachievers, the business leader should "be direct and honest. . . . [W]hen employees fall short, you have to have the courage to walk your talk, to confront the issue and make the change. . . . Just as you have to have the courage to take out your weak players, you must take care of your great achievers no matter what, because if you don't, they'll walk."[32] For example, MetLife asks managers to use a lifeboat ranking for their team, and the bottom 20 percent are either placed on probation or lose their jobs.[33] In contrast, political leaders need not be as concerned with high economic achievers; defenders of the free market will say that successful economic actors are best left alone, social democrats will say that high achievers should pay a relatively high share of taxes, but both sides agree that political leaders need not devote all (or most) of their time to considering the interests of successful and high-status members of the political community. Nor should political leaders "take out" the weak members of the political community because they do not contribute to the overall good of the state. Quite the opposite: political thinkers from Mencius to Rawls argue that political leaders need to be particularly concerned with the plight of the disadvantaged.[34] Finally, innovation is more important for business: in a cutthroat capitalist world, most businesses must innovate to compete; in government, innovation may not be the number one priority, and the state won't go "out of business" if it doesn't innovate.

Another key difference is that business leaders need not be overly concerned with the well-being of the society in which they operate, nor need they be overly concerned with respecting its traditions and historical heritage. To the extent that social responsibility is part of a business enterprise, it should not interfere with its core profit-making mission. Hence, most corporations today maintain a clear dichotomy between profit-making and social responsibility functions, which are managed separately. Moreover, it is common for corporate social responsibility functions to be aligned as much as possible with initiatives to further maximize profit. For example, a bank may sponsor an international sporting event to increase brand recognition among the public, or a mining company may invest in social infrastructure for remote communities to facilitate access to nearby mineral resources.[35]

Corporate social responsibility need not always serve commercial interests, but when the good of the company conflicts with the wider social good, the former has priority. If a bank can increase its profit at some cost to the social whole, it will normally be expected to do so. It is the task of government regulators, not CEOs, to try to minimize damage to the overall society. If a company can make substantially more profit by moving its operations abroad or by being taken over by a foreign company, it can do so. Business leaders need to be concerned with the greater social good if it affects the profitability of the firm, but they need not otherwise be patriotic or attached to a particular society.[36] Hence, it is not uncommon to appoint foreigners to head large companies, even in supposedly xenophobic societies such as Japan. In contrast, the leader of a political community, no matter what the form of government, needs to be from that community. In the past, colonial powers appointed overlords to rule over foreign lands, but it would not be acceptable today. At a minimum, a political leader must be seen to be a patriotic member of the political community.

Max Weber's "Politics as Vocation"

In short, political leaders face quite distinct challenges that require distinct abilities and virtues. So what exactly are the qualities of good political leaders? The most influential twentieth-century work on the qualities of political leadership is Max Weber's essay "Politics as a Vocation," first delivered as a lecture to the Free Students Union at the University of Munich in 1919. He begins the essay with the famous definition of the state as a human community that (successfully) claims the monopoly of the legitimate use of physical force within a given territory. He then invokes the equally famous distinction between traditional, charismatic, and legal sources of legitimacy (meaning the different ways that domination is seen to be morally justified by the ruled), and he specifies that his lecture is concerned with the qualities of leaders that dominate by charisma, that is, domination by virtue of the devotion of those who obey the purely personal charisma of the leader: "Devotion to the charisma of the prophet, or the leader in war, or to the great demagogue in the ecclesia or in parliament, means that the leader is personally recognized as the innerly 'called' leader of men. Men do not obey him by virtue of tradition or statute, but because they believe in him. If he is more than an upstart of the moment, the leader lives for his cause and 'strives for his work.' The devotion of his disciples, his followers, his personal party friends is oriented to his person and to its qualities."

But political leaders with the "inner charismatic qualities that make a leader" are a specific breed. A political leader must live *for* politics and make politics his life, and not just live *off* politics, meaning that politics is viewed primarily as a source of income.[37] Political officials can be transferred, dismissed, or at least temporarily withdrawn, in contrast to administrative officials in the bureaucracy who develop specialized expertise through long years of preparatory training. The political leader must take exclusive personal responsibility for what he does, in contrast to the civil servant who must execute conscientiously the order of the superior authorities, even if it appears wrong to him. The political leader enjoys the feeling of power: "the knowledge of influencing men, of participating in power over them, and above all, the feeling of holding in one's hands a nerve fiber of historically important events." But the good political leader will also ask "through what qualities can I hope to do justice to this power."

Weber says that three preeminent qualities are decisive for the politician: passion, a feeling of responsibility, and a sense of proportion. Passion matters, in the sense not of emotional excitation but rather of devotion to a cause. The political leader must also make responsibility to this cause the guiding star of action. And a sense of proportion is needed to "let realities work upon him with inner concentration and calmness. Hence his *distance* to things and men." The question for the good political leader, in short, "is simply how can warm passion and a cool sense of proportion be forged together in one and the same soul?" In the case of the bad political leader, "the striving for power ceases to be *objective* and becomes purely personal self-gratification, instead of exclusively entering the service of 'the cause.' For ultimately there are only two kinds of deadly sins in politics: lack of objectivity and—often but not identical with it—irresponsibility. Vanity, the need personally to stand in the foreground as much as possible, strongly tempts the politician to commit one or both of these sins."

The good politician should be guided by an "ethic of responsibility," meaning he has to give an account of the foreseeable results of his actions, not simply by an "ethic of ultimate ends" that only values good intentions. An ethic of ultimate ends provides guidance as to which ends are right, but it cannot stand alone without consideration of results. The political leader must be prepared to use morally dubious means for good results: "The world is governed by demons and that he who lets himself in for politics, that is, for power and force as means, contracts with diabolical powers and for his action it is not true that good can follow only from good and evil only from evil, but that often the opposite is true. Anyone who fails to see this is, indeed, a political infant." Whoever wants to engage in politics as a vocation has to realize these ethical paradoxes and accept responsibility for the results: "He who seeks the salvation of the soul, of his own or of others, should not seek it along the path of politics, for the quite different tasks of politics can only be solved by violence."[38]

In short, politics is the art of compromise and decision making based on social benefits and weighed against costs and backed up by the instruments of violence, so political action cannot solely be guided by convictions. Political leaders must take into account all that is at stake in making a political decision and accept responsibility for the outcomes. Political leaders most likely to satisfy these requirements will have both passion for politics driven primarily by moral conviction and a cool-headed ability to consider diverse perspectives and make use of the instruments of violence for the sake of less-than-perfect political decisions.

Weber's analysis helps us think further about how political leadership differs from other forms of leadership. But the requirements of political leadership will also vary according to different political contexts.[39] It is hard to blame Weber for the general character of his account of the qualities of the good political leader (he was delivering a lecture, and only a few lines speak directly to the topic), but even his general remarks do not apply in certain contexts. Weber's account of the charismatic political leader seems more applicable in times of warfare or violent civil strife. A wartime leader needs to be driven by conviction and to dominate people by the power of charisma. He also needs to solve problems by resorting to violence and take personal responsibility for the outcomes.

In the context of a modernizing, largely peaceful society characterized by collective leadership such as China, the desired traits of a leader are likely to be different, perhaps closer to the characteristics of what Weber calls the "civil servant," with long periods of preparatory training and intellectual knowledge of different disciplines. Hence, when wartime heroes try to govern in peaceful times, from the First Emperor of Qin to Mao Zedong and Robert Mugabe, they often turn out to be disasters.

Weber's distinction between the political leader who decides and the civil servant who implements is also context-specific. In imperial

China (as Weber recognizes), there was no distinction between civil servants and political leaders: the successful examination candidates were put on the road to be political leaders with the power to decide on matters affecting the lives of millions of people (although they were still supposed to serve, in an ultimate sense, at the behest of the emperor). In contemporary China, the public service examinations (misleadingly translated as "civil service examinations") are also steppingstones to political power; there are not separate tracks for political officials and civil servants.[40] Nor does Weber distinguish between the qualities required of political leaders at different levels of government; in a huge country such as China, for example, superior intellectual ability (not mentioned by Weber) may be particularly important for central-level political leaders, which may not be the case for village leaders. In the Ming dynasty, for example, government officials in the capital had to meet more demanding evaluation requirements than those outside.[41]

Today, prospective officials for posts at higher levels of government in China are tested for different abilities than those at lower levels: the public service examinations for lower levels of government test for the ability to implement the goals of the organization and the ability to resolve problems (as well as reading comprehension and writing expression), but the exams for higher levels of government (subprovincial and above) also test for the ability to "comprehensively analyze" (analyzing all parts of the contents, standpoints, or questions of the given information and to make reasonable inferences or evaluation) and the ability to "raise and resolve problems" (based on the understanding and analysis of the given information, use one's own practical or living experience to find and define problems, provide evaluation or trade-offs, and propose a solution plan or course of action).[42] Upper-level cadres are also typically expected to have a university education.[43]

In short, context matters. If the aim is to discuss the abilities and virtues of a good leader, it is important not just to differentiate between leadership in politics and other spheres of social life, but also between different kinds of political leaders in different places and times. So here's the context I have in mind: the qualities required of political leaders selected by nondemocratic mechanisms at higher levels of government in large, modernizing countries with relatively secure territorial boundaries. In reality, China is the only country that comes close to fitting that description, but there is a large gap between the meritocratic ideal described here and the reality in contemporary China; the point of discussing an ideal is to provide standards for reform.

Given the focus on political meritocracies, I will not discuss qualities that may be more appropriate for political leaders in democratic societies, such as a very thick skin, the ability to think quickly on one's feet, the need to exaggerate differences with political opponents and to give the same partisan stump speech with the same apparent degree of enthusiasm repeatedly during the campaign season, as well as the ability to switch to a more inclusive political discourse that seeks to explain and justify policies to the public after election victory.[44] Nor will I discuss in any detail what those leaders should do because China is a large and complex country with different needs and priorities in different times and places,[45] and any informed answer depends partly on what the Chinese people actually want. Hence, I will assume that leaders should seek to promote the well-being of the people, but beyond that my discussion of the qualities required of leaders in a political meritocracy is meant to be compatible with many different theories and views regarding the purposes of government (see section 4). In each section, I will begin by discussing general qualities of political leadership in political meritocracies, followed by a discussion of qualities that may be more China-specific. I will also propose nondemocratic mechanisms that increase the likelihood of selecting and promoting political leaders with those qualities.

2. On the Need for Intellectual Ability

Which abilities matter for public officials also depends on the context. In ancient times of incessant warfare, physical abilities were most important: for example, the Warring States thinker Shang Yang proposed that soldiers should be promoted based on the number of decapitated heads of enemy soldiers.[46] In today's world, intellectual abilities matter more.[47] A political leader needs to understand complex arguments and make decisions based on knowledge of the latest developments in a number of interconnected disciplines that bear on the policy-making process: economics, science, international relations, psychology, and so on. In addition, sound decision making requires a global outlook. Globalization and technological innovation in the past few decades have made the world increasingly interconnected, with the result that financial, political, social, and environmental shocks spread faster and become more disruptive.[48] To ensure social stability and sustained growth, political leaders need to be adaptable, agile, and responsive to looming global risks.[49] Hence, it is insufficient to rely on well-crafted national political institutions and laws: an ability to understand the world and respond to rapid changes in a risk-prone world in an informed and intelligent way is an essential requirement of what it means to be an effective political leader today, and arguably the qualities of political leaders matter more than ever before in human history.

Singapore, once again, has been ahead of the curve. Its leaders have long emphasized intellectual ability. As Singapore's founding father Lee Kuan Yew put it, "I am sorry if I am constantly preoccupied with what the near-geniuses and the above average are going to do. But I am convinced that it is they who ultimately decide the shape of things to come."[50] Lee himself graduated with a rare double first-class honors degree from Cambridge University, and his son Lee Hsien Loong (the current prime minister) graduated from the same university by scoring twelve more alphas than his nearest competitor (which had never been seen in the history of Tripos at Cambridge). It should not be surprising that Singapore has institutionalized a rigorous system for the recruitment of political talent that starts with the search for high academic achievers in the school system, followed by a battery of examinations at key stages in the selection and promotion process. Almost all of Singapore's key political decision makers have stellar academic backgrounds, which surely helps to explain why Singapore's policy-making process is usually supported by social scientific research and knowledge of best practices abroad, perhaps more so than any other political community. China has been learning from Singapore in this respect, as well as looking to its own past as inspiration for meritocratic reform.

A Mechanism for Recruiting Political Officials with Intellectual Ability: The Imperial Examination System

The idea of using exams as a mechanism to search for political talent might seem odd to Westerners, but it has deep roots in Chinese political culture. As we saw, the principle of political meritocracy—the appointing of officials according to merit rather than their pedigree—was shared by every major intellectual current in the preimperial period. Yet thinkers argued over not just the content of merit but also the kinds of mechanisms necessary to identify political merit. The establishment and institutionalization of the examination system largely settled the latter debate in imperial China, with even harsh critics of the examination system such as Zhu Xi (1130–1200) agreeing that the examinations were necessary for selecting political officials.[51]

Emperor Wu of Han (r. 141–87 BCE) started an early form of the imperial examinations: local officials would select candidates to take part in an examination on the Confucian classics, from which he would select officials to serve by his side. There were other avenues for promotion, but examinations were specifically designed to broaden access to government service for the local elites. During the Eastern Han (25–220 CE), examinations for talent were used to screen candidates to ensure competence in specialized fields, such as flood control and foreign policy, and the Imperial University expanded to the point that it significantly influenced composition of the officialdom. But local magnates objected to state-based competitive examinations and argued in favor of promoting the people according to their moral behavior, as judged by neighbors and approved by local officials. Recruitment on the basis of local recommendations was adopted at the very end of the Han and continued to dominate the process of selecting officials for the next three hundred years or so. As power devolved to the local communities with the court rubber-stamping local recommendations, the composition of the elite turned into a powerful hereditary aristocracy closed to outsiders, and examinations gradually lost their prestige.[52]

Examinations were revived and expanded during the Sui (581–618) and Tang (618–907) dynasties with the aim of discontinuing aristocratic rule and reconfirming the right of the throne to have the final say in determining one's rank. Recruitment in the imperial government became an imperial prerogative rather than a duty to be performed by lower levels, and selection by recommendation was replaced by selection by examination. The tests—the world's first standardized tests based on merit—were designed as objective measures to evaluate the educational attainment and merit of the examinees, as part of the process of final selections and appointments to political office. In the Tang period, examinations became a necessary condition for officialdom for the first time in Chinese (or human) history: candidates for political office took qualifying examinations, and then underwent a selection process that evaluated moral character and determined the level of appointment.[53] The examination system was consolidated under the Song dynasty, and examinations became the primary channel for entry into officialdom: all successful candidates examined in the capital were automatically appointed to government offices.[54] Song rulers also implemented institutional reforms of the examination system that were to characterize the institutional form of the examinations for the next millennium, such as creating three levels of examinations and establishing a triennial schedule for the examinations.[55]

The examination system was briefly interrupted at the beginning of the (Mongol) Yuan dynasty (1280–1368), but the dynasty belatedly renewed the examination system in 1313. The Yuan rulers incorporated aspects of Song dynasty "Learning of the Way" (or Neo-Confucianism) in the examination curriculum, though the examination system was still a minor avenue for entry into officialdom. The system matured under the Ming: for the first time, examination success at the provincial level opened the way to an official career. Neo-Confucian ideas about moral thought and classical statecraft served as important models for the examination curriculum (and intellectual orthodoxy more generally) during both the Ming and (Manchu) Qing dynasties.[56] The examination system also spread to Korea and Vietnam as a means of drawing in (and maintaining a grip on) top national talent.[57]

Although the meritocratic idea of selecting officials by means of examinations was often flawed in practice, particularly toward the end of dynasties,[58] the whole system was challenged as a result of humiliating military defeats at the hands of French, British, and Japanese powers in the second half of the nineteenth century. The main question became

how to build up China's national power by relying on popular mobilization for collective purposes, and Western-style education designed for mass mobilization rather than bureaucratic recruitment was seen as key for popular mobilization.[59] Hence, the examination system was abolished in 1905 on the grounds that it was incompatible with the quest for national power. At the same moment, ironically, the Western world was beginning to embrace meritocratic examinations as a means of modernizing its political systems,[60] but with one crucial difference: examinations were employed to select civil servants with the task of implementing the decisions of democratically elected officials, not for selecting political officials with the power to decide on a wide range of matters affecting the political community.[61]

The longevity and global influence of the examination system can be explained because of its social advantages. First, and most obvious, the imperial examination system was relatively fair and impartial as a method for selecting political officials with superior abilities compared to political systems that selected rulers on the basis of race, sex, family ties, or social connections. In the transformation from the Tang to the Song, the Chinese state established the examination system at least partly with the aim of challenging the educational and political monopoly held by aristocratic families. In the Song dynasty, the emperors expanded the examinations and the government school system to counter the influence of military aristocrats, quadrupling the number of those who passed the exams and broadening the social base of scholar-officials. As Song dynasty founder Emperor Taizu (r. 960–976) put it, "The country has fastened upon examinations to select scholars, choosing men to become officials. Since picking and ranking men in the public court is preferable to [receiving their] thanks for favors in private halls, this will serve to rectify customs that have been lacking."[62] To ensure fairness in the examination process, Song rulers instituted measures that are still used today, such as blind grading (papers were recopied in order not to allow biases by revealing the candidate by his calligraphy).[63] In practice, the system was often plagued by cheating that undermined the claims of impartiality and fairness (especially in certain periods, such as the late Northern Song, the late Ming, and the late Qing), but in its better moments the imperial examination system (arguably) reduced the influence of arbitrary factors in the political talent selection process compared to other systems in other places at the same time. In contemporary China, examinations for political officials play a similar role. It is true that several top political leaders are the children ("princelings") of leading political families from China's revolutionary era, but they began their ascension to power before the establishment (or revival) of the examination process for selecting political officials in the 1990s. Given the ultracompetitive nature of university and public service examinations that are increasingly viewed as necessary stages for the political recruitment process, it is likely that there will be a declining percentage of "princelings" in the political system in two or three decades.

Second, the examination system allowed for more social mobility than less meritocratic systems. As the censor—a political official with the task of criticizing mistaken government policies—Wang Ji put it in the tenth century, "If examination selection is not strict the powerful will struggle to be foremost and the orphans and poor will have difficulty advancing."[64] Records from the Song dynasty indicate the possibility of impressive upward mobility through imperial examinations: in 1148, for example, 330 people successfully passed the national examinations, and of the 279 graduates with family information on record, 157 had no forebears in the government.[65] That said, the reality did not always (or even usually) match up to the myth of the poor peasant boy who makes it good on the basis of ability and hard work.[66] Benjamin Elman argues that true social mobility was never the goal of state policy in late imperial China (1400–1900). Success at examinations had literary requirements, which effectively excluded most peasants, artisans, and clerks (women were formally excluded). The literary requirements meant that only the children of wealthy families could compete for examination success, and social circulation was mainly an unexpected consequence of upward (and downward) movement between elites (gentry, merchants, and military men) and (upper) political elites with degrees. To the (limited) extent there was upward political mobility from lower classes, it was normally first via commercial wealth, and then success at examinations, and the process normally took more than one generation.[67] In contemporary China, examinations are theoretically open to all citizens and most people are literate, but class background still influences outcomes because the process of studying for examinations tends to be time-consuming and costly, requiring leisure and tutors that poor families cannot afford.[68]

Third, the imperial examination system provided an element of social and political stability. The state could capture the loyalty of local-level elites who succeeded at the exams, thus ensuring the integration of the Chinese state and countering tendencies toward regional autonomy and the breakup of the centralized system (in late imperial China, the examination system distributed its prizes according to provincial and prefectural quotas, which meant that imperial officials were recruited from the whole country, in numbers proportionally to each province's population). Although only a tiny percentage of those who entered the examination competition could realistically expect to climb to the top of the ladder, even a minor examination success allowed an individual to join the broad body of literati who were understood to be potential officials and thus were granted social privileges and high social status.[69] As for the 95 percent who failed to become officials of any sort, the authority of the classical language necessary for examination preparation produced literates of high social status who engaged in professions such as medicine, teaching, astronomy, printing, and publishing.[70] And even those who truly felt that they were "failures" could invest hope in their children: the relative fairness of the examinations beginning in the Song dynasty meant that any elite male could expect that his offspring could earn the right to join the officialdom.[71] The evolving regional and geographical penetration of the exams from the capital (in the Tang dynasty) to the provinces (in the Song dynasty) down to the fifteen hundred counties (in the Ming–Qing dynasties) meant that local elites and ambitious would-be members of those elites across the whole of China learned and assimilated similar values. In short, the examination system gave both "winners" and "losers" a stake in the system, notwithstanding a few famous cases of examination failures who became outlaws, rebels, and disenchanted poets.[72]

Last but not least, the fact that through examinations the central government greatly favored literary studies and advanced civilians to important posts (including, from the Song dynasty on, to important military posts) meant that military officers, with their concern for physical power, were kept subordinate to civilians and helps to explain why there were fewer attempts by the military to seize power (from the Song on) than in other societies.[73] The examination system was perhaps the key tool for the imperial system to consolidate its social, political, and cultural influence, and abolition of the examination system in 1905 had the unexpected consequence of accelerating the demise of the whole imperial system.[74] Today, the (re)establishment of an examination system for the selection of political officials has not been accompanied by other features of the imperial system (such as monarchy), and there are many other ways of making a mark in Chinese society, but the perceived fairness of the examination system (relative to feasible alternatives) can still help to provide an important element of legitimacy, and hence stability, to the political system.

Finally, the examination system served to limit abuses of political power. Preimperial thinkers, as noted, believed that political power should be distributed on the basis of ability and virtue. Yet they also believed in monarchy, and the monarch owed his position to birth rather than merit. That would not pose a problem in an ideal world with an all-wise sage-king: as Xunzi put it, "The [True] Son of Heaven is the most respectable in terms of his power and position and has no rivals in Heaven. . . . His morality is pure; his knowledge and kindness are extremely clear."[75] Yet it was only too obvious that actually existing monarchs were mediocre in comparison; even Mencius, the most idealistic thinker of the era, said that the True Monarch arrives only once in five hundred years (and in his own day, Mencius noted, they had already been waiting seven hundred years; 2B.13).[76] So the question was how to ensure that inept rulers would not cause irreparable damage to the state in the interim (i.e., most of the time). Xunzi proposed a seemingly ingenious solution: the sovereign, while ostensibly omnipotent, should relegate most of his everyday tasks to meritorious aides: "The ruler works hard in looking [for proper officials] and is at rest when employing them."[77] But Xunzi could not foresee the huge administrative apparatus required of a large imperial state, and the idea of one person appointing and selecting all meritorious officials was not practicable in imperial China.[78] The imperial examination system solved this problem because it proved to be a relatively efficient mechanism for selecting political officials to exercise power (and deselecting the vast majority). Political officials could check the power of weak and incompetent rulers (and do the work that even the best rulers could not do due to lack of time and expertise).[79] Although the emperor had the ultimate say over the examination system, in the long term modifications were not possible without the elite's consent.[80] In contemporary China, national examinations limit the power of the political elite by limiting access to examination success; the university entrance examination system, regarded as a steppingstone for political success, is flawed in many ways but is perhaps the least corrupt political institution in China.

Whatever the merits of the imperial examination system, it was far from perfect as a mechanism to select political rulers with ability and virtue. Critic after critic questioned the careerist approach to learning and asked whether examinations test for the right kind of intellectual ability required for informed and intelligent political decision making. In the late 1060s, the radical reformer Wang Anshi removed the traditional poetry composition sections from the imperial examinations on the grounds of irrelevance to the official functions of government office. Wang argued for a more practical teaching curriculum that required changing the content of the exams and reforming the school system. But his opponents bitterly complained about unprecedented ideological control over the curriculum that was even less helpful for selecting talented public officials—"Today in all prefectures and counties, there are no entrance examinations which test the student's ability to write. The first thing the examiners look for is whether or not the candidate's essays refer to subjects currently tabooed. If the language of the candidate's subjects touches on such tabooed subjects, then no matter how well he has written, they are not to pass him."[81]

There were similar criticisms in later times. The eight-legged essay that had to be mastered to pass the imperial examinations during the Ming and Qing dynasties was formulated around a rigid artificial structure that tested, among other things, the examinees' ability to insert classical allusions and idioms at the places deemed appropriate. Here too, the rigidity of the examination system was mercilessly skewered by critics: as the seventeenth-century essayist Zhang Dai put it, the finest of scholars would "find no use for their arsenal of talents and knowledge" unless they joined the pack, "submissive in manner, limited in scope, stale in words, poor in attire, with internal feeling rotted away. . . . [Those who passed] were either old men waiting for death, or naïve youth who understood nothing" (Zhang Dai himself never passed the provincial examinations that would have permitted him to sit for the national examinations in Beijing; he plunged into depression and settled for the life of a private scholar and aesthete).[82] In short, it is far from obvious that the imperial examination system actually tested for high-caliber political talent.[83]

But is the problem with the examination system per se, or with the content and form of the imperial examination system? Today, examinations testing for government positions can and should be designed without aiming for ideological uniformity and rigid adherence to proper form. In fact, today's public service examinations in China are more like IQ tests,[84] designed to filter out those without superior analytical skills[85] (it is highly unlikely that someone like Sarah Palin or Toronto's former mayor Rob Ford could pass such examinations).[86] They also ask candidates to answer policy-related questions, with the aim of identifying candidates who can look at complex matters from different perspectives rather than through a rigid ideological lens.[87]

This is not to deny that the public service exams can be improved. For one thing, there may be a need to test for the ability to make predictions: policy makers at the highest levels of government need to wrestle with the complexities of the world and make plausible predictions about what will happen next. Social scientific research suggests that the art of making predictions depends less on expertise in a particular field and toiling devotedly within one tradition and more on knowing many things from an eclectic array of traditions and accepting ambiguity and contradiction as inevitable features of life.[88] Hence, exams should test for a wide range of knowledge in different disciplines and traditions, they should not simply be IQ tests. That said, some disciplines clearly bear on public policy—economics, environmental science, and international relations—so it makes sense to give extra weight to basic knowledge of those disciplines. Testing for knowledge of the latest research on cognitive biases is helpful, so that leaders know how to exert effort designed to minimize biases in decision making.[89] Exams should also test for basic knowledge of history so that future leaders have knowledge of political decision making in the past (both what worked and what didn't) that may still be relevant today.[90] There is evidence that bilinguals have a heightened ability to monitor the environment—a useful quality for political leaders—which may be a case for testing of a second language.[91] Last but not least, basic knowledge of the Confucian classics would be particularly helpful in the Chinese context (and elsewhere too, but several of the key texts have not yet been translated): the classics are a rich repository of cultural knowledge about how to act well in politics (and society more generally). In any case, the Confucian classics should be recommended over study of the Marxist classics that are singularly devoid of discussion about the good qualities of political rulers and what they ought to do.[92]

In sum, today's world requires political leaders with superior intellectual abilities—analytical skills and knowledge of different disciplines and traditions—and an examination system can help to test for such abilities. Of course, the examination system is a flawed mechanism. It is hard to settle disputes about what should be the content of exams in noncontroversial ways. The question of how to select the examiners may be controversial.[93] But all political selection mechanisms are flawed (controversy cannot be avoided), and the aim is to maximize advantages and minimize disadvantages relative to other systems. Clearly there is a need for more social scientific research to shed further light on the question of how best to test for intellectual abilities required for political decision making.[94] But it seems hard to dispute the fact that, however imperfect, exams can at least filter out candidates who lack basic analytical abilities and knowledge of the world required for informed and morally justified political decision making at the highest levels of government. In a large-scale society, the examination system is the fairest and most efficient way of selecting public officials with above-average intellectual ability.[95] As we will see, however, examinations cannot do as well at filtering out candidates who lack the basic social skills and virtues that are also required of political decision makers.

3. On the Need for Social Skills

Intellectual ability is important for political leaders, but it may not be the most important quality. The intellectual abilities required for serious academic research—the need to publicly engage with the best counterarguments available, the willingness to challenge orthodoxy, to make mistakes if they help to push the boundaries of what we know, and to articulate original ideas even if they are misunderstood or underappreciated at the time they are made—are not necessarily the abilities required of political leaders.[96] We are familiar with the stereotype of the academic nerd—the semi-autistic physicist or economist with an IQ off the charts—who cannot deal with people in a "normal" way. The academic nerd is not likely to be an effective political leader. Here too, Singapore's political meritocracy is an instructive example. In the past, leaders were selected mainly according to high performance in disciplines such as economics and engineering. But the wooden and bookish manner of its political leaders alienates much of the population, especially the youth, which has been energized and politicized by new social media. In response, a growing number of critics argue that the ruling party needs to expand its narrowly technical and academic notion of merit, in part to recognize the importance for political success of communicative talent and emotional intelligence.[97]

Clearly, a first-class mind is not sufficient for political leadership. But it may not even be necessary. Oliver Wendell Holmes famously said that Franklin D. Roosevelt had a second-class intellect but a first-class temperament.[98] What mattered, as Bill Clinton writes, is that Roosevelt surrounded himself with brilliant people who knew more about particular subjects than he did, and allowed them to argue with one another—and with him—as they searched for the right policies.[99] For political success, in other words, it is not necessary to be able to produce and systematize original ideas (perhaps the most important characteristic of a first-class mind), but the leader must appoint talented advisors and be sufficiently intelligent to at least recognize what counts as a good argument for the purpose of policy making. Even political leaders with what look like first-class minds, such as Lee Kuan Yew, recognize the importance of appointing talented advisors and encouraging them to do much of the thinking and arguing about the right policies.[100]

But what does it mean to have a "first-class temperament" necessary for political success? Again, the answer will differ from context to context, and the temperament required of a political leader in a state of war may be different from that required in a state of peace (although

FDR was one of the few leaders to be successful in both contexts). But which social skills matter in times of peace? Writings about leadership in politics rarely draw on systematic research, but research in business studies can shed some light. As discussed in section 1, there are key differences between the qualities required for business and political leaders, but some qualities appropriate for leadership in business may be transferable to the world of politics. Daniel Goleman analyzed competency models from 188 companies and found that "the most effective leaders are alike in one crucial way: They all have a high degree of what has come to be known as emotional intelligence." More specifically, a group of five skills enabled the best leaders to maximize their own and their followers' performance: self-awareness (knowing one's strengths, weaknesses, drives, values, and impact on others); self-regulation (controlling or redirecting disruptive impulses and moods); motivation (relishing achievement for its own sake); empathy (understanding other people's emotional makeup); and social skill (building rapport with others to move them in desired directions). The more leaders had such skills, the better the performance of the companies. Cognitive skills such as big-picture thinking and long-term vision also matter, but emotional intelligence proved to be twice as important as IQ and technical skills. Moreover, "emotional intelligence played an increasingly important role at the highest level of the company, where differences in technical skills are of negligible importance. In other words, the higher the rank of a person considered to be a star performer, the more emotional intelligence capabilities showed up as the reason for his or her effectiveness."

Such findings may not be directly applicable to the question of what makes an effective political leader, but there are relevant parallels: for example, the reasons empathy is particularly important as a component of leadership in business—"the increasing use of teams; the rapid pace of globalization; and the growing need to retain talent"[101]—also apply to leadership in politics. To the extent that there are differences between the requirements of leadership in the business and political worlds, they do not necessarily undermine, and may in fact reinforce, the case for emotional intelligence. For example, the fact that political leaders of large countries need to deal with an even larger and more comprehensive group of stakeholders than most business leaders means that social skills may be even more important in politics. A political leader needs not just to communicate, cooperate, and compromise with colleagues, but also inspire and persuade diverse sectors of society and (to a lesser extent) members of the international community.

Given that social skills matter for effective political leadership,[102] the next question is what mechanisms can increase the likelihood of selecting political leaders with superior social skills. One advantage of democracy is that it is difficult, if not impossible, to be elected without superior social skills: the campaign process involves constant dealing with people, and voters tend to reward leaders with good social skills. In a political meritocracy without one person, one vote to choose top leaders, the answer is less obvious. Exams can test for intellectual ability (if imperfectly), but it is harder to test for social skills. Exams can reward candidates who are persistent and work hard, but it doesn't follow that exam takers can work well with other people to get things done. Questions can ask test takers to consider policy issues or ethical dilemmas from different perspectives in order to filter out candidates congenitally unable to articulate plausible arguments from different points of view (Hitler could have been weeded out),[103] but most intelligent people can answer such questions whether or not they can think well from other perspectives in real-world situations. In China, it may be particularly important for exams to test for knowledge of Chinese history—if there's one way to describe literate Chinese, it's the sense of being part of a great historical tradition, and much of the Chinese language turns on the invocation of the right historical allusion or phrase in the right context; hence, a leading public official who is largely ignorant of Chinese history is unlikely to be able to persuade his or her colleagues, no matter how brilliant the policy proposal—but historical knowledge on exams cannot filter out the socially insensitive nerds from the political officials with social skills. Testing for another language might also help to determine the ability to think from another's perspective (at least, many of the world's monolingual tyrants could have been filtered out), but there is a need for social scientific research to show that those who speak more than one language have superior ability to think from the perspective of other people.[104] Psychological exams that test for the traits of effective leaders in the business world have fallen into disfavor.[105] An intelligent person can learn the literature on social skills and score highly on exams without being able to practice those skills in the social world.

So what can be done? One possibility is to require evidence of administrative competence as a qualification for examination candidates, since good performance at lower levels of government suggests that the potential leader has good social skills.[106] The historian Qian Mu pointed to the advantages of political meritocracy in the Han dynasty: candidates for literary examinations mostly came from aristocratic families that provided them with adequate knowledge and familiarity with the rules of politics and ritual propriety, hence successful examination candidates were already fairly well equipped with the social and practical skills required for political success.[107] As a consequence, the Han dynasty avoided the problem of overly scholastic successful examination candidates in later dynasties. But such qualifications for examinations undermine the ideal that all citizens should have an equal opportunity to participate in public service. The obvious solution is to require evidence of administrative (or political) competence *after*, not before exams. That is, examination success should not be a sufficient qualification for high political office: examination success needs to be followed by evidence of good performance at lower levels of government as a condition for further promotion up the chain of political command.[108]

But how can we measure good performance of political leaders? In business, as mentioned, the answer is relatively straightforward: good performers contribute to the profitability of the company, and the more they contribute to profit, the better they perform.[109] In government, what counts as good performance is intensely controversial, and the answer depends at least partly on what recipients of policies think, not just what government leaders regard as good performance. That said, it is possible to measure the performance of political leaders in relatively objective ways under certain conditions. Consider the case of China over the past three decades or so. The key priority of government—to reduce poverty—has been widely shared among both leaders and people. And since economic growth is an essential condition for the reduction of poverty, government officials were often promoted according to the level of economic growth in their district.[110] At least partly as a result of this promotion mechanism, China has seen perhaps the single most impressive poverty alleviation achievement in human history.[111]

the World Bank estimates that the poverty rate fell from 85 percent to 15 percent between 1981 and 2005, equivalent to six hundred million people being lifted out of poverty.[112]

Needless to say, the personnel promotion system has not always worked according to the standard of good economic performance. At the local township level, promotion often depends on personal relationships.[113] The selection mechanism for posts at the central level is still somewhat opaque and may rely more on patronage than economic performance.[114] According to a report issued by the CCP's own Organization Department, nearly 25 percent of cadres see the official promotion procedures as "going through the motions" to mask the fact that decisions have already been made at a high level.[115] Overall, however, considerable evidence indicates that China's officials are increasingly selected based on performance.[116]

The more serious problem is that the appropriate standard for measuring performance needs to change. Now that hundreds of millions of Chinese have been lifted out of poverty, what should the government do for them? The task of government becomes more complex, with more diverse interests and values and greater demands for political participation, and the unqualified pursuit of economic growth is no longer the widely accepted criterion for good performance. And what counts as good performance can no longer just be determined from the top: what people want and think matters more than before in terms of shaping the government's priorities. Moreover, the no-holds-barred pursuit of economic growth is now often seen as actively harmful to the polity. Most obvious, China's growth has come at the expense of the environment and people's well-being,[117] with pollution now surpassing land disputes as the leading cause of social unrest in China.[118] And rewarding public officials almost exclusively on the basis of short-term economic growth has contributed to a chaotic urbanization process that has filled China with nearly empty "ghost cities."[119]

In response, academics have urged a more holistic approach to measuring government performance that takes into account multiple indicators that contribute to sustainable human development.[120] The Chinese government itself has allowed for experimentation—as party secretary of Jiangsu, for example, Li Yuanchao (now vice-president) assessed local officials in terms of performance measured by social and environmental factors, as opposed to purely economic ones. In the country as a whole, Chinese leaders have elevated environmental priorities through the cadre evaluation system that sets explicit environmental targets.[121] The problem, however, is that the more holistic the standard, the more controversial it becomes. The government can and does make extensive use of polling data and relies on social media to stay well-informed about public opinion (see concluding thoughts, section 1), but what if different groups of people prioritize different needs and the majority's priorities conflict with expert views about governmental priorities? How should it be determined which factor counts more, in what proportion to other factors, and who gets to decide on the holistic standard? Even if the holistic standard is widely agreed on by the government and the people affected by the policies, it is far more difficult to measure performance in areas such as environmental sustainability—should government officials be penalized for failing to anticipate pollution problems that spill over from neighboring jurisdictions?—with the result that short-term economic growth often becomes the default way of measuring "successful" performance, regardless of the social costs.[122] In short, performance at lower levels of government is an important indicator of the social skills required for good performance at higher levels of government but it becomes more difficult to measure performance in noncontroversial ways once the government's priorities move beyond a sole focus on poverty reduction as measured by economic growth. Hence, there is an increased need for more objective ways of measuring social skills required of top political leaders that can supplement the increasingly subjective attempts to measure performance at lower levels of government.

A Mechanism for Promoting Political Officials with Social Skills: Taking Traits Seriously

A company or organization that favors seniority is commonly thought to undermine a commitment to promotion on the basis of merit. But what if it turns out that the social skills required for leadership correlate with age? Then it makes sense to promote people who are older. From a Confucian standpoint, it seems obvious that social skills such as self-awareness, self-regulation, and empathy normally increase as our life experience deepens. As we age, we experience different roles (such as caring for elderly parents) and deepen our experience performing particular roles (a teacher with five years' experience should be better than a brand new teacher) that increase our ability to understand and cooperate with different kinds of people for the purpose of achieving desired ends, so long as we maintain the quest for self-improvement and our desire for social interaction. As it turns out, scientific research largely bears out this Confucian insight: "One thing is certain: Emotional intelligence increases with age."[123] Fredda Blanchard-Fields's research compares the way young adults and older adults respond to situations of stress and "her results show that older adults are more socially astute than younger people when it comes to sizing up an emotionally conflicting situation. They are better able to make decisions that preserve an interpersonal relationship. . . . And she has found that as we grow older, we grow more emotionally supple—we are able to adjust to changing situations on the basis of our emotional intelligence and prior experience, and therefore make better decisions (on average) than do young people."[124] Other research shows that older adults seem particularly good at quickly letting go of negative emotion because they value social relationships more than the ego satisfaction that comes from rupturing them.[125] Being older, in short, improves one's chances of developing superior social skills.

The political implications for a meritocratic selection process should be obvious: it is best to promote older officials who are more likely to have superior social skills necessary to get things done.[126] That said, older adults suffer from cognitive declines as they enter their sixties and seventies,[127] so it also makes sense to have age limits for political leaders. The not-so-young may also suffer from declines in energy level and physical health; hence, a good case can be made for collective leadership at the highest level of government because the decline of any one leader would not be so problematic. The current Chinese system of collective leadership seems to have more or less struck the right balance between rewarding improvements in social skills while taking into account cognitive and physical decline:[128] seniority plays an important role in influencing selection to the ruling Standing Committee of the Politburo but there is an informal retirement age of seventy, with the result that most members are in their mid-sixties.[129]

It is worth keeping in mind that there are many exceptions to the rule that social intelligence increases with age; hence, age should be only one factor influencing the selection of political officials. A minority of spots can be reserved for innovative younger leaders (see chapter 3, section 2) and younger leaders can play an important role in an advisory capacity. But political selection mechanisms are necessarily imperfect, and social scientific research (as well as philosophical argumentation) can help to reduce imperfections: given the well-documented tendency for our social skills to improve as we age, a good case can be made that age should count in the evaluation process as a proxy for the social skills required for effective political decision making.

Gender is another good proxy for social skills. CEOs interviewed about different leadership styles said women were more collaborative, better listeners, more relationship oriented, and more empathetic and reasonable.[130] Neuroscientists have shown that women make less risky and more empathetic decisions in stressful circumstances, which may explain why large-cap global corporations with at least one woman on their boards outperformed comparable companies with all-male boards by 26 percent in the years directly preceding and following the 2007–2008 financial crisis.[131] In another study, researchers analyzed the 360-degree leadership evaluations of more than 7,280 executives, which had been filled out by their peers, bosses, and subordinates. The analysis revealed that at every management level, women were rated higher than men, and the higher the level, the wider the gap. Women rated higher on twelve of the sixteen competencies that the researchers identified as most important to overall leadership effectiveness, including social skills such as "develops others," "inspires and motivates others," "builds relationships," "engages in collaboration and teamwork," "communicates powerfully and prolifically," and "connects the group to the outside world." Yet the data also showed that the higher the level, the higher the proportion of men. In other words, the best people—women—are not being promoted. The researchers draw the conclusion that "by adding more women the overall effectiveness of the leadership team would go up. Organizations go outside to recruit effective leaders when in many cases they may well have internal people who could rise to fill the position that is vacant."[132]

Again, we need to be cautious about drawing direct implications from business to politics. But the same sorts of social skills needed for effective leadership in large companies are likely to be even more important for political leaders of large countries, given the greater importance of communication, cooperation, and compromise in politics. As one CEO interviewed about differences in leadership styles put it, "When you've got a complex project involving multiple layers, you need a leader who is collaborative, and more often than not I have found that leader to be a woman."[133] In government, the tasks are often more complex and require more collaboration. In short, there is a strong case for women in government: if the concern is to select political leaders with superior social skills, it is generally better to choose a woman.[134] Yet most political leadership positions are occupied by men, especially at the higher levels. In China, the trend is going from bad to worse: as China's most influential editor notes, "the percentage of women among the top leaders in the Chinese government, especially among members and alternate members of the Central Committee of the Chinese Communist Party, shrank from 11.4 percent in 1977 to 7.6 percent in 2002. While women can be found serving as officials in more than 80 percent of the country's provincial-level governments, only about 8 percent have a woman as head of the government."[135]

So what should be done? First, we must be clear about the sources of discrimination so they can be corrected. The "motherhood penalty"—the assumption that mothers tend to be less competent and less committed—has been well documented and such biases almost certainly contribute to discrimination against women in politics.[136] The "motherhood penalty" can be overcome if a performance review shows that a mother had demonstrated a heroic level of commitment to a previous job,[137] but clearly women have a huge hurdle to overcome before they can be treated as men's equals in the promotion process, not to mention given special privileges on account of their superior social skills. Hence, there may be a need for enforceable laws specifying goals that aim to increase the proportion of women in government: Nepal's 2007 constitution stipulated that at least 33 percent of candidates in parliamentary elections must be women, and as a result the country has the highest proportion of women in government (30 percent) in the Asian region.[138] In the case of China, preference should be given to women in the selection and promotion process for political leaders, other things being (roughly) equal.[139] If China can substantially increase its proportion of women in government, the government will be more effective at doing what it's supposed to do. But what exactly is the government supposed to do? At this point, our discussion of political leadership needs to take a more explicitly normative turn.

4. On the Need for Virtue

A leader with superior intellectual and social skills is potentially the worst kind of leader, because he or she can figure out the best way of realizing immoral purposes. Clearly any theory of leadership that leaves out ethics is deficient.[140] Adolf Hitler's singular skills as an orator set him above his National Socialist colleagues, and he could hold a crowd rapt for hours with his speeches.[141] Had his oratorical skills been matched by intellectual brilliance, he might have figured out more effective war strategies and (God forbid) maybe even won the war. On a less worrisome scale, sociopaths—those devoid of any conscience—can and do achieve social success by means of rational cost-benefit analysis of how to manipulate people for their own advantage. With superior ability to understand other people and to plan the likely consequences of different paths of action, they can outmaneuver other people to get what they want. The problem is that sociopaths completely lack compassion and feeling for fellow human beings, and only rational calculation about their own interests stops them from harming other people. As a successful law professor put it,

> Remorse is alien to me. I have a penchant for deceit. I am generally free of entangling and irrational emotions. I am strategic and canny, intelligent and confident. . . . Yet I am not motivated or constrained by the same things that most good people are. . . . [As a child], I envisioned the people in my life as robots that turned off when I wasn't directly interacting with them. . . . I have never killed anyone, but I have certainly wanted to. I

> may have a disorder, but I am not crazy. In a world filled with gloomy, mediocre nothings populating a go-nowhere rat race, people are attracted to my exceptionalism like moths to a flame.[142]

The Chinese Legalist thinker Han Fei (c. 280–233 BCE) argued that political leaders should act like rational sociopaths. He wrote a political handbook for power-hungry rulers, and argued that state power needed to be strengthened by means of harsh laws and punishments. His aim was nothing less than total state control, and he stressed over and over again that moral considerations should not get in the way.[143] The ruthless king of Qin ascended to the throne in 246 BCE and drew on Han Fei's advice to conquer and rule all of China under the title of First Emperor of the Qin dynasty. This dynasty was short-lived, however, and the First Emperor became infamous in Chinese history for his excessive cruelty and megalomania and Legalism fell into disrepute. Less than a century later, the Han dynasty ruler Emperor Wu (r. 141–87 BCE) officially endorsed (a reinterpreted version of) Confucianism as the reigning political philosophy, and Confucianism became the mainstream political tradition in subsequent imperial history.

Like debates in Western political theory, Confucians argue endlessly about which people (if any) matter most,[144] what is meant by the good of the people,[145] and how the government should seek the good of the people,[146] but they share the assumption that power ought to be exercised in the interest of the ruled, not the rulers.[147] The pragmatic ideas of Legalist thinkers influenced governance practices in imperial China (including, arguably, the examination system), but they were supposed to be used for the moral purpose of benefitting the people.[148] In the "communist" era, Mao Zedong openly praised Legalist-style methods,[149] but he also agreed that the government ought to serve the people. In short, the sine qua non of any theory of good government (in the Chinese context and, arguably, elsewhere) is that political leaders should use the power of the state to promote the good of the people rather than for personal benefit. Political rulers also need superior intellectual abilities and social skills, but they should use those skills to benefit the people. The question, then, is what sorts of mechanisms are

most likely to produce political rulers with the motivation to promote the good of the people?

Immanuel Kant famously argued that "the problem of setting up a state can be solved even by a nation of devils."[150] So long as the institutions are designed to produce good outcomes, the self-seeking inclinations of individuals will be neutralized or eliminated. In contemporary democracies, however, it is widely recognized that the quality of citizens also matters.[151] If voters are ignorant or narrowly self-interested, elections will not produce desirable outcomes (see chapter 1, section 1). It is also recognized that the quality of political leaders matters, and the task of political candidates is to persuade voters of their commitment to work for the common good. Hence, candidates for political leadership must have the oratorical skills to persuade voters that they will seek their good. The power of speaking has long roots in the history of Western civilization. In Greek antiquity, delivering speeches was a primary means to achieve legal and political goals, and politicians had to rely on oration to persuade one another and the people of their intentions and ambitions. Masters of oration from ancient Greece and Rome served as inspiration for later generations of political leaders, and delivering speeches has been an integral part of public life in the West. In contemporary democratic societies, oratorical skill is of utmost importance for running campaigns, directing movements, and managing crises in order to galvanize voters' support.[152]

In East Asian societies with a Confucian heritage, by contrast, verbal fluency is not held in high regard.[153] As Jin Li explains, the emphasis has been on action rather than words: verbal craftiness is viewed as an impediment to moral self-cultivation because "(1) a glib tongue divorces the mind from the heart, (2) flattering speech undermines sincerity, and (3) boastful speech lacks humility."[154] Hence, "we could easily name a long list of great speakers in the West, but we could name *none* in East Asia, not even after an ardent search through the triumphant democracies of Japan, Korea, and Taiwan, where eloquence of public speaking is supposed to matter."[155] In short, the problem with electoral democracy in an East Asian context is not just that voters often lack the knowledge and motivation to support the common good (like voters elsewhere; see chapter 1, section 1) but also that there is a strong cultural bias against the main mechanism employed by political leaders in the West—eloquent speech—to try to persuade voters that they are motivated by the common good.[156]

In a political meritocracy without democratic elections and without a tradition of eloquent speech, which mechanisms can increase the likelihood that political leaders will be motivated to seek the good of the people? Here too, debates in imperial China centered on the pros and cons of the examination system and what could be done with the power of the written word. Defenders of the examination system argued that it can help to select political officials with superior virtue. The key argument is that studying the Confucian classics improves the virtue of the learner. As the Tang court put it:

> Now the Classics are the subtle pointers of the most intelligent men and the affairs that were possible for the sages; with them, one can make heaven-and-earth constant, regulate yin and yang, rectify social norms, and promote morality. On the outside they show how to benefit everything in the world, yet on the inside they contain behaviors for being good as a person. Those who learn them will grow; those who do not learn will fall. When in the great enterprise of governing the ruler honors [these texts], he completes his imperial virtue. . . . Thus it is said, "when one is compliant and sincere, it is thanks to the teaching of the *Songs*; when he sees the larger picture and can think ahead, it is thanks to the teaching of the *Documents*; when he is accommodating and harmonious, it is thanks to the teaching of the *Music*; when he is reverent and respectful, it is thanks to the teaching of the *Rites*; and when he writes judgments and finds analogies between cases, it is thanks to the teaching of the *Spring and Autumn Annals*."[157]

Hence, by testing knowledge of the Confucian classics, the examinations also test the moral virtue of the candidates.

Critics argued otherwise. Most famously, the Song dynasty Confucian scholar Zhu Xi argued that exams test the wrong kind of knowledge: they should test not just knowledge of the classics themselves but also knowledge of interpretations and the candidate's own interpretation of the classics.[158] Others argued that the problem lies with the examination system per se: the Tang dynasty Confucian official Lu Zhi (754–805 CE) argued that "if examinations are used for selection, people will engage in crafty hypocrisy and as a result the righteous man of principle will seldom get promoted."[159] In other words, it is easy for intelligent candidates to fake virtue in examinations by making what appear to be ethically correct judgments and arguments, but it takes a leap of faith to think that successful candidates will be virtuous once they have political power.

In today's China, there are similar doubts about the examination system as a mechanism to select political leaders committed to the public good. Success in the public service examinations means automatic appointment to government offices (these appointments are usually for office staff positions, unlike the Song practice in which the top *jinshi* holders could immediately enter relatively high positions). Over the past few years, however, the moral quality of public servants appears to have deteriorated (see chapter 3, section 1), and the government recently proposed measures for ethical screening in the national examinations for public servants that would take a candidate's virtue into consideration: according to one report, "candidates who lack political integrity, a sense of responsibility, and a willingness to serve the public will not be allowed to become public servants."[160] But such criteria are vague and hard to measure, and formal policies have not yet been implemented for screening candidates' moral character.[161] One possibility (not being considered at the moment) would be to reintroduce more systematic testing on the Confucian classics with a rich discourse about virtuous political leaders. Although such tests would likely be an improvement on the status quo,[162] even the most committed Confucians concede that examination on the classics is not a sufficient test for political virtue.[163] So what are other possible mechanisms?

If the aim is to identify rulers willing to serve the community, a minimum condition is to deselect those who have clearly harmed the community. Hence, candidates with criminal records, especially convictions for serious crimes such as murder and rape, should be banned from public office. In democratic countries such as India and Ukraine, many politicians do not meet even this minimal standard,[164] but China's political leaders could not hold political office if they were found guilty of such crimes. In China, it is widely assumed that being filial to one's parents is a necessary step in learning other-regarding behavior and extending morality outside the family,[165] so it makes sense to bar candidates who have violated basic expectations of filial piety. The selection process for public servants has recently been reformed with this criterion in mind on an experimental basis in Qufu city.[166] Most obvious, perhaps, officials accused of corruption should be deselected from the political system. Here lies the biggest gap between ideal and practice, as the Chinese government itself recognizes (for further discussion, see chapter 3, section 1).

A more positive way of assessing commitment to serve the people is to gauge the extent to which candidates have been willing to sacrifice their own interests on behalf of the country. In China's revolutionary past, such candidates were fairly easy to identify: war heroes who put their lives at risk to serve the country clearly demonstrated commitment to public service. Today, however, it is harder to identify public-spirited heroes. Arguably, political dissidents such as Liu Xiaobo who knowingly risk imprisonment for the sake of promoting political ideals come closest, but they are not likely to be given opportunities to serve as political rulers unless the whole political system collapses (not to mention the fact that they do not represent large constituencies even among independent intellectuals, in comparison to, say, Nelson Mandela, Vaclav Havel, and Aung San Suu Kyi at the time they were imprisoned).[167]

One way of showing willingness to experience harm for the sake of the public is to do volunteer work in poor and remote rural areas for long periods.[168] Among public officials, perhaps the clearest sign of willingness to experience harm on behalf of the community is the willingness to stick to the one-child policy. Although wealthy Chinese often pay fines so that they can have more than one child, few if any top political leaders have violated the one-child rule. (How many politicians in the West would be willing to sacrifice their personal interests in this way?) But the challenge now is to increase the population to maintain a sufficient proportion of productive citizens needed to support China's rapidly aging population, and the one-child policy is being loosened and will likely be abolished in the near future.[169] Low salaries for public servants are justified on the grounds that Chinese officials should be willing to sacrifice their personal interests for the sake of serving the community; as Xi Jinping put it, "If you go into politics, it mustn't be for money. . . . [Y]ou must give up any thought of personal advantage."[170] But given the extent of corruption in the political system (see chapter 3, section 1) and the fact that many people join the party to obtain material benefits,[171] few will argue that the system works as it's supposed to. If such mechanisms designed to increase the likelihood of recruiting and promoting public officials committed to serving the public are far from sufficient, then what else is there?

A Mechanism for Selecting Political Officials with Virtue: Selection by Peers

Confucius, had he been aware of the possibility, would probably not have endorsed the examination system as a method for determining the moral character of a candidate. To assess a person, he says, we must carefully observe his actions and motives: "The Master said: 'See what a man does; watch his motives; examine what he is at ease with. How can a man conceal his character? How can a man conceal his character?'" (2.10). The Tang dynasty official Lu Zhi (mentioned earlier) agrees with Confucius that the only way to assess a person is to get to know him for an extended period of time and from all angles. On this basis, he argues in favor of recommendation by elders and officials "as the method of selection and promotion. This method was adopted for many benefits: it verifies clearly the actual political/administrative performance of the officials, extends the range of talent selection, encourages the cultivation of virtuous conduct and performance, and, lastly, puts the ambition due to pride to rest."[172]

The philosopher Joseph Chan defends a contemporary variant of Lu's model. Chan argues for a house of government consisting of senior public servants selected by those who know them best: colleagues, senior secretarial staff, and experienced journalists who can evaluate the candidates' public spiritedness, sense of responsibility, fairness, integrity, and civility.[173] Chan's proposal may be workable in the context of a small society like Hong Kong, where public officials are aware of one another's moral character and the pool of selectors is relatively small. In the context of a huge and populous country such as China, however, the proposal is both too rigid and not rigid enough. It is too rigid in the sense that the group of selectors is closely tied to the Hong Kong context. As Chan recognizes, the "proposal was developed against the background of Hong Kong's political institutions, including its statutory bodies and government advisory bodies, rather than those of China as a whole."[174] In greater China, different combinations of subordinates, peers, and superiors at different levels of government will have different levels of exposure and different insights into the moral character of candidates, and it seems too rigid to confine the group of selectors to colleagues, senior secretarial staff, and experienced journalists.[175] On the other hand, Chan's proposal is not rigid enough because it seems to favor certain groups over others in a way that would leave much room for abuse in a political context characterized by corruption and excessive reliance on human relations (*guanxi*). In mainland China, there is a need for a more rigorous and systematic way of assessing moral character that does not seem to arbitrarily favor certain groups (e.g., "experienced journalists") over others.

So who should have a say in assessing the moral character of candidates, and in what proportion? The principle that moral character is best assessed via close acquaintance and careful observation over prolonged periods in different settings is a good starting point. In practice, the candidate's peers—meaning public officials holding posts at the same level in the political hierarchy—normally have had the most prolonged interaction with candidates, and hence should have the most say in assessing their moral characters.[176] High peer ratings can and should be the most important factor in determining whether the candidate possesses the moral qualities necessary for further promotion up the chain of political command.[177] But the views of subordinates and superiors should also be taken into account. Peers can be envious of talented colleagues, in which case the views of superiors (who have less reason to feel jealous) should be given some weight. And subordinates can be in a good position to observe features of moral character due to their position in the hierarchy: for example, they can notice if candidates are amiable and deferent to superiors and rude and unhelpful to subordinates, implying that the candidate cares more about personal ambition than about treating others well. Given the need for a more rigorous and systematic way of assessing moral character, it might be best to settle on something like a 60:20:20 ratio for assessment of moral character, with 60 percent of the weighting given to peers and 20 percent each given to superiors and subordinates.[178] Although this ratio (or any ratio) is somewhat arbitrary and may be difficult to enforce to the letter (or the number), the advantage of a clear and transparent system for assessing moral character is that it reduces the possibility of even more arbitrary assessments that characterize the actually existing political meritocracy in China.

To be fair, the peer rating system seems to work well at the very highest level of government in China. About 370 members and alternative members of the party's Central Committee cast preferences for the party's decision-making Politburo, currently a twenty-five-member body, and the Politburo Standing Committee, its innermost cabinet, currently with seven members.[179] In the run-up to the 2012 selection process, the outgoing president, Hu Jintao, favored Li Keqiang as his successor, but Xi Jinping was ranked highest in an internal survey of national senior leaders and therefore Xi was selected as president.[180] At lower levels of government, however, the views of superiors tend to have the most weight in promotion decisions,[181] with the result that the system favors conservative and cautious candidates over risk-takers and candidates with new ideas that challenge the "normal" way of doing things as established by superiors. Hence, there may be unnecessary attachment to the status quo long after its practical utility has expired.[182] Even more worrisome, the system may reward public officials who curry favor with their superiors by less than ethical means,[183] and those who spend time serving the public rather than their superiors may be disadvantaged in the promotion process. Hence, there is a need to implement and rigorously enforce a promotion system that gives extra weight to the assessment of peers rather than superiors. Such meritocratic reforms, arguably, would do more political good than the kinds of electoral reforms that have been the subject of countless articles and books in academic and journalistic writings on Chinese politics.

In sum, I have argued that high-level political leaders in large, peaceful, and modernizing meritocratic states need to be strong in terms of intellectual ability, social skills, and virtue. Note, however, that political leaders need not be at the top of the scale on any one dimension. Theoretical physicists are likely to have greater intellectual ability, top business leaders may have stronger social skills,[184] and religious leaders may be more self-sacrificing and virtuous. What makes *political* leaders distinctive, however, is that they should be above average on all three dimensions. That said, not all qualities matter equally. A degree of virtue is indispensable; without any desire to serve the public, a political leader can put his or her intelligence and social skills to disastrous uses. Next comes social skills, because a political leader needs to be able to persuade fellow leaders as well as members of the public. In last place comes intellectual ability: a certain degree of intelligence is necessary to process information and recognize what counts as a good argument, but policy suggestions and original thinking can come from a group of talented advisors and experts. The relative importance of each quality will also depend on the political priorities of the time. In the early days of China's economic reform, GDP growth mattered most; hence it was most important to select and promote government officials with the right social skills to get things done. But now that corruption is widely viewed as a mortal threat to the political system (see chapter 3, section 1), more emphasis should be placed on the moral character of political officials. To repeat, a certain degree of virtue is always necessary, but now it matters even more than before.

This chapter, I freely confess, is not only a theoretical exercise about which qualities matter for leaders in political meritocracies and which mechanisms are most likely to select and promote leaders with such qualities. I had the Chinese context in mind and I tried to answer the question of how to improve China's evolving meritocratic system. Hence, I developed an argument about a feasible and desirable political meritocracy in the context of a large, peaceful, and modernizing meritocratic state that was used as a standard for evaluating China's actually existing meritocratic system. My conclusion is that China can and should improve its meritocratic system, but it must do so within the system: a meritocratic system can be explicitly designed to increase the likelihood that political leaders have the motivation and ability to enact sound policies, and in that sense China has a clear advantage over electoral democracies that leave the whole thing up to the whims of the people unconstrained by the lessons of philosophy, history, and social

science. But any defense of political meritocracy needs to address the question of how to minimize the disadvantages of the system, not just the question of how to maximize its advantages. The next chapter will discuss the main disadvantages of political meritocracy and suggest ways of minimizing them in a contemporary Chinese context.

CHAPTER 3

What's Wrong with Political Meritocracy

In theory, political meritocracy sounds like a good idea. Of course the political system should be designed to choose rulers with superior ability and virtue. Who would prefer to be governed by incompetent and corrupt rulers? But good ideas can be disastrous if they are implemented in a world composed of imperfect people with different values and interests competing for scarce resources. The Great Leap Forward seemed like a good idea—let's skip competitive individualistic capitalism and move straight to a world of material abundance and equality for all—but it led to a famine resulting in tens of millions of deaths. The Cultural Revolution also seemed like a good idea—participatory, bottom-up democracy without any social hierarchies—but it led to ten years of insanity. So the question is whether it is possible to implement political meritocracy in ways that won't go wrong. Electoral democracy may not guarantee superior rulers, but at least voters can get rid of their rulers if it turns out they made a bad choice. And curbing democracy in favor of a political mechanism explicitly designed to choose superior rulers who rule for the people's interests seems too risky without strong countermeasures designed to prevent rulers from doing bad things.

Plato's *Republic* is perhaps the most widely read book in Western political theory, but his arguments in favor of rule by philosopher kings and queens are so extreme that few people today read the work for insights about how to select political rulers. Perhaps the most outlandish argument is that a just regime requires the abolition of private property and the family for the "guardian" class to guarantee that rulers serve the political community instead of their own private selfish interests.[1] In an influential essay on *The Republic*, Allan Bloom speculates that Plato's views "are the absurd conceits of a comic poet who only suggested them in order to ridicule them."[2] By showing the impossibility of a utopian political meritocracy, Plato (according to Bloom) sought to provide a subtle defense of democracy as a practicable second-best alternative. Even philosophers benefit from a democracy: they may not have political power or high social status, but at least they have freedom of speech, which allows the pursuit of truth.

The most influential English-language work on meritocracy in the twentieth century was a more explicit political satire. In a book titled *The Rise of the Meritocracy*, first published in 1957, the sociologist Michael Young argued that any attempt to institutionalize a system of rewarding people according to their merit (defined as IQ plus effort) would lead to a brave new world in which an intellectual elite could justify their relative power and prosperity by saying that the outcome was fair because they actually were better than others: "If the rich and powerful were encouraged by the general culture to believe that they fully deserved all they had, how arrogant they could become, how ruthless in pursuing their own advantage. . . . If [ordinary people] think themselves inferior, if they think they deserve on merit to have less worldly goods and less worldly power than a select minority, they can be damaged in their own self-esteem, and generally demoralized."[3] Young's book sold hundreds of thousands of copies and made the term *meritocracy* toxic for succeeding generations of political theorists. Starting from the 1960s, the key issue for theorists became the question of how to promote a society of equals. Hierarchies may be necessary in a modern, complex society, but theorists in the Western world generally agreed that we should regard all hierarchies as morally problematic and definitely not attempt to institutionalize them in the political system.

More specifically, Young's work points to three key problems typically associated with any attempt to implement political meritocracy: (1) political rulers chosen on the basis of their superior ability are likely to abuse their power; (2) political hierarchies may become frozen and undermine social mobility; and (3) it is difficult to legitimize the system to those outside the power structure.[4] In this chapter, I will discuss possible ways of addressing those problems in the context of a large, modernizing, and peaceful society that aims to institutionalize political meritocracy. As in chapter 2, I have contemporary China in mind, and I will assume that electoral democracy is not a realistic possibility in the foreseeable future; hence, I will ask if it's possible to fix what's wrong with political meritocracy without electoral democracy.

1. The Problem of Corruption

The most obvious problem facing any system of political meritocracy is that meritocratically selected rulers are likely to abuse their power. If rulers are not chosen by the people, and if the people cannot change their rulers (other than by extreme means such as violent rebellion), what prevents the rulers from serving their own interests instead of the interests of the community? Whatever we think of the arguments against electoral democracy, it is a good means of checking the power of rulers because they can be changed at election time.[5] Hence, it should not be surprising that there are widespread abuses of power in China. Perhaps the most serious problem is official corruption—the abuse of public office for private gains. The overall level of corruption has exploded over the past three decades,[6] and it has become a more visible political problem in the past few years due to the glare of social media and more conspicuous consumption by political elites. Upon assuming power, President Xi Jinping recognized that corruption threatens the stability of the entire political system and he has made combating corruption the government's top priority.[7] Clearly corruption undermines not just the legitimacy of the Communist Party but also the whole aim of building a political meritocracy composed of public-spirited rulers. Is it possible to combat corruption in a meritocratic system without the mother of all checks, namely, competitive elections that empower voters to get rid of bad leaders?

In fact, electoral democracy is not always (or even usually) a strong bulwark against corruption. According to Transparency International, democratic countries such as Indonesia and India are perceived as more corrupt than China;[8] in the case of Indonesia, corruption seems to have worsened since the advent of political democratization.[9] In Taiwan, the authoritarian Kuomintang (KMT) leader Chiang Ching-kuo cleaned up what had been one of the most corrupt systems in world history, but corruption worsened once the system democratized under Lee Teng-hui.[10] What does seem to help combat corruption is the level of economic development:[11] wealthier countries, including countries without fully free and fair elections for top leaders such as Singapore, Qatar, and the United Arab Emirates, tend to be less corrupt. In his book *China Modernizes*, Randall Peerenboom argues that the quality of governance in the East Asian region, including control of corruption, improves along with level of economic development.[12] Within China, wealthier parts such as Shanghai tend to be less corrupt than poor areas in the rural hinterland. Other factors do influence the level of corruption—one study found that Chinese provinces with greater anticorruption efforts, higher educational attainment, historic influence from Anglo-American church universities, greater openness, more access to media, higher relative wages of government employees, and a greater representation of women in the legislature are markedly less corrupt[13]—but high GDP per capita is still the best bulwark against corruption.[14] So why not just wait a few decades when (assuming an optimistic economic growth scenario) China will have become a wealthy country? Put differently, why are Chinese leaders so worried about corruption now? After all, the United States had high levels of corruption when it was going through its industrialization in the late nineteenth and early twentieth centuries, but political leaders didn't worry that the whole political system was under threat of collapse.

The main reason for worry in China is related to the meritocratic system.[15] In a democracy, leaders get their legitimacy from being chosen by the people, and the people can change their leaders in the next election if they aren't satisfied. If the next batch of leaders is still corrupt, to a certain extent the people need to blame themselves. Corruption in a democracy doesn't mean that the political system is not democratic. In a political meritocracy such as China, by contrast, the system is supposed to select leaders with superior virtue, meaning that rulers are supposed to use power to serve the political community, not themselves. In other words, the higher the level of political corruption, the less meritocratic the political system. Put negatively, the regime will lack legitimacy if its leaders are seen to be corrupt. Hence, Chinese leaders are not wrong to think that corruption threatens the whole political system.

Such views are not mere theoretical speculation: the CCP won the hearts and minds of the (majority of) Chinese people in its civil war with the KMT at least partly, if not mainly, because it was perceived to be far less corrupt. From the viewpoint of regime survival, it is indeed alarming that corruption in mainland China seems to have reached levels similar to those of prerevolutionary China under KMT rule. Moreover, Yan Sun has argued that it was corruption, rather than the demand for democracy, that lay at the root of the social dissatisfaction that led to the Tiananmen protest movement of 1989.[16] Over the past two decades, most dissatisfaction in China was directed at corruption by lower-level officials, but the Bo Xilai and Zhou Yongkang cases point to rot at the top that more directly threatens the foundations of the political system.[17] The same goes for reports by *Bloomberg* and the *New York Times* that exposed the extravagant fortunes accumulated by family members of China's top political elite. The Chinese government reacted by closing down websites of "unfriendly" foreign media, but such stopgap measures can only postpone the day of reckoning.[18] In short, it is clear that meritocratically selected leaders have more incentive to clean up corruption than democratically elected leaders, if only because regime survival depends on it.[19] But the question remains—is it possible to address the problem of corruption by means other than electoral democracy? To answer this question, we need to understand the root causes of political corruption in China and consider ways of addressing the problems.

The most obvious cause of corruption is the absence of independent checks on the power of the government; without the rule of law, how is it possible to curb the power of corrupt government officials? That said, it is not correct to assume that Chinese officials exercise limitless power and rule with dictatorial impunity. The Han dynasty devised institutions aiming to decentralize, check, and control the power of the emperor that shaped the course of subsequent imperial history, including independent institutions for the training of Confucian scholars.[20] The rule of avoidance prohibited officials from serving in their home areas in order to avoid conflict between local ties and pursuit of the common good. Political posts could not normally be handed down to the next generation unless sons succeeded in the examination process. Of course, the emperor stood at the apex of political power, but the emperor did not rule with totalizing, unchecked power. Censors were entrusted with the task of checking administrators at each level to prevent corruption and malfeasance, and they sometimes directed their criticisms at the emperor himself.[21] The examination system also served the check the emperor's power.[22] Even symbolically, the emperor was not, so to speak, number one: words designating the emperor on examinations had to be written two spaces above the text, but the emperor's parents and ancestors were held to be more important and words referring to them were raised three spaces above the text.[23] As a child, the emperor was educated in the Confucian virtues and court historians subsequently aimed to monitor almost every aspect of the emperor's conduct and virtue: in the words of a petition to Emperor Shenzong by Lü Gongzhu, filed in 1085, "each single action and each word of a ruler has to be written down by a historian. If you [the ruler] display a lack of virtue, it is not only to the disadvantage of the people but its recording in the histories will serve as a source of ridicule for countless generations. Therefore you should rise early and go to bed late, work hard and refine your self-cultivation, rule righteously and justly and control your heart in agreement with the rites. The most minute goodness should be practiced, the smallest evil should be eliminated."[24] Contemporary political theorists argue that such Confucian disciplinary mechanisms could be adapted to fit government structures in modern-day political systems; they may not make rulers into paragons of virtue, but at least they can help to prevent abuses of power.[25]

Nonetheless, it should be recognized that the emperor in imperial China was not formally restrained by separate powers. Hence, emperors could, and sometimes did, ignore informal constitutional norms if it was in their interest to do so.[26] As Francis Fukuyama notes, "under capricious or incompetent sovereigns, the enormous powers granted them often undermined the effectiveness of the administrative system. The empress Wu purged the bureaucracy and packed it with her own unqualified supporters; the emperor Taizu abolished the prime ministership and locked his successors into this awkward system; the emperor ignored the bureaucracy altogether and government collapsed. The Chinese recognize this as the problem of the 'bad emperor.'"[27] Fukuyama adds that "things are not all that different in contemporary China," but the current political system in China has taken measures to solve the problem of the "bad emperor." The principle of collective leadership, term limits, and the introduction of a mandatory retirement age prevents leaders from doing as much damage as emperors of the past (and modern "emperors" such as Mao Zedong). As Yuri Pines explains, "these safeguards may also preclude top executives' remaining in office after becoming physically or mentally debilitated, as occurred with the first generation of CPC [Communist Party of China] leaders. Current chief executives undergo lengthy processes of recruitment, training, and socialization into the top leadership, which renders them incomparably fitter for their tasks than were the majority of the emperors."[28]

Still, the basic problem has not changed: there are no independent legal or political institutions with the formal power to investigate or check the power of the collective leadership.[29] When anticorruption bloggers and transparency advocates are imprisoned,[30] it seems hard to deny that the regime is concerned with the interests of the rulers rather than the ruled.[31] The problem of one bad emperor may have been solved,[32] but not the problem of how to avoid several bad leaders at the top of a rotten system. And today, there aren't censors, court historians, or Confucian educators to pressure rulers into doing the right thing.

In contemporary China, the CCP has tried to combat corruption in its own way. China's governing system has two parallel hierarchies—a state hierarchy and a party hierarchy—operating on all five administrative levels of the system (the political center, the province, the prefecture, the county, and the township). The state hierarchy is made of three different branches—an administration, a judiciary, and a parliament (a People's Congress and a People's Political Consultative Conference)—that are supposed to check one another. The CCP is supposed to bring consistency to the various levels of government as well as providing a further check on the abuse of state power. At each level of the hierarchy, a CCP committee sits parallel to the state. In practice the party makes important strategic and personnel decisions, and officials in decision-making positions (particularly at the higher levels) are usually party members. Hence, the big question is how to check abuses by party cadres who exercise the most power. The CCP's Central Discipline Inspection Commission is the most important institution for rooting out corruption and malfeasance among party cadres but it does not seem to be sufficient. In recent years, the commission has been very aggressive—in 2011 it conducted formal investigations into 137,859 cases that resulted in disciplinary actions or legal convictions against party officials, a nearly fourfold increase since the years before 1989, when corruption was one of the main issues that drove the Tiananmen protests[33]—yet perceptions of the level of corruption in the party have only worsened.[34] The discipline inspection mechanisms have been streamlined with more independent power to investigate abuses by local officials and more clarity about who is in charge of anticorruption work,[35] but clearly there is a need for even more substantial changes to the political system if corruption is to be contained to the point that it no longer poses a threat to the survival of the regime.[36]

But can changes be made without full-scale political democratization in the form of one person, one vote to choose top political leaders? In fact, the experience of contemporary societies shows that there are several ways of curbing corruption without elections that make leaders accountable to the people. Nondemocratic Hong Kong relies on a powerful and independent anticorruption agency, the rule of law, and a relatively free press. Less-than-democratic Singapore relies on high salaries and an independent anticorruption agency. For that matter, democratic countries also rely on extensive monitoring systems to curb the power of their elected leaders, such as "public integrity commissions, judicial activism, local courts, workplace tribunals, consensus conferences, parliaments for minorities, public interest litigation, citizens' juries, citizens' assemblies, independent public inquiries, think-tanks, experts' reports, participatory budgeting, vigils, 'blogging' and other novel forms of media scrutiny."[37]

Obviously there is a need for China to draw on such practices and institutions. The emergence of independent anticorruption fighters using social media to expose official malfeasance is an encouraging sign, but whistleblowers also face serious risks of retaliation.[38] Budget reform, including fiscal transparency, has contributed to the fight against corruption, though there is room for improvement.[39] Another encouraging sign is the increased willingness to experiment with anticorruption mechanisms in different parts of China: for example, the government has launched an experimental scheme in (parts of) the province of Guangdong to force public officials to disclose their assets.[40] But such measures face substantial opposition, and they do not address the problem of family members drawing on political connections to accumulate wealth in semilegal ways.[41] The most far-reaching step would be to institutionalize an independent nationwide anticorruption agency similar to the Hong Kong model.[42] It is more difficult to establish effective anticorruption bureaus at the national level (because it's harder to monitor officials in a big and diverse country), but the government can experiment with more independent institutions at lower levels.[43] A more radical solution at the local level—designed to prevent the *mai guan* (buying a government post) phenomenon that is more prevalent at lower levels and in poor regions[44]—would be to simply decide on appointments by lots, as was done under Emperor Wanli.[45] At the very least, there should be more transparency in the selection and promotion process of public officials.[46] All these measures will help to curb corruption and defuse popular anger and they can be implemented without going the way of electoral democracy for China's top leaders.

The second cause of corruption is related to economic development and the transition to a market economy. On the one hand, privatization gives rise to rent-seeking: in the mixed public-private economy, officials have the power to vet and approve applications for land acquisition and construction projects.[47] On the other hand, state control of the economy also gives rise to rent-seeking: state-owned enterprises (SOEs) fight to maintain their monopolistic powers and have billions of dollars to distribute to advance their agendas, and government ministries, divided and at odds with one another, are overly keen to accommodate SOEs' requests.[48] Moreover, the closed nature of SOEs undermines meritocracy in the economic realm: as Zheng Yongnian puts it, the "management layers [of SOEs] from top to bottom are filled with relatives and friends of officials. An ordinary person, even if they are extraordinarily talented, has a hard time penetrating the networks of the state enterprises."[49]

So what can be done? The government has successfully decreased the number of corruption cases related to the internal administrative process (embezzlement and misappropriation of public funds) by means such as strengthening the merit-based public service system, improvement of the budgeting and auditing system, fiscal recentralization and better monitoring of local governments' activities, and progress in anticorruption regulation and enforcement. At the same time, Chinese corruption has made a transition from being an administrative issue to being a public–private transactional problem, with a steep increase in bribery involving both public and private parties.[50] Clearly there is a need to reduce dependence between public and private parties and establish clearer boundaries between the two sectors.

Imperial China may offer some lessons: Tang dynasty law prohibited merchants and artisans from social intercourse with officials, banned the upper echelons of the public service from entering urban markets, and forbade merchants and artisans from sitting for the public service exams and holding public office.[51] Such drastic measures may be difficult to implement today, but imposing some limits on social interaction between public and private officials can help: for example, Zhang Lu suggests that China can learn from an anticorruption law in South Korea passed in 2001 that forbids public officials and business persons from playing golf together;[52] in the case of China, such measures can perhaps be extended to other social settings conducive to corruption, such as karaoke parlors.

Most important, policies that induce more competition in commercial and political markets could help to reduce corruption:[53] in November 2013, the Third Plenum resolved that the market should play a "decisive" role in the allocation of resources, and if the deeds match the rhetoric corruption can be substantially reduced.[54] In addition, "public–private partnerships between the government and the civil society, for example involving nongovernmental organizations and private organizations in designing and implementing anticorruption policies, would be helpful to curb bribery."[55] Finally, what look like corrupt practices can simply be legalized. In the United States, commercial interests legally influence elected politicians by means of campaign contributions and lobbying between elections. The large majority of Americans believe such practices violate the public interest,[56] and yet few Americans think that they undermine the value of the constitutional system as a whole. In a nondemocratic system (such as China), however, legalization of systemic political corruption would not solve the legitimacy problem. Still, legalization of small-scale corruption can

help: for example, the Korean government passed a law in 2011 forbidding gifts to public officials worth more than 180 rmb (approx. U.S.$30), thus providing a clear guideline about the limits of "bribery."[57] Such small gifts for public officials would not be viewed as morally obscene in a Chinese context, especially if they were legalized. Finally, a general amnesty can be granted to all corrupt officials, with serious policing of the boundaries between public and private, with activity provided to allow them to start afresh.[58] Again, none of these measures require democracy in the form of one person, one vote.

The third cause of corruption is the low salaries of public officials. China's President Xi Jinping makes an annual salary of roughly U.S. $19,000, compared to U.S. President Barack Obama's $400,000 a year. Former Prime Minister Wen Jiabao's similarly meager salary did not prevent his family members from accumulating a hidden trove of wealth estimated at $2.7 billion. Fallen political leader Bo Xilai had an official salary of $1,600 a month but his family owned assets valued at $130 million.[59] Lower-level officials earn less, and yet they often seem to be far wealthier than people who earn much more.

Why is it that government officials often do not seem satisfied with low salaries? In a revolutionary period, when political leaders and their followers are fully committed to an ideal, corruption will be minuscule. But such times do not last long, and corruption cannot be avoided if material benefits are insufficient to cover the basic needs of officials and their family members. And corruption can worsen with economic development: market reforms brought about the emergence of private property and a growing disparity between public service and private wealth. There is more money in the system, and public officials compare themselves negatively to those doing well in the private sector. Plus, the cost of living has gone up exponentially and—to be charitable—the cost of caring for needy family members often cannot be covered by official salaries. Hence, public officials have the motivation to abuse their public position for private (and family) gain, and punishing a few corrupt officials is not likely to help so long as salaries remain so low. The connection between low salaries and high levels of corruption is familiar to students of Chinese history: in the Ming dynasty, when officials' salaries were the lowest and anticorruption campaigns were the fiercest, the level of corruption stubbornly remained the highest.[60]

The solution seems obvious,[61] and it's the same solution put forward by Wang Anshi (1021–1086) in the Song dynasty: "The rate of salaries paid nowadays is generally too low. . . . What people want is a decent life, to earn a good reputation, gain a distinguished title, and get good pay."[62]

The Most Highly Paid Public Officials in the World

As Singapore's economy improved over the years, the government found it increasingly difficult to attract and retain its ministers and top public service officers. Various policies to close the gap between private- and public-sector salaries were explored and implemented. In 1994, the government decided to benchmark the salaries of ministers and top civil servants to the salaries of top earners in the private sector. The formula was revised in 2007 to peg the salaries of ministers and permanent secretaries to two-thirds of the median salary of the top eight earners in six professions. According to the government, economic globalization had created a single worldwide market for talent and government scholars were keenly sought by top global companies like McKinsey & Co. and Goldman Sachs. With the salary revision the annual pay of entry-level ministers and senior permanent secretaries went up from $1.2 million to $1.6 million, and that of the prime minister went from $2.5 million to $3.1 million. Top performers in the elite Administrative Service, which identifies high-potential talent early on and grooms them for top generalist posts, at age thirty-two would be paid up to $361,000 a year.[63]

The advantages of benchmarking compensation in order to keep pace with the private section are obvious: as the Boston Consulting Group puts it, "it ensures that a talented public servant is not unfairly penalized for choosing a career in the public sector, and reduces the temptation to engage in corrupt practices."[64] Of course, the government is also aware that the policy is politically sensitive and may not be feasible in a "pure" electoral democracy with critical media and the serious possibility of being voted out of power: in his 2000 National Day Rally, then Prime Minister Goh Chok Tong said, "Many Western leaders told me in private that they envied our system of Ministers' pay. But they also said that if they tried to implement it in their own countries, they would be booted out."[65] Notwithstanding the government's staunch defense of the policy and less-than-democratic political institutions, the market-based salary system has proven to be highly controversial in Singapore, particularly at a time when the gap between rich and poor increased dramatically and the myth of equal opportunity began to be seen as, well, a myth, by Singapore's disadvantaged (not to mention the fact that several members of the Lee family have been in positions of economic and political power).[66] During the 2011 general elections, the policy became a major issue (especially on social media sites) and the government won "only" 60 percent of the popular vote and it lost six parliamentary seats. In response, the government reduced ministers' salaries by 40 percent, and bonuses were linked not just with high economic performance but to the economic state of the poorest Singaporeans. The ruling People's Action Party also acknowledged that politicians should be motivated at least partly by "the ethos of political service and sacrifice,"[67] not just by selfish material interests. Even after the cuts, however, the salaries of Singapore's ministers are the highest in the world.

In the case of China, it is clear that the salaries of public officials need to be substantially increased to reduce the temptation to engage in corrupt practices.[68] One solution is to peg salaries to market rates.[69] To further deter any temptation for favoritism or abuse, the large bulk of compensation should be made in cash rather than in the form of allowances or benefits (in the case of Singapore, all compensation is payable in cash except for minimal health-care benefits).[70] Relative to Singapore, however, China is poor and cannot afford Singapore-style salaries. Moreover, it has a huge pool of talent and need not worry as much about losing talent to the private sector. China also has a long tradition of public service and a more deeply rooted sense of national identity, and the ethos of serving the political community should play a relatively important role in motivating public servants. So salaries need to increase, but not to Singapore-style levels.

In any case, money per se is not sufficient to deter corruption.[71] This brings us to the fourth cause of corruption in China: lack of ethics. Strict Legalist and utilitarian thinkers dismiss such considerations: as a contemporary philosopher puts it, "the law and a code of enforced ethics can regulate behavior more readily and pervasively than any ordinary ethics can."[72] So long as the right combination of incentives—rewards for good behavior and punishment for bad behavior—are in place, then public officials will do the right thing. But it is difficult and expensive for outsiders to ensure that public officials are always being conscientious. The law cannot specify moral behavior in all circumstances, and less-than-conscientious public officials can serve their own interests at the cost of the public good in ways that do not directly (or obviously) violate the letter of the law.

Even when the law is clear, it is not always easy to enforce.[73] There is no way of monitoring people at all times and places: only internal self-regulation can restrain bad behavior when nobody is watching. A Confucian classic—the *Zhongyong* (Book of the Mean)—emphasizes that the mark of an exemplary person is what he or she does in private. In other words, guardians need to watch themselves. Even analysts of American political culture—famed for its suspicion of political power—recognize that the ultimate restraints on abuses of the public trust must come from within: "The checks that hold the President in line are internal rather than external. His conscience and training, his sense of history and desire to be judged well by it, his awareness of the need to pace himself lest he collapse under the burden—all join to halt him far short of the kind of deed that destroys a President's 'fame and power.'"[74] At the end of the day, corruption in China can be substantially curtailed only if it is seen to be deeply shameful and being clean is seen to be a matter of honor for public officials.[75] As Kwame Anthony Appiah puts it, honor "motivates the people to act well, whether or not anyone is watching, because honorable people care about being *worthy* of respect and not just about being respected."[76] Footbinding, despite its long history in China, was brought to a swift end more than a century ago when the practice began to be seen as shameful for the people involved and the nation as a whole.[77] What will it take for corruption to be seen as similarly shameful?

The CCP is officially communist in orientation and its cadres are supposed to be motivated (and constrained) by Marxist ideology: as President Xi Jinping put it, "the Party's cadres should be firm followers of the Communist ideal, true believers of Marxism and devoted fighters for the socialism with Chinese characteristics. . . . They must serve the people heart and soul, exercise their power carefully and resist corruption. . . . A CPC official's integrity will not grow with the years of service and promotion of his post but with persistent efforts to discipline himself and study Marxist classics and theories of the socialism with Chinese characteristics."[78] The problem is that Marxism is basically dead as a motivating ideology in contemporary China; the more cadres are forced to study the Marxist classics, the more cynical they will become. Equally serious, the Marxist classics offer little insight into ethical behavior by public officials.[79] Karl Marx, in his voluminous writings, has nothing to say about the self-cultivation of public officials. To the extent that texts in the Chinese Marxist tradition ("socialism with Chinese characteristics") offer insights on the ethical behavior of public officials, they owe more to Confucianism than to Marxism.[80] So why not directly revive the Confucian tradition as the main source of moral education for public officials? Influential Chinese intellectuals have long been calling for such steps.[81] In fact, President Xi has named Confucianism—along with Buddhism and Taoism—as one of the "traditional cultures" that can help fill an ethical void that has allowed corruption to flourish and he has invoked Confucian values in a speech on party members' moral training and standards.[82] Qufu, the home of Confucian culture, is experimenting with an educational program that emphasizes more teaching of Confucianism in public schools. And Communist Party schools often teach the Confucian classics to public officials. But the party has yet to take the formal step of officially replacing communism with Confucianism.[83]

There are many ways of abusing political power, but I have focused my discussion on the issue of corruption because it is widely acknowledged—by the government, the people, and scholars—as the most serious threat facing the political system in China. In a democracy, corruption won't threaten the whole system, but it can make or break a political meritocracy. The good news (for a meritocratic regime) is that there are many ways of combating corruption without going the way of one person, one vote to choose leaders: establishing independent checks on political power, reducing dependence between the public and private sectors, increasing the salaries of public officials, and implementing a more systematic program in Confucian moral education can help to eradicate corruption. Let's now turn to the second key problem associated with the attempt to realize a meritocratic political system.

2. The Problem of Ossification

According to the meritocratic ideal, a political system should aim to select and promote leaders with superior ability and virtue. In the Warring States period, the market for political talent was basically international. Scholars roamed from state to state hoping to persuade rulers of their superior qualities and be chosen to serve as ministers and advisors. As Mencius put it, "if a ruler gives honor to men of talents and employs the able, so that offices shall all be filled by individuals of distinction and mark, then all the scholars of All-under-Heaven will be pleased, and wish to stand in his court" (2A.5). Moreover, the political system should aim to choose the best, regardless of class background. Xunzi expressed this idea: "Promote the worthy and capable without regard to seniority; dismiss the unfit and incapable without hesitation. . . . Although they may be the descendants of kings and dukes or scholar-officials and counselors, if they are incapable of devotedly observing the requirements of ritual principles and justice, they should be relegated to the position of commoners. Although they may be descendants of commoners, if they have acquired learning, are upright in conduct, and can adhere to ritual principles, they should be promoted to the post of prime minister, scholar-official, or counselor" (9.1; see also 9.4). Around the same period in a different part of the world, Plato extended meritocratic principles to two other groups. First, the very top ruler(s) should also be chosen according to merit (Xunzi did not extend meritocracy to the position of king). Second, women should also have the opportunity to be rulers. In short, the meritocratic ideal is that everyone should have an equal opportunity to serve as a political official regardless of social background, and the political system should aim to choose the most able and virtuous among the contenders.

Early defenders of political meritocracy were ahead of their time, but today political meritocracies endorse the ideal that the political system should draw on as wide a talent pool as possible (with the exception that the top positions are reserved for citizens). Given the wide distribution of talents in society, one would therefore expect that political leaders in meritocratic systems such as China and Singapore would come from diverse social backgrounds. In reality, however, political hierarchies are increasingly composed of elites from a narrow social background. This leads to the problem that the political selection process may be missing out on talent from other sectors of the population; political meritocracy is not as good as it could be. But confining political leadership to a narrow social circle leads to even more serious problems that threaten the viability of the whole system.

First, the political elite downplays social background and luck and can easily become convinced of its inherent superiority, with the consequence that it looks down on the "losers" in a supposedly fair competitive race to the top. Here too, the case of Singapore is telling. Former top civil servant Ngiam Tong Dow has noticed "a particular brand of elite arrogance creeping in. Some civil servants behave like they have a mandate from the emperor. We think we are little Lee Kuan Yews."[84] Talented scholars come to feel they are deserving winners in tough competition and they often develop a disdainful attitude toward ordinary people. In one notorious case, a humanities scholar from an elite junior college wrote a blog criticizing a young executive who expressed concerns about competition from foreigners and the lack of opportunities for older workers: "We are a tyranny of the capable and the clever. . . . [I]f you're not good enough, life will kick you in the balls, that's just how things go. . . . [P]lease, get out of my elite uncaring face." This blog created a public uproar and the blogger's father—a scholar and member of parliament—intervened on behalf of his daughter: "If you cut through the insensitivity of the language, her basic point is reasonable, that a well-educated university graduate who works for a multinational company should not be bemoaning the Government and get on with the challenges of life. Nonetheless, I have counseled her to learn from it. Some people cannot take the brutal truth and that sort of language." The publication of the father's interview caused even more general unhappiness because he implied that he continued to believe in the "brutal truth."[85] In the popular mind, the word *meritocracy* has become code for elitism of the kind that focuses on winning and maximizing rewards for the winners, while downplaying factors that limit opportunities for the disadvantaged.[86]

In his 1957 satirical book on meritocracy (set in the year 2033), Michael Young predicted that meritocratically selected leaders would become arrogant and detached from the rest of society: "some members of the meritocracy, as most moderate reformers admit, have become so impressed with their own importance as to lose sympathy with the people whom they govern, and so tactless that even people of low caliber have been unnecessarily offended." He also predicted the solution: "The schools and universities are endeavoring to instill a more proper sense of humility."[87] Faced with declining popular support, Singapore's political leaders have rebranded the ruling ideology as "compassionate meritocracy." In striking contrast to Lee Kuan Yew's less-than-humble political discourse, his son, Prime Minister Lee Hsien Loong, emphasizes that political leaders must "serve with humility. Let us do the right things and do things right, but never be self-righteous or arrogant. Being humble also means accepting that government does not have all the answers."[88] In short, government leaders should be humble and sympathize with the people, not look down on them. But is sympathy sufficient?

Political Elitism in France

The École Nationale d'Administration (ENA), created in 1945 by Charles de Gaulle, is an institution explicitly designed to realize political meritocracy. It aims to select the country's intellectual political elite regardless of social background and train them for public service. Admission to ENA is based on perhaps the most rigorous and grueling set of examinations in the world. The candidates need to take five written exams (in public law, economy, general knowledge, a summary of documents in either European law and policies or social law and policies, and a fifth exam to be chosen by the candidate from subjects ranging from math to language); then the candidates with the highest marks take five oral exams (in public finance, international politics, European or social issues, foreign language, and the famous forty-five-minute-long Grand Oral, open to the public, during which any question can be asked, including personal questions), and one test in sports fitness. Fewer than one hundred are chosen every year. Following two years of ultracompetitive education and training at the ENA, the graduates are numerically ranked according to academic performance. They are basically guaranteed jobs in the civil service, and the top fifteen performers almost always choose to enter one of three administrative corps: the Conseil d'État, the Inspection des finances, or the Cour des comptes. The reason is simple: these corps serve as platforms for prestigious careers in administration, business, and politics.[89] Unlike parliamentary systems in the United Kingdom and Canada, the boundaries between the civil service and political leadership are fluid: civil servants who are elected or appointed to a political position do not have to resign their position in the civil service, and if they are not reelected or appointed, they may ask for reintegration into their service. Hence, several leading politicians are ENA alumni, including French presidents (Valéry Giscard d'Estaing, Jacques Chirac, and François Hollande) and prime ministers (Laurent Fabius, Michel Rocard, Edouard Balladur, Alain Juppé, Lionel Jospin, and Dominique de Villepin). Typically, one-third to one-half of every French cabinet since the 1960s (with the exception of the Sarkozy administration) is composed of ENA alumni. That said, only 3 percent of ENA alumni go into politics: 80 percent of alumni work in the civil service and the rest enter the private sector.[90]

The education at ENA is meant to produce generalists who can be skilled at administration, politics, and business. They are supposed to be good at problem solving without worrying about the glare of media attention. They learn values such as impartiality toward all citizens, loyalty to the democratic government, and ethical usage of public funds. They are supposed to be competent technocrats with the ability to deal with extremely complex administrative issues without ever forgetting that policies apply to real flesh-and-blood people. In short, the ideal ENA graduate is both a technocrat and a humanist.[91] The ENA is successful in the sense that the graduates often serve in positions of power and derive self-esteem from service to the public.[92]

Unfortunately, the public image of ENA graduates is less positive. They are increasingly viewed as arrogant, detached from the rest of society, and more concerned with serving their own career interests than serving the public. And the reality is that ENA graduates increasingly come from privileged backgrounds. Among 2011 graduates, 50 percent had a parent working in the national education sector, and only 3 out of 81 had a working-class background.[93] At the start, ENA graduates came from diverse social backgrounds (including former President Chirac, from a farmer's family). But it is increasingly difficult for those from underprivileged backgrounds to have a shot at the ENA: a self-perpetuating elite of the wealthy and the white provide their own children with the social skills, financial support, and cultural knowledge to pass the entrance exams, which are normally undertaken after an extra two years of intensive study in preparatory schools.[94] The result is a relatively homogenous cohort of graduates, and the current director of the ENA, Bernard Boucault, spells out the implications for administering the country: "To have a good comprehension of the needs of society, the administration must come from the whole of society. I realize it's a contested point, but no matter how open or talented the person, there are some things that can be known only from personal experience."[95]

The basic problem is that humble political discourse expressing sympathy with the people, however sincere, is insufficient to motivate policy making on behalf of the people, especially disadvantaged sectors of the population. That is, policy making on behalf of the people depends not just on sympathy but also on social background. Political decision making, especially at higher levels of government, involves trade-offs between different goods, and politicians are more likely to fight for the interests of people from their own background when faced with competing considerations. This is not to deny that some people can transcend their class backgrounds—even Karl Marx allowed for the possibility that capitalists (such as Engels) can take the side of the proletariat—but it is not likely that an entire social group will do so. And if a political elite composed of people from a particular social background does make a special effort to help people from other backgrounds, the rulers may still lack the knowledge required to enact policies that benefit other groups. Even with thorough briefings by brilliant political advisors, leaders born into wealthy and privileged families will lack the knowledge that comes from lived experience within a particular social setting.[96] Hence, the fact that political elites are composed of an increasingly narrow and wealthy sector of the population is a worrying phenomenon.[97] Whatever the rhetoric about sympathy for the disadvantaged, such leaders will often lack sufficient motivation and knowledge to fight for their interests.[98] In short, the more political leaders come from diverse social backgrounds, the better the quality of policy making.

So what can be done? In a democracy, the problem is not so difficult to solve, at least on the surface. In France, for example, people will not vote for ENA graduates viewed as privileged elites with neither the motivation nor the knowledge required to work for the interests of the public. Nicolas Sarkozy was elected at least partly because he was viewed as different from the ENA-molded political elite; the people wanted a leader who looked more like them, stronger in emotional quotient than intellect.[99] More worrisome, the far right Front National leader Marine Le Pen defeated an ENA graduate, Jean-François Cope, in a cantonal election with populist rhetoric that verged on hatred: "What contempt! What arrogance! This arrogance, Mr. Cope, will lead to you to being thrown out of politics. The French people will turn their backs on you. The candidates of the Front National are students, unemployed. They are also mothers of families and workers. All those you turned your back to. Of course, they are not ENA graduates. Ah, we prefer to mingle with ENA graduates and high functionaries. Well, all that is finished."[100] Whether or not the alternative to rule by ENA graduates is far-right populism, it seems likely that fewer ENA graduates will be going into politics.[101]

In a political meritocracy, the question of how to deal with closed and self-perpetuating political elites is less straightforward. The only way to remedy the problem of a ruling class largely composed of people from a privileged background is to improve representation of diverse social groupings within the political elite. In Singapore, there are various constraints on the democratic process and the government will not lose power in the foreseeable future, but the ruling party has reacted to falling popular support by implementing policies such as limiting legacy-based admission in schools and extending scholarship opportunities to nonelite schools and a more diverse range of students in order to equalize opportunities and eventually increase the representation of underprivileged classes in the political elite.[102] In 2002, the CCP did take a major step designed to increase representation of diverse social classes within its ranks: it accepted capitalists as members (Mao and Marx must be turning in their graves, but the point was to recognize that capitalists can help with policy making appropriate for market reforms.[103] But other social classes have not fared as well.

The CCP aims to select excellent persons from diverse social sectors, but it selects fewer farmers and workers and an increasing proportion of members are highly educated overachievers.[104] The problem is that it is difficult for families without the economic resources to pay for tutors and extra classes that increase the likelihood of success on the ultracompetitive national entrance examinations.[105] Hence, the students at elite universities that serve as key entrance points to political leadership are increasingly composed of families from privileged backgrounds. One short-term way to deal with this problem is to implement quotas for students from underprivileged backgrounds.[106] Such measures will be controversial because they conflict with the aim of meritocratic selection that is blind to social background,[107] but applicants from minority groups are admitted to universities with lower scores on the national university entrance examinations and such programs can be extended to economically deprived students.[108]

There may also be a need for quotas for disadvantaged sectors of the population throughout the promotion process. In China, the CCP has implemented institutional rules to systematically promote ethnic minorities into its leadership, but the higher the party rank, the fewer the proportion of ethnic minorities.[109] At the highest levels of government, spots can be set aside for minority groups with different religions and people from economically deprived backgrounds, even if they didn't rise through the political system (of course, they would also have to be talented in ways relevant for high-level political decision making, such as superior analytical ability).[110] With respect to religious groups, the case for representation is clear: only sincere adherents of a religion can really know what's best for their religion. But people from economically deprived backgrounds also tend to have special insight into the needs and wants of people from their background,[111] and they should be more represented in the system as well.[112] Ultimately, the best solution is to reduce income gaps and inequalities of opportunity in society at large so that people from wealthy and powerful families have fewer advantages in the meritocratic competition for political power.[113] In other words, a relatively equal society is less likely to be ruled by a political elite composed of people from a privileged background, assuming that the process of selection and promotion of political leaders is done in a meritocratic way blind to social background.[114] Political meritocracy depends on a high degree of economic equality.

But such measures still won't be sufficient to deal with the problem of rigid and inflexible political hierarchies. Even if political leaders come from diverse sectors of society, there will still be a problem if they are chosen according to a rigid definition of merit that does not change along with new circumstances that require different kinds of leaders with different qualities. In Michael Young's dystopic meritocracy, the influence of social background has been minimized, but since leaders are chosen according to a narrow definition of merit—IQ scores plus effort—the result is a ruling class that lacks social skills and public-spiritedness. In France, Marxist-inspired sociologists who argued that rewarding abstract skills like mathematics would neutralize the influence of parents and social origin on school success helped to shape (and justify) a selection system for elite universities that emphasizes mathematical skills—only the top 5 percent of secondary-school students in math even have a chance at landing spots at top universities. As a consequence, French elites tend to be strong in analytical ability but weak at working with teams, listening to others, and practical problem-solving skills, as well as prone to arrogance because they come to believe that their success is due to their excellence without giving credit to the influence of luck and social background.[115] In China, the political elite is more diverse than, say, family-run dictatorships in North Korea and the Middle East, and such diversity is key to its success. But measurement of merit in the promotion process within the CCP over the past couple of decades has largely been confined to economic growth. To the extent that other factors have come into play, perhaps the most important has been the willingness to please and get along with political superiors.[116]

Hence, the rigorous, multiyear talent selection process has discouraged risk-taking, and relatively creative and original minds may have been weeded out early because they have offended people or challenged the "normal way of doing things."

In the previous chapter (section 3), I argued that there should be more diverse criteria for the selection of top leaders that would result in a more diverse ruling class, including more gender balance. But the criteria suggested may still be too rigid: in today's ever-changing world, any selection process needs to leave room for new definitions of merit. Again, such arguments are not mere idle speculation. In the Warring States period, the Qin state's success was in part related to its ability to maintain multiple avenues of social and political advancement, but the loss of this diversity after it unified China and established the first dynasty hastened Qin's collapse. Yuri Pines draws the implications for today's CCP: "Insofar as manifold routes of individual advancement are maintained, the system may be expected to be fairer, more dynamic, and more adaptable overall to changes than a too perfectly organized one, which would always be prone to ossification."[117] Diversity of avenues of entrance would preserve the flexibility that is particularly important in today's fast-changing world.

Hence, the CCP needs not just to seek expansion to include ambitious and high-achieving representatives of currently marginalized groups, but also to allow for multiple avenues of entering the top levels based on different ideas of merit so as to promote people with more differentiated experience. This is not to deny the advantage of a relatively stable and rule-bound system of promotion based on transparent criteria of merit, especially at higher levels of government. But a minority of places—including in the Standing Committee of the Politburo—should be reserved for excellent performers who succeed outside the mainstream system of selection and promotion, even for non–party members. So for example, the top leadership can include a younger person with excellent understanding of modern technology and its social implications, an expert in foreign cultures who has spent considerable time abroad, a capitalist who has proved good at money-making as well as philanthropy, and/or an expert in military affairs. As Pines notes, the Qing incorporation of the bannermen into officialdom proved a very good gamble that diversified the pool of talent and made the administration far more effective than was the case under the Ming, when the examinations were the exclusive way upward.[118]

But how to know which people will be most useful for political decision making in the future? In other words, how to identify new sources of political merit? Here John Stuart Mill's utilitarian arguments for freedom of speech are helpful. Freedom of speech matters not just because it helps to identify *what* is important,[119] but also because it helps us to identify *who* is important. Mill argued that the freedom of speech allows for a range of choice that enables us to choose the wise and noble among us. Everyone gains from the "experiments of living" of the few, and if some "eccentrics" are willing to find out at their own risk what new and better ways of life there might be, we should all be grateful, not resentful.[120] Mill had in mind a democratic context where educated citizens would choose the new members of the ruling elite in democratic elections, but his point that freedom of speech is necessary to identify unconventional sources of merit appropriate for new circumstances is also valid in the context of a political meritocracy.[121]

Equally important, new sources of merit, and new ways of measuring merit, can be identified by means of experimentation at subcentral levels of government. Here the Chinese political system has demonstrated clear advantages relative to constitutional democracies with rigid divisions of power between different levels of government. In a federal system, for example, what works well in one subunit cannot necessarily be generalized to the rest of the country if the central government does not have the constitutional power to do so.[122] But the power to spread desirable local innovations is an important advantage of Chinese-style political meritocracy.[123] As the authors of *China Experiments* explain,

> Local experiments are the hallmark of how China has undertaken all sorts of reforms since the end of the Mao era in the late 1970s. China's massive transformations over the past three decades are the result of multi-layered and incremental change rather than top-down shock-therapy style reform. . . . The benefits of this experimentalist approach are clear: Given the size of the country and the relatively underdeveloped nature of its government institutions, the repercussions of implementing a

> policy and getting it wrong are massive, and not easy to correct. The socioeconomic variations across the country also demand flexibility rather than a one-size-fits-all approach. The decentralized, experimentalist strategy allows the center to set an overall objective, but also allows localities to test ideas through pilot projects in different places, to gain experience from the ground up. The pilots that end up being nationalized are first endorsed by central authorities, and their adoption is then promoted through official announcements and press conferences, as well as visits and exchanges with other regions.[124]

The real source of dynamism in China is that the government usually takes a hands-off approach to dealing with local affairs, except when they prove to be particularly innovative and effective at dealing with social problems, in which case the central government seeks to generalize good policies elsewhere, to the extent conditions allow. Trial experiments started with economic reform and more recently the government has embarked on experiments dealing with tricky governance issues.[125] In order to prevent the ossification of merit-based political hierarchies, such experiments from provincial down to township levels can and should include different ways of assessing merit and the successful experiments can be scaled up to higher levels of government.[126]

In short, I have argued that there are three problems related to the ossification of political hierarchies and suggested some possible responses short of electoral democracy for top leaders. Political elites prone to arrogance should strive to be humble and sympathetic to the people. Political elites prone to selecting people from their own social grouping should strive for representation of diverse social groups in government. And political elites prone to selecting people according to the same criteria of merit that defined themselves as the best should make room for differentiated standards of merit. At the end of the day, political elites need to combat the tendency to self-love. Why should they care about this argument? The lessons from Chinese history are clear: the ossification of political meritocracy is just as threatening to the system as systemic corruption. But perhaps there is something even more threatening to the system.

3. The Problem of Legitimacy

Political legitimacy, according to Jean-Marc Coicaud, "is defined as the governed recognizing the right of the governors to lead and, to a certain extent, their entitlement to the perks of power."[127] Put simply, a government is legitimate when it is morally justified in the eyes of the people.[128] It is not easy to measure legitimacy: do we use qualitative interviews with people from different social groups, survey data, or elections? And what counts as legitimate: the views of educated people, a majority of the people, or does everybody have to agree? What is clearer, perhaps, is when the governors lack legitimacy: they are overthrown in a revolution or must use brutal violence to put down popular uprisings. In fact, "legitimacy usually enters the analytical picture when it is missing or deficient. Only when a regime is being manifestly challenged by its citizens/subjects/beneficiaries do political scientists tend to invoke legitimacy as a cause for the crisis. When it is functioning well, legitimacy recedes into the background. Persons take it for granted that the actions of their authorities are 'proper,' 'normal' or 'justified.'"[129]

In the case of China, the study of legitimacy took off in the early 1990s. Again, the reason is political: the CCP rulers used extreme violence to put down a popular demand for change on 4 June 1989, and it seemed clear that a regime with legitimacy would not have resorted to such means. The more a regime is legitimate—that is, seen as morally justified in the eyes of the people—the less it has to rely on coercion to get its way.

It also seemed clear—especially to Western analysts—that the regime was doomed. As happened in Russia and Eastern Europe after the collapse of the Soviet empire (and more recently in the Middle East), the people would sooner or later demand the freedom to organize political parties and the right to vote for their political leaders. In the short term, there may be "democratic reversals" in the form of military coups (as in Egypt), but nondemocratic alternatives cannot last long. Liberal democracy, as Francis Fukuyama famously put it, is the "end of history"; no other regime type could be legitimate in a modern or modernizing society. Max Weber's equally famous distinction between three ideal types of legitimate authority also seemed to point the way to liberal democracy. The first type—traditional authority—seemed to have collapsed along with the Qing dynasty in 1911. The second type—charismatic authority—was dying along with Mao Zedong and the other heroes of the Chinese revolution. The third type—rational/legal authority—seemed to be inevitable along with China's economic modernization, with liberal democracy as the only viable regime type that could operate according to a rational-legal structure of authority. The recent political history of economically developed East Asian societies with a Confucian heritage seemed to lend further support to the view that liberal democracy will eventually triumph in China. Japan, South Korea, and Taiwan proved that there is no incompatibility between a Confucian legacy and democratic forms of rule. They all lifted restrictions on political speech and mobilization and adopted democracy in the form of one person, one vote for the country's political rulers, thus setting the apparent path for modernizing China.[130]

Yet China's single-party state structure didn't collapse. If anything, it seemed to strengthen since the early 1990s, and now liberal democracy seems to be further off than ever. Survey after survey shows that the regime enjoys substantial popular support. As Wang Shaoguang puts it, "since the 1990s Western scholars (or scholars born in China and working in the West) have carried out many large-scale surveys into the legitimacy of Chinese political power. . . . By now scholars familiar with the field have virtually all arrived at a consensus: The degree of legitimacy of the Chinese political system is very high."[131] Initially, Wang adds, "the high degree of acceptance of the regime was interpreted by many Western scholars as a result of the respondents being afraid to tell the truth. As a result later surveys added various mechanisms to prevent people being questioned from telling lies (such as providing options: 'don't know' or 'no response'). But the results of each survey were always the same."[132] There is little doubt that the large majority of Chinese consider the current political system to be the appropriate system for their country. In fact, Chinese citizens trust their political institutions more than in any of the eight societies included in a recent Asian Barometer Survey, including democratic societies such as Japan, South Korea, the Philippines, and Taiwan.[133]

This is not to deny the fact of widespread social discontent in China. According to one estimate, there were 180,000 "mass incidents"—everything from strikes to riots and demonstrations—in 2010, twice as many as in 2006.[134] And the government has been devoting massive resources to public security—624.4 billion yuan spent in 2011, more than a quarter more than was spent in 2009[135]—suggesting that discontent is getting more widespread. But this discontent is largely directed at the lower levels of government. As Tony Saich explains, "citizens 'disaggregate' the state and, although they express high levels of satisfaction with the central government, satisfaction declines with each lower level of government. While in 2009, 95.9 per cent were either relatively or extremely satisfied with the central government, this dropped to 61.5 per cent at the local level."[136] He Baogang uses more colorful language to account for this phenomenon in the eyes of the people: "In popular terms, the central governmental officials are the saviors, in the province they are close relatives, in the county they are good people, in the township they are villains, and in the village they are the enemy."[137]

One apparent paradox is that Chinese citizens profess faith in democracy while endorsing nondemocratic rule. As Shi Tianjian and Lu Jie put it, however, "democracy in the minds of ordinary Chinese may not match the meaning defined in the liberal democracy discourse; rather, it is based on the guardianship discourse."[138] Put simply, there is a widely shared view that democracy means government for the people (by elites), rather than government by the people.[139] So if the Chinese government "serves the people," it is democratic. Surveys do show support for elections, but those elections should not be accompanied by multiparty politics organized around competing interests: "While 84% of respondents agreed or strongly agreed with having elections for national leaders, only 16.3% agreed or strongly agreed with multiparty competition."[140] Western analysts may complain that recent talk of "intraparty democracy" within the CCP is not truly democratic because it precludes multiparty competitive politics, but the majority of Chinese people may not be using the same standard to evaluate "democratic" progress.

In short, the Chinese government has managed to achieve a high degree of political legitimacy (in the sense that the people think the government is morally justified) without adopting democracy in the sense of free and fair competitive elections for the country's leaders. So how exactly did the government achieve legitimacy without electoral democracy? Put differently, what are the main sources of nondemocratic legitimacy in China? The CCP has drawn on three sources of nondemocratic legitimacy: nationalism, performance legitimacy, and political meritocracy. Although all three sources of legitimacy have been important at different times to a certain extent, nationalism was most important in the early days of the regime, performance legitimacy in the first couple of decades of the reform era, and political meritocracy is becoming an increasingly important source of legitimacy. The question is whether these sources of legitimacy will be sufficient in the future.

An important part of legitimacy is something we can call "ideological legitimacy": the state or regime seeks to be seen as morally justified in the eyes of the people by virtue of certain ideas that it instantiates and expresses in its educational system, political speeches, and public policies. The CCP was of course founded on communist or Marxist principles, as revised and reinterpreted by Lenin and Mao, and it derives much of its legitimacy by virtue of its ability to live up to those principles. The problem now is that few Chinese believe in Marxism. As Jiang Qing puts it, "the practice of Marxism-Leninism in mainland China over the past thirty years proves not only that it is incapable of solving China's problems but, on the contrary, has delayed the course of modernization. . . . Despite the fact that those in power in modern China have made strenuous efforts to defend Marxism-Leninism's monopoly on power, hoping to use power to maintain the unique authority that Marxism-Leninism enjoyed formerly as the 'national doctrine,' middle and lower levels of authority—especially the youth—no longer trust Marxism-Leninism."[141] This is not to deny that some socialist values such as the need to secure material welfare for people still resonate in society. Arguably, however, they resonate at least partly because they are similar to earlier traditional political values (see below). Nor is it to deny that there are worthwhile contemporary experiments in land reform inspired at least partly by socialist values.[142] But it still seems fair to say that the CCP has managed to secure political legitimacy despite, not because of, its official Marxist ideology. Much of that "ideological legitimacy" has come from a turn to nationalism, with the CCP as the main vehicle and protector of Chinese nationalism.

Winning Hearts and Minds by War

Nationalism is a foreign import. Traditional Chinese political culture was shaped by a more global political vision, with the ideal being a unified world without territorial boundaries governed by a wise and virtuous sage-king. In imperial China, the political elites tended to view their "country" as the center of the world. But that all changed once China was subject to the incursions of Western and Japanese imperial powers from the mid-nineteenth century. For nearly one hundred years—the "century of humiliation"—China was subject to one military defeat after another, and the country was plunged into poverty and civil war. Chinese elites became preoccupied with the painful reality that their polity was peripheral within the expanding Westphalian international order. If China was to survive, it had to adjust to this new system.[143] In practice, it meant the need to strengthen the state, almost at the cost of all other concerns. As Chiang Kai-shek put it in 1947, "during the past hundred years, the citizens of the entire country, suffering under the yoke of the unequal treaties which gave foreigners special 'concessions' and extra-territorial status in China, were unanimous that the national humiliation be avenged, and the state be made strong."[144] As we know, the CCP rather than the KMT successfully avenged "national humiliation," and Mao Zedong's famous declaration in 1949 that "the Chinese people have stood up" put a symbolic end to abuse and bullying by foreign powers.[145]

The establishment of a relatively strong and secure Chinese state under the leadership of the CCP meant that China had less to worry about survival qua political community. However, the Korean War, instability in minority regions, and the break with the Soviet Union (not to mention a degree of paranoia among ruling elites) continued to foster a form of nationalism built on resentment. Global condemnation of the Tiananmen Square crackdown and the collapse of the Soviet empire made the regime even more sensitive about "outside interference," and the regime intensified its promotion of "patriotic education" in schools, with constant reminders of "humiliation" at the hands of foreign powers and the need for a strong centralized CCP leadership to protect the Chinese nation from outside interference.[146] Such "patriotic education" continues to this day: as vice-president, Xi Jinping emphasized that "we suffered over a century of national weakness, oppression and humiliation,"[147] and shortly after taking power as president he issued a call to realize "the cause of national rejuvenation" that seemed to coincide with increased assertiveness of territorial claims over contested islands.

It's worth asking if resentful nationalism is sustainable.[148] One risk to CCP rule is that people who have been subject to patriotic education turn against the regime for failing to stand up to foreign interference as much as it should. Best-selling books such as *China Can Say No* are not so implicitly critical of the regime for being "soft" in the way it deals with Japan, Taiwan, and the West. Popular newspapers such as the *Global Times* are viewed as "nationalistic" by outsiders, but much of their censorship is directed at excessively belligerent and hawkish expressions of nationalism. Anti-Japanese demonstrations are reined in by the authorities for fear that they can get out of hand. Bellicose nationalism is almost universally rejected by Chinese intellectuals,[149] but it resonates more at the popular level (and in military circles) and may well go beyond what the government intends. The government may be able to rein in discontent, but one can imagine scenarios that could spell danger for the regime, such as a military encounter with Taiwan and its foreign protectors that "humiliates" mainland China.

Setting aside moral concerns, the best-case scenario from a regime survival point of view is for China to win a war. Like, say, the British victory over Argentina in the Falklands War, success in war could help the regime that led the war.[150] On the other hand, the eventual loss of support for Margaret Thatcher's conservative government also shows that nationalist legitimacy grounded in military exploits does not last long. In times of peace, people more clearly distinguish between the good of the nation and the good of the ruling party, and the government can gain the trust of the population more by exercising moral power than military force.[151] This is not to imply that nationalism will go away as a legitimizing force in times of peace. But nationalism will take "softer" forms, drawing on pride in culture and history rather than victory in war and resentment against foreigners.[152] The CCP does recognize the importance of "soft" nationalism in times of peace. As Jyrki Kallio puts it, "tradition and history have become the Chinese Communist Party's tools of choice for bolstering its legitimacy. The Party is attempting to patch the chinks in its rusting spiritual-ideological armor with a concoction of handpicked values from traditional schools of thought, especially Confucianism."[153] The government has been stressing Confucian values such as harmony and filial piety in its political speeches. The 2008 Olympics in Beijing highlighted Confucian themes, quoting the *Analects* of Confucius at the opening ceremony, and downplayed any references to China's experiment with communism. Cadres at the Communist Party School in Shanghai proudly tell visitors that the main building is modeled on a Confucian scholar's desk. Abroad, the government has been promoting Confucianism via branches of the Confucius Institute, a Chinese language and culture center similar to Germany's Goethe Institute.

But the government cannot successfully promote "soft" nationalism of this sort on its own: Chinese intellectuals also seek to put forward their own interpretations of the national good and whatever the government says will not be credible (at home and abroad) if they are left out of the process. Scholars such as Jiang Qing and Kang Xiaoguang have been calling for an official embrace of Confucianism,[154] but the government has resisted because it still officially adheres to Marxism.[155] And the debate is not confined to Confucianism: a group of liberal, Christian, socialist, and Confucian scholars who "love the land of China and are loyal to its people" recently met in Oxford and signed a document endorsing values meant to inspire the future development of China.[156]

The point here is that independent intellectuals and other groups outside the government distinguish between the national good and the good of the ruling party, and they seek to put forward their own definitions of the national good; the idea that the party solely embodies the national good is passé. In short, "hard" nationalism justifying CCP rule grounded in military victory that unified China after years of poverty, chaos, and bullying by foreign powers cannot forever win the hearts and minds of the people. To the (limited) extent that nationalism will continue to serve as a source of legitimacy in times of peace, the government will have to make way for a more participatory and open society that allows diverse forces to join the conversation about what constitutes the national good. Nationalism won't go away, but it won't help the CCP as much as it used to.

If nationalism has a short history in China, the idea that the government has an obligation to improve people's material well-being has much deeper roots.[157] According to the *Analects* of Confucius, the government has an obligation to secure the conditions for people's basic means of subsistence and intellectual/moral development. In cases of conflict, however, the former has priority: "Ranyou drove the Master's carriage on a trip to Wey. The Master said: 'What a huge population!' Ranyou said: 'When the people are so numerous, what more can be done for them?' The Master said, 'Make them prosperous.' Ranyou asked, 'When the people are prosperous, what more can be done for them?' The Master replied, 'Educate them'" (13.9).[158] This does not mean the blind pursuit of a higher GDP. The main obligation is to help the needy: "Exemplary persons help out the needy; they do not make the rich richer" (6.4; see also 16.1). One important reason for helping the needy is that poverty is conducive to negative emotions, whereas wealth makes it easier to act in ethical ways: "To be poor without feeling resentful is difficult; to be rich without feeling arrogant is easy" (14.11).[159]

Mencius echoes these concerns. People must be educated so that they can develop their moral natures. First, however, the government must provide for their basic means of subsistence so that they won't go morally astray:

> The people will not have dependable feelings if they are without dependable means of support. Lacking dependable means of support, they will go astray and fall into excesses, stopping at nothing. To punish them after they have fallen foul of the law is to set a trap for the people. How can a humane person set a trap for the people? Hence when determining what means of support the people should have, a clear-sighted ruler ensures that these are sufficient for the care of parents and for the support of wives and children, so that the people will always have sufficient food in good years and escape starvation in bad; only then does he drive them towards goodness. In this way, the people will find it easy to follow him. (1A.7; see also 3A.3)[160]

There is no point promoting moral behavior if people are worried about their next meal. Thus, the government's first priority is to secure the basic means of subsistence of the people. If the government succeeds in doing so—in lifting people out of a state of poverty—then it will gain the hearts and minds of the people (i.e., it will have political legitimacy). Such legitimacy depends on the performance of the government, not the procedure used for choosing government officials or the participation of the people in government.

The idea that the government has the obligation to secure basic material welfare for all members of the state informed policy and helps to explain why dynasties lasted as long as they did. According to Yanqi Tong, "disaster prevention, especially flood control and disaster maintenance, fell squarely on the shoulders of the government, due to the enormous scale of the project. The first emperor of the Xia dynasty (twenty-first century–sixteenth century BCE), Da Yu, became a legend for his achievements in flood control." His achievements are still used to illustrate the role the government should play today: "Every Chinese knows from childhood that Da Yu was so devoted to his work in flood control that he passed his home three times and never went in."[161]

In the Ming and Qing dynasties, the state protected farmers against subsistence uncertainties by means of local community granaries. As R. Bin Wong notes, "the explicit logic of community granaries put responsibility for the creation and maintenance of these institutions in the hands of the local people. The state's willingness to depend on the gentry and others to promote local grain reserves assumed a basic commitment to subsistence security as a key element in social stability."[162] When disasters struck, the grain storage was opened and the state also supported victims by giving relief money to those who could not afford coffins and even by helping families to "buy back" children who had been sold in desperate circumstances. The government also had an obligation to take charge of postdisaster reconstruction by means such as reducing or eliminating taxes for the disaster victims, payment for the transportation of the affected population to return to their deserted lands, and providing crop seeds and other funds for the farmers to resume production.[163] In the Qing dynasty, the penal code explicitly secured the right to food by punishing local officials who failed to provide aid to the needy.[164]

As paramount leader of the People's Republic of China from 1978 to 1992, Deng Xiaoping realized that nationalism and revolutionary energy were not sufficient to sustain people's faith in the CCP. In line with traditional ideas about how to win hearts and minds, the government needed to provide for the people's material well-being. Hence, Deng embarked on market reforms meant to improve economic performance (including a substantial reduction in military expenditures). Mao might have been horrified,[165] but Marx himself argued that capitalism is necessary to develop the productive forces. The result is well known. China became one of the fastest-growing economies in the world for more than thirty years, and the post-reform era has seen perhaps the single most impressive poverty alleviation achievement in human history.[166]

The question, however, is whether performance legitimacy is sustainable. What happens when things go wrong? Here too, history offers some insights. In traditional China, people judged the performance of the state not just in terms of its economic performance, but also in terms of how well it does at dealing with crises, and the same is true today. Given the general view that the Chinese state did an adequate if not admirable job dealing with crises such as the Asian financial crisis (1997), the Wenchuan earthquake (2008), and the global financial crisis (2007–2008), we should not be surprised that the legitimacy of the regime increased over the past few years. The same is true of the way the Chinese state dealt with tensions over Taiwan: when tensions were defused, the legitimacy of the Chinese state increased. There is no reason to define performance exclusively in terms of rates of economic growth or poverty alleviation.

Nor should we expect that things will necessarily go wrong when there are crises: it depends on perceptions of the state's responsibility for crises and its willingness and ability to deal with them.[167] We can expect performance legitimacy to break down when the state is held responsible for bad performance in times of crisis. One reason for the widespread popular outrage at the high-speed rail crash in Wenzhou (July 2011) is that the state was seen to take much pride in its ability to build a network of high-speed rail in record time and subsequently was viewed as covering up the aftermath of the crash. Hence, the government was seen as being at least partly responsible for the crash—valuing high-profile expensive projects at the expense of safety and concern for lives—and it further lost credibility for its seemingly heartless response to the crash. Such events may not lead to the "end of the dynasty." But a prolonged economic crisis that undermines faith in the government's economic performance combined with perceptions of a heavy-handed or incompetent response to a social crisis or natural disaster may be the tipping point.

There is another reason to question whether performance legitimacy is sustainable. It may be easier to justify strong government when the key priority is widely shared among both leaders and the people, such as the elimination of poverty in the past three decades. But what happens after the government successfully provides the conditions that allow people to secure basic material welfare? At that point, the work of government becomes more complex, and there is more of a need for input from various social forces to help formulate policy. As Wang Shaoguang puts it, "in China today, socioeconomic polarization; urbanization; and increases in literacy, education, and media exposure have conspired to give rise to enhanced aspirations in decision-making. If groups within society cannot find institutionalized channels through which they can express their needs and interests, their repressed discontent could erupt in violence. . . . In the long run, as the variety and complexity of interests being articulated increase, the time will come for the country to replace its monopolistic structure of interest aggregation with a competitive one."[168] In short, good performance by political leaders per se is not likely to provide long-term stability in China. More input by "the people" in the form of institutionalized participation may be necessary.[169]

The third source of nondemocratic legitimacy—political meritocracy—also has ancient roots (as has been emphasized throughout this book). But it is the newest source of legitimacy for the CCP. For one thing, the establishment of a rigorous selection and promotion process for public service officials has a relatively short history in the People's Republic of China, starting from the early 1990s. Moreover, the CCP has been cautious about promoting political meritocracy as an ideal because it coexists uneasily with egalitarian communist ideology: Maoism valued the social contributions of farmers and workers over those of intellectuals and educators. And the idea that a society should be governed by a political elite explicitly conflicts with Marx's egalitarian ideal of a "higher communist" society where the state would have withered away. Confucians, by way of contrast, are explicit that even an ideal society would need to be governed by leaders of above-average moral and political talent: the ideal of "the Great Way" (*da dao*) in the *Record of Rites* (*Liji*), a work compiled during the Han dynasty on the basis of older materials, is described as an age when the world worked for the interests of all people (*tian xia wei gong*) and this famous line is immediately followed by an ideal of political meritocracy in which "the worthy and the able were promoted to office" (*xuan xian yu neng*). But the ruling party is called the Chinese Communist Party, not the Chinese Confucian Party.

Nonetheless, the CCP is fully aware that political meritocracy can help to justify its rule. Recent survey data shows that there is widespread support for the ideal of political meritocracy in East Asian societies with a Confucian heritage that affects the way people conceive of government. As Doh Chull Shin explains, "Attachment to paternalistic meritocracy contributes significantly to understanding democracy in substantive terms, while it has an equal negative effect on understanding democracy in procedural terms."[170] As mentioned, Shi Tianjian and Lu Jie found that the majority of Chinese people endorse "guardianship discourse," defined as the need to "identify high-quality politicians who care about people's demands, take people's interests into consideration when making decisions, and choose good policies on behalf of their people and society" over liberal democracy discourse that privileges procedural arrangements ensuring people's rights to participate in politics and choose their leaders.[171] Moreover, Shi Tianjian shows that attachment to Confucian political values has been increasing in China since the 1990s.[172]

To the extent that the CCP continues to transform itself into a more meritocratic political organization, it should therefore be seen as more legitimate in the eyes of the Chinese people. Of course, the meritocratic system also needs to be made somewhat transparent, so people will have a better understanding of the system and respect for those who succeed in the ultracompetitive talent-selection process. Hence, it should not be surprising that there is more discussion of political meritocracy in Chinese political discourse, both in official circles and by independent academics. And for popular consumption, a slick cartoon video in Chinese and English contrasting the selection of leaders in

Western democracies and Chinese meritocracy was produced in October 2013 and immediately went viral, with more than ten million viewings in a couple of weeks,[173] if only because it coincided with the shutdown of government in the United States that exposed the downside of democracy.

Still, it is questionable whether a legitimacy founded solely (or mainly) on political meritocracy is sustainable. Although it's true that most social grievances are directed at lower levels of government, they are also accompanied by a rise of humble petitions in which disgruntled citizens from all over China travel to Beijing to file complaints at the central government office against local officials. Ho-fung Hung noted a similar pattern in the mid-Qing and argues that such patterns of protest are rooted in a Confucian conception of authority and justice.[174] Under this conception, abused subjects count on the emperor as the loving patriarch to redress injustice, as children abused by parents might look to their grandparents for paternalistic protection. Although this attitude has shielded the imperial center from popular unrest and helped it survive major social crises, it also contains the seeds of instability: "This 'safety valve' for the central authorities only worked when the subjects generally trusted their rulers were legitimate and morally righteous. Such trust could disappear easily, sometimes because of rumors about the emperor's promiscuity, or sometimes because of the emperor's perceived failure in performing critical functions. . . . [W]e should not be surprised if an unexpected singular event—such as a major economic blunder, a scandal involving the highest leaders or defeat in a geopolitical conflict—abruptly displaces the popular trust in the central government and precipitates a breakdown of the party-state."[175]

Even if the government succeeds in limiting the corruption of high-level political leaders (or at least, limiting the perception of corruption at the top), the problem of legitimacy in a political meritocracy won't be solved given that the people have high moral expectations of their leaders. It may be only a slight exaggeration to suggest that a Clinton-like sex scandal involving, say, members of the Standing Committee of the Politburo could fundamentally undermine popular support for the political system. Even a serious scandal involving a family member of a ruler can topple the regime: Mencius famously argued that a ruler whose father had committed a murder should resign from his post and flee the country with his father (VIIA.35), suggesting not just that family obligations can have priority over political ones, but also that the immoral behavior of a family member could taint a ruler to the point that he would lose the moral authority to rule.

The deepest problem with a pure form of political meritocracy is that it is hard to justify to ambitious and public-spirited people outside the system.[176] During the course of research for this book, I found that the surest way to get a critical perspective on the public service examinations is to ask those who failed the exams (i.e., the large majority). In imperial China, the examination "failures" still had high social status in local communities and could often obtain valued employment by virtue of having prepared for the imperial examinations.[177] But today, those who fail the public service examinations get nothing.

So the question is how to justify the meritocratic system to examination failures and more generally to ambitious citizens who seek to make a positive difference in Chinese society without going through the official selection and promotion process for political leaders. One way is to emphasize that being a professional public official is not the only way to make a positive difference in society: farmers, family caretakers, manual workers, medical doctors, and NGO activists all contribute to the social good.[178] The government can and should highlight the achievements of individuals and social groups outside the political system, for example by subsidizing television shows that reward outstanding social contributions.[179] Political leaders should be humble and explicitly recognize that other social groups and citizens may be superior in terms of intellectual ability and virtue.[180] Most important, perhaps, "nonpolitical" social contributors can and should be rewarded economically, at least as much as public officials. In other words, those without political power at the top can and should view themselves as "winners" so long as they make a contribution to the public good; unequal political power need not violate one's sense of (equal) social worth.[181]

Still, in a society with a Confucian heritage, it seems likely that political leaders will continue to have the highest social status. So the government must take measures to expand political participation. The CCP can continue to co-opt ambitious representatives of diverse social groups, but not all potentially subversive types can be or want to be co-opted. The government can also provide more opportunities for political participation by non–party members, especially at lower levels of government, but the big question is how to placate the critics of meritocracy at the top. Ultimately, the only way is to show without a shadow of a doubt that the people support political meritocracy. In other words, democracy may be necessary to legitimize meritocracy.

In this chapter, I have discussed the three main problems of political meritocracy with the Chinese context in mind and suggested possible solutions that do not require electoral democracy for the country's most powerful rulers. The problem of corruption can be addressed by mechanisms such as independent supervisory institutions, higher salaries for public officials, and improved moral education. The problem of ossification of political hierarchies can be addressed by means of humble political discourse, opening the ruling party to diverse social groups, more freedom of speech, and allowing for the possibility of selecting different kinds of political leaders according to new ideas of political merit. The problem of legitimacy, however, can only be addressed by means of democratic reforms, including some form of explicit consent by the people. The question, therefore, is how to reconcile political meritocracy and democracy. The next chapter will discuss the pros and cons of different models of "democratic meritocracy."

CHAPTER 4

Three Models of Democratic Meritocracy

Political meritocracy—the idea that a political system should aim to select and promote leaders with superior ability and virtue—sounds a bit dubious on first hearing. Both Plato and Confucius argued for a form of political meritocracy that effectively excludes the majority from political power. Yet nobody argues for establishing a purely meritocratic political community today. For one thing, it would be hard to persuade people that they should be totally excluded from political power. Plato himself recognized the need to propagate a "Noble Lie" that the Guardians deserve absolute power because they have gold in their souls, unlike everybody else. Regimes like North Korea can propagate such myths about the quasi-divine status of their rulers,[1] but no modern open society can get away with it. No ruler is so great that he or she should rule depoliticized masses without accountability. It is hard to imagine a modern government today that can be seen as legitimate in the eyes of the people without any form of democracy. We are all democrats today.

Yet it takes only a brief moment of reflection to realize that political meritocracy is also a good thing. Political leaders have power over us, and no rational person would want to be ruled by an incompetent leader who lacks a basic understanding of the key issues that should inform policy making. What if a geographically challenged president mixes up North and South Korea and presses the wrong button in a moment of crisis? Ideally, our leaders should have a good understanding of the world, and the better the understanding, the better the policy making. In the same vein, no rational person would want to be ruled by an immoral leader. Who would choose a corrupt and murderous ruler over a leader with compassion and integrity? Ideally, our leaders should be committed to the common good, that is, they should do their best to promote policies that benefit all those affected by their policies, and the more they can do that, the better the policy making. In short, it is rational to believe that our political leaders should have superior ability and virtue. We are all meritocrats today.

So the question is how to reconcile democracy and meritocracy. In the last chapter, I argued that sustainable political meritocracy requires features typical of democratic societies: the rule of law to check corruption and abuses of power, and freedom of speech and political experimentation to prevent the ossification of political hierarchies. In principle, there should not be a problem. However, I also argued that political meritocracies will find it difficult if not impossible to solve the legitimacy problem without giving the people the right to political participation. And here the solution is not so obvious. How is it possible to reconcile a meritocratic mechanism designed to select superior political leaders with a democratic mechanism designed to let the people choose their leaders? That is, how can political meritocracy be reconciled with widespread political participation? In this chapter, I will discuss three models of democratic meritocracy: (1) a model that combines democracy and meritocracy at the level of the voter; (2) a horizontal model that combines democracy and meritocracy at the level of central political institutions; and (3) a vertical model with political meritocracy at the level of the central government and democracy at the local level. Whatever the philosophical merits of the first model, it is a nonstarter from a political point of view. I have been a strong defender of the second model for nearly two decades. I have changed my mind, however, and now I think the third model is best. This chapter will explain why.

1. Voting for the Wise and the Virtuous

What we think of as the distinguishing mark of democracy today—elections—first arose as a response to the need for meritocracy. In ancient Athens, the birthplace of democracy, most political officers (with the exception of generals and other military officers) were appointed by lottery. The use of the lottery, according to Aristotle, "is regarded as democratic, and the use of vote as oligarchical."[2] Voting was meant to provide a meritocratic check on the system, with would-be rulers having to persuade the electorate that they have the ability and motivation to rule well. Eventually, voting itself came to be viewed as democratic, and the argument for electoral democracy won out over the system of random selection. Today, hardly anybody argues for the selection of political officials by means of the lottery, even if random selection might make the political system more democratic in the sense that all citizens have a truly equal opportunity to rule.[3] Rather than let the roll of the dice decide who will be leaders, ordinary citizens can be trusted to make sensible choices of capable leaders. If people want able and virtuous political leaders, they will vote for them at election time. Let the people decide!

The problem with this view is that ordinary citizens often lack the competence and motivation to make sound, morally informed political judgments. In the most infamous case, the Nazis gathered enough electoral support to become the largest political party and the effective governing power in 1933.[4] Today, an often-heard argument among Chinese intellectuals is that China cannot implement democracy now because relatively uneducated rural people—about half the population—lack the wisdom to make good political decisions. The assumption is that people will improve their ability to vote in rational ways once they are more educated and urbanized. But even this assumption may be too optimistic. The problem of the irrational voter is not confined to poor, rural societies. In relatively wealthy, urbanized, and educated societies like the United States, many voters still vote in irrational ways.[5] Drawing on extensive empirical research, Bryan Caplan shows that American voters often misunderstand their own interests.[6] And when they do understand their interests, they tend to vote according to their short-term economic interests ("voting their pocketbooks," in popular parlance). From a moral point of view, people should vote for the common good, because their votes affect other people, not just themselves.[7] Even when voters vote according to the common good of the voting public, such decision making can have disastrous consequences for future generations and people living outside the state who are affected by the policies of government (consider global warming). In contemporary democracies, one is hard pressed to find citizens who vote for leaders most likely to take into account the interests and needs of all those affected by the policies of the government. Is the solution then to tamper with the voting system so as to increase the likelihood that voters will vote for meritorious leaders who take a longer-term, morally informed approach to political decision making?

John Stuart Mill's Proposal for a Plural Voting Scheme

Mill's *Considerations on Representative Government* (1861) is rightly considered a classic in democratic theory. He argued for universal suffrage on the grounds that "it is a personal injustice to withhold from any one, unless for the prevention of greater evils, the ordinary privilege of having his voice reckoned in the disposal of affairs in which he has the same interest as other people." Moreover, the right to vote can make people more public-spirited than they would otherwise be:

> It is by political discussion that the manual laborer, whose employment is routine, and whose way of life brings him in contact with no variety of impressions, circumstances, or ideas, is taught that remote causes, and events which take place far off, have a most sensible effect even on his personal interests; and it is from political discussion, and collective political action, that one whose daily occupations concentrate his interests in a small circle round himself, learns to feel for and with his fellow-citizens, and becomes consciously a member of a great community. But political discussions fly over the heads of those who have no votes, and are not endeavoring to acquire them.

Just as members of a jury learn to deliberate about the interests of other people, so voters engaged in political discussion learn to deliberate and take into account the interests of the whole political community. In his own day, the vote was restricted to propertied males, and Mill forcefully argued for the extension of the suffrage to women and (taxpaying) workers.[8]

Mill also recognized that not all voters are equally moral and rational:

> Though everyone ought to have a voice—that everyone should have an equal voice is a totally different proposition. When two persons who have a joint interest in any business, differ in opinion, does justice require that both opinions should be held of exactly equal value? If with equal virtue, one is superior to the other in knowledge and intelligence—or if with equal intelligence, one excels the other in virtue—the opinion, the judgment, of the higher moral or intellectual being, is worth more than that of the inferior: and if the institutions of the country virtually assert that they are of the same value, they assert a thing which is not. One of the two, as the better or wiser man, has a claim to superior weight.

Given inequalities in intelligence and morality, not all voters should have an equal say in the political process. Mill proposed that two or more votes be given to graduates of universities and members of professions that require more use of reason; the right to extra votes would also be open to anyone who passed a voluntary examination that "might prove that he came up to the standard of knowledge and ability laid down as sufficient."[9]

Mill was a progressive in his own day, but he was only partly on the right side of history. Over the following century, the franchise has been extended to all adult citizens in electoral democracies, but the idea that wiser and more virtuous voters should get extra votes is widely viewed as beyond the moral pale. Singapore's founding father, Lee Kuan Yew, did put forward a proposal in Mill's vein (I do not mean to imply that Lee shares other aspects of Mill's ethical outlook). Lee questioned whether the one person, one vote system is the best way to select a "government of the best men." Young men bent on immediate gratification are more likely to vote in a capricious way, not taking into account the interests of others, and elderly people are also focused on the short term, supporting policies such as free health care that could harm the economic prospects of future generations. So why not give two votes to middle-aged family men who are more likely to be cautious and to consider the interests of their children? Lee's proposal was put forward in 1994—after he had retired as premier—and it was viewed as another example of the sort of political elitism that is increasingly rejected by Singaporeans today.[10]

So what exactly is wrong with proposals for giving extra votes to certain groups of citizens? It seems hard to argue with the premise that not everyone is equally able and willing to vote in a sensible manner. The problem is not so much philosophical as political. Mill himself was not rigid about the implementation of his proposal for plural votes: what matters is that "the distinctions and gradations are not made arbitrarily, but are such as can be understood and accepted by the general conscience and understanding."[11] But it is hard to imagine any distinctions and gradations that "can be accepted by the general conscience and understanding." Selecting target groups of "rational" voters is a rough and unreliable procedure, and those denied equal democratic rights are likely to perceive the denial as an official insult issued by public authority.[12] Even if people recognize that they are not equal in terms of the capacity and motivation to vote in a sensible way, they will object to being officially treated as less than equals in the political process and will reject the decisions of whoever decides to deprive them of an equal vote.[13] If the ruling party decides who gets the extra votes, citizens may think that the government is motivated by a desire to select the groups most likely to perpetuate its dominance.[14] Even if the proposal for plural votes is implemented at the start without much controversy, it could easily become corrupted in the democratic process: political parties would promise special favors to groups with extra votes, and elected officials might try to award extra votes to their own constituencies, regardless of merit. And there are no obvious alternatives to letting politicians decide such matters. Caplan proposes tests of economic competence for voters to remedy the problem of voter irrationality,[15] but who would trust an "independent" body of economists to identify the groups most likely to vote for competent and public-spirited rulers? Even if it were feasible, who would appoint this body? And why limit the tests to questions about economics, given that many people are also ill informed about many other matters with policy implications, such as international relations and environmental science?[16] Plus, the target group of sensible voters may change over time, so the body of social science experts would have to revise the "extra-voting" rules at every election. Mill himself recognized that his proposal for plural voting "is so unfamiliar to elections in Parliament, that it is not likely to be soon or willingly adopted"[17] but he didn't recognize that the political problem of making the proposal accepted by those denied extra votes means that it will never be willingly accepted in a democratic context. So let's turn to other proposals for reconciling democracy and meritocracy.

2. A Horizontal Model: Democracy and Meritocracy at the Top

Instead of trying to reconcile democracy and meritocracy at the level of the voting public, several political thinkers have proposed combining the advantages of meritocracy and democracy at the level of central political institutions. A properly designed constitutional system should have institutions that both reflect the need to choose leaders on the democratic basis of one person, one vote, as well as institutions that reflect the need for meritorious leaders with above-average ability and virtue. But can these two desiderata be combined?

Perhaps the most influential proposal for a horizontal model combining democracy and meritocracy at the top was put forward by Sun Yat-sen. Sun died in 1925, before the split between the KMT (Kuomintang) and the CCP (Chinese Communist Party) that led to the civil war in China and separate political systems in mainland China and Taiwan. He cofounded the KMT and served as its first leader, and promoted active cooperation with the CCP in 1923 with the aim of achieving a unified, democratic country. Hence, he is regarded as a "founding father" by both sides: in Taiwan, he is referred to as the "father of the nation" and in mainland China as the "forerunner of the democratic revolution."

Taiwan, however, has been more faithful to Sun's political vision. According to Sun, a democratic constitutional system should incorporate democracy in the form of voting as well as checks and balances.

He favored three separate branches of government—the legislative, executive, and judicial—similar to the U.S. constitutional system. However, Sun argued that the U.S. constitutional system was flawed and the "future constitution of the Republic of China" should incorporate two additional branches that borrow and modernize institutions from imperial China. One is an independent Supervisory branch, similar to the Censorate in imperial China but freed from its dependence on the monarchy. It would also be an improvement on the U.S. constitutional system: "In the United States, the supervisory power rests with Congress, which has frequently made arbitrary use of it to coerce the executive branch into doing its bidding." The other—more pertinent for our purposes—is an Examination branch. Sun was critical of U.S. democracy because of the low quality of its politicians: "With respect to elections, those endowed with eloquence ingratiated themselves with the public and won elections, while those endowed with learning and ideals but lacking eloquence were ignored. Consequently, members of America's House of Representatives have often been foolish and ignorant people who have made its history quite ridiculous." To remedy the problem, Sun argued for an independent Examination branch, similar to China's imperial state examination system but freed from dependence on the arbitrary rule of the monarch: "The future constitution of the Republic of China must provide for an independent branch expressly responsible for public service examinations. Furthermore, all officials, however high their rank, must undergo examinations in order to determine their qualifications. Whether elected or not, officials must pass those examinations before assuming office. This procedure will eliminate such evils as blind obedience, electoral abuses, and favoritism."[18] In short, democracy and meritocracy can be combined by requiring that political leaders chosen by the people pass exams that test competence. The independent Examination branch is meant to ensure that the examination process will not be influenced by political considerations.

Sun's ideal of a five-branch constitution influenced the KMT-designed 1946 constitution, including the creation of an Exam Yuan. Sun himself favored a six-year period of political tutelage before Chinese citizens be given the right to vote, and the KMT took a few decades longer than Sun had anticipated, but today Taiwanese leaders are chosen by one person, one vote. However, the Exam Yuan has never truly realized the functions envisioned by the original designer. It has been basically serving as an organ for the selection, promotion, and other duties related to civil servants, but elected officials have not had to pass any exams before assuming office. In other words, Taiwan's constitutional system more closely reflects the "Western" distinction between elected officials chosen by the people and meritocratically selected civil servants who are supposed to implement the decisions of democratically elected officials. Again, the reasons have more to do with politics than philosophy. For one thing, elected officials may worry that the need to take examinations set by an independent branch of government will cause them to lose power. More fundamentally, the citizens themselves would find it hard to accept the idea that elected politicians should pass exams before assuming office because its effect would be to exclude from political power politicians who fail examinations, no matter how popular they may be.[19] It is difficult to imagine that a government that excludes the people's chosen leaders could achieve much legitimacy in the eyes of the people: consider a situation where somebody elected with 80 percent of the vote but who fails examinations is replaced with a successful examination candidate who received only 20 percent of the vote. The people would be up in arms!

Just as it seems politically impossible to subject voters to tests that aim for quality control, so it seems politically impossible to subject elected politicians to such tests. In a democratic context, the legitimacy of the political leaders comes from the fact that they are chosen by the people, and the people will not accept any constraints on their right to choose leaders by means of one person, one vote. But what about the possibility of separate political institutions with separate functions and separate sources of legitimacy? One institution could be composed of democratically elected political leaders, and another institution composed of leaders selected by a mechanism that explicitly tests for ability and virtue. The democratic institution would derive its legitimacy by virtue of the fact that its leaders are chosen by the people, and the meritocratic institution would derive its legitimacy by virtue of the fact that its leaders have superior competence and virtue. The people could choose their leaders as they see fit, and the political community would also benefit from having competent and qualified rulers.

Friedrich Hayek, the twentieth-century economist and philosopher best known for his defense of classical liberalism, put forward an intriguing political proposal for a bicameral legislature combining democracy and meritocracy in *Law, Legislation, and Liberty* (1973). Hayek was more a liberal than a democrat,[20] and he worried first and foremost about the abuses of state power. The main task of government is to protect and promote individual liberty, and government institutions should be designed for that purpose. A single, democratically elected assembly is likely to exercise untrammeled power and to abuse the rights of minorities. It would be inimical to the protection of individual liberty—what Hayek calls "justice." Hence, Hayek argues for a separation of legislative powers at the highest levels of government. In a chapter titled "A Model Constitution," Hayek puts forward a model of an ideal government, with the powers of a democratically elected representative assembly balanced and constrained by another representative body entrusted "with the task of stating the general rules of just conduct." The chamber responsible for legislating laws of general application and providing for the general rules of conduct could only be effective if its members are selected on the basis of merit, as opposed to being chosen on the basis of one person, one vote. Its representatives would rule for a single term of fifteen years without being constrained or controlled by any one party or group. They would be at least forty-five years old, with a proven track record of achievement, elected by people at least forty-five years old, and would not have to worry about pandering to the electorate because they could not be reelected and they would be assured of continued public employment after they retire from the chamber.[21]

Hayek's proposal has never come close to being realized, and it is worth asking why. One reason is that Hayek's vision of a limited role for government is highly controversial: besides protecting individual liberty, most people today accept that the state should also have other aims, such as providing opportunities for disadvantaged sectors of the population. But the key reason is that Hayek underestimates the commitment to democracy, at least in Western countries. Today, democracy in the form of one person, one vote is valued not just because it is a means for liberal aims such as the protection of individual liberty. It is valued for a whole range of historical, psychological, and philosophical reasons with the result that few citizens in established democracies question the idea that political decision makers chosen on the basis of one person, one vote should have the ultimate controlling power, including the power to "state the general rules of just conduct."[22] The idea that political decision makers chosen by means other than one person, one vote should have the power to debate and decide on a wide range of issues affecting the political community in ways that override the decisions of democratically elected decision makers is anathema to the political sensibilities of citizens in established democracies. Even the idea that democratically elected leaders can choose unelected officials—such as U.S. Supreme Court justices—with the power to make decisions in accordance with a tightly circumscribed mandate (such as interpreting a constitution) is controversial today;[23] what is clear is that any powers beyond that role, such as the powers of Hayek's second chamber, would be deemed fundamentally antidemocratic.

Consider recent proposals to reform the House of Lords in the United Kingdom. Its powers are far more limited than Hayek's second chamber. The House of Lords has the power to delay bills passed by the House of Commons for one year, though it rarely exercises this power. More commonly, it operates as a revising body, refining bills from the lower chamber by filling in the details and closing the loopholes. It generally performs that task with admirable competence and nonpartisanship. Its debates are elegant, nonadversarial, and informative, and sometimes lead to significant amendments. Many of its members have a depth of experience often lacking in the relative youngsters occupying the House of Commons.[24]

Nonetheless, it lacks legitimacy in the eyes of the people because its members do not have sufficient democratic legitimacy. Tony Blair's Labour government tried to replace hereditary peers with individuals of great distinction (such as eminent academics), but even an assembly of meritocrats appointed by democratically elected politicians has proven to be too controversial: all three of Britain's leading parties support some sort of plan to reform the House of Lords by replacing its appointed and hereditary membership with a mostly elected chamber.[25] In theory, as Martin Wolf argues, a good case can be made for an assembly composed of eminent individuals that derive their legitimacy primarily by virtue of their competence, even if its powers are simply to raise the level of political discourse and provide an element of expertise lacking in an electoral assembly.[26] But neither voters nor political parties are likely to support such proposals in democratic countries: any sort of effort to institutionalize a house of government that circumscribes the power of politicians elected on the basis of one person, one vote seems doomed to failure in democratic countries that have come to uphold the system of one person, one vote as an almost sacred political value.[27]

That said, the case for a meritocratic assembly might be easier to make in countries that place more value on political meritocracy. In China, political surveys show strong attachment to "guardianship discourse," defined as the need to identify high-quality rulers who enact good policies on behalf of their people and society, over liberal democratic discourse that privileges procedural arrangements ensuring people's rights to participate in politics and choose their leaders.[28] So perhaps it makes more sense to put forward proposals that combine democracy and meritocracy at the highest levels of government in the Chinese context. Any proposal needs to be both desirable and realistic if it is to serve as a standard for guiding political reform, and such proposals are more realistic in countries that place a high value on political meritocracy.

Jiang Qing's Proposal for a Tricameral Legislature

Jiang Qing (b. 1952) is one of the most original and influential Confucian political theorists in mainland China. He is a normative thinker and his theory of legitimacy is a normative one: he defines legitimacy as morally justified rule; his main concern is not the social scientific question of what kind of rule happens to be regarded as morally justified in the eyes of the people. And his main target is the democratic theory of legitimacy as developed by liberal democratic theorists from Locke on, namely, that a state is legitimate if it has secured the consent of the people. Although democracy—a form of government that grants ultimate controlling power to democratically elected representatives—is built on the separation of powers, the separation, Jiang argues, is a matter of implementation rather than legitimization. In a democracy, legitimacy is based on the sovereignty of the people. But Jiang objects to the idea that there is only one source of legitimacy. He claims that the modern notion of sovereignty of the people is similar in form to the medieval notion of the sovereignty of God, but with the content changed from God to the people: "In fact, the sovereignty of the people is simply the secular equivalent of the sovereignty of God."[29]

In political practice, the overemphasis on popular sovereignty translates into the politics of desire: "in a democracy, political choices are always down to the desires and interests of the electorate." This leads to two problems. First, the will of the people may not be moral: it could endorse racism, imperialism, or fascism. Second, when there is a clash between the short-term interests of the populace and their long-term interests or the common interests of all humankind, the former have political priority. Jiang specifically worries about the ecological crisis. It is difficult if not impossible for democratically elected governments to implement policies that curb energy usage in the interests of future generations and foreigners. If China were to follow the American model in terms of per capita carbon emissions, for example, the world would be damaged beyond repair. But "it is impossible for Green Parties to fully—through legitimization and implementation—realize ecological values in a Western democracy, without radical change in both the theory and structure of Western democracy." Hence, a political system must place more emphasis on what Jiang calls "sacred values" that are concerned with the well-being of the environment, the welfare of future generations, and humanity as a whole.

Jiang's political alternative is the Confucian "way of the humane authority" (*wang dao*). The question of political legitimacy, he argues, is central to Confucian constitutionalism. He defines legitimacy as "the deciding factor in determining whether a ruler has the right to rule or not." But unlike Western-style democracy, there is more than one source of legitimacy. According to the Gongyang commentary (a commentary on the *Spring and Autumn Annals* allegedly compiled by Confucius himself that chronicled the history of the state of Lu from 722 to 481 BCE), political power must have three kinds of legitimacy—that of heaven, earth, and the human—for it to be justified. The legitimacy of heaven refers to a transcendent ruling will and a sacred sense of natural morality. The legitimacy of earth refers to a legitimacy that comes from history and culture. And the legitimacy of the human refers to the will of the people, which determines whether the people will obey political authorities. All three forms of legitimacy must be in equilibrium, but Jiang notes that the equilibrium is not one of equality. According to the *Book of Changes*, the multiplicity of things comes from the one principle of heaven, hence the sacred legitimacy of the way of heaven is prior to both the cultural legitimacy of the way of earth and that of the popular will of the human way.

In ancient times, the "way of the humane authority" was implemented by the monarchical rule of the sage-kings of the three dynasties (Xia/Shang/Zhou). But changes in historical circumstances necessitate changes in the form of rule. Today, the will of the people must be given an institutional form that was lacking in the past, though it should be constrained and balanced by institutional arrangements meant to implement the other two forms of legitimacy. Hence, Jiang argues that the "way of the humane authority" should be implemented by means of a tricameral legislature that corresponds to the three forms of legitimacy: a House of the People (*shuminyuan*) that represents popular legitimacy, a House of Exemplary Persons (*tongruyuan*) that represents sacred legitimacy, and a House of the Nation (*guotiyuan*) that represents cultural legitimacy.

Jiang goes into more institutional detail. The members of the House of the People "are chosen according to the norms and processes of Western democratic parliaments," including universal suffrage and election from functional constituencies. The leader of the House of Exemplary Persons is a great scholar proposed by the Confucian scholars. The candidates for membership are nominated by the scholars, and then they are examined on their knowledge of the Confucian classics and assessed following a trial period of administration at lower-level parliaments, like the examination and recommendation systems used in China in the past. The leader of the House of the Nation should be a direct descendant of Confucius, who would select from "among the great sages of the past, descendants of the rulers, descendants of famous people, of patriots, university professors of Chinese history, retired top officials, judges and diplomats, worthy people from society as well as representatives of Daoism, Buddhism, Tibetan Buddhism, and Christianity."

Each house deliberates in its own way and may not interfere in the running of the others. Jiang addresses the key issue of how to deal with political gridlock that may arise as a result of conflicts between the three houses of parliament. He says that a bill must pass at least two of the houses to become law. The priority of sacred legitimacy is expressed in the veto power exercised by the House of Exemplary Persons. However, Jiang notes that the power of the House of Exemplary Persons is restrained by the other two houses: for example, "if they propose a bill restricting religious freedom, the People and the Nation will oppose it and it will not become law." In that sense, it differs from the Council of Guardians in theocratic Iran, where the sacred is the only form of legitimacy and "and so at the level of implementation the Council of Guardians has power over the Assembly and is not subject to its restraint."

Jiang's proposal for a House of Exemplary Persons helps us to think about how to institutionalize the principle of political meritocracy, but it is justified with reference to highly controversial transcendent values. Such a foundation is not acceptable to those who view Confucianism as primarily social rather than religious ethics, not to mention those indifferent or hostile to the Confucian tradition.[30] But we can borrow Rawls's strategy of striving for an overlapping consensus on politics based on different versions of a comprehensive system of (religious or secular) value.[31] Jiang and his critics, in other words, can agree to disagree about the justification for the House of Exemplary Persons: for Jiang and his supporters, it could be justified with reference to a transcendent Heaven, and for nonreligious Confucians and non-Confucians it could be justified on secular grounds. Politically speaking, what matters is to secure agreement on what the institution is supposed to do: to deliberate about and act on behalf of the interests and needs of nonvoters such as future generations and people living outside the boundaries of the state who are affected by the policies of the government. In practice, one of the main tasks of the House of Exemplary Persons would be to consider the long-term environmental consequences of policies that are normally neglected or underemphasized in democratic decision making since voters tend to care about their own interests first and foremost. If there is agreement on the main tasks of the house, it would also be easier to secure agreement on the

criteria for choosing the meritocratically selected leaders who are supposed to represent voters. Given that they are supposed to focus on the needs of future generations and foreigners, for example, it may not be too controversial to suggest that they should be tested for basic knowledge of environmental science and international affairs.

Still, one may wonder if Jiang's proposal for a powerful House of Exemplary Persons is realistic. Most obviously, it is far removed from the current political reality in China, hence the proposal may not satisfy the criterion that a political theory should serve as a realistic standard for guiding political reform. But rapid and unexpected change is not impossible—the Soviet Union did collapse far sooner than most analysts expected—so one cannot rule out the possibility of a moment of major constitutional change in China.

Let's imagine that there is substantial political support for a modified version of Jiang's proposal. Even then, however, Jiang's proposal may not be realistic. Here's why. Jiang's proposal includes a house of government with members selected on the basis of one person, one vote.[32] But once some political leaders are chosen on the basis of one person, one vote, it is almost inevitable that those leaders will be seen as the legitimate political leaders by the people who elect them and any proposal to subordinate their power to institutions with meritocratically chosen leaders is likely to be rejected by the people themselves. Even political cultures that value political meritocracy rapidly change and come to support democracy in the form of one person, one vote once the change is made. People in East Asian societies that adopted democratic forms of rule—from Japan to South Korea and Taiwan—all came to develop a preference for democracy over paternalistic Confucian legacies after the institutionalization of democracy,[33] and East Asian democracies with a Confucian heritage have not been plagued by military coups that (temporarily?) reverse democratic gains in the Middle East and elsewhere. So democracy in the form of one person, one vote really is the end of history, but in the bad sense that it cannot be improved. The sad fact is that citizens in electoral democracies won't even question their right to choose their political rulers, no matter how intellectually incompetent or morally insensitive their political judgment may be.[34]

If we want something better than one person, one vote—such as a political institution that secures the interests of future generations, with the power to complement, and sometimes override, the decisions of politicians elected by one person, one vote—it cannot be done in the form of proposals for bicameral or tricameral legislatures, no matter what the context. Jiang Qing is typically criticized for being too antidemocratic,[35] but the irony is that his proposal is too democratic: if his proposal for a tricameral legislature were implemented, the slippery slope toward a powerful House of the People could not be stopped and the House of Exemplary Persons (as well as the House of the Nation) would almost certainly be marginalized, if not made completely irrelevant. The same goes for other recent proposals that seek to combine democratic and meritocratic chambers at the highest levels of government, such as Nicolas Berggruen and Nathan Gardels's template for intelligent governance, Bai Tongdong's proposal for a bicameral legislature with one democratically elected house and one meritocratic house composed of deputies selected on the basis of exams and performance at lower levels of government, and Joseph Chan's proposal for a democratic house and a meritocratic house composed of retired civil servants with a proven record of public experience.[36]

And now I must confess the same goes for my own proposal of a bicameral legislature with one democratic house and one meritocratic house composed of deputies selected by examinations. I have been arguing for modified forms of a proposal for a bicameral legislature since the mid-1990s. In 1999, I predicted a constitutional moment in China in the year 2007 when such proposals could be taken seriously. That year went by without any hint of political interest. In the Chinese translation, I changed the year to 2017. But now I realize that the problem is not just that I was overly optimistic in anticipating major constitutional change in China at the highest levels of government. The problem is that such proposals could not be consolidated even if they were tried! Just like the House of Lords, any sort of meritocratic chamber is almost certain to be progressively weakened once some political leaders are chosen on the basis of one person, one vote. So does that mean that we should abandon efforts to combine democracy and meritocracy? Yes, at the top. But that's not the only possibility. The other possibility is so obvious that somehow political theorists have been blind to it until very recently.

3. A Vertical Model: Democracy at the Bottom, Meritocracy at the Top

Political theorists speculating about China's political future have largely concentrated on the question of how to reconcile democracy and meritocracy at the central level of government. The main point has been to provide a set of standards to evaluate China's political reform. But standards must be desirable as well as feasible, and we have seen that there are two reasons to doubt the feasibility of horizontal models that reconcile democracy and meritocracy: (1) the model is too far removed from China's current political reality, and (2) even if it were implemented, it could not be consolidated. But there is a third reason to object to the horizontal model: democracy works best at the local level.[37] Earlier political thinkers—from Aristotle to Rousseau and Montesquieu—all converged on the argument that democracy works best in small communities, but somehow this point has been obscured from modern political thought and practice.[38] In small communities, people have more knowledge of the ability and virtue of the leaders they choose. The issues at the local level are usually relatively straightforward and easy to understand: do we need to upgrade the local school or the hospital? People often have more of a stake in local affairs, and what they do is more likely to affect outcomes. Given the moral imperative to vote in accordance with the common good—since our votes affect not just ourselves, but other people—it is easier to generate a sense of community at the local level. Finally, mistakes are less costly at the local level: it is not the end of the world if local citizens decide to spend more funds on a new road that turns out to be unnecessary; but it might be the end of the world if big countries launch nuclear war or ignore the perils of global warming.[39]

In the Chinese context, there is widespread support for the idea of democracy at the local level. The Chinese government introduced direct village elections in 1988 to maintain social order and combat corruption of leaders. In 1998, direct village committee elections were made mandatory in the whole country, and by 2008 more than nine hundred million Chinese farmers had exercised the right to vote.[40] Of course such elections are not free of problems. There have been worries about the quality of decision making and the extent to which local elections really curb the power of local cadres and wealthy elites. In response, the government has backed experiments with deliberative democracy at the local level.[41] Such experiments hold the promise of aiding the democratic education process and securing more fair representation. In short, all sides pretty much agree that the solution to the problems with local-level democracy lies in more democracy, not less.[42]

As an empirical matter, local-level electoral democracy has not generated a widespread sense that voting is something "sacred" that should be extended to higher levels of government.[43] The psychological feeling of empowerment is strongest at the national level, when voters see themselves as choosing the most powerful leaders of the political community, and the further we go down the chain of political command, the less voters feel empowered.[44] But the normative question is whether democracy at the local level should be extended to higher levels of government. Most Western analysts criticize the Chinese government precisely for the lack of extension to higher levels of government since the early 1990s. Given that they associate (explicitly or not) political reform with democratic reform (in the form of competitive elections), the typical view—among political scientists and leading media outlets in Western countries—is that there has been no political reform in China over the past couple of decades or so.[45] But this view is false. Over the past three decades or so, China has evolved a sophisticated and comprehensive system for selecting and promoting political talent at higher levels of government: political meritocracy, in short. Aspiring government officials normally pass the public service examinations, with thousands of applicants competing for single spots, and they must perform well at lower levels of government, with more rigorous tests and evaluations at each step of the way, to move further up the chain of political command. Of course, the system is flawed in practice, and selection and promotion of public officials is often influenced by factors other than the ability and virtue of the candidate.[46] But there is little doubt that the political system has been substantially "meritocratized" over the past couple of decades and the political impact of "meritocratization" has been far more substantial than the widely reported and researched local-level elections. Yet somehow—until very recently—the "meritocratization" of the political system in China has fallen under the radar screen of major media outlets and academic researchers have not paid sufficient attention to it. I confess I missed it as well, despite having lived in Beijing for nearly a decade. A meeting with a top Chinese leader, however, helped change my mind.

A Meeting with Minister Li Yuanchao

In May 2012, I was fortunate to participate in the first annual Peace and Development Forum near the Great Wall in Beijing. Academics and political leaders had instructive discussions about China's political system, as well as even more instructive informal discussions during the breaks. On the last day, the academics were invited to a dialogue session with Mr. Li Yuanchao, then Minister of the Organization Department of the Communist Party of China Central Committee (the following year, Mr. Li was appointed vice-president of China). Fascinated by the discussion about political meritocracy at the forum, I asked Minister Li which criteria are used to judge ability and virtue during the process of recruiting and promoting government officials. Mr. Li replied that the criteria depend on the level of government. At lower levels, close connection with the people is particularly important. At the higher levels, more emphasis is placed on rationality since cadres need to take multiple factors into account and decision making involves a much broader area of governance, but virtues such as concern for the people and a practical attitude also matter. Cadres are also expected to set a model of corruption-free rule.

To illustrate the rigorous (meritocratic) nature of selection at higher levels of government, Minister Li described the procedure used to select the Secretary General of the Organization Department of the Communist Party of China Central Committee. First, there was a nomination process, including retired cadres. Those who received many nominations could move to the next stage. Next, there was an examination, including questions such as how to be a good Secretary General. More than ten people took the exam, and the list was narrowed to five people.

To ensure that the process was fair, the examination papers were put in the corridor for all to judge the results. Then, there was an oral examination with an interview panel composed of ministers, vice-ministers, and university professors. To ensure transparency and fairness, ordinary cadres who work for the General Secretary were in the room, which allowed them to supervise the whole process. Three candidates with the highest scores were selected for the next stage. Then, the department of personnel led an inspection team to look into the performance and virtue of the candidates, with more emphasis placed on virtue. Two people were recommended for the next stage. The final decision was made by a committee of twelve ministers who each had a vote, and the candidate had to have at least eight votes to succeed. If the required number of votes was not secured the first time, the ministers discussed further until two-thirds could agree on a candidate.

Mr. Li has a point. Why do we think there is a "one-size-fits-all" solution to the question of how to select political leaders? Western-style democrats tend to think that the same selection process—democratic elections—should be used to select leaders at all levels of government, from the village to the highest level of government. But surely that's too simplistic! In a large, populous, modernizing country, it seems eminently reasonable to assume that different criteria for selection and promotion should apply at different levels of government. At the local level, democracy is desirable. But the process should become more meritocratic as we go further up the chain of command. At the central level, the issues are more complex, and we need leaders with a good understanding of economics, science, international relations, history, and, yes, political philosophy. They should also be constantly willing to learn and upgrade their skills, particularly in a globalized world that changes faster than at any previous time in human history. The issues also matter more from a moral point of view, given that policies can affect not just "the people," but future generations, ancestors, people living outside the country, and the natural world. Hence, the leaders should have a long-term outlook that takes into account the interests of all those affected by government policies, not just those with the loudest and most emotional voices. In short, it matters more at the central level for leaders to have superior ability and virtue—to be more "rational," as Mr. Li put it—and the political selection system should be explicitly designed to choose such leaders. At the bottom democracy is desirable, but at the top meritocracy is desirable. Rather than think in horizontal terms about how to reconcile democracy and meritocracy, we should think in vertical terms.

The advantages of "actually existing" meritocracy in the CCP are clear. Cadres are put through a grueling process of talent selection, and only those with an excellent record of past performance are likely to make it to the highest levels of government. The training process includes programs for public administration at various levels of government, consulting experts, learning from best practices abroad, rotational career postings though different sectors, as well as the cultivation of virtues such as compassion for the disadvantaged by means such as limited periods of work in poor rural areas.[47] Moreover, this kind of meritocratic selection process is likely to work only in the context of a one-party state. In a multiparty system, there is no assurance that performance at lower levels of government will be rewarded at higher levels, and there is no strong incentive to train cadres so that they have experience at higher levels, because the key personnel can change with a government led by a different party. So even talented leaders, like President Obama, can make many "beginner's mistakes" once they assume rule because they have not been properly trained to assume command at the highest levels of government.[48] Top leaders in China are not likely to make such mistakes because of their decades-long experience and training. The fact that decision making at the highest levels is by committee—the Standing Committee of the Politburo (currently with seven members)—also ensures that no one person with outlandish and uninformed views can set wrongheaded policies (such as Lee Kuan Yew's policies in Singapore favoring births by educated women that were based on eugenics theories rejected by most scientists).

Once Chinese leaders reach positions of political power, they can react more quickly to crises (such as the financial crisis of 2007–2008) and undertake great infrastructure projects that underpin economic development. Meritocratically selected leaders can make long-term-oriented decisions that consider the interests of all relevant stakeholders, including future generations and people living outside the state.[49] In multiparty democracies with leaders chosen on the basis of competitive elections, by contrast, leaders need to worry about the next election and they are more likely to make decisions influenced by short-term political considerations that bear on their chances of getting reelected. Democratically elected leaders are more vulnerable to the lobbying of powerful special interests, and the interests of nonvoters affected by policies, such as future generations, are not likely to be taken seriously if they conflict with the interests of voters and campaign funders. At the very least, meritocratically selected leaders have more time to think about such issues; they need not waste time and money campaigning for votes and giving the same speech over and over again.

Moreover, the fact that the real power holders in Western-style democracies are supposed to be those chosen by the people in elections often means that "bureaucrats" are not considered to be important; hence, less talent goes into the bureaucracy. This flaw may be particularly clear in the American political system, where the top layers of the bureaucracy are selected by elected leaders—about 10 percent of the posts in the federal government are allocated on the basis of political patronage, and such political appointments amount to two hundred thousand individuals, many of whom hold senior positions in the bureaucracy[50]—and there is less incentive for ambitious and talented people to take permanent jobs in the mid to lower levels of the bureaucracy.[51] In contrast, the Chinese political system does not clearly distinguish between "bureaucrats" and "power-holders" and thus ambitious people of talent are not discouraged from joining the political system at the lower levels, with the hope of moving upward.[52]

Of course, "actually existing meritocracy" is flawed, just like every other political system. The success of meritocracy in China is obvious: China's rulers have presided over the single most impressive poverty alleviation achievement in history, with several hundred million people being lifted out of poverty over the past few decades. Equally obvious, however, some problems in China—corruption, the gap between rich and poor, environmental degradation, abuses of power by political officials, harsh measures for dealing with political dissent, overly powerful state-run enterprises that distort the economic system, repression of religious expression in Tibet and Xinjiang, discrimination against women—seem to have become worse while the political system has become more meritocratic. Part of the problem is that China lacks democracy at various levels of government that could help check abuses of power and provide more opportunities for political expression by marginalized groups. But part of the problem is also that political meritocracy has been insufficiently developed in China. The political system needs to be further "meritocratized" so that government officials are selected and promoted on the basis of ability and morality rather than political connections, wealth, and family background. And the right formula for judging improvement should be, more or less, the vertical model of democratic meritocracy: democracy at the bottom, with the system becoming progressively more meritocratic at higher levels of government.[53]

Still, defenders of political meritocracy at the top must confront the problem of legitimacy. As argued in chapter 3 (section 3), the nondemocratic sources of political legitimacy that underpinned rule of the CCP will prove to be increasingly difficult to sustain. In the context of a relatively peaceful, modernizing country such as China, more input by "the people" in the form of institutionalized participation and the articulation of interests and non-mainstream values may be necessary. In response, the Chinese government has recently implemented mechanisms that allow for more consultation and deliberation,[54] but such responses won't be sufficient. Social critics call for more radical measures, such as bold steps toward intraparty elections, autonomous organizations of workers and farmers, judicial independence, and opening of the mainstream media.[55] But even these steps won't be sufficient: at the end of the day, the government can show that it's legitimate only by showing that it has the consent of the people. One response is to silence political critics and throw them in jail. But the more the government relies on harsh measures of this sort, the more it will lose support. At some point in the not too distant future, there will be a need for more freedom of political speech, democracy at higher levels of government, and more independent social organizations. But defenders of political meritocracy need to draw the line at one person, one vote and multiparty competition for top leaders because democracy at the top will wreck the whole system.[56] Is it possible to secure the people's support for a more open society and increased political participation but without going the way of "Western-style" democracy?[57] In other words,

is it possible to secure some form of explicit consent by the people without electoral democracy at the top?

A Referendum against Electoral Democracy

The political history of Chile in the second half of the twentieth century offers food for thought. Army General Augusto Pinochet took power on 11 September 1973 in a violent coup d'état that deposed the democratically elected President Salvador Allende. For the next sixteen years, Pinochet ruled as Supreme Leader of the Nation. Pinochet presided over a period of substantial economic growth, but he faced increased pressure to open up politically. In addition to domestic pressure for reform, the international context had changed: the Soviet Union under Mikhail Gorbachev—the supposed sponsor of the communist "subversives"—had itself initiated the *glasnost* and *perestroika* democratic reforms. In 1987, Pope John Paul II visited Chile and called on religious forces to actively fight for the restoration of democracy. The following year, Pinochet succumbed to pressure and called a national referendum on his rule. If the majority voted "yes," Pinochet would have remained in power for another eight years.

The referendum was heavily stacked in Pinochet's favor. In the pre-Internet age, the opposition had only fifteen minutes of media time per night for twenty-seven days to make its case for "no." Yet Pinochet lost the referendum, with nearly 56 percent of the population voting "no." As depicted in the Oscar-nominated film *No,* the opposition won (at least partly) by employing lighthearted marketing techniques that pointed the way to a "happy" future rather than by reminding the population of the Pinochet regime's grim history of human rights abuses.[58] Following his defeat at the polls, Pinochet wanted to retain power, but he was pushed out of power when the heads of the branches of Chile's military refused to support him, thus paving the way for the restoration of democracy in that country.

In the case of China, leading political scientists predict that China will need to implement some form of electoral democracy and multiparty rule (at the top) within the next decade or two.[59] If China does face a major constitutional moment, however, there is a more desirable and, arguably, more realistic, possibility. What if the CCP were to follow Pinochet's example and call a referendum, asking the Chinese people to vote "yes" in favor of a more open form of political meritocracy, with more freedom of political speech and more freedom to form social organizations, but without one person, one vote to choose top leaders and without the freedom to form political organizations that explicitly challenge CCP rule? A victory for the "yes" could provide an important element of democratic legitimacy to the system. Critics inside China alleging that the Chinese regime is fundamentally unstable or illegitimate because it lacks the support of the people would be silenced by the people, and the government need not worry about their social impact.[60] A "yes" vote would also be a big coup for China's soft power: the rest of the world would realize that the political system is indeed endorsed by the majority of Chinese citizens and sets a good model for political reform. The dominant narrative in global media coverage would change from "what's wrong with China's political system?" to "what can we learn from China's political system?"

Of course, the CCP would be taking a major risk by calling such a referendum: after all, Pinochet lost! But the Chinese case is different. For one thing, the country is not ruled by a military dictator responsible for killing thousands of people. True, in a more open environment, the "no" side in China could remind people of the CCP's human rights abuses in recent history. But the Chilean case shows that reminders of a dark past are not sufficient; the democratic opposition would also need to mount an optimistic case for China's political future. And here the opposition would have a harder case. Unlike in Chile, many intellectuals would argue for the "yes" side. The referendum would be calling for public support of a morally desirable, largely homegrown model of political rule, one that could legitimately serve as a source of pride for the people.

Still, there is a worry. Given that voters consistently show irrational behavior at election time (see chapter 1, section 1), why should we expect them to be more rational in a referendum? But elections are different. Referenda on key constitutional changes tend to generate extensive deliberation and relatively informed debate; it is difficult, if not impossible, to mobilize the same level of interest and enthusiasm on the part of the voter in regular elections.[61] The meritocrat may still want to place voting restrictions to ensure a more rational process: voters could be subject to tests of economic competence; extra votes could be given to educated people; more votes could be given to voters with young children; and so on. But such efforts would be viewed as attempts to rig the system to get the desired result, and the "referendum" is not likely to provide sufficient democratic legitimation even if restrictions are minimal and designed to ensure a more rational voting process rather than victory for the rulers. So the referendum must be free and fair, which increases the risk. In short, there are good reasons to be cautious, and the Chinese government need not call a referendum now that it enjoys substantial support from nondemocratic sources of legitimacy as measured by political survey results and (the lack of) unrest directed at the central government. But, to repeat, things may change in a decade or two, and if the government faces another choice between, say, maintaining stability by means of June 4th–style repression and a referendum that clearly shows that the people endorse the political system, the latter option is (needless to say) more humane.[62]

From the perspective of defenders of political meritocracy, an equally serious risk is that the people get used to the idea that the state's political system should be decided by referendum, and there might be another call for a referendum in a few years, even if the result is positive the first time around. In Uganda, for example, a referendum that restricted political parties (in order to curb sectarian tensions) was approved by the people in 1986, but citizens voted to restore the multiparty system in a subsequent referendum in 2000.[63] One solution is to specify a time period in the referendum itself—say, fifty years—long enough to provide stability for the recruitment and training of meritocratically selected leaders but without binding the people to perpetual CCP-style meritocratic rule.[64] The question itself can be formulated in terms of an ideal meant to guide political reform within a specified time period: for example, "Do you endorse vertical democratic meritocracy as an ideal that will guide political reform over the next fifty years?"[65] It may not be possible to win over "pure" democrats, but a strong "yes" vote could provide sufficient democratic legitimacy to ensure a long-lasting political meritocracy.

My argument in this chapter has been influenced by greater understanding and appreciation of the Chinese approach to political reform over the past three decades: a version of the vertical model of democratic meritocracy, with democracy at the bottom, experimentation in the middle, and meritocracy at the top, which we can term the "China model." Still, I want to emphasize that this book is not a defense of the status quo. There is a large gap between the reality of political reform and the ideals underpinning reform, and I will conclude this book by distinguishing between the two and suggesting ways of closing the gap.

Concluding Thoughts
Realizing the China Model

The China model is a phrase widely employed to describe China's approach to economic development and governance since the era of reform in the late 1970s. Although the phrase means different things to different people,[1] it generally refers to China's approach to the establishment of free-market capitalism under the umbrella of an authoritarian one-party state that emphasizes political stability above all else. In short, the China model is a combination of economic freedom and political oppression.[2] But trying to understand contemporary China in terms of these two characteristics is highly misleading. As an economic model, it is true that China has established aspects of a free-market economy, in which labor, capital, and commodities flow increasingly freely. But the state still keeps ultimate control over strategic sectors of the economy and a large range of core industries, including utilities, transportation, telecommunications, finance, and the media.[3] To be more precise, the People's Republic of China has a mixed economy with a three-tier enterprise system consisting of large, central government firms; hybrid local and foreign firms; and small-scale capitalism.[4]

The assumption that oppressive authoritarian rule is the key political characteristic of the China model is equally misleading. It is true that the Chinese government spends lavishly on the security apparatus to preserve social stability and resorts to harsh measures to put down perceived threats to one-party rule. It is also true that the CCP is the motor of political reform and it will not enact reform likely to lead to the party's demise. But the reform era has been characterized by an evolving three-pronged approach to political governance that cannot be accurately captured by labeling China a "bad" authoritarian regime similar in nature to, say, dictatorships in North Korea and the Middle East. Since the model—democracy at the bottom, experimentation in the middle, and meritocracy at the top—is unique to China, we can call it the "China model." The China model—referring here to political governance rather than an approach to economic reform—is both a reality and an ideal. It is a reality that has characterized China's approach to political reform over the past three decades or so. It is also an ideal that can be used as a standard to evaluate political reform and to suggest areas of possible improvement.[5] In chapter 4, I argued that vertical democratic meritocracy is a politically realistic and morally desirable way of combining political meritocracy and democracy. But Chinese-style vertical democratic meritocracy ("the China model") also includes a middle plank of experimentation between local and central government. What I say should not be too controversial, but scholars have yet to provide a detailed analysis of the model, let alone sketch out the basic planks. So let me describe the key features of the China model both as a reality and as an ideal, while recognizing the need for more detailed academic analysis in future research. I will end with some thoughts about the possibility of exporting the China model to other countries.

1. The Reality of Political Reform

The first plank of the China model is democracy at the bottom. Arguably, the idea of local democracy has historical roots in Zhu Xi's Neo-Confucian project, based on local voluntary institutions such as the community compact, community granaries, and local academies, which envisioned a decentralized network of self-governing communities as the foundation of social order and political stability.[6] But community associations were to be led by local literati; Song dynasty Neo-Confucians did not envision the possibility that farmers and women would have an equal say in choosing community leaders (and an equal right to be chosen as leaders). In modern China, the emergence of village self-governance came about largely as a reaction to the chaotic situation created by the collapse of the commune system. In late 1980, villages in Guangxi province began to establish village committees as a kind of self-governing association. A major breakthrough occurred when the new constitution adopted in 1982 included a clause defining the village committee and residents' committee as self-governing organizations of the masses in rural and urban areas, respectively, including the provision that officeholders should be selected by election. In the 1980s, the question of whether the village committee was to be used as a means to reorganize rural society became a major item of contention; proponents argued that village committees could restore orderly social life to the rural areas and exert a degree of control over corrupt cadres at the grassroots level, but local cadres worried that village committees could become a significant force capable of countering the state and party organizations. In 1987, a "provisional law" on village committees was adopted by the National People's Congress Standing Committee, and for the next decade more than eight hundred thousand village committees were set up. A new national law on village committees adopted in 1998 consolidated the various practices of the previous decade and specified the conditions for free and fair elections: a committee with a total membership between three and seven members (depending on the size of the village) would serve for a term of three years; the members would have to be directly elected by villagers age eighteen or older; nominations of candidates must be made directly by registered voters and the elections must be competitive (the number of candidates must exceed that of the seats to be returned); the secret ballot system must be used; and the law specified a mechanism to dismiss the village committee members in cases of wrongdoing.[7]

By 1996, balloting had been carried out in every province. Turnout rates have been generally high (in many locations reportedly more than 90 percent), and surveys and direct observation by international monitors show that the conduct of elections (including nomination procedures, competitiveness, and secret balloting) has improved over time.[8] Acutely aware of international criticism of its human rights record following the crackdown against the Tiananmen Square demonstrators in June 1989 and the need to boost its democratic credentials, the Chinese government has been keen to take foreign academics, journalists, and donor representatives to view such elections.[9] As a result, democracy at the local level is perhaps the most widely researched plank of China's political reform over the past couple of decades, and definitely the plank that has received the most international attention. Early enthusiasm on the part of some China watchers that village elections would pave the way for a Western-style democratic transformation of China has since given way to a more sober assessment of reality—the power of elected leaders is checked by village committees and township governments, and the CCP has no intention of expanding an electoral system based on one person, one vote all the way to the top—but as we will see, the general trend is that local elections have become more free and fair.

The second plank of the China model is experimentation between local and central levels of government: to be more precise, the central government checks which policies work at the subcentral level before spreading them throughout the country. Here too, there are historical antecedents in imperial China. For example, a new population census system implemented in the Sui dynasty was first tried by a county official, who was subsequently promoted to the central administration.[10] In the modern era, experimentation in the sense that central policy makers encourage local officials to try out new ways of problem solving and then feed the local experiences back into the national policy formulation was systematically carried out by the CCP from its earliest days. But the idea that local experimentation is necessary to find new policy solutions owes nothing to Marxist-Leninist ideology. Rather, CCP leaders were influenced by John Dewey's pleas for social experimentation and "learning by doing," as well as earlier Confucian ideas about teaching by example and learning through role models. The CCP was not unique: the KMT and the Confucian thinker Liang Shuming also introduced experiments in rural reform in the Republican era. But the CCP tied experimentation to the idea that a strong central power should decide what works and what doesn't. Localized experimentation was also motivated by necessity: the CCP did not have sufficient numbers of well-trained rural cadres to dispatch to hundreds of thousands of villages and lacked the capacity for standardized policy implementation. Hence, the revolutionary process had to be driven from scattered base areas, and an elaborate mode of local policy experimentation under central guidance was developed in the context of experiments with land reform in the Communist base areas. Mao Zedong and Deng Zihui initiated controlled experimentation based on the establishment of "model villages," dissemination of "model experiences," and progressive refinement of policies in the course of expansion. After the intensification of Japanese military campaigns, a base area behind enemy lines in Taihang under the leadership of Deng Xiaoping introduced experiments with land reform as well as a new "bottom-up work style" based on consultation with the populace. In 1951, two years after the establishment of the PRC, the party's guidelines on land reform were consolidated into six steps, "of which steps 2 to 6 are crucial to Chinese-style policy experimentation to the present day: (1) train work team cadres and send them down to localities; (2) carry out model experiments; (3) accomplish breakthroughs in a key point; (4) broaden the campaign from point to surface; (5) integrate point and surface with regard to the applied measures; (6) unfold the campaign in steady steps."[11]

But policy experimentation of this sort soon came to an end. From the mid-1950s to the mid-1970s, feverish ideological campaigns were launched in the whole country, and there was no political room for generating new policy approaches through decentralized experimentation; the only option was standardized implementation and swift total compliance with Mao's directives. To the extent there were local models, they were meant to serve as instantiations of preconceived, centrally imposed ideas to be emulated by the rest of the country, not as open-ended experiments meant to generate novel policy instruments. Arguably, national disasters such as the Great Leap Forward and the Cultural Revolution could have been avoided had the CCP stuck with its earlier policy of decentralized experimentation as a test for what works and what doesn't.

The policy of experimenting with subcentral policy alternatives—what Sebastian Hellman terms "experimentation under hierarchy"[12]—was revived in the post-Mao reform era. Deng Xiaoping redefined the main mission of the CCP from achieving communism to achieving rapid economic growth, and the CCP reactivated a repertoire of policy experimentation meant to serve that purpose. Policy experimentation took several forms, the most internationally famous of which was the Shenzhen Special Economic Zone, which tested controversial policies such as land auctions, wholly foreign-owned companies, and labor-market liberalization that were then applied to the rest of China.[13] The advantages of "experimentation under hierarchy" are clear—the CCP can start market reforms with initial trials in sensitive areas, it can detect hitherto hidden problems and make adjustments before they spread to the whole country, and the economy can develop without major ideological and social conflicts[14]—but continued economic growth over the past three decades brought about increasingly complex governance challenges, from inequality and growing demands for social insurance to pollution and corruption.

In response, the range of policy innovations pioneered at subcentral levels has expanded beyond the economic sphere into administrative, social, and political realms.[15] In the 2002–2007 period, a wide variety of experiments dealt with pressing rural issues such as the marketing of rural products, reduction of taxes and levies, land management, and cooperative health care. As of 2007, seventy-two cities have the status of "experimental point for comprehensive reform."[16] Some cities are empowered to experiment with renewable energy and others with different ways of reducing income gaps among residents.[17] Other experiments defy common assumptions about authoritarian rule, such as exploring ways of harnessing nonstate actors to provide health care for the elderly and rights for migrant workers, using transparency as a governance tool to curb corruption, and improving accountability by allowing citizens to request information.[18] Different Chinese cities are also experimenting with different ways of evaluating the performance of public officials. The city of Foshan, for example, is "giving the public a direct role in evaluating the performance of officials. Under the city's new points-based evaluation system, 15% of officials will be assessed via an online questionnaire. Officials who score badly will have their pay docked; those who score well will receive bonuses. A further 10% of points will be awarded for public service, while just 5% will be awarded for economic growth. The aim is to reverse one of the key problems currently afflicting local governance—that officials are incentivized to chase investment and GDP growth, not to optimize the delivery of public services."[19] And starting in 2014, more than seventy smaller Chinese cities and counties have dropped GDP as a performance metric for government officials in an effort to shift the focus to environmental protection and poverty reduction.[20]

In short, experimentation with different forms of economic, social, and political reform in between the local and central levels of government, including the question of how best to select and promote government officials, is key to explaining China's adaptability and success over the past three decades.[21] In contrast to the experience of other countries "such as India, where 'the corpses of pilot projects litter the management field,' Chinese-style experimentation managed to transform many pilot projects into full-scale operational programs that cover a broad policy spectrum ranging from economic regulation to organizational reforms within the Communist Party."[22] Notwithstanding its economic, social, and political importance in China's reform era, however, experimentation in the middle has not been as well researched as democracy at the bottom.[23]

The third plank of the China model is meritocracy at the top. Political meritocracy has a long history in China, as discussed throughout this book. Its modern incarnation dates from the post-Mao reform era; let's turn to its recent history in more detail.[24] Following the chaos of the Cultural Revolution, China's leaders decided that public officials should have the managerial skills, professional knowledge, and broad understanding of China and the world necessary to lead the country to full modernity and global prominence.[25] Hence, party leaders emphasized that the selection and promotion of cadres should be based on expertise rather than revolutionary energy. The government established a competitive national university entrance examination system in the late 1970s, and the first step for most officials is to be admitted to university. Then they must be admitted to the party—students compete fiercely to join the party, and usually the party selects students with high academic achievement and leadership qualities, preferably from elite universities.[26] In the early 1990s, the government established nationwide ultracompetitive public service examinations (including written and oral tests),[27] and today most aspiring officials must succeed at these examinations after they graduate from university.[28] There is more emphasis on technical competence for appointment to posts in the government system compared to recruitment for positions in the CCP hierarchy,[29] but there are not separate tracks for professional civil servants and political officials,[30] and appointment to posts for successful candidates depends on level of education and experience.

The most important provisions for the management of cadres above the county/division level (*xianchu ji*) are contained in the "Regulation on Selection and Appointment of Party and Government Leading Cadres" issued in 2002 by the CCP Organization Department. There are requirements of education and experience for appointment and promotion to political posts; generally, the higher the level, the more demanding the requirements. To be promoted to leading party and government posts at the section (village)-head level, officials must have at least a college diploma and have worked at a deputy post for more than two years. To be promoted to posts higher than the county (division) level, candidates must have held at least two positions at lower-level organs, and candidates who are promoted from deputy to head generally must have worked at the deputy post for more than two years. Leading cadres at the bureau level (*ju, si, ting*) or above should have at least a bachelor's degree.[31] Once a year, the Organization Department reviews quantitative performance records for each official in the higher grades, carries out interviews with superiors, peers, and subordinates, vets the official's personal conduct, and uses public-opinion surveys to assess the public's general satisfaction or dissatisfaction with that official's performance.[32] Committees then discuss the data and promote the winners.

To get to the top, party officials must typically start from leadership at a primary-level office and then be promoted successively to the township level, a county division, a department bureau, and the province/ministry level. A public official aiming to reach the position of vice-minister has to be promoted from senior member to deputy section chief, section chief, division chief, deputy division chief, division chief, deputy bureau chief, bureau chief, and vice-minister.[33] If one meets the minimum length of service at each rank, one needs at least twenty years to reach the position of vice-minister. During this process, officials are typically rotated through the civil service, state-owned enterprises, and government-affiliated social organizations such as universities and community groups, as well as serving in different parts of the country. The top candidates are sent for further training at party and administrative schools in China, and many promising officials are sent to top universities abroad to learn best administrative practices from around the world. Out of seven million leading cadres, only one out of 140,000 makes it to the province/ministry level. A select few move up the ranks and make it to the party's Central Committee and then the twenty-five-member Politburo. The members at the very apex of political power—the Standing Committee of the Politburo—must normally have served as governors or party secretaries of two provinces, each the size and population of most countries. In short, top leaders must pass through a battery of merit-based tests and accumulate decades of extensive and diverse administrative experience. In contrast, as Eric X. Li puts it, "a person with Barack Obama's pre-presidential professional experience would not even be the manager of a small county in China's system."[34] Notwithstanding its importance for understanding China's reforms and future political prospects, political meritocracy is perhaps the least-studied aspect of the China model.[35]

The three planks of the China model point to different ways of selecting and promoting leaders at different levels of government, but there is overlap between them (in addition to the fact that the CCP designed and implemented the whole system). The first plank—democracy at the bottom—includes elements of experimentation and meritocracy: electoral democracy at the bottom started off as an experiment in selected villages before it was generalized to the rest of the country; and there is a meritocratic check on the system in the form of a party secretary at the village level appointed from above who is often more educated than elected leaders and has the task of trying to ensure the implementation of center-driven policies that may be unpopular, such as birth control and land acquisition. The second plank—experimentation in the middle—includes forms of democracy and meritocracy: there have been democratic elections in selected townships in Sichuan province and experiments with democratic practices such as public-opinion polling as part of the evaluation process for cadres at higher levels of government;[36] and meritocratically selected leaders at the top often decide which experiments to carry out and which ones should be generalized to other parts of the country. The third plank—meritocracy at the top—includes forms of democracy and experimentation: there has been increased use of democratic practices such as contested intra-party balloting to select and promote leaders at high levels of government; meritocratic practices such as open and competitive examinations for public officials started as pilot projects in certain provinces and central administrative organs in the late 1980s before they were spread to the rest of the country,[37] and there has even been experimentation with different practices and institutions at the very top, such as varying the number of spots on the Standing Committee of the Politburo to suit different needs at different times. Overall, however, political reform over the past three decades has been informed by commitment to the general principles of the China model: the lower the level of government, the more democratic the political system; experimentation is more likely to take place, including experiments with brand new practices and institutions, in between the lowest and highest levels of government; and the higher the level of government, the more meritocratic the political system.

2. The Ideal of Political Reform

The China model is not simply a reality that has informed political reform over the past three decades. It is also informed by ideals that can be used to evaluate the reality and point to better ways of doing things. We have to ask about the moral purpose of democracy, experimentation, and meritocracy, whether actually existing practices, laws, and institutions are implemented in accordance with what makes those political goods valuable in the first place, and, if not, how the reality can be improved in ways that are politically realistic and morally desirable. So let's turn to a discussion of what makes each plank of the China model morally desirable, along with some suggestions of how the inevitable gap between reality and the ideal can be reduced.

Democratic elections are valuable if the leaders (1) are chosen in free and fair elections (otherwise the leaders do not represent the will of the people); (2) exercise real power (otherwise elections are a waste of time

and money), and (3) exercise power in ways that serve the interests of the community (as opposed to serving the interests of the leaders or a small segment of the community). In the case of village elections in China, however, there is a substantial gap between reality and the ideal. For one thing, village-level elections are not always free and fair. Candidates have rigged elections through voting blocs, bribes, or threats. The government itself recognizes the problem and has tried to fix it. A 2009 government circular urged candidates to practice fair play in direct elections of village heads amid complaints of bribery and other dirty tricks to win votes: the "bribery situation is grave and seriously harms the impartiality of elections," it said, warning that criminal penalties will be enforced against those who try to win votes from villagers with money, violence, or intimidation and against those who cheat in vote counts.[38] The government has also promoted the use of nomination procedures, competitiveness, and secret balloting to improve the chances of access to power via free and fair elections. Overall, "electoral procedures have improved greatly in the past two decades and a good number of competitive and reasonably fair elections have been held."[39]

Access to power does not always (or even usually) translate into the exercise of power, however. In other words, even if villagers can express their preferences on voting day, it doesn't follow that their representatives exercise real power: the key problem is that their power is checked by the village party secretaries and township governments.[40] When there is a very clear separation between the personnel of the non–party members of the elected village committees and the village party secretaries, it is easy for the latter to dominate; and when there is overlap, the preferences of the superiors at the township level who have authority over the party secretary can easily outweigh the preferences of the voters (or the elected leaders can be co-opted in the party).[41] That said, a recent empirical study found that branch committees of the CCP, traditionally the centers of power in the villages, increasingly share their authority with elected villagers' committees.[42]

Still, we must ask not only whether elected leaders exercise real power but also whether they exercise the right kind of power, namely, power that benefits the community. Here too, the record is mixed. The good news is that village elections in rural China have increased the share of public expenditures and reduced the share of administrative costs in the village budget.[43] And when the administrative boundaries of local government overlap with solidary groups such as temples, lineages, or tribes, local officials are more likely to perform well because providing public goods and services earns them moral standing among fellow group members as well as the help of other local elites in implementing state policies.[44] However, elections can also serve to strengthen the position of dominant clans at the cost of the weaker members of society.[45] Empirical studies in India show that decentralization could lead to elite capture at the local level if the financing of public goods provision is not properly designed, and the same is true in China: rising business elites have been found to dominate village elections and can use their material power to steer the village committee to adopt pro-rich policies. So what can be done? Deliberative polling—randomly chosen citizens advised by experts make policy recommendations—is one way to curb the power of the rich and increase the likelihood of fair distribution of public goods.[46] In 2005, the Wenling township in Zhejiang province implemented a form of deliberative polling: randomly chosen citizens were invited to review the proposed government budget and to recommend budget priorities.[47] Unfortunately, this innovation in local governance has expanded to only one county within the province due to lack of support from higher-level political authorities,[48] leading us to the next issue: the gap between the reality and the ideal of experimentation.

Experimentation is morally desirable only if successful experiments are expanded and failures are discontinued. The problem, however, is that central political authorities decide what works and what doesn't, and their decisions are often guided less by social scientific knowledge and moral considerations than by "an intensely politicized process driven by competing interests, ideological frictions, personal rivalries, tactical opportunism or ad hoc policy compromises."[49] In the case of failed experiments, the good news is that they are typically phased out and silently stopped;[50] higher authorities are unlikely to seek to spread them throughout the country. In the case of local experiments specifically tailored to the development needs of a special context,[51] all the higher authorities need to do is refrain from excessive interference.[52]

The bigger challenge is to generalize local innovations that could benefit other parts of the country because replicating and scaling up experiments in institutional innovation requires the support of a central leader with the power and the motivation to overcome powerful groups that benefit from the status quo. Again, Chinese history offers some useful lessons. The empress dowager supported Li Hongzhang's self-strengthening projects at the provincial level in the 1860s, but her court failed to broaden and intensify localized reform efforts into a comprehensive, empirewide initiative,[53] with the result that China fell behind Japan in the quest for economic and military modernization. Conversely, experiments in market reform in the late 1970s were generalized to the rest of the country because they had the strong backing of Deng Xiaoping, and experiments in village elections in the early 1980s were generalized because they had the strong backing of Peng Zhen, then vice-chairman of the National People's Congress Standing Committee.[54] As party secretary of Jiangsu, Li Yuanchao experimented with a procedure for soliciting public opinion and intraparty elections for township party secretaries, and such experiments with "intraparty democracy"[55] were replicated at least partly (if not mainly) because of the support of the central authorities (Li is a longtime colleague and confidante of the then-president Hu Jintao).[56]

On the other hand, experiments that seem promising have yet to be generalized because central authorities lack sufficient power and motivation to overcome vested interests. The case of deliberative polling has already been discussed. The Tianjin eco-city, a government-to-government project between Singapore and China meant to showcase an environmentally friendly and resource-conserving form of urban development,[57] has not (yet?) proven to be successful at least partly because of competition from nearby development projects.[58] Competition between experimental zones can be the source of economic dynamism,[59] but high-level government support is needed to replicate and scale up experiments dealing with social justice or governance issues that do not have clear economic benefits for (or that go against the interests of) powerful groups. The experiment with free speech and the rule of law in Hong Kong is another example that has yet to be generalized in other parts of China.[60] The same goes for experiments with asset disclosure of government officials in Guangzhou meant to combat corruption and the protection of religious freedoms in Tibetan-populated areas of Qinghai and Sichuan.[61]

Even seemingly successful experiments can be relabeled as failures and discontinued with a change of central government leadership. For example, Li Yuanchao's experiments with standardizing the process of evaluating the performance of public officials by means of greater reliance on competitive voting and examinations for purposes of promotion have been deemphasized since the change of leadership in 2012. There may be good reasons for the change. The emphasis on voting often poisoned relations between candidates, honest and humble candidates who did not "sell themselves" well and those who resolved problems that required taking on vested interests were unduly penalized, and the process of designing the voting process and setting standards was often abused by powerful patrons to increase the likelihood of predetermined outcomes. Today, voting is not emphasized as much as qualitative interviews and an evaluation of work results. The emphasis on exams was also reduced because exams were seen as unduly rewarding good exam takers; writing ability is still strongly valued for purposes of promotion, but more in the sense of the ability to write useful reports addressing real problems. Hence, examinations have largely been discontinued as a way of assessing performance beyond the initial hiring phase. The whole emphasis on standardization often conflicted with relevance for the job, which requires more local variation in terms of evaluating what counts as good performance; for example, poor parts of China should reward officials that contribute to poverty reduction, but environmental sustainability should matter more in wealthier parts. The need to combat corruption means that Central Commission for Discipline Inspection should be given a greater role in evaluating the virtue of officials being considered for promotion. Last but not least, the need for complex voting and examinations procedures at each step of the promotion process substantially increased the cost to the public coffers.[62] Nonetheless, the fact that these changes took place after the change of leadership makes it hard to entirely dispel the worry that they were partly driven by political rather than scientific considerations.[63]

In short, the experimentation with innovative policies meant to address new challenges is desirable if successful experiments are consistently replicated and scaled up to other parts of the country, but high-level authorities often lack the power and motivation to do political battle on behalf of innovations that threaten powerful groups. The political obstacles may be particularly acute in the case of experiments with new ways of evaluating the performance of officials because those promoted under the old ways often have a vested (and perhaps psychological) interest in maintaining the status quo. So what can be done? Public pressure can help: various pilot programs in rural health care reforms carried out since the 1980s were scaled up to a national reform program only after the SARS epidemic in 2003 triggered massive public criticism.[64] To deal with controversial cases in a more scientific way, the government can set up an advisory body of experts in the social sciences with the mandate to evaluate the advantages and disadvantages of ongoing experiments in different parts of the country. If experts are chosen at random from, say, the nation's twenty leading universities, the advisory body would be seen as disinterested and could make recommendations based on moral considerations and social scientific knowledge.[65] If politically sensitive experiments are deemed to be successful by a body of independent experts, well-intentioned reformers in the central government would have the moral authority to promote the experiments and need not take full responsibility for promoting innovations that trample on vested interests.[66]

The third plank of China's political reform—political meritocracy at the top—is desirable if leaders are selected and promoted on the basis of superior ability and virtue. The practice, however, often deviates from the ideal. The most glaring gap is the political dominance of "princelings": several of China's top leaders, including President Xi Jinping, are the descendants of prominent and influential senior Communist officials.[67] In a meritocratic system with equal opportunity to rise to the top, one would expect fewer leaders with family ties to past leaders.[68] But the princelings began their rise before the institutionalization of examinations for public officials in the early 1990s and they were initially selected because of their relatively high level of education and reformist leanings, not to maintain the status quo; such conditions are unlikely to be reproduced in the future.[69] Moreover, the avoidance system—an antinepotism mechanism with roots in imperial China that forbids officials with kinship or other relations to work in the same office—was extended to all public officials in 1991,[70] so examples of blatant nepotism have decreased.[71]

Today, arguably, the more serious challenge to China's political meritocracy is that cadres are often promoted on the basis of loyalty to political superiors,[72] although here too superiors are increasingly expected to pay greater attention to political merit rather than just rewarding personal friends.[73] But this leads to the normative question of what constitutes political merit. In chapter 2, I drew on history, philosophy, and social scientific research to put forward morally desirable and politically realistic suggestions about which qualities matter most for political leaders in the context of a large, relatively peaceful, and modernizing political meritocracy such as China. More specifically, I discussed the intellectual abilities, social skills, and virtues required of political leaders and suggested mechanisms that could be implemented to increase the likelihood of selecting and promoting leaders with these qualities. These findings were then used as a standard for evaluating China's actually existing meritocratic system and I argued that China can improve its meritocratic system by means of exams that more effectively test for politically relevant intellectual abilities, by selecting and promoting more women into leadership positions to increase the likelihood that leaders have the social skills required for effective policy making, and by more systematic use of a peer-review system (as opposed to letting superiors decide) to promote political officials motivated by the desire to serve the public.

But even well-designed political meritocracies are prone to failings in practice, and in chapter 3 I discussed three key problems with political meritocracy and suggested possible solutions with the contemporary Chinese context in mind. The problem of corruption can be addressed by means of mechanisms such as independent supervisory institutions, higher salaries, and improved moral education. The problem of ossification of political hierarchies can be addressed by means of humble political discourse, opening the ruling party to diverse social groups, more freedom of speech, and allowing for the possibility of different kinds of political leaders selected according to new ideas of political merit. The problem of legitimacy can be addressed by means of democratic reforms, including some form of explicit consent by the people. In chapter 4, I argued that vertical democratic meritocracy (political meritocracy at the top, democracy at the bottom) is the best way of reconciling political meritocracy and electoral democracy in a large country and suggested that China's leaders may need to put vertical democratic meritocracy to a referendum some time in the future in order to boost the democratic legitimacy of the political system. In short, there is a large gap between the ideal and the reality of political meritocracy in China, but it is possible (and desirable) to substantially reduce the gap without instituting electoral democracy at the top.

3. Beyond China

China has carried out a model of political reform since the late 1970s that is both a reality and an ideal that can be used to judge further improvement. It's worth asking if the model can be exported elsewhere. The main limitation is that the model itself is the hybrid product of a historical experience unique to China. The practice of village elections has roots in earlier ideas about village self-governance, but electoral democracy was invented and borrowed from the West. Experimentation at local levels was carried out in imperial China, but it was first systematized into a workable policy by the CCP from the 1930s to the 1950s. The idea and practice of political meritocracy is central to Chinese political culture and China has proved to be fertile ground for its reestablishment in the reform era. Clearly the whole package—democracy at the bottom, experimentation in the middle, meritocracy at the top—cannot readily be adopted by countries with a different history and culture. Moreover, it is a workable model only in a large and diverse country that is committed to a peaceful form of social and economic modernization under the guidance of meritocratically selected leaders. And the whole thing can be implemented only by a ruling organization similar to the CCP. Other than perhaps Vietnam, no country comes close to fitting the requirements for successful establishment of the "China model."

But the different planks of the model can be selectively adopted. The practice of free and fair elections at the local level is widely adopted in the world, and even countries that have no plan to establish electoral democracy at the highest level of government can and should consider adopting democracy at local levels, just as China has done. The practice of experimentation in between central and local levels of government is difficult to implement in democratic contexts because experiments can take decades to bear fruit and elected politicians worried about the next election tend to have shorter time horizons. Also, the same party may not control the different levels of government and the top may not have the power to launch pilot projects in the whole country, particularly with regard to experiments in political reform.[74] Even with the same party in power at different levels of government, experimentation in the middle is not likely to be workable in a rigid federal system that enshrines strict divisions of powers among different levels of government because such experimentation is premised on the assumption that the central government has the power to generalize successful experiments to other parts of the country. And experimentation in the middle assumes a relatively large country (it wouldn't work in Singapore).[75] Here too, Vietnam is perhaps the only country that comes close to meeting these requirements.[76]

Political meritocracy at the top is the foundation of the China model, but it is also the most difficult to export. Citizens in electoral democracies are committed to the practice of one person, one vote to choose top leaders and it is hard to imagine getting elected on a platform for "meritocratization" of democratic political systems that would involve curtailing people's equal right to vote. Even the idea that civil servants need to pass examinations to be hired is intensely controversial in countries such as the United States, never mind the idea that political officials must do so.[77] One cannot rule out scenarios, either pessimistic (e.g., nuclear war, global warming, major terrorist attacks) or optimistic (e.g., mechanization of necessary labor with more opportunities for creative work, discovery of new sources of renewable energy), that radically change political outlooks in several decades' time, but for the moment democratic constitutional systems appear to be stable. Still, the positive qualities of political leaders in meritocratic systems can inspire voter preferences in democratic systems (e.g., voters can seek to elect political leaders with the traits of leaders in meritocratic systems) and elected leaders can seek to model themselves and implement policies according to what works in meritocratic systems. Perhaps the best hope for defenders of political meritocracy is the fact that many countries have yet to consolidate electoral democracy at the top, and China can assist other countries seeking to build up meritocratic rule.[78] Just as the United States promotes democracy abroad via government-funded foundations like the National Endowment for Democracy, so the Chinese government can fund an institution—let's call it the National Endowment for Meritocracy—that would fund experiments in political meritocracy designed to improve governance in other countries. In terms of its foreign policy, China should make it explicit that it seeks special ties with political meritocracies abroad, if only to answer the criticism that its foreign policy is purely motivated by mercantile concerns.

At the end of the day, however, political meritocracy will work as a form of "soft power" only if China sets a good model for others: that is, it must practice political meritocracy at home. As China closes the gap between the ideal and the reality of political meritocracy, the true nature of the system will become more apparent to outsiders. At the moment, however, China's harsh treatment of its domestic critics and minority groups in western China grabs media headlines abroad, and it is difficult for defenders of political meritocracy to counter the criticism that coercion lies at the heart of its political system. Hence, as Pan Wei puts it, the Chinese state should become less oppressive and more tolerant.[79] Last but not least, the CCP also needs to change its name so that it better corresponds to the institutional reality of the organization, as well as to what it aspires to be. In fact, the CCP is neither Communist nor a party. Few Chinese, including members of the CCP, believe that the CCP is leading the march to higher communism.[80] Political meritocracy was valued neither by Marx nor by Mao, and Lenin's idea of the vanguard party was also different.[81] With eighty-six million members, including card-carrying capitalists, the party is not a political party among others. It is a pluralistic organization composed of meritocratically selected members of different groups and classes, and it aims to represent the whole country.[82] A more accurate name might be the Chinese Meritocratic Union (*Zhongguo xianneng lianmeng*). A more politically correct name—given the importance of the term *democracy* (*minzhu*) in official Chinese political discourse and among independent Chinese intellectuals, as well as the fact that the political system as a whole incorporates democratic characteristics[83]—might be the

Union of Democratic Meritocrats (*Minzhu xianneng lianmeng*). A change of public discourse can also help to close the gap between the ideal and the reality of political meritocracy because the government becomes more obliged to move some way toward realizing stated aspirations.[84] In short, the challenge for the Chinese government is not simply to walk the meritocratic walk; it should also talk the talk.[85]

NOTES

Introduction

1. See the video at: http://world.time.com/2013/10/17/whats-the-secret-to-chinas-incredible-success/.

2. Daniel Bell, "On Meritocracy and Equality," *National Affairs* 29 (Fall 1972): 66–67. Bell (no relation) was one of the few major American thinkers in the post–World War II era to defend the idea of political meritocracy. He also put forward a proposal for a "House of Counselors" composed of a group of experienced and disinterested political leaders ready to act for the common good (Bell, "The Old War: After Ideology, Corruption," *New Republic*, 23 and 30 Aug. 1993). Bell had a special knack for tapping into the zeitgeist but in this case he was both behind and ahead of his time.

3. It could be argued that the ideal of merit was discredited because of its abuses. But other ideals, such as government by popular consent, have also been abused without discrediting the ideal itself. As Joseph F. Kett explains (with reference to the American context), "Most Americans doubt that their vote really counts and suspect that powerful offstage interests shape policy more than do the voters, but nearly all of them defend government by consent. Today merit and consent, each an ideal of the founding fathers, nevertheless provoke different reactions. Evidence of the failings of popular consent scarcely ruffles the ideal, while evidence of the difficulties encountered in implementing merit provides derision of the ideal." One might be more skeptical of the ideal of merit if attempts to implement it always (or usually) led to negative consequences, but Kett argues otherwise: "Throughout the course of our history, invocations of merit have served many hitherto excluded groups in their demand for equal rights." Kett, *Merit: The History of a Founding Ideal from the American Revolution to the 21st Century* (Ithaca, N.Y.: Cornell University Press, 2013), pp. 261–262.

4. See, e.g., Nicolas Berggruen and Nathan Gardels, *Intelligent Governance for the 21st Century: A Middle Way between West and East* (Cambridge: Polity Press, 2012).

5. See Stephen Macedo, "Meritocratic Democracy: Learning from the American Constitution," and Philip Pettit, "Meritocratic Representation," both in *The East Asian Challenge for Democracy: Political Meritocracy in Comparative Perspective*, ed. Daniel A. Bell and Chenyang Li (New York: Cambridge University Press, 2013). Debates over judicial review and the U.S. Supreme Court suggest that the lines are not

always so clear between what counts as "political" and what counts as "judicial," but in principle judges are not supposed to exercise political power.

6. Of course, the theoretical distinction between elected politicians who decide and civil servants who implement is often violated in practice, as the satirical British television show *Yes, Minister* reminds us.

7. In 1958, the English sociologist Michael Young coined the term *meritocracy* in a political satire that was meant to discredit the ideal, but he conflated political and economic meritocracy. Young, *The Rise of the Meritocracy* (London: Thames and Hudson, 1958). The Chinese term for political meritocracy—贤能政治 *(xianneng zhengzhi)*—more clearly refers to the idea that the political system should aim to choose leaders with superior ability and virtue rather than an economic principle governing the distribution of wealth in society.

8. Karl Marx, *The Critique of the Gotha Program* (1875, part I) (http://www.marxists.org/archive/marx/works/1875/gotha/ch01.htm).

9. John Rawls, *A Theory of Justice* (Oxford: Clarendon Press, 1972), p. 100.

10. Cited in Jordan Weissmann, "Ben Bernanke to Princeton Grads: The World Isn't Fair (and You All Got Lucky)," *The Atlantic*, 3 June 2013.

11. Similarly, I do not mean to justify any particular view regarding "meritocracy" in education unless the question of how to distribute places in the educational system bears on the issue of how to establish a morally desirable and politically realistic form of political meritocracy.

12. What if China's one-party state collapses and is replaced by "Western-style" electoral democracy, as happened in the Soviet Union? In such an (improbable) event, the democratic system is still likely to be influenced by key aspects of Chinese political culture (just as Vladimir Putin's Russia has "restored" key aspects of Russian political culture), especially its commitment to political meritocracy, so what I say in this book in favor of political meritocracy may still be (at least partly) relevant.

13. China is formally a multiparty state under the leadership of the Chinese Communist Party, but the eight officially registered minor political parties are not supposed to compete for political power with the CCP.

14. I haven't responded to any of these critiques (except for one particularly unfair article that contained misleading information about my wife) because I realized that any response would need to be very detailed to be persuasive. I've faced the same problem whenever I've presented parts of this book at seminars and lectures at universities around the world: if I present, say, chapter 2, the questions and comments will inevitably turn to issues raised in chapters 3 and 4; if it's about chapter 4, then people want to talk about issues raised in chapters 1 and 3, etc. Hence (and I apologize if this sounds pompous), I literally had to write a whole book to answer the criticisms.

15. Another reason is that I value university presses at leading Anglo-American universities: their procedures for publication express a commitment to academic freedom and academic meritocracy; the same cannot always be said of publishers in other countries.

16. In the case of democratic countries, I have in mind reforms of the type sug-

gested in Berggruen and Gardels's book *Intelligent Governance for the 21st Century*, which are meant to be built on democratic foundations. My aim is *not* to undermine faith in electoral democracy in countries that have implemented such systems, if only because the practical alternatives tend to be military dictatorship or authoritarian populism. Also, political meritocracy (unlike electoral democracy) cannot be established overnight; it requires decades of work. In the case of China, the practical alternative to electoral democracy (in the foreseeable future) is political meritocracy because such arguments resonate with its dominant political culture and the government has been (re)establishing an (imperfect) form of political meritocracy over the past three decades or so and it can be improved on the basis of the current model (see concluding thoughts).

17. To be more precise: there is a wide range of political views in China, and my book falls somewhere in the middle range of the ideological spectrum: leftists (defenders of socialism and Chinese-style democracy) are likely to object to the proposal for a referendum and more freedom of political speech, and rightists (defenders of capitalism and liberal democracy) are likely to object to the strong critique of electoral democracy at the top.

Chapter 1
Is Democracy the Least Bad Political System?

1. To be more precise, there is also widespread agreement on the value of basic human rights and prohibitions against slavery, genocide, murder, torture, prolonged arbitrary detention, and systematic racial discrimination, as well as the idea that all citizens should be equal before the law in criminal cases. But such values are also endorsed in contemporary China at the level of principle (in imperial China, by way of contrast, a group of elites, such as successful exam takers, were given special exemptions from criminal punishment simply by virtue of their social status; I do not know of any modern Chinese thinkers, including Confucians, who seek to revive that form of inequality). In this book, I do not mean to question the value of basic human rights or equality before the law in criminal cases (quite the opposite: I wholeheartedly endorse such values). My concern here is only to evaluate the desirability of choosing political leaders by means of one person, one vote.

2. See, e.g., John Keane, *The Life and Death of Democracy* (London: Simon and Schuster, 2009).

3. Samuel P. Huntington, *Political Order in Changing Societies*, new ed. (New Haven, Conn.: Yale University Press, 2006).

4. Even prodemocracy movement leaders from the late 1980s such as Fang Lizhi "expressed only horror at a democratic formula that would give equal voting rights to peasants" (Vivienne Shue, "China: Transition Postponed?" *Problems of Communism* 41, nos. 1–2 [Jan.–Apr. 1992]: 163).

5. Yu Keping, *Democracy Is a Good Thing* (Washington, D.C.: Brookings Institution Press, 2009), and http://www.chinausfocus.com/political-social-development/the

-case-for-an-orderly-democracy-in-china/. For a mild critique, see Gao Minzheng, "Zhongguoshi minzhu ye shi ge hao dongxi—You 'Minzhu shi ge hao dongxi' yinfa de ji dian sikao" [Chinese-Style Democracy Is Also a Good Thing—A Few Thoughts Sparked by "Democracy Is a Good Thing"], *Tansuo yu zhengming* 11 (2013): 4–10.

6. Yu Chongsheng, "Cha'e xuanju: Zhongguoshi minzhu de yingran zhi lu" [Multi-Candidate Elections: A Necessary Way for Chinese-Style Democracy], *Tansuo yu zhengming* 5, no. 271 (2012): 56–59.

7. Ma Ling, "Daiyizhi dui minzhu de fenjie: Minzhu xuanju, minzhu juece he minzhu jiandu" [An Analysis of Representative Democracy: Democratic Elections, Democratic Decision Making, and Democratic Supervision], *Zhanlue yu guanli* 5, no. 6 (2012): 27–38.

8. Again, not all Chinese intellectuals share this view: as we will see, Confucian-inspired thinkers seek to defend strong meritocratic checks on electoral democracy. For a comprehensive account of the academic debates about democracy in China, see Émilie Frenkiel, *Parler politique en Chine: Les intellectuels chinois pour ou contre la démocratie* [Talking about Politics in China: Chinese Intellectuals for or against Democracy] (Paris: Presses Universitaires de France, 2014).

9. I do not mean to imply that a long history is sufficient to justify a social practice (consider the long history of slavery). But a long history is often taken to be an argument in favor of social practices that do not, on reflection, seem straightforwardly bad or good (in contrast, it makes sense to withhold judgment about a controversial event without a very long history).

10. I add "preferably" because, at least in the case of university presidents, the experience need not always be in the same field: for example, Janet Napolitano was appointed president of the University of California system in July 2013 (at least partly) on the basis of her track record running organizations as governor of Arizona and secretary of homeland security.

11. Similarly, few people other than experts in human rights law know that the Universal Declaration of Human Rights specifies that "the will of the people shall be the basis of the authority of government; this will shall be expressed in periodic and genuine elections which shall be by universal and equal suffrage and shall be held by secret vote or by equivalent voting procedures" (Article 21 (3)).

12. In fact, knowledge of debates in political science may undermine faith in democracy. The harshest criticism of electoral democracy as a political ideal in China is often made by Chinese intellectuals with PhDs in political science from leading American universities (Ren Jiantao, "Jiazhi yinni yu zhishi niuqu: Liu mei zhengzhixue boshi dui minzhu de juchi" [Hidden Values and Distortion of Knowledge: The Rejection of Democracy by Chinese Scholars Who Have Received Ph.D.s in Political Science in the United States], *Zhanlue yu guanli* 1 [2012]). The author of the article is highly critical of such scholars who supposedly exaggerate the weaknesses of electoral democracy in the United States and the strengths of "Chinese-style" democracy in China.

13. For an account of the long and contested history of the expansion of the fran-

chise in the United States, see Alexander Keyssar, *The Right to Vote: The Contested History of Democracy in the United States* (New York: Basic Books, 2009).

14. For an account of the way the history of the popular sovereign has displaced, while borrowing from, the revelatory character of the Judeo-Christian God (thus helping to explain why many citizens are willing to sacrifice for the state), see Paul W. Kahn, *Putting Liberalism in Its Place* (Princeton, N.J.: Princeton University Press, 2005).

15. In principle, political equality can take other forms; for example, everybody can have the equal right to take exams that put citizens on the road to political power.

16. As Alexis de Tocqueville put it, the "ceaseless agitation which democratic government has introduced into the political world influences all social discourse. . . . I have no doubt that the democratic institutions of the United States, joined to the physical constitution of the country, are the cause (not the direct, as is so often asserted, but the indirect cause) of the prodigious commercial activity of the inhabitants" (https://www.marxists.org/reference/archive/de-tocqueville/democracy-america/ch14.htm). But the argument that only democratic-style political energy translates into social and economic energy is not so straightforward. Social energy is hard to measure, but even the most casual observer of contemporary China cannot fail to notice the ceaseless motion and social tumult that may also have been characteristic of the United States in Tocqueville's day. If the rate of economic growth is the key measurement of economic energy, then both Singapore and China have outperformed democratic countries over the past three decades. An oft-heard argument is that China will require democracy to allow for more innovation and the creativity that underpins economic growth at higher levels of development, but indicators of innovation such as the number of Chinese invention patents filed abroad have been rising sharply since 2003 ("Chinese Patents: Ever More Inventive," *The Economist*, 24 May 2014; see also "The China Wave: Chinese Management Ideas Are Beginning to Get the Attention They Deserve," *The Economist*, 13 Sept. 2014).

17. This sentiment won't be as strong in a country without elections to choose top leaders and where people generally support political meritocracy (as in China; see chapter 3, section 3), but people become more attached to electoral democracy once it's in place because those "downgraded" in any attempt to modify or abolish the system will be viewed as "losers" and will object to the change. On the other hand, strong minorities (as in Thailand) and perhaps even majorities (Egypt?) may favor military coups if electoral democracy fails to deliver the promised goods.

18. I confess I don't find any of these reasons psychologically compelling from a personal point of view: I haven't voted for political leaders since I left Canada nearly three decades ago and I neither miss it nor feel that my human dignity has been undermined as a result. For those of us who care about political influence, perhaps influence via means such as teaching and writing is sufficient psychological compensation for lack of voting rights.

19. Such arguments are made not only within the liberal or deontological traditions: Joseph Chan argues from a "Confucian perfectionist" viewpoint that elections

express the ideal of mutual commitment and trust. See Chan, *Confucian Perfectionism: A Political Philosophy for Modern Times* (Princeton, N.J.: Princeton University Press, 2014), chs. 3–4.

20. See Jason Brennan, "Political Liberty: Who Needs It?" *Social Philosophy and Policy* 29 (2012): 1–27. For a critique of influential arguments on behalf of majority rule, see Mathias Risse, "Arguing for Majority Rule," *Journal of Political Philosophy* 12, no. 1 (2004): 41–64.

21. Richard Miller, "How Does Political Equality Matter? Mencius Meets Walt Whitman," paper presented at the "Philosophy and Public Policy" Colloquium, Wuhan University, 22–23 Mar. 2014. Miller himself defends political equality on the noninstrumental grounds that citizens denied political equality will feel humiliated and insulted, but such views owe much to the American historical experience that deprived African Americans of the vote. It's unclear why it's a problem if people do not feel insulted by being denied an equal vote and if they feel they derive sufficient benefits from a nondemocratic system. Should we say that Chinese people suffer from a collective form of false consciousness if they are generally supportive of political meritocracy—see chapter 3, section 3—and are well aware of the alternatives?

22. Doh Chull Shin, *Confucianism and Democratization in East Asia* (Cambridge: Cambridge University Press, 2011), p. 322. See also the discussion in my book *East Meets West: Human Rights and Democracy in East Asia* (Princeton, N.J.: Princeton University Press, 2000), ch. 3.

23. It was not Churchill's original intent: he made this remark in the House of Commons in 1947 after he had been voted out of power (in 1945) and had reason to feel somewhat bitter (http://wais.stanford.edu/Democracy/democracy_DemocracyAndChurchill(090503).html).

24. Jason Brennan, *The Ethics of Voting* (Princeton, N.J.: Princeton University Press, 2011), p. 76.

25. Amartya Sen, *Democracy as Freedom* (New York: Anchor, 1999).

26. See Thomas Christiano, "An Instrumental Argument for a Human Right to Democracy," *Philosophy and Public Affairs* 39, no. 2 (2011): 163–164.

27. The rate of malnutrition among children in India is almost five times greater than that in China. See http://www.worldbank.org/en/news/feature/2013/05/13/helping-india-combat-persistently-high-rates-of-malnutrition.

28. From a moral point of view, the tendency to go to war is less problematic if the wars are just. A defender of U.S. foreign policy might argue that China is free riding on an international order that lets the United States do the dirty work (fighting just wars). But both liberals and Confucians would agree that some American-led wars, such as the invasion of Iraq in 2003, have been unjust. See the discussion in my book *Beyond Liberal Democracy: Political Thinking for an East Asian Context* (Princeton, N.J.: Princeton University Press, 2006), ch. 2.

29. See http://www.cartercenter.org/peace/democracy/des.html.

30. Paul Collier, *Wars, Guns, and Votes: Democracy in Dangerous Places* (London: Vintage, 2010), pp. 28–36, 225.

31. Of course, power and influence are not the same as success in promoting human well-being. Nordic countries typically rank at the top of global indexes measuring human well-being, but it makes little sense to compare China with resource-rich and relatively homogenous countries of a few million people. That said, I do discuss tiny Singapore in this book because Singapore-style political meritocracy has been influential in China, and I do not mean to deny that China can also learn from aspects of the political experience of Nordic countries.

32. I should also add a personal reason: it may not be obvious from the criticisms of the American political system that are about to follow, but I have a special affection for the United States (my father and son were both born in the United States, and, yes, some of my best friends are Americans). In other words, I write about the United States because I care about it and hope it improves.

33. See my introduction to *The East Asian Challenge for Democracy.*

34. I do not focus on *all* key drawbacks: for an argument, put forward by political theorists of the past but still relevant today, that the norms of democracy (such as transparency) conflict with the demands of security, see Rahul Sagar, "Presaging the Moderns: Demosthenes' Critique of Popular Government," *Journal of Politics* 71, no. 4 (Oct. 2009): 1394–1405.

35. Michael Mann, *The Dark Side of Democracy: Explaining Ethnic Cleansing* (Cambridge: Cambridge University Press, 2005), esp. chs. 1, 3, and 17.

36. Josiah Ober, *Political Dissent in Democratic Athens: Intellectual Critics of Popular Rule* (Princeton, N.J.: Princeton University Press, 1998), p. 345.

37. I say "generally" because constitutionally enshrined rights in liberal democracies are meant to protect individuals against the whims of majority decision making on the assumption that people are not always rational.

38. Classical economics has also been founded on the assumption that people are rational and know what they want. This assumption has been the subject of much criticism of late, with even Alan Greenspan conceding that as Fed chairman he was too sanguine about the ability of financial institutions to act rationally and prudently, and he now gives much greater weight to the role of "animal spirits." See Greenspan, *The Map and the Territory: Risk, Human Nature, and the Future of Forecasting* (New York: Penguin, 2013).

39. See Brennan, *The Ethics of Voting*, ch. 5.

40. Ibid., p. 127 and ch. 7.

41. Bai Tongdong, "A Confucian Hybrid Regime: How Does It Work and Why Is It Superior?" in *The East Asian Challenge for Democracy*, p. 61. One can imagine optimistic scenarios in the future similar to Karl Marx's version of communism—machines or robots do most of the necessary labor and we are freed to exercise our creative talents—but more pessimistic scenarios (e.g., domination by machines) seem just as likely.

42. Brennan, *The Ethics of Voting*, p. 165.

43. Daniel Kahneman, *Thinking, Fast and Slow* (London: Penguin, 2011), pp. 258, 259, 256–257, 417–418.

44. Brennan, *The Ethics of Voting*, pp. 163–164. On the political ignorance of voters in France, see “Pourquoi Voter?” [Why Vote?], *Books* 31 (Apr. 2012): 29.

45. Brennan, *The Ethics of Voting*, p. 10. The fact that Republicans and Democrats tend to attribute false (bad) motives to their opponents, no matter how irrational, is explained by a well-documented “partisan bias” that activates the part of the brain involved in processing emotions. As the lead scientist on one such study put it: “We did not see any increased activation of the parts of the brain normally engaged during reasoning. What we saw instead was a network of emotion circuits lighting up, including circuits hypothesized to be involved in regulating emotion, and circuits known to be involved in resolving conflicts. None of the circuits involved in conscious reasoning were particularly engaged. Essentially, it appears as if partisans twirl the cognitive kaleidoscope until they get the conclusions they want, and then they get massively reinforced for it, with the elimination of negative emotional states and the activation of positive ones.” Cited in Denise D. Cummins, *Good Thinking: Seven Powerful Ideas That Influence the Way We Think* (Cambridge: Cambridge University Press, 2012), p. 120.

46. Jonah Goldberg, “Public Lacks Grasp of Obamacare,” *USA Today*, 30 Sept. 2013.

47. Bryan Caplan, *The Myth of the Rational Voter: Why Democracies Choose Bad Policies* (Princeton, N.J.: Princeton University Press, 2007), p. 10. Kahneman’s finding that entrepreneurs tend to be overly optimistic is not necessarily inconsistent with Caplan’s findings of a pessimistic bias among voters at large: it could be that the minority of optimists become entrepreneurs.

48. Nicholas Kristof, “No. 1 Neglected Topic: Climate Change,” *New York Times*, 20 Jan. 2014.

49. See http://www.huffingtonpost.com/2013/07/23/evolution-god_n_3640658.html.

50. Cited in Jamie Terence Kelly, *Framing Democracy: A Behavioral Approach to Democratic Theory* (Princeton, N.J.: Princeton University Press, 2012), p. 77.

51. David Leonhardt, “When the Crowd Isn’t Wise,” *New York Times*, 8 July 2012 (reporting the findings of Nate Silver).

52. Brennan, *The Ethics of Voting*, p. 171.

53. Ibid., p. 103. For more on the special conditions required for Aristotle’s argument on behalf of collective wisdom to be effective, see Mathias Risse, “The Virtuous Group—Foundations for the ‘Argument from the Wisdom of the Multitude,’ ” *Canadian Journal of Philosophy* 31, no. 1 (Mar. 2001): 53–84. See also Josiah Ober, “Democracy’s Wisdom: An Aristotelian Middle Way for Collective Judgment,” *American Political Science Review* 107, no. 1 (Feb. 2013): 104–122.

54. Lexington, “The China-Bashing Syndrome,” *The Economist*, 14 July 2012.

55. Brennan, *The Ethics of Voting*, p. 10.

56. See my book *Beyond Liberal Democracy*, ch. 7.

57. Kahneman, *Thinking, Fast and Slow*, p. 262.

58. Nicolas Berggruen and Nathan Gardels, “Political Meritocracy and Direct

Democracy: A Hybrid Experiment in California," in *The East Asian Challenge for Democracy*. See also their book *Intelligent Governance for the 21st Century*, ch. 6.

59. Mark Henderson, *The Geek Manifesto: Why Science Matters* (London: Corgi Books, 2012), pp, 38, 22. See also John Allen Paulos, "Why Don't Americans Elect Scientists?" *New York Times*, 13 Feb. 2012.

60. David Dobbs, "Appendix: A Geek Manifesto for America," in Henderson, *The Geek Manifesto*, p. 321.

61. Sharon LaFraniere, "China and Cheap Tires," *New York Times*, 3 Oct. 2012.

62. I do not mean to imply that voters and political decision makers should always listen to experts, but experts should have disproportionate political input when their results are more reliable. See Harry Collins and Robert Evans, *Rethinking Expertise* (Chicago: University of Chicago Press, 2009), pp. 135–136.

63. John Stuart Mill, "Considerations on Representative Government" [orig. pub. 1861], in *Collected Works of John Stuart Mill*, ed. J. M. Robson (Toronto: University of Toronto Press, 1977), ch. 3.

64. Brennan, "Political Liberty: Who Needs It?" p. 24 (referring to Diana Mutz, *Hearing the Other Side: Deliberative versus Participatory Democracy* [Cambridge: Cambridge University Press, 2006]). For some contrary evidence showing that there is widespread willingness to deliberate in the United States and that people who are less likely to participate in traditional nonpartisan politics are most interested in deliberative participation, see Michael A. Noblo et al., "Who Wants to Deliberate—and Why?" Faculty Research Working Paper Series, Kennedy School, Harvard University, Sept. 2009. But these findings draw on the highly atypical experiment of an invitation to deliberate with their member of the U.S. House of Representatives.

65. Kelly, *Framing Democracy*, p. 121. Some interventions designed to overcome cognitive biases may not be so costly or complicated: for example, politicians get away with avoiding tough questions by exploiting the fact that people have finite attention spans, but research has shown that posting a summary of the question on screen during the answer helps people to detect artful dodges (Todd Rogers and Michael I. Norton, "A Way to Stop Dodges," *New York Times*, 3 Oct. 2012). On the other hand, a recent study by Amanda Friesen and Aleksander Ksiazkiewicz comparing identical and genetic twins points to a source of political bias that may be particularly difficult to overcome: "the correlation between religious importance and conservatism is driven primarily, but usually not exclusively, by genetic factors. . . . If these predispositions are, as Friesen and Ksiazkiewicz argue, to some degree genetically rooted, they may not lend themselves to rational debate and compromise" (Thomas B. Edsall, "How Much Do Our Genes Influence Our Political Beliefs?" *New York Times*, 8 July 2014). Put differently, it is not impossible to change genetically rooted predispositions, but it requires prolonged conscious effort and careful weighing of arguments, and most people lack the time, motivation, and cognitive skills to do so.

66. Brennan, *The Ethics of Voting*, p. 182. To be frank, these tips seem somewhat half-baked: unlike the rest of the book, they are presented in a superconfident way without any empirical evidence suggesting that they will be effective.

67. Ibid., p. 68.

68. "Free Exchange," *The Economist*, 12 Jan. 2013.

69. Robert B. Albritton and Thawilwadee Bureekul, "Developing Democracy under a New Constitution in Thailand," in *How East Asians View Democracy*, ed. Yun-Han Chu, Larry Diamond, Andrew J. Nathan, and Doh Chull Shin (New York: Columbia University Press, 2008), p. 123.

70. Jason Brennan, "The Right to a Competent Electorate," *Philosophical Quarterly* 61, no. 245 (2011): 724.

71. Brennan's proposal may be more appropriate for China, where the political culture is less anti-elitist and the central government has the power to carry out local experimentation that can be scaled up (see concluding thoughts).

72. See also chapter 4, section 2.

73. See my book *East Meets West*, ch. 3.

74. Cited in Han Fook Kwang, Warren Fernandez, and Sumiko Tan, *Lee Kuan Yew: The Man and His Ideas* (Singapore: Times Editions, 1998), p. 315.

75. Cited in Edwin Lee, *Singapore: The Unexpected Nation* (Singapore: ISEAS, 2008), p. 547. Prime Minister Lee does not make explicit the contrast—repeatedly made in the *Analects of Confucius*—between the *junzi* (exemplary person) and the *xiao ren* (petty person) because political leaders could not refer to citizens as *xiao ren* without arousing needless controversy. A charitable interpretation of Lee's point is that political leaders in a meritocracy should be evaluated by the standards of the *junzi*, whereas ordinary citizens need not be evaluated according to such lofty standards.

76. See Benjamin Wong, "Political Meritocracy in Singapore: Lessons from the PAP Government," in *The East Asian Challenge for Democracy*.

77. Lee Kuan Yew, *From Third World to First: The Singapore Story, 1965–2000* (New York: Harper, 2000).

78. Eugene K. B. Tan, "Re-engaging Chineseness: Political, Economic and Cultural Imperatives of Nation-Building in Singapore," *China Quarterly* 175 (Sept. 2003): 756.

79. Cited in Han, Fernandez, and Tan, *Lee Kuan Yew*, p. 134.

80. Kenneth Paul Tan, "Meritocracy and Political Liberalization in Singapore," in *The East Asian Challenge for Democracy*. It is worth noting that the Singapore regime advocates both political and economic meritocracy (see the introduction) and the negative connotations of the term are also the result of growing doubts about economic meritocracy in Singapore.

81. For a detailed interpretation of the 2011 election results, see Kevin Y. L. Tan and Terence Lee, eds., *Voting in Change: Politics of Singapore's 2011 General Election* (Singapore: Ethos Books, 2011).

82. See, e.g., Yan Cang, "Xinjiapo moshi de xingcheng yu chixu" [The Formation and Continuance of the Singapore Model], *Wenhua zongheng*, Apr. 2013, pp. 46–51.

83. Since 1992, for example, more than twelve thousand Chinese officials at the rank of county mayor or above have gone through executive training programs and

postgraduate programs in managerial economics and public administration at Nanyang Technological University, and many are now influential decision makers in the Chinese government.

84. See, e.g., Song Xiongwei, "*Xuexi Shibao* kan wen jieshao Xinjiapo zhizhengdang zhenggai jingyan" [*Study Times* Introduces Singaporean Political Parties' Experience of Political Reforms], *Tencent News*, 22 Oct. 2012. Retrieved from http://news.qq.com/a/20121022/000098.htm.

85. David Runciman argues that China's rival political model is one of the four major challenges facing democracy. Runciman, *The Confidence Trap: A History of Democracy in Crisis from World War I to the Present* (Princeton, N.J.: Princeton University Press, 2013), pp. 318–323.

86. Ober, *Political Dissent in Democratic Athens*, pp. 304, 341.

87. Macedo, "Meritocratic Democracy."

88. Jacob S. Hacker and Paul Pierson, *Winner-Take-All Politics: How Washington Made the Rich Richer—and Turned Its Back on the Middle Class* (New York: Simon and Schuster, 2010), p. 76.

89. John P. McCormick, *Machiavellian Democracy* (Cambridge: Cambridge University Press, 2011), p. 179.

90. Cited in Hacker and Pierson, *Winner-Take-All Politics*, p. 77

91. John Kay, "A Tyranny of the Minority in an Age of Single-Issue Obsessives," *Financial Times*, 12 June 2013.

92. Hacker and Pierson, *Winner-Take-All Politics*, p. 3.

93. Charles A. Kupchan, "The Democratic Malaise," *Foreign Affairs* 91, no. 1 (Jan./Feb. 2012): 64.

94. Hacker and Pierson, *Winner-Take-All Politics*, p. 6. For detailed evidence that economic elites and organized groups representing business interests have substantial independent impacts on U.S. government policy, while average citizens and mass-based interest groups have little or no independent influence, see Martin Gilens and Benjamin I. Page, "Testing Theories of American Politics: Elites, Interest Groups, and Average Citizens," *Perspectives on Politics* 12, no. 3 (Sept. 2014): 564–581.

Another important cause of economic inequality in the United States is related to education: during the first eight decades of the twentieth century, the increase in the supply of educated workers was greater than the technologically induced demand for them, which had the effect of boosting income for most people and lowering inequality, but the reverse has been true for the past three decades. Claudia Goldin and Laurence F. Katz, *The Race between Education and Technology* (Cambridge, Mass.: Harvard University Press, 2010).

95. Bob Herbert, "Fast Track to Inequality," *New York Times*, 1 Nov. 2010. This is not to suggest that the superrich are necessarily incapable of looking beyond their economic self-interest: Warren Buffett wrote an op-ed in the *New York Times* that ends with this stirring paragraph: "My friends and I have been coddled long enough by a billionaire-friendly Congress. It's time for our government to get serious about

shared sacrifice. Billionaires like me should pay more taxes" ("Stop Coddling the Super-rich," *New York Times*, 15 Aug. 2011).

96. Chrystia Freeland, "The Self-Destruction of the 1 Percent," *New York Times*, 13 Oct. 2012.

97. "Census: U.S. Poverty Rate Spikes, Nearly 50 Million Americans Affected," CBS, 15 Nov. 2012.

98. "Extreme Poverty in the United States, 1996 to 2011," National Poverty Center, Feb. 2012.

99. http://opinionator.blogs.nytimes.com/2013/05/29/why-cant-america-be-sweden/.

100. Michael Lewis, *The Big Short* (London: Penguin, 2010), pp. 23, 74, 130–131, 176, 179, 214, 258.

101. http://opinionator.blogs.nytimes.com/2013/05/29/why-cant-america-be-sweden/.

102. Christopher Hayes, *Twilight of the Elites: America after Meritocracy* (New York: Crown, 2012), pp. 62, 63. See also Timothy Noah, *The Great Divergence: America's Growing Inequality Crisis and What We Can Do about It* (New York: Bloomsbury Press, 2012), pp. 28–29. That said, recent support for the Occupy movement and the unexpected runaway success of Thomas Piketty's tome *Capital in the Twenty-First Century*, trans. Arthur Goldhammer (Cambridge, Mass.: Belknap Press, 2014) point to a significant shift in American public opinion about inequality and (lack of) opportunity in American society.

103. Hacker and Pierson, *Winner-Take-All Politics*, pp. 101–102. See also Jeffrey Edward Green, *The Eyes of the People: Democracy in an Age of Spectatorship* (Oxford: Oxford University Press, 2011).

104. Consider the differential impact of mass demonstrations in different types of political systems. In nondemocratic Hong Kong, more than a half million people took to the streets in 2003 to protest a proposed national security law, and the government was forced to withdraw the proposal. In democratic Montreal, more than a half million people took to the streets in 2012 to protest a plan to increase university fees, and the government could divert political pressure with the argument that the people should wait till the elections to enact change.

105. Hayes, *Twilight of the Elites*, pp. 60–62.

106. Richard G. Wilkinson, *The Impact of Inequality: How to Make Sick Societies Healthier* (New York: New Press, 2005). See also Richard G. Wilkinson and Kate Pickett, *The Spirit Level: Why Equal Societies Almost Always Do Better* (London: Allen Lane, 2009).

107. Noah, *The Great Divergence*, ch. 11.

108. See the references in McCormick, *Machiavellian Democracy*, p. 171n10.

109. Ibid., p. 181.

110. "Going Swimmingly," *The Economist*, 23 Apr. 2011, p. 67.

111. Marie-Claire Bergère, *Chine: Le nouveau capitalisme d'État* (Paris: Fayard, 2013).

112. A wide-ranging survey of Chinese family wealth and living habits by Peking University estimated China's Gini coefficient to be .49 (still very high—the United States had a Gini coefficient of .45 in 2007—but lower than the .51 the United States had in 2010). Edward Wong, "Survey in China Shows Wide Income Gap," *New York Times*, 19 July 2013. Singapore's Gini coefficient worsened from .425 in 1998 to .478 in 2009. Lam Peng Er, "The Voters Speak: Voices, Choices and Implications," in *Voting in Change: Politics of Singapore's 2011 General Election*, ed. Kevin Y. L. Tan and Terence Lee (Singapore: Ethos Books, 2011), p. 186.

113. Martin King Whyte, "Soaring Income Gaps: China in Comparative Perspective," *Daedalus* 143, no. 2 (Spring 2014): 39–52.

114. Traditional Marxists, of course, would advocate not reform but revolution, that is, violent overthrow of the economic ruling class. But such voices are few and far between in both China and the United States.

115. I've developed this argument, drawing on the philosophy of Xunzi and supported with examples from East Asian societies, in my book *China's New Confucianism: Political Thinking for an East Asian Context* (Princeton, N.J.: Princeton University Press, 2008), ch. 3. For a similar argument with an example from American politics, see Jonathan Haidt, "Reasons Matter (When Intuitions Don't Object)," *New York Times*, 7 Oct. 2012.

116. Noah, *The Great Divergence*, p. 193.

117. Chrystia Freeland, "Superrich with Political Prowess," *New York Times*, 1 Mar. 2013. See also Daniel Goleman, "Rich People Just Care Less," *New York Times*, 5 Oct. 2013.

118. This is not to imply that CEOs of multinational corporations do not try to morally justify their lack of national allegiance or attachment to democracy: see my comment from Davos, http://www.huffingtonpost.com/daniel-a-bell/memo-from-davos_b_1232758.html.

119. Hacker and Pierson, *Winner-Take-All Politics*, pp. 83–86.

120. Of course, there are also vested interests in China, such as powerful state enterprises with economic interests that attempt to block reform. But China's leaders have successfully taken on such interests in the past—such as Jiang Zemin and Zhu Rongji's efforts to remove the military from business activities and fight protectionist resistance against China's bid to join the World Trade Organization—and the party leadership unveiled a plan to embark on an ambitious project of market-based reform designed to tackle vested interests at the Third Plenum in November 2013 (only time will tell if the plan will succeed).

121. Needless to say, political leaders dispatched to disadvantaged regions should be sent for limited terms, unlike during the Cultural Revolution, when "sent-down youths" had no hope of return and often became demoralized and alienated.

122. Other groups of nonvoters are affected by the policies of the voting community, such as animals and ancestors. Since humans often abuse animals for their own needs, Sue Donaldson and Will Kymlicka argue for the need to appoint special legislators with the task of arguing on behalf of animals' interests. Donaldson and Kym-

licka, *Zoopolis: A Political Theory of Animal Rights* (Oxford: Oxford University Press, 2011). In ancient China, the dead were considered at least as important as the living, and an important part of political activity involved ceremonies connected with ancestor worship. Ch'ien Mu, *Traditional Government in Imperial China: A Critical Analysis*, trans. Chu-tu Hsueh and George O. Totten (Hong Kong: Chinese University Press, 1982), p. 7. The same is true in parts of sub-Saharan Africa today: see John Mbiti, "'Ancestors' (Ancestral Spirits) as Aspects of African Ontology and Genealogy," paper presented at the Chinese/African Philosophy Colloquium, Shanghai Jiaotong University, 10–12 May 2013. In the case of China, Jiang Qing argues for a government agency with the special task of maintaining cultural continuity of a nation's traditions that can serve, at least partly, to ensure representation for dead ancestors. Jiang, *A Confucian Constitutional Order: How China's Ancient Past Can Shape Its Political Future*, ed. Daniel A. Bell and Fan Ruiping; trans. Edmund Ryden (Princeton, N.J.: Princeton University Press, 2012), ch. 1.

123. For a more detailed argument along the same lines, see Mathias Risse, *On Global Justice* (Princeton, N.J.: Princeton University Press, 2012), ch. 17. In the contemporary East Asian context, Cho Il Yun argues that incomplete democratic consolidation, combined with the political salience of national identity, sparked a process of intergroup competition among domestic political actors, through which the foreign policy orientation of the three East Asian democracies (Taiwan, Japan, and South Korea) became belligerent, thereby unnecessarily increasing regional tensions. Cho, "Democratic Instability: Democratic Consolidation, National Identity and Security Dynamics in East Asia," *Foreign Policy Analysis* 8, no. 2 (Apr. 2012): 191–213.

124. Darius Rejali, *Torture and Democracy* (Princeton, N.J.: Princeton University Press, 2007), pp. 45, 3, 56, 46, 57. Surprisingly, Thomas Christiano's otherwise comprehensive review article of empirical results showing that there is a negative relationship between democracy and the violation of rights of personal integrity (including the right not to be tortured) at the domestic level does not even mention the possibility that such an optimistic finding can be (at least partly) explained by the fact that democracies carry out their dirty work against noncitizens and outsource torture to other countries. See Christiano, "An Instrumental Argument for a Human Right to Democracy," sec. III.

125. For details, see my book *Beyond Liberal Democracy*, ch. 11.

126. Anne Loveband, "Positioning the Product: Indonesian Migrant Women Workers in Contemporary Taiwan," Working Papers Series, no. 43, City University of University of Hong Kong, Apr. 2003, p. 3.

127. Christian Joppke (noting the findings of Virginia Guiraudon), "The Evolution of Alien Rights in the United States, Germany, and the European Union," in *Citizenship Today*, ed. T. Alexander Aleinikoff and Douglas Klusmeyer (Washington, D.C.: Carnegie Endowment for International Peace, 2001), p. 56.

128. Berggruen and Gardels, *Intelligent Governance for the 21st Century*, p. 9. See also Fareed Zakaria, "Can America Be Fixed? The New Crisis of Democracy," *Foreign Affairs* 92, no. 1 (Jan./Feb. 2013): 22–33.

129. Nikos Konstandaras, "The Kindness of Strangers," *New York Times*, 28 Apr. 2010. In Greece, "the first thing a government does in an election year is to pull the tax collectors off the streets." Cited in Michael Lewis, *Boomerang: The Biggest Bust* (London: Penguin, 2011), p. 49.

130. On the dangers to future generations posed by an unaffordable security system in the United States, see Thomas L. Friedman, "Sorry, Kids. We Ate It All," *New York Times*, 15 Oct. 2013. Public pension obligations also pose serious threats to cities, including wealthy cities such as San Jose, California. See Allysia Finley, "A Liberal Mugged by Pension Reality," *Wall Street Journal*, 2 Dec. 2013.

131. Tim Mulgan, *Ethics for a Broken World: Imagining Philosophy after Catastrophe* (Montreal: McGill–Queen's University Press, 2011), p. 213. See also Runciman, *The Confidence Trap*, pp. 313–318.

132. See Julia Baird, "Australia's Politics of Global Warming," *New York Times*, 15 Nov. 2013.

133. Mulgan, *Ethics for a Broken World*, p. 217. See also Philippe Schmitter, "Further Thoughts on Political Strategies for Sustainable Development" (unpublished manuscript).

134. Hungary did establish the institution of an ombudsman for future generations in 2007 that looked relatively powerful on paper, but it has had very limited impact and its powers were watered down by a populist government in 2012 (http://mosur.czp.cuni.cz/images/2013/Converge/Converge-POSTER-JNO_3.pdf). Even Norway—the most harmonious society in the world (see appendix 1 at http://press.princeton.edu/titles/10418.html)—has resisted such proposals. Dag Hariede, director of the Norwegian Humanistic Academy and former leader of the biggest environmental organization in Norway, proposed an institution with the task of advising democratically elected politicians about the likely impact of policies on future generations, but this proposal—for an advisory body!—has not been supported by any of Norway's major political parties.

135. One objection to such proposals is that it is extremely difficult to claim that we can know what future people would want. But as the 2013 United Nations report on "Intergenerational Solidarity and the Needs of Future Generations" puts it, "a broader agreement exists . . . that there are some basic rights (to life, health, subsistence, peace, etc.) that would be relevant and important to people as biological human beings at any time in the future, and that these rights should be protected by the present generation insofar as it has the power to do so" (http://sustainabledevelopment.un.org/content/documents/2006future.pdf, article 22). We can assume without much controversy that people in Bangladesh do not want to be impoverished or driven to civil war as a result of massive flooding caused by global warming.

136. Huang Zongxi, *Waiting for the Dawn: A Plan for the Prince*, trans. Wm. Theodore de Bary (New York: Columbia University Press, 1993), p. 83.

137. The contemporary Confucian thinker Jiang Qing has advocated reviving this practice in contemporary China: see Daniel A. Bell and Avner de-Shalit, *The Spirit of*

Cities: Why the Identity of a City Matters in a Global Age (Princeton, N.J.: Princeton University Press, 2011), p. 160.

138. Huang, *Waiting for the Dawn*, p. 113.

139. I have modified a proposal put forward in my book *Beyond Liberal Democracy*, ch. 6. For a similar proposal, see Sheng Hong, *Jingjixue jingshen* [The Spirit of Economics] (Guangzhou: Guangdong Jingji, 1999), pp. 143–144. See also the proposals discussed in chapter 4, section 2.

140. Singapore Constitution, art. 19(2)(g)(iv).

141. See Kevin Tan and Lam Peng Er, eds., *Managing Political Change in Singapore: The Elected Presidency* (London: Routledge, 1997).

142. See Chandran Nair, *Consumptionomics: Asia's Role in Reshaping Capitalism and Saving the Planet* (Oxford: Infinite Ideas Limited, 2011).

143. Richard Stone, "Climate Talks Still at Impasse, China Buffs Its Green Reputation," *Science*, 15 Oct. 2010, p. 305. But Bill Dodson argues that China's central planning approach to implementing alternative energy sources led to overcapacity issues across the sector. Dodson, *China Fast Forward: The Technologies, Green Industries and Innovations Driving the Mainland's Future* (Singapore: John Wiley & Sons, 2012), ch. 7.

144. Juan Cole, "China Installed More Solar Power in 2013 Than the US Has in Its Whole History," *Informed Consent*, 25 Jan. 2014. See also J. Matthew Roney, "China Leads World to Solar Power Record in 2013," *Earth Policy Institute*, 18 June 2014.

145. Of course, more can be done: for policy suggestions on improving China's electric vehicle policy, see Wang Tao, "Recharging China's Electric Vehicle Policy," Carnegie–Tsinghua Center for Global Policy, 2013.

146. "China Province Plans Huge Carbon Market," *New York Times*, 28 Nov. 2013; Dodson, *China Fast Forward*, pp. 159–160; Dirk Forrister and Paul Bledsoe, "Pollution Economics," *New York Times*, 9 Aug. 2013. For as yet unrealized suggestions, see the *China Greentech Report 2013: China at a Crossroads* (http://www.report.china-greentech.com).

147. Pang Chao, "Ji daqi wuran fangzhi mubiao zerenshu, PM2.5 kongzhi cheng yueshuxing zhibiao" [The Hebei Government Signed the Air Pollution Control Responsibility Contract; PM2.5 Control Has Become an Obligatory Target], *Xinhuanet News*, 29 Sept. 2013. See also "Chinese Shift: Put the Environment above GDP Growth," *World Post*, 22 Feb. 2014.

148. Jørgen Delman, "Fragmented Authoritarianism and Climate Change Politics at the City Level in China: Post-corporatism by Design or Default?" (unpublished manuscript).

149. Leslie Hook and Pilita Clark, "China Weighs Cap on Carbon Emissions," *Financial Times*, 28 May 2013. Jørgen Delman argues that China played a constructive role at the Copenhagen Climate Summit in 2009 ("China's 'Radicalism at the Center': Regime Legitimation through Climate Politics and Climate Governance,"

Journal of Chinese Political Science 16, no. 2 [June 2011]: 183–205), which provides a reason to expect more constructive contributions in the future.

150. Cited in Elizabeth Rosenthal and Andrew W. Lehren, "Carbon Credits Gone Awry Raise Output of Harmful Gas," *New York Times*, 8 Aug. 2012. In April 2014, the government adopted sweeping changes to the country's environmental laws that give authorities stronger enforcement powers against polluting companies, authorize detention of negligent executives, provide protection for whistleblowers, and set penalties for officials who fail to enforce laws. Benjamin van Rooij and Alex Wang, "China's Pollution Challenge," *New York Times*, 20 May 2014; "Green Teeth," *The Economist*, 17 May 2014.

151. "Browner, but Greener," *The Economist*, 1 Feb. 2014 (referring to the Environmental Performance Index, a joint product of Yale and Columbia universities, http://epi.yale.edu/epi); Kelly Sims Gallagher and Qi Ye, "Climate and Clean Energy," in *Debating China: The U.S.–China Relationship in Ten Conversations*, ed. Nina Hadigan (Oxford: Oxford University Press, 2014), esp. pp. 117–122.

152. See Joy Y. Zhang and Michael Barr, *Green Politics in China: Environmental Governance and State–Society Relations* (London: Pluto Press, 2013).

153. Edward Wong, "China's Climate Plans Raise Many Questions," *New York Times*, 13 Nov. 2014.

154. Even without the presidency, Republicans can sabotage the deal: "Mitch McConnell has already said that he will use his new powers as majority leader in 2015 to launch a full-scale attack on the EPA rules on power-plant pollution—if that attack is successful, it would be all but impossible for the U.S. to meet its carbon-reduction commitment." Jeff Goodell, "The Secret Deal to Save the Planet," *Rolling Stone*, 9 Dec. 2014, http://www.rollingstone.com/politics/news/the-secret-deal-to-save-the-planet-20141209?page=4.

155. Stefan Wurster compares democracies and autocracies in terms of strong ecological sustainability and concludes that "democracies display significant deficits . . . in overcoming long-term environmental problems for which there are no cheap technical solutions, but which must be rectified by means of fundamental changes in lifestyles and economy. As the empirical analysis shows, most democracies have difficulties in including future interest into their current decision-making processes (because of the short-lived political timeframe), despite their stable institutional framework and their measures protecting against the degeneration of power. In addition, their steering ability does not often seem sufficient to overcome current stakeholder interests that resist moves towards strong ecological sustainability." Wurster, "Comparing Ecological Sustainability in Autocracies and Democracies," *Contemporary Politics* 19, no. 1 (2013): 89. Wurster also concludes that "the performance results for strong sustainability do not provide any evidence for the general superiority of autocratic regimes," but he does not distinguish between meritocratic and nonmeritocratic "autocratic" regimes. Perhaps a comparison of meritocratic and democratic regimes at similar levels of economic development would show that meritocratic regimes do better in terms of strong sustainability.

156. Cited in Kwasi Wiredu, "Democracy by Consensus: Some Conceptual Considerations," *Philosophical Papers* 30, no. 3 (Nov. 2001): 228.

157. For an empirical study showing that competitive elections indirectly reduce voters' feelings of trust and efficacy, see Thomas L. Brunell, "Ideological Representation and Competitive Congressional Elections," *Electoral Studies* 28, no. 3 (Sept. 2009): 448–457.

158. See Albert H. Y. Chen, "Mediation, Litigation, and Justice: Confucian Reflections in a Modern Liberal Society," in *Confucianism for the Modern World*, ed. Daniel A. Bell and Hahm Chaibong (Cambridge: Cambridge University Press, 2003), pp. 257–287. A recent report criticizes family law in Canada for the destructive effect of the adversarial system on couples who are vulnerable and prone to go on the attack, arguing that judges, lawyers, and law schools must embrace a culture of mediation and settlement. Kirk Makin, "Court Told to Overhaul Family Law," *Globe and Mail*, 27 Mar. 2013.

159. For example, the "constitutions" of some small-scale co-ops in New York City force residents to make decisions by means of voting rather than striving for consensus, which can needlessly poison relations (I testify here from personal experience).

160. This is not to imply that adherence to the value of harmony always, or even usually, prevented disharmonious social and political outcomes: ancient Chinese history was rife with divisiveness and bitter struggles (see, e.g., Ari Levine, *Divided by a Common Language: Factional Conflicts in Late Northern Song China* [Honolulu: University of Hawai'i Press, 2008]). As always, there was a gap between the ideal and reality, but the point is that the ideal of harmony sets a standard for evaluating political progress and regress.

161. See Wei Xiaohong and Li Qingyuan, "The Confucian Value of Harmony and Its Influence on Chinese Social interaction," *Cross-Cultural Communication* 9 (2013): 60–66. See also the empirical evidence cited in Thaddeus Metz, "Values in China as Compared to Africa: Two Conceptions of Harmony" (forthcoming).

162. Po-Keung Ip, "Harmony as Happiness? Social Harmony in Two Chinese Societies," *Social Indicators Research*, 117, no. 3 (2014), sec. 2.1.

163. Joseph Henrich, Steven J. Heine, and Ara Norenzayan, "The Weirdest People in the World?" *Behavioral and Brain Sciences* 33 (2010): 61–135.

164. To be more precise, there are parallels to the ideal of harmony in some Western countries—for example, the ideal of solidarity in Nordic countries and in France, and of communitarianism in North America—but they tend to be buried beneath individualistic understandings, especially in the U.S. case. See Robert Bellah, Richard Madsen, William Sullivan, and Ann Swidler, *Habits of the Heart* (Berkeley: University of California Press, 1985).

165. See appendix 1 at http://press.princeton.edu/titles/10418.html for a more detailed discussion.

166. As noted earlier, Xunzi also argued that we can improve morally through participation in common rituals and other forms of moral education.

167. Cummins, *Good Thinking*, pp. 75, 25. On the basis of studies that show that

we reward cooperation more generously and punish defection more severely than predicted by standard game-theoretic analyses, Cummins questions the assumptions of mainstream economic theory based on self-interest (p. 19). For more evidence from neuroscience in favor of Mencius's view of human nature, see Edward Slingerland, *Trying Not to Try: The Art and Science of Spontaneity* (New York: Crown, 2014), p. 117.

168. One study found that bonobos, among the primates most closely related to humans, will share their food with a stranger, and even give up their own meal, if the stranger offers them social interaction. "Observatory: Milk of Human Kindness Also Found in Bonobos," *New York Times*, 7 Jan. 2013. For a book-length argument that primates display other-regarding morality, see Frans de Waal, *The Bonobo and the Atheist: In Search of Humanism among the Primates* (New York: Norton, 2013). More anecdotally, pet owners will testify that dogs and cats can show empathetic behavior when the owner is ill.

169. Mencius, IA.7.

170. Martha C. Nussbaum, *Not for Profit: Why Democracy Needs the Humanities* (Princeton, N.J.: Princeton University Press, 2010), pp. 36, 43–44.

171. Ibid.

172. See, e.g., Amy Gutmann and Dennis Thompson, *Democracy and Disagreement* (Cambridge, Mass.: Harvard University Press, 1998).

173. Research shows that we need to be quiet and attentive if we want to tap into our deeper emotions such as empathy, but technologies such as the Internet constantly interrupt and distract us, hence dampening empathy and encouraging the immediate expression of whatever is on our minds, with the result that a lot of nastiness gets expressed that would not have been expressed before. Nicholas Carr, *The Shallows: What the Internet Is Doing to Our Brains* (New York: Norton, 2011).

174. Wiredu, "Democracy by Consensus," pp. 227–244.

175. Berrgruen and Gardels, *Intelligent Governance for the 21st Century*, p. 121.

176. Wiredu, "Democracy by Consensus," p. 243. Wiredu doesn't say this, but presumably open competition by political parties outside of this setting would be disallowed.

177. G.W.F. Hegel, *Elements of the Philosophy of Right*, trans. H. B. Nisbet (Cambridge: Cambridge University Press, 1991), sec. 303; see also sec. 308.

178. See the discussion in my book *East Meets West*, pp. 294–299.

179. A research report undertaken in 2006 found that 74.9 percent of the people surveyed perceived Chinese society as harmonious (cited in Ip, "Harmony as Happiness?" p. 733). According to the Harmony Index (see appendix 1 at http://press.princeton.edu/titles/10418.html), population size is the key factor limiting the possibility of establishing a harmonious society, but China is the least unharmonious among countries with a population of more than one hundred million people (unlike many other global indicators biased in favor of democracy by using the extent of democracy as a key measurement of well-being, the Harmony Index was deliberately designed so that political liberty in the form of one person, one vote is not heavily

weighted as a measurement of social harmony, the point being to allow for a less biased comparison of democracies and political meritocracies along the dimension of social harmony).

180. In the case of Taiwan, David C. Schak argues that democratization has given rise to more civility, especially other-regarding behavior toward strangers in public space. Schak, "The Development of Civility in Taiwan," *Pacific Affairs* 82, no. 3 (Fall 2009): 447–465. Schak argues, in a Mencian vein, that predemocratic governments did lay the foundation for civility "by overseeing the conditions which brought a rise from a poor to a prosperous, highly educated and sophisticated population in two generations" (p. 464). An issue not addressed in the article is whether nation-based democratization in Taiwan contributed to more nation-based civility based at least partly on increased hostility directed toward people outside the nation (especially mainland China).

181. See concluding thoughts.

182. Again, I focus on elections because Westerners tend to think they are necessary for selecting political leaders at all levels of government, but I do not mean to imply that people think electoral democracy is a sufficient condition for a well-functioning democratic regime (certainly, that "minimal" view of democracy is rejected by most political theorists). Moreover, the key political debate between "the West" and "China" takes place over the value of electoral democracy because other features of democracies said to enhance good policy making such as public consultation and deliberation are far less controversial in China, including in official circles.

Chapter 2
On the Selection of Good Leaders in a Political Meritocracy

1. Cited in *International Herald Tribune*, 9–10 Nov. 1991.

2. Cited in Barbara Crossette, "U.N. Survey Finds Rich-Poor Gap Widening," *New York Times*, 15 July 1996.

3. See, e.g., Joanne Bauer and Daniel A. Bell, eds., *The East Asian Challenge for Human Rights* (New York: Cambridge University Press, 1999).

4. See Kim Dae Jung, "Is Culture Destiny? The Myth of Asian's Anti-Democratic Values," *Foreign Affairs* 73, no. 6 (Nov./Dec. 1994).

5. The Singapore government does invoke the need for more positive virtues such as the willingness to serve, but there is no attempt to systematically measure and evaluate government officials according to such criteria. "Zhiding jizhi tigao zhengfu jigou chengxin" [Promulgate Mechanisms to Improve the Integrity of the Government], *Lianhe zaobao*, 2 Oct. 2013.

6. For discussion of Singapore's anticorruption strategy, see Jon S. T. Quah, *Combating Corruption Singapore-Style: Lessons for Other Asian Countries*, Maryland Series in Contemporary Asian Studies, no. 2 (Baltimore: School of Law, University of Maryland, 2007).

7. "'Compassionate Meritocracy' Key to Future," *New Paper*, 21 Aug. 2013.

8. Yuri Pines, "Between Merit and Pedigree: Evolution of the Concept of 'Elevating the Worthy' in Pre-imperial China," in *The East Asian Challenge for Democracy.*

9. Thomas Jefferson to John Adams, *The Founders' Constitution* (Chicago: University of Chicago Press, 2000), vol. 1, ch. 15, document 61 (http://press-pubs.uchicago.edu/founders/documents/v1ch15s61.html).

10. Similarly, such debates came to an end in South Korea since the adoption of electoral democracy in the form of one person, one vote: few if any articles or books (in either English or Korean) about political meritocracy in Korea have been published over the past three decades, notwithstanding the importance of political meritocracy in Korean political culture. Doh Chull Shin's book *Confucianism and Democratization in East Asia* discusses the topic but in the context of debates about democratization.

11. For discussion of the desirable qualities of various kinds of actors in the American political system—qualities meant above all to strengthen the democratic process—see Andrew Sabl, *Ruling Passions: Political Offices and Democratic Ethics* (Princeton, N.J.: Princeton University Press, 2002).

12. Wang Guoliang, "Rujia xianneng zhengzhi sixiang yu Zhongguo xianneng tuiju zhidu de fazhan" [The Political Theory of Confucian Meritocracy and the Development of a Meritocratic Recommendation System in China], *Wenshizhe* 3, no. 336 (2013): 24–31.

13. See Hong Xiao and Chenyang Li, "China's Meritocratic Examinations and the Ideal of Virtuous Talents," in *The East Asian Challenge for Democracy.* See also concluding thoughts.

14. John P. Burns and Wang Xiaoqi, "Civil Service Reform in China: Impacts on Civil Servants' Behavior," *China Quarterly* 201 (2010): 69, 76–77.

15. Sander A. Flaum and Jonathon A. Flaum, with Mechele Flaum, *The 100-Mile Walk: A Father and a Son Find the Essence of Leadership* (New York: American Management Association, 2006), p. 1.

16. George Yeo, "China and the Catholic Church," *The Globalist*, 1 Aug. 2013.

17. It is worth noting that the main point of George Yeo's article is to urge rapprochement between the two organizations.

18. St. Gregory the Great, *The Book of Pastoral Rule*, trans. George E. Demacopoulos (Crestwood, N.Y.: St. Vladimir's Seminary Press, 2007), p. 43.

19. Ibid., p. 74.

20. This is not meant to be a critique of George Yeo's role on a special commission to advise the Vatican (http://www.channelnewsasia.com/news/singapore/george-yeo-appointed-to/750222.html): his task is to advise in matters of administration and governance, not to serve as a leader of the Catholic Church concerned with spiritual formation of the flock.

21. John Glenn wrote a supportive foreword for the book on the grounds that it can "help inspire young people to get involved in public service leadership positions," on the apparent assumption that what works in business will also work in government.

22. "Interview with Jack Welch," *Piers Morgan Tonight*, CNN, 11 June 2011 (http://transcripts.cnn.com/TRANSCRIPTS/1106/11/pmt.01.html).

23. Sek-loong Tan, "Realizing Political Meritocracy: Lessons from Business," paper prepared for the Center for International and Comparative Political Philosophy, Tsinghua University, 20 July 2011. Sek-loong Tan is a business consultant who advises both private and public entities on governance issues.

24. See Gabriel Wildau, "Beijing Identifies SOEs for Reform Pilot," *Financial Times*, 16 July 2014; Richard Silk, Liyan Qi, and Grace Zhu, "Beijing Moves to Overhaul State Firms," *Wall Street Journal*, 16 July 2014.

25. "Will a New Round of Reforms Shake Up State Firms?" *Week in China* (HSBC weekly newsletter), 25 July 2014.

26. For an overview of how the (Central) Department of Organization selects and promotes cadres, see *Zhongguo xinwen zhoukan*, 8 Sept. 2014 (http://www.duwanjuan.cn/zhong_zu_bu_ru_he_xuan_guan_yuan). For a more cynical take, see Richard McGregor, *The Party: The Secret World of China's Communist Rulers* (London: Penguin, 2010), ch. 3.

27. As John Micklethwait and Adrian Wooldridge put it, "the bureaucrats who return from the SOEs know how to run things better. If state capitalism allows politicians to shape companies, it also allows companies to shape politicians." Micklethwait and Wooldridge, *The Fourth Revolution: The Global Race to Reinvent the State* (New York: Penguin, 2014), p. 152.

28. Paul Thomas, *Performance Measurement, Reporting, Obstacles and Accountability: Recent Trends and Future Directions* (Canberra: ANU E Press, 2006), pp. 1, 51–53, 55.

29. Ibid., pp. 9, 19.

30. Cited in Noel M. Tichy and Stratford Sherman, *Control Your Destiny or Someone Else Will* (New York: Random House, 1994), p. 105.

31. Jonathan Powell, *The New Machiavelli: How to Wield Power in the Modern World* (London: Vintage Books, 2010), p. 54.

32. Flaum and Flaum, *The 100-Mile Walk*, pp. 41, 42.

33. Ibid., p. 103.

34. Another reason that political leaders might need to be more compassionate than business leaders is that they can use—and hence misuse—the coercive apparatus of the state. If a political leader decides to "take out" the weak members of the political community, the implications are much more ominous.

35. Tan, "Realizing Political Meritocracy: Lessons from Business," p. 4.

36. I do not mean to imply that leaders of multinational corporations are indifferent to moral concerns, but they are more likely to appeal to universal moral considerations that trump the national good in cases of conflict (see http://www.huffingtonpost.com/daniel-a-bell/memo-from-davos_b_1232758.html).

37. Philippe Schmitter argues that political leaders in democratic societies have come to be viewed as living *off* politics rather than *for* politics, thus contributing to a sharp decline in the prestige of and trust in politicians. See Schmitter, "Reflections

on Political Meritocracy: Its Manipulation and Transformation," in *The East Asian Challenge for Democracy*.

38. All quotations are from the English translation of Weber's lecture: http://anthropos-lab.net/wp/wp-content/uploads/2011/12/Weber-Politics-as-a-Vocation.pdf. I stick to male pronouns here because Weber probably had male politicians in mind.

39. Similarly, it is a mistake to think that all business organizations require the same types of leaders. Even within the same industry, different companies have different cultures and histories that require different abilities. For example, star analysts who switch from one Wall Street investment bank to another often suffer an immediate and lasting decline in performance because their earlier excellence depended heavily on their former firms' organizational cultures and networks. Boris Groysberg, *Chasing Stars: The Myth of Talent and the Portability of Performance* (Princeton, N.J.: Princeton University Press, 2010).

40. In Singapore, the distinction is not so rigid: for example, the Civil Service College has the task (among others) to prepare reports that provide new ideas and influence policies; it is not meant simply to train civil servants who implement policies. Also, leading civil servants in Singapore often go into politics, which is rarely the case in the United Kingdom and Canada. That said, the Singaporean government is considering drawing a sharper distinction between the civil service and politics by, e.g., imposing a waiting period before civil servants can be given political appointments. (I am grateful for discussions with officials at Singapore's Civil Service College.)

41. Chen Guoping, "Mingdai guanyuan kaohe zhidu shulun" [On the Assessment System of Public Officials in the Ming Dynasty], *Zhongguo zhengfayuan xuebao* 1 (1993): 92–96.

42. *Zhongyang jiguan jiqi zhishu jigou 2013 niandu kaoshi luyong gongwuyuan gonggong kemu kaoshi dagang* [2013 National Public Service Examination Syllabus for Central-Level Organs and Direct Subordinate Organizations], available at http://bm.scs.gov.cn/2013/UserControl/download/2013zkjz.rar.

43. *Dangzheng lingdao ganbu xuanba renyong tiaoli* [Regulations on the Selection and Appointment of Cadres of the CCP], 2014-1-15, 8.4, available at http://news.xinhuanet.com/politics/2014-01/15/c_118985244.htm.

44. For discussion of the qualities required of the democratic leader, see John Kane and Haig Patapan, *The Democratic Leader: How Democracy Defines, Empowers, and Limits Its Leaders* (New York: Oxford University Press, 2012). Note, however, that there are important differences between presidential and parliamentary systems: in a parliamentary system, the prime minister can lose the post if she or he loses the support of her/his party, and hence faces more pressure to conform to party discipline. Commenting on the Canadian case, Michael Ignatieff writes: "Where it [democracy] isn't so healthy is in the place that should be the very temple of our democracy, the House of Commons. I can't remember a speech I heard in five years that was actually meant to persuade, though I heard dozens that faithfully recited party talking points" (Ignatieff, *Fire and Ashes: Success and Failure in Politics* [Cambridge, Mass.: Harvard University Press, 2013], pp. 95–96; see also p. 134). That said, even some presidential

candidates speak openly about retaining partisan biases if elected as leaders of the state—e.g., Turkish presidential candidate Recep Tayyip Erdoğan said, "I will not be an impartial president" (*Daily News,* 9 July 2014).

45. For example, poverty reduction was the overriding goal in the early days of economic reform, and now more attention is paid to distributive issues and environmental sustainability, although China's poorer regions still emphasize poverty reduction as the key priority.

46. Pines, "Between Merit and Pedigree."

47. Again, I have upper levels of government in mind as the relevant context. At lower levels, physical strength still matters, as I was reminded recently when I visited a village north of Beijing and the (physically imposing) party secretary had to literally force himself into a home to break up a fight. Such considerations also help to explain why there may be more open discrimination against female cadres at the local level.

48. Joshua Cooper Ramo, *The Age of the Unthinkable: Why the New World Disorder Constantly Surprises Us* (New York: Back Bay Books, 2009).

49. See *Global Risks 2012*, 7th ed. (Geneva: World Economic Forum, 2012).

50. Cited in Benjamin Wong and Xunming Huang, "Political Legitimacy in Singapore," *Politics and Policy* 38, no. 3 (2010): 523–543.

51. To be more precise, Zhu Xi condemned examinations because they encourage an instrumental approach to learning, but he said that 30 percent of time can be given to study for examinations. Chu Hsi, *Learning to Be a Sage*, trans. Daniel K. Gardner (Berkeley: University of California Press, 1990), p. 19. See also Hilde de Weerdt, *Competition over Content: Negotiating Standards for the Civil Service Examinations in Imperial China (1127–1279)* (Cambridge, Mass.: Harvard University Asia Center, 2007), p. 385.

52. This paragraph draws on an email sent by Yuri Pines. See also Dennis Graffin, "Reinventing China: Pseudobureaucracy in the Early Southern Dynasties," in *State and Society in Early Medieval China*, ed. Albert Dien (Stanford, Calif.: Stanford University Press, 1990), pp. 139–170, esp. pp. 145–155.

53. Benjamin Elman, *A Cultural History of Civil Examinations in Late Imperial China* (Berkeley: University of California Press, 2000), p. 7. On examinations under the Tang, see also Penelope A. Herbert, *Examine the Honest, Appraise the Able: Contemporary Assessments of Civil Service Selection in Early T'ang China* (Canberra: Faculty of Asian Studies, Australian National University Press, 1988).

54. In the thirteen-hundred-year history of imperial examinations from the Sui dynasty onward, the Song dynasty practice of directly appointing successful examination candidates to government posts is an exception to the rule that examination success needed to be followed by other tests and evaluations, but even a top score in the national-level examinations (*jinshi*) in the Song did not guarantee a good career because it was tacitly assumed that the literary skills of successful examinees did not automatically translate into the qualities required of top government officials.

55. John W. Chaffee, *The Thorny Gates of Learning in Sung China*, new ed. (Albany: State University of New York Press, 1995), p. xxii.

56. Benjamin A. Elman, "A Society in Motion: Unexpected Consequences of Political Meritocracy in Late Imperial China, 1400–1900," in *The East Asian Challenge for Democracy*.

57. Japan also used the Chinese imperial examination system as a model in the Heian period (794–1185), but the influence affected only the minor nobility and was replaced by the hereditary system during the Samurai era. Liu Haifeng, "Influence of China's Imperial Examinations on Japan, Korea, and Vietnam," *Frontiers of Philosophy in China* 2, no. 4 (Oct. 2007): 493–512.

58. See, e.g., Lawrence Lok Cheung Zhang, "Power for a Price: Office Purchase, Elite Families, and Status Maintenance in Qing China," PhD dissertation, Harvard University, 2010. Zhang shows that about 25 percent of the time people gained access to official positions by paying for it (even when they already had examination degrees), and this figure rose substantially toward the end of the dynasty, resulting in a debasement of the examination degree and contributing to wider political destabilization toward the end of the Qing period.

59. Alexander Woodside, *Lost Modernities: China, Vietnam, Korea, and the Hazards of World History* (Cambridge, Mass.: Harvard University Press, 2006), pp. 10–11.

60. Liu Haifeng, "Kejuzhi yu xianneng zhiguo chuantong" [The Imperial Examination System and the Tradition of Building a Meritocratic State], paper presented at conference "Quanguo zhengzhi ruxue he xiandai shijie taolun" [Political Confucianism and Its Contemporary Significance in China and the World], Tsinghua University, 27–28 Oct. 2012; Liu Haifeng, "Kejuzhi dui xifang kaoshi zhidu yingxiang xintan" [A New Exploration of the Influence of the Imperial Examination System on Western Examination Systems], *Zhongguo shehui kexue* 5 (2001): 188–208.

61. Again, there was no distinction between civil servants and political officials in imperial China. Hence, I use the term *imperial examinations* to translate *keju*. The usual translation in English—"civil examinations"—makes sense to experts in Chinese imperial history because "civil examinations" is meant to contrast with "military examinations " that were held to recruit army officers, but for most (Anglophone) readers *civil* brings up the misleading connotation of a civil servant who is supposed to implement the policies of political officials. For a similar point, see Bai Tongdong, *China: The Political Philosophy of the Middle Kingdom* (London: Zed Books, 2012), p. 167. For the same reason, I do not use the term *bureaucracy* to characterize imperial China's political system, because it connotes the idea of specialized bureaucrats who implement the decisions of political officials. It is true, as Francis Fukuyama notes, that China's political system shared some features of modern bureaucracy identified by Max Weber, such as the practice of impersonally selecting candidates on the basis of qualifications and salaried offices treated as careers (Fukuyama, *The Origins of Political Order: From Prehuman Times to the French Revolution* [New York: Farrar, Straus, and Giroux, 2011], p. 134), but it also differed in important ways: starting from the Song dynasty, the successful national examinations candidates were generalists (the top *jinshi* degree holders all held one degree, whereas previously there had been various degrees in different subjects), not specialists who held offices defined by func-

tional area with a clearly defined area of competence (the Song did continue multiple examination systems below the national level, but the *jinshi* had preferential access to the top offices and hence were more prestigious than other exams), and they often had the political power to exercise authority in a wide range of affairs (they were subject in principle to the authority of the monarch, but the monarch, if only for reasons of lack of time, more often than not reigned rather than ruled; see Yuri Pines, *The Everlasting Empire: The Political Culture of Ancient China and Its Imperial Legacy* [Princeton, N.J.: Princeton University Press, 2012], ch. 2).

62. Cited in Chaffee, *The Thorny Gates of Learning in Sung China*, p. 49.

63. Elman, *A Cultural History of Civil Examinations in Late Imperial China*, p. 14.

64. Cited from Chaffee, *The Thorny Gates of Learning in Sung China*, p. 99.

65. Xiao and Li, "China's Meritocratic Examinations and the Ideal of Virtuous Talents," p. 343.

66. It could be argued that the Ottoman administrative system "was a model of meritocracy" and provided even more social mobility than the Chinese imperial examination system because slaves taken in the child levy from the empire's Christian subjects—the main source of recruitment into imperial service between the fourteenth and late sixteenth centuries—"had been selected for their physical grace, strength, and intelligence. During their training they underwent constant scrutiny. Only the most qualified were sent on to schools where they were trained to be officials and generals." Justin McCarthy, *The Ottoman Turks* (London: Longman, 1997), p. 126; see also Colin Imber, *The Ottoman Empire*, 2nd ed. (Houndmills: Palgrave Macmillan, 2009), esp. ch. 3. The "continual ability to draw the best men" may help to explain the longevity of the Ottoman Empire (Karen Barkey, *Empire of Difference: The Ottomans in Comparative Perspective* [Cambridge: Cambridge University Press, 2008], p. 19), but slavery should (needless to say) not be viewed as a morally desirable starting point when comparing social mobility in different meritocratic bureaucracies. Another important difference with imperial China is that physical abilities were given extra weight in the Ottoman administrative system because there was no clear distinction between civil government and military command (Imber, *The Ottoman Empire*, p. 330). And when late nineteenth-century Ottoman Empire reformers argued for more meritocracy and less nepotism, they proposed "recruitment based only on merit measured by objective and standardized examinations." Doğan Gürpinar, *Ottoman Imperial Diplomacy: A Political, Social and Cultural History* (London: I. B. Tauris, 2014), p. 90.

67. See Elman, "A Society in Motion." The archives indicate that peasants, traders, and artisans, who made up 90 percent of the population, were not among the fifty thousand Ming–Qing male palace graduates. Benjamin A. Elman, *Civil Examinations and Meritocracy in Late Imperial China* (Cambridge, Mass.: Harvard University Press, 2013), p. 320.

68. The second-tier universities offer more opportunities to students from poorer

backgrounds because they do not require high scores on the national university examinations.

69. Pines, *The Everlasting Empire*, pp. 113–114.

70. Elman, "A Society in Motion," p. 205.

71. Pines, *The Everlasting Empire*, p. 114.

72. For a list of uprisings led by examination failures, see Ichisada Miyazaki, *China's Examination Hell: The Civil Service Examinations of Imperial China*, trans. Conrad Schirokauer (New Haven, Conn.: Yale University Press, 1976), pp. 122–124. And the rebels did not always abandon the idea of examinations: the leader of the Taiping Rebellion Hong Xiuquan (who had repeatedly failed to become a licentiate) attempted to overthrow the Qing dynasty in the mid-nineteenth century but he also instituted an examination process. Elman, *Civil Examinations and Meritocracy in Late Imperial China*, pp. 302–305.

73. Miyazaki, *China's Examination Hell*, p. 127.

74. Elman, "A Society in Motion."

75. Cited from Pines, *The Everlasting Empire*, p. 51.

76. Confucian thinkers held similar views in imperial China: Song dynasty Neo-Confucians concluded that not a single emperor had met the appropriate moral standard, implying that the emperor and the court were not the final arbiters of how people should act and think. Peter K. Bol, *Neo-Confucianism in History* (Cambridge, Mass.: Harvard University Asia Center, 2008), pp. 129–130.

77. Cited from Pines, *The Everlasting Empire*, p. 52.

78. Xunzi argued that the ruler should select a chancellor whose task is to select other officials, but he still seemed to assume that one person could do all the work.

79. In fact, talented emperors felt disempowered by the system to their personal detriment: one famous case is the Ming emperor Wanli, who received an excellent Confucian education from the best tutors in the land, but once he realized that he was largely confined to symbolic duties (and literally confined to the Forbidden City), he become uncooperative and helped to bring about the end of the Ming dynasty. See Ray Huang, *1587, a Year of No Significance: The Ming Dynasty in Decline* (New Haven, Conn.: Yale University Press, 1981).

80. Elman, *A Cultural History of Civil Examinations in Late Imperial China*, pp. 173–238.

81. Cited from Chaffee, *The Thorny Gates of Learning in Sung China*, p. 79.

82. Cited in Jonathan D. Spence, *Return to Dragon Mountain: Memories of a Late Qing Man* (New York: Penguin, 2007), p. 51. See also Wu Jingzi, *The Scholars*, trans. Yang Xianyi and Gladys Yang (New York: Columbia University Press, 1992).

83. Adam Yuen-Chung Lui, "Syllabus of the Provincial Examination (Hsiang-shih) under the Early Ch'ing (1644–1795)," *Modern Asian Studies* (Cambridge University Press) 8, no. 3 (1974): 391–396.

84. For past examinations, see http://www.gjgwy.org/gwykszt/ (*Quanguo gongwuyuan kaoshi wang* [National Public Service Examinations Network]). The third

and fourth parts of the *xingzheng nengli ceshi* [Administrative Ability Test] test math and reasoning abilities, similar to IQ tests.

85. That said, lower-level governments in the 1990s were authorized to provide public service employment for demobilized soldiers without going through a competitive selection process. Burns and Xiaoqi, "Civil Service Reform in China," pp. 67–68. But such public servants are unlikely to be promoted without participating in a competitive selection process.

86. Arguably, some political leaders who are perceived to be relatively successful, such as Ronald Reagan, would not have made the cut on such exams. Any system has flaws, and the benefits of filtering out those who lack good analytical skills and the ability to think about policy questions from diverse perspectives may be worth the cost.

87. The dissertation test (*shenlun*), especially the analytical writing part, requires thoughtful analysis.

88. See Philip E. Tetlock, *Expert Political Judgment: How Good Is It? How Can We Know?* (Princeton, N.J.: Princeton University Press, 2005), p. 2; and Michael C. Horowitz and Philip E. Tetlock, "Trending Upward: How the Intelligence Community Can Better See into the Future," *Foreign Policy*, 6 Sept. 2012.

89. Given that so much scientific and academic material is written in English, perhaps exams should also test for reading knowledge of English. On the other hand, advisors of top political leaders can translate and provide summaries of key articles and books.

90. The Song dynasty thinker Ye Shi advocated "utilitarian" knowledge, with emphasis on historical analysis of institutions in order to learn from past failures. Dieter Kuhn, *The Age of Confucian Rule: The Song Transformation of China* (Cambridge, Mass.: Harvard University Press, 2009), p. 105.

91. Yudhijit Bhattacharjee, "Why Bilinguals Are Smarter," *New York Times*, 17 Mar. 2012.

92. I do not mean to imply that only Confucian classics offer insights into what ought to be the good qualities of leaders: the texts of Legalists, for example, offer relevant insights for times of warfare and Marxist classics may also be useful in the sense that they offer insights into the workings of capitalist economies that can be helpful for political leaders. Moreover, it may be necessary to revise what counts as a classic for political purposes in order to deemphasize works that easily lend themselves to misuses similar to, say, the Kangxi emperor's use of Yijing divination to make decisions on matters relating to punishment and foreign policy. See Richard J. Smith, *The I Ching: A Biography* (Princeton, N.J.: Princeton University Press, 2012), pp. 114–120. My argument is that there should be more systematic testing of the Confucian classics with historical and normative lessons for rulers today, not that testing should be confined to them.

93. One way to minimize controversy would be to select examiners for high-level political positions by means of random selection from among university professors in various disciplines.

94. One reason the examination system as a method for the selection of political talent has been underresearched is that political science departments in Western societies have focused so much energy on researching democratic elections. Greater awareness of the need to research mechanisms of political meritocracy in China (along with more funding for research of China-specific issues) should help to remedy the situation.

95. Still, it is important to keep in mind that what separates the few at the top from those directly below depends on luck more than anything else. (I make this point because Chinese media often seem to make a fetish of the top performers—see, e.g., the cover of the *Bejing qingnian bao*, 24 June 2014, with the photos and brief bios of those who scored highest on the university entrance examinations in Beijing.) Moreover, I would surmise that students at top universities such as Peking University and Tsinghua University often end up with more higher-level jobs than, say, students from Shandong University who scored a tiny fraction lower on the university entrance examinations, because of the increased opportunities and social networking offered to students at top universities rather than superior intellectual ability.

96. For a similar point, see Ignatieff, *Fire and Ashes*, pp. 170–171.

97. Tan, "Meritocracy and Political Liberalization in Singapore." See also chapter 1, section 1.

98. Roy Jenkins made the same remark about Tony Blair, another relatively successful politician according to the judgment of Jonathan Powell, Blair's chief of staff from 1994 to 2007. See Powell, *The New Machiavelli*, p. 32.

99. Bill Clinton, "The Legacy of FDR," *Time*, 24 June 2009 (http://content.time.com/time/specials/packages/article/0,28804,1906802_1906838_1906981,00.html). Similarly, Sander A. Flaum writes, "Among the people I would call true leaders . . . there is consensus that when it comes to people, you need to recruit, develop, and reward people who are as smart or smarter than you are. And I would add that you have to accept their pushback and have the courage to push back at them in order to help them be more than they imagined they ever could be" (*The 100 Mile-Walk*, pp. 24–25).

100. Lee delegated much of the policy-oriented thinking to brilliant advisors such as Goh Keng Swee, who is often referred to as the architect of Singapore's economic and social success. See Tilak Doshi and Peter Coclanis, "The Economic Architect: Goh Keng Swee," and Kian-Woon Kwok, "The Social Architect: Goh Keng Swee," both in Peng Er Lam and Kevin Tan, eds., *Lee's Lieutenants: Singapore's Old Guard* (St. Leonards, N.S.W.: Allen & Unwin, 1999). My wife worked for a Singaporean think tank headed by Goh Keng Swee in the early 1990s, and I can personally testify to his brilliance. Even after Goh's retirement from politics, Lee Kuan Yew met him once a week to bounce ideas off him.

101. Daniel Goleman, "What Makes a Leader?" in *On Leadership* (Boston: Harvard Business Review Press, 2011), pp. 1, 3, 17. See also Daniel Goleman, Richard Boyatzis, and Annie McKee, *Primal Leadership: Realizing the Power of Emotional Intelligence* (Boston: Harvard Business School Press, 2002).

102. Here I use the term *social skills* more broadly to refer to what Goleman calls "emotional intelligence."

103. A recent study found that people performed better on tests measuring empathy, social perception, and emotional intelligence after reading literary fiction (David Comer Kidd and Emanuele Castano, "Reading Literary Fiction Improves Theory of Mind," *Science*, 18 Oct. 2013, pp. 377–380), which may be a case for testing for knowledge of literary fiction on public service exams.

104. At a minimum, knowledge of another language is necessary to communicate with members of the minority groups who may not be fluent in the national language: hence, candidates for public service in Xinjiang are now required to be bilingual. "Xinjiang Government Job Candidates Required to Be Bilingual," *Xinhua*, 1 May 2010.

105. Robert Goffee and Gareth Jones, "Why Should Anyone Be Led by You?" in *On Leadership*, p. 85.

106. I do not mean to deny that good performance may also be indicative of other qualities required of good leaders in a modernizing and largely peaceful political meritocracy, such as intellectual ability and virtue, but perhaps the link is clearer in the case of emotional intelligence, which is necessary to effectively cooperate with people and hence get things done.

107. Qian Mu, *Guoshi xinlun* [New Studies of Chinese History] (Taipei: Dongda Publishing, 2004), p. 249. Qian does not emphasize the downside: local magnates hijacked the dynasty and caused the severest systemic crisis of imperial rule in its history.

108. Again, the norm in Chinese imperial history, with the exception of *jinshi* examinations in the Song dynasty, is that examination success needed to be followed by further evaluations for promotion to high government posts.

109. I say "relatively straightforward" because even good performance in business is not so clear. For example, an investment bank like Goldman Sachs tends to distribute its highest rewards to bankers and traders who contribute in measurable ways to the profitability of the firm, as one would expect. But its employees within the "Federation"—lawyers, accountants, and others who perform supportive but necessary functions for the bank—are rewarded on less tangible criteria, such as the ability to manage people in harmonious ways.

110. Hongbin Li and Li-An Zhou, "Political Turnover and Economic Performance: The Incentive Role of Personnel Control in China," *Journal of Public Economics* 89 (2005): 1743–1762. This article concludes that the likelihood of promotion of provincial leaders increases with their economic performance, hence supporting "the hypothesis that the Chinese economy is run in such a way that provincial leaders act like middle managers of a large corporation" (pp. 1760–1761).

111. On the causal link between the promotion mechanism for officials mainly based on economic growth and the outcome of economic growth, see Qiao Kunyuan, "Wo guo guanyuan jinsheng jinbiaosai jizhi de zai kaocha: Lai zi sheng, shi liang ji zhengfu de zhengju" [A Reexamination of the Mechanism for Competitive Promo-

tion in China: Evidence from Provincial and Municipal Governments," *Caijing yanjiu* 39, no. 4 (Apr. 2013): 123–133; Zhou Li'an, "Zhongguo difang guanyuan de jinsheng jinbiaosai moshi yanjiu" [Research on Model of Competitive Promotion of Local Chinese Officials], *Jingji yanjiu* 7 (2007): 36–50; and David J. Bulman, "Promotion-Based Incentives for Growth: Evidence from the County Level in Jiangsu and Anhui," paper presented at the Association for Asian Studies Annual Conference, San Diego, Mar. 2013.

112. http://www.globalissues.org/article/4/poverty-around-the-world#WorldBanksPovertyEstimatesRevised.

113. Ouyang Jing, "'Guanxi' ruhe, yuanhe yingxiang jiceng guanyuan jinsheng" [How Personal Relations Influence the Promotion of Grassroots Officials in a Differentiated Model Association], *Gansu xingzheng xueyuan xuebao* 1 (2012): 4–14. One can surmise that "drinking ability" (*jiuliang*) is a key mediating variable: good drinking ability is often viewed favorably by local officials (I can say from personal experience that local government officials often inquire about one's drinking ability at mealtime), which can improve relations with peers and superiors, which can, in turn, positively influence prospects for promotion. This hypothesis—admittedly hard to test—could also help to explain why men, on the (arguable) assumption that typically their drinking ability is superior to women's, find it easier to be get promoted at the local level. The discrimination affecting women at lower stages of their career does not continue once they reach the rank of mayor—see Pierre F. Landry, *Decentralized Authoritarianism in China: The Communist Party's Control of Local Elites in the Post-Mao Era* (Cambridge: Cambridge University Press, 2008), p. 108—perhaps (at least partly) because higher-ranking cadres do not have the time for long drinking sessions with colleagues.

114. See Victor Shih, Christopher Adolf, and Mingxing Liu, "Getting Ahead in the Communist Party: Explaining the Advancements of Central Committee Members in China," *American Political Science Review* 106 (Feb. 2012): 166–187; Ma Liang, "Guanyuan jinsheng jili yu zhengfu jixiao mubiao shezhi: Zhongguo shengji mianban shuju de shizheng yanjiu" [Promotion Incentives of Government Officials and Government Performance Target-Setting: An Empirical Analysis of Provincial Panel Data in China], *Gonggong guanli xuebao* 10, no. 2 (Apr. 2013): 28–39; and Ciqi Mei, "Bringing the Politics Back In: Political Incentives and Policy Distortion in China," PhD dissertation, University of Maryland, College Park, 2009, ch. 2, p. 83. At the very highest level, however—the Politburo Standing Committee—age and institutional rules had the greatest influence in deciding the appointment of leaders in 2012. Candidates' patron–client ties with senior leaders also played a role (but not always in a positive direction), and powerful family background either did not matter or had negative effects on the chances of being promoted to the highest level. Jinghan Zeng, "What Matters Most in Selecting Top Chinese Leaders," *Journal of Chinese Political Science* 18 (2013): 223–239. Moreover, the criteria for assessment of public officials tend to become more complex at higher levels—the case for the promotion of officials solely based on economic performance is even weaker at higher levels of govern-

ment—so it may not be a bad thing that promotion based on economic performance matters less at higher levels of government.

115. Russell Leigh Moses, "China's Big Challenge: Dissension in the Communist Party Ranks," *Wall Street Journal* (China real-time blog), 8 July 2014. That said, democratic societies with a Confucian heritage fare even worse: results of a large-scale survey of civil servants in seven countries show that 55.9 percent of respondents in mainland China agreed that their departments uphold merit principles in hiring as against only 35 percent in South Korea and 35.3 percent in Taiwan. Ora-orn Poocharoen and Alex Brillantes, "Meritocracy in Asia Pacific: Status, Issues, and Challenges," *Review of Public Personnel Administration* 33 (Apr. 2013): 148. The culture of *guanxi* (relations) rather than the political system is perhaps a key underlying factor explaining lapses from meritocracy in the government.

116. See John P. Burns, "The CCP's Nomenklatura System as a Leadership Selection System: An Evaluation," in *The Chinese Communist Party in Reform*, ed. Kjeld Erik Brodsgaard and Zheng Yongnian (London: Routledge, 2006), p. 39; and Landry, *Decentralized Authoritarianism in China*, esp. ch. 3 (on the promotion of mayors).

117. See, e.g., Tao Ran, Lu Xi, Su Fubing, and Wang Hui, "Diqu jingzheng geju yanbian xia de zhongguo zhuangui: Caizheng jili he fazhan moshi fansi" [China's Transition under Evolving Patterns of Regional Competition: Reflections on Financial Incentives and China's Development Model], *Jingji yanjiu* 7 (2009): 21–33.

118. "China to Curb Cars, Coal and Steel to Eliminate Heavily Polluted Days in Decade," *Star World*, 12 Sept. 2013.

119. Tan Haojun, "Zhongguo 'xincheng' bian 'kongcheng.' Pigu shui lai ca?" ["New City" Becomes "Empty City": Who Will Deal with It?], *Lianhe zaobao*, 13 Sept. 2013, p. 24. For a map of "ghost cities" in China, see http://english.caixin.com/2014-10-17/100739980.html.

120. Hou Zanhua, "Lun zhuanbian jingji fazhan fangshi de zhengzhi dongli—Ji yu difang zhengfu dongli queshi de shijiao" [An Analysis of the Political Motivation for the Transformation of Economic Development—from the Perspective of the Lack of Motivation in the Local Government], *Yunnan shehui kexue* 4 (2012): 61–65.

121. Alex Wang, "The Search for Sustainable Legitimacy: Environmental Law and Bureaucracy in China," *Harvard Environmental Law Review* 37 (2013): 365–440.

122. Qiao, "Wo guo guanyuan jinsheng jinbiaosai jizhi de zai kaocha: Lai zi sheng, shi liang ji zhengfu de zhengju" [A Reexamination of the Mechanism for Competitive Promotion in China: Evidence from Provincial and Municipal Governments], p. 132. Li Yonggang and Guan Yue suggest replacing "competing for higher GDP" with "competition for harmony" as the standard for rewarding public officials, but without specifying how to measure harmony. Li Yonggang and Guan Yue, "Difang guanyuan jingzheng de zhengzhi jinbiaosai moxing ji qi youhua" [The Model for Competitive Promotion of Local Officials and Its Optimization], *Jiangsu xingzheng xueyuanbao* 2, no. 56 (2011): 73–78. For ideas about how to measure harmony, see appendix 1 at http://press.princeton.edu/titles/10418.html.

123. Goleman, "What Makes a Leader?" p. 8. That said, culture may also matter:

in Japan, wise reasoning (what I call social skills), including taking into account the perspectives of others, recognizing that events can unfold in different ways, recognizing the limits of one's own knowledge, and searching for compromise, increased with age among Americans but not among Japanese (who scored at a high level regardless of their age). I. Grossman, M. Karasawa, S. Izumi, J. Na, M. Varnum, S. Kitayama, and R. Nisbett, "Aging and Wisdom: Culture Matters," *Psychological Science* 23, no. 10 (2012): 1059–1066.

124. Stephen S. Hall, *Wisdom: From Philosophy to Neuroscience* (New York: Vintage Books, 2010), pp. 228–229.

125. Cited in ibid., p. 255. For more evidence that men (in the case of this study) become emotionally attuned as they grow older, see also George E. Vaillant, *Triumphs of Experience: The Men of the Harvard Grant Study* (Cambridge, Mass.: Harvard University Press, 2012).

126. The implication that young people should be barred from high-level political posts does not sound so reactionary if one is reminded of the fanaticism of youth-led political movements, from German and Italian fascists to the Red Guards of the Cultural Revolution. Such youth movements may have been manipulated by more elderly political leaders, but they were often led by young people: as Walter Laqueur notes, "In 1933, Adolf Hitler was in his forties, but his closest followers were all very young: Joseph Goebbels was 36; Heinrich Himmler, head of the terror machine, was 33; his deputy, Reinhard Heydrich, 29, and Adolf Eichmann, the engineer of the Holocaust, a mere 27." Laqueur, "The Weimar Union: Europe, Back to the 30s," *New Republic*, 2 Aug. 2012, p. 16.

127. Hall, *Wisdom*, p. 228. Fluid intelligence, or the ability to solve novel, abstract problems that make relatively little use of real-world information, begins to decline in the early twenties and continues to decline thereafter (hence, mathematicians and others who work with symbolic, abstract materials for which they must invent novel solutions often do their best work before age thirty). Richard E. Nisbett, *Intelligence and How to Get It: Why Schools and Cultures Count* (New York: Norton, 2009), pp. 7–10. Bilingualism has been shown to postpone dementia by approximately five years (E. Bialystok, F.I.M. Craik, M.A. Binns, L. Ossher, and M. Freedman, "Effects of Bilingualism on the Age of Onset and Progression of MCI and AD: Evidence from Executive Function Tests," *Neuropsychology* 28, no. 2 [2014]: 290), so perhaps bilingual political leaders should be allowed to retire a few years later, other things being equal.

128. Arguably, the U.S. founding fathers also established a good model of setting age limits for political positions on the assumption that wisdom increases with age: according to the U.S. Constitution, a person must be at least thirty-five to be president or vice-president (given shorter life expectancy in the eighteenth century, the equivalent today would be about fifty), thirty to be a senator, and twenty-five to be a congressional representative. The principle that age requirements should increase with the importance of the political position is a good one, though I surmise it would be difficult to argue for such requirements in contemporary American society, given the dominance of a populist, anti-elitist ethos and the celebration of youthful ways of life.

129. Susan Shirk, "Age of China's New Leaders May Have Been Key to Their Selection," *China File*, 15 Nov. 2012.

130. Boris Groysberg and Katherine Connolly, "Great Leaders Who Make the Mix Work," *Harvard Business Review*, Sept. 2013, p. 72. Insights from brain research may help to explain gender differences in decision making: "Men's brains have approximately 6.5 times more gray matter than women's and women's brains have approximately 10 times more white matter than men's. Because gray matter characterizes information processing centers and white matter facilitates the connections among those centers, scientists theorize that those differences might explain why men tend to excel in tasks that depend on sheer processing while women show relative strength in tasks that call for assimilating and integrating disparate pieces of information. What's more, the cord connecting the left and right lobes is 10 percent thicker, on average, in female brains. And women have wider peripheral vision than men do." Cathy Benko and Bill Pelster, "How Women Decide," *Harvard Business Review*, Sept. 2013, p. 80.

131. Therese Huston, "Are Women Better Decision Makers?" *New York Times*, 17 Oct. 2014.

132. Zenger Folkman, "A Study in Leadership: Women Do It Better Than Men," 2012 (http://www.zfco.com/media/articles/ZFCo.WP.WomenBetterThanMen.033012.pdf). The study is discussed in "Women in the Workplace: A Research Roundup," *Harvard Business Review*, Sept. 2013, p. 89. See also Nicholas D. Kristof, "Twitter, Women and Power," *New York Times*, 25 Oct. 2013.

133. Quoted in Groysberg and Connolly, "Great Leaders Who Make the Mix Work," p. 73.

134. I do not know of any systematic comparisons of the performance of male and female political leaders, but studies in other fields bear on the question: Brad Barber and Terrance Odean gained access to the trading activity in more than thirty-five thousand households and found that men not only trade more than women but do so from a false faith in their own financial judgment (see Lewis, *Boomerang*, p. 37). Michael Lewis draws on this finding to note that "one of the distinctive traits of Iceland's [financial] disaster . . . is how little women had to do with it" (ibid.). In 2009, the nearly all-male Independence Party was voted out of power and replaced by the mostly female Social Democrats, led by Johanna Sigurdardottir, Iceland's first female prime minister and the world's first openly gay head of state (she is married to another woman).

135. Hu Shuli, "Changing Realities for Asian Women Leaders," *Global Asia* 6, no. 3 (Fall 2011): 17. Hu Shuli is the (female) editor-in-chief of the influential Caixin Media group, where more than 60 percent of the newsroom staff are women (ibid., p. 18). See also Frank N. Pieke, *The Good Communist: Elite Training and State Building in Today's China* (Cambridge: Cambridge University Press, 2009), pp. 152–153. For a more optimistic picture of how China's women fare globally in terms of political power, see Li Yunhe, "Zhongguo funu diwei shijie paiming lingxian" [China's Leading Position in the World Rankings for Women], *Renmin wang*, 8 Mar. 2012 (http://bbs1.people.com.cn/postDetail.do?boardId=2&treeView=1&view=2&id=117538704).

136. The same holds true, I regret to say, in Chinese academia. My female PhD students have a harder time finding academic jobs than my male students do, and male professors are often strikingly open that the "motherhood penalty" is the main reason. Given that most female professors are bound by law to have only one child (not to mention the fact that Chinese grandparents often help with child-rearing), the bias against female applicants makes even less sense than elsewhere.

137. Shelly J. Correll, "Minimizing the Motherhood Penalty: What Works, What Doesn't and Why?" paper presented at conference on "Gender & Work: Challenging Conventional Wisdom," Harvard Business School, 28 Feb.–1 Mar. 2013 (http://www.hbs.edu/faculty/conferences/2013-w50-research-symposium/Documents/correll.pdf). The study is discussed in "Women in the Workplace: A Research Roundup," *Harvard Business Review*, Sept. 2013, p. 88.

138. David Arkless, "The Secret to Asia's Long-Term Prosperity? Improving Roles for Women at Work," *Global Asia* 6, no. 3 (Fall 2011): 14.

139. Again, the practice is often the opposite of what it's supposed to be. For example, women are less likely to be recruited to the foreign ministry even if they score as well as men on written examinations because it is felt that men can do better at dealing with male diplomats and political leaders in patriarchal Arab and African countries. In other words, Chinese women are penalized because of patriarchal prejudices elsewhere.

140. An obvious point, perhaps, but it is striking how little of the (English-language) literature on leadership has focused on ethics. Deborah L. Rhode, "Introduction," in *Moral Leadership: The Theory and Practice of Power, Judgment and Policy* (San Francisco: John Wiley & Sons, 2006), p. 5. The very idea of moral expertise hasn't been much discussed in contemporary Anglophone philosophical literature (Justin Tiwald, "On Treating Political Authorities as Moral Experts: Deliberative Autonomy from a Confucian Point of View," unpublished manuscript), so the question of what it would mean for political authorities to have superior morality hasn't been much of a subject of academic debate (again, in Anglophone circles; it has been the subject of debate in the Confucian tradition, although the Anglophone debates about political Confucianism tend to be about the relationship between Confucianism and democracy or political equality).

141. A. N. Wilson, *Hitler* (New York: Basic Books, 2012).

142. M. E. Thomas, "Confessions of a Sociopath," *Psychology Today*, May/June 2011, pp. 52–60.

143. For more nuanced interpretations of Han Fei's thought, see Paul R. Goldin, ed., *Dao Companion to the Philosophy of Han Fei* (Dordrecht: Springer, 2013); and the articles in the special issue "Legalist Philosophy of Han Fei," *Journal of Chinese Philosophy* 38, no. 1 (Mar. 2011).

144. Some Confucian thinkers argue that the commitment to *tian xia* (the whole world) means that political rulers should be more concerned with the fate of the whole world than the fate of one country (e.g., Gan Chunsong, *Chonghui Wangdao: Rujia yu shijie zhixu* [A Return to the Way of the Humane Authority: Confucianism

and the World Order] [Shanghai: Huadong shifan daxue chubanshe, 2012]), whereas others argue that the idea of graded love justifies special commitment to a country (see my essay "Reconciling Confucianism and Nationalism," forthcoming in the *Journal of Chinese Philosophy*). At a minimum, Confucians agree that rulers should not seek the bad of any group of people: hence the theory that the ruler should seek the good of people, even if some deserve special treatment, rules out Nazi-like racist theories that some people ought to be exterminated.

145. My own Confucian-inspired view is that the people have a fundamental interest in leading harmonious lives, and hence the government ought to prioritize social harmony (see appendix 1 at http://press.princeton.edu/titles/10418.html). For another Confucian-inspired theory, see Ruiping Fan, "Confucian Meritocracy for Contemporary China," in *The East Asian Challenge for Democracy*. But the broad idea that the purpose of government is to promote the good of the people is compatible with both views as well as many other more specific theories about the purposes of government (for a similar point, see Brennan, *The Ethics of Voting*, pp. 117–118).

146. In contrast to "Legalists," Confucians argue that governments should lead first and foremost by virtue and ritual (or what many today call "soft power"), not harsh laws and punishments (see the Analects 2.3). But more pragmatic Confucian thinkers such as Xunzi argued that harsh punishments and immoral means are sometimes required in politics.

147. For a modern-day Confucian-inspired defense of the "service conception of political authority"—the point of political authority is to serve the ruled and the political rights attached to this authority are justified by the contribution they make to the betterment of people's lives—see Chan, *Confucian Perfectionism*, ch. 1.

148. Although the well-being of the governed was not a major concern for Legalist thinkers, a charitable interpreter could argue that Legalists stressed the need for laws that provide order because stability benefits the people. See Henrique Schneider, "Legalism: Chinese-Style Constitutionalism?" *Journal of Chinese Philosophy* 38, no. 1 (Mar. 2011): esp. 50–59.

149. As a first-year student in middle school, Mao wrote an essay praising the harsh ruling system of Legalism (http://www.worldfuturefund.org/wffmaster/Reading/China/Mao%20on%20Shang%20Yang.htm) and he (in)famously compared himself to Qin Shihuang in 1958. Zhengyuan Fu, *Autocratic Tradition and Chinese Politics* (Cambridge: Cambridge University Press, 1993), p. 187.

150. Immanuel Kant, "Perpetual Peace," in *Kant: Political Writings*, ed. Hans Reiss and trans. H. B. Nisbet (Cambridge: Cambridge University Press, 1991), p. 112.

151. See Chan, *Confucian Perfectionism*, p. 86.

152. Although studies show that highly extroverted U.S. presidents are perceived as more effective, a recent study (from the business world) suggests that in certain situations an introvert may make the better boss. Adam M. Grant, Francesca Gino, and David A. Hoffman, "The Hidden Advantages of Quiet Bosses," *Harvard Business Review*, Dec. 2010, p. 28.

153. This is not to deny that there were also critics of verbal fluency in Western

societies: Montaigne, for example, deliberately kept his speeches brief and his anecdotes concise on the grounds that slowness opened the way to wisdom and sound judgment, and his open admission of memory failings "was a direct challenge to the Renaissance ideal of oratory and rhetoric" (Sarah Bakewell, *How to Live or A Life of Montaigne in One Question and Twenty Attempts at an Answer* [New York: Other Press, 2010], p. 70). On the Renaissance ideal of the perfect orator, see Baldassare Castiglione, *The Book of the Courtier*, trans. Sir Thomas Hoby, introduction by Walter Raleigh (London: David Nutt, 1900, orig. pub. 1561), esp. pp. lxii, 368–377.

154. Jin Li, *Cultural Foundations of Learning: East and West* (Cambridge: Cambridge University Press, 2012), p. 297; I have also drawn on pp. 281 and 282.

155. Ibid., p. 296. The military strategist and statesman Zhuge Liang (181–234) may be an exception in ancient times (perhaps oratorical skills matter more for leaders who need to inspire their troops). Singapore's Lee Kuan Yew may be an exception in modern times, but he was educated in law at Cambridge and is eloquent primarily in English, and he also happens to be the leading political voice in favor of political meritocracy over democracy. In mainland China today, it is more common to see news reports of political leaders (including very top leaders) assiduously taking notes than giving speeches (think of the contrast with Western politicians!).

156. Albert Galvany argues that China's cultural aversion to eloquent speech started during the Warring States period, when eloquence was a legitimate means of ensuring one's promotion. Galvany, "Sly Mouths and Silver Tongues: The Dynamics of Psychological Persuasion in Ancient China," *Extrême-Orient, Extrême-Occident* 34 (2012): 15–41. This aversion focuses on eloquent speech as a means of self-marketing, which is precisely the main usage of eloquent speech in electoral democracies.

157. Cited in Bol, *Neo-Confucianism in History*, pp. 47–48. For a similar defense of the classics as the ultimate source of moral wisdom from the Song dynasty, see the passage cited in Chaffee, *The Thorny Gates of Learning in Sung China*, pp. 4–5. Another defense of the examination system as a way of testing for morality is the argument that a person's handwriting reveals his or her moral quality (see, e.g., the Tang dynasty passage cited in Xiao and Li, "China's Meritocratic Examinations and the Ideal of Virtuous Talents," p. 344.). I leave aside this argument because it is somewhat out of date: today, many people use computers to write and it is no longer so common (unfortunately, perhaps) to express one's personality and feelings via handwriting.

158. See Xiao and Li, "China's Meritocratic Examinations and the Ideal of Virtuous Talents," p. 354.

159. Cited in Joseph Chan, "Political Meritocracy and Meritorious Rule: A Confucian Perspective," in *The East Asian Challenge for Democracy*, p. 45.

160. Cited in Xiao and Li, "China's Meritocratic Examinations and the Ideal of Virtuous Talents," p. 350.

161. Tan Fuxuan, "Xin xingshi xia jiaqiang ganbu de de kaohe pingjia wenti yanjiu" [Research on Strengthening Moral Evaluation in the Selection of Cadres under New Conditions], *Xiandai rencai* 6 (2010) (http://www.cnki.com.cn/Article/CJFDTotal-XDRC201006014.htm). The new regulations on the selection and appointment

of cadres do specify that virtue should come before ability (*Dangzheng lingdao ganbu xuanba renyong tiaoli* [Regulations on the Selection and Appointment of Cadres of the CCP], 2014–1-15, 2.2; and for regional experiments with increased emphasis on virtue in the selection of young cadres, see "Xuanba nianqing ganbu, yan le!" [On the More Rigorous Selection of Young Cadres], *Zhongguo qingnian bao*, 22 Aug. 2014), but it remains unclear how virtue is to be assessed and measured.

162. Plus, there is no reason to be bound by earlier definitions of what counts as the classics. Zhu Xi chose the *Zhongyong* [Doctrine of the Mean] as one of the four Confucian classics that were used to test potential public officials from the Yuan dynasty onward, but he may have been motivated to select this relatively metaphysical text to counter the challenge of Buddhism. Today, it might make more sense to select a text—such as the *Yueji* [Record of Music] in the *Liji* [Book of Rites]—that more directly discusses ways of achieving a harmonious society using the arts without extensive discussion of contestable metaphysical foundations.

163. See, e.g., Jiang Qing, "Xianneng zhengzhi de zhidu jiagou: 'Rujiao xianzheng' dui minzhuxianzheng de chaoyue yu xina" [The System and Structure of Political Meritocracy: How Confucian Constitutionalism Transcends and Learns from Democratic Politics], paper presented at conference "Quanguo zhengzhi ruxue he xiandai shijie taolun" [Political Confucianism and Its Contemporary Significance in China and the World], Tsinghua University, 27–28 Oct. 2012.

164. Criminals are attracted to elective office not just because it offers opportunities for corruption but also because it provides immunity from prosecution (Collier, *Wars, Guns, and Votes*, p. 27). In India, 162 out of 543 members of the lower house have criminal records, but the Supreme Court recently ruled that sitting MPs will henceforth be disqualified upon conviction in serious criminal cases (http://www.ft.com/intl/cms/s/0/4ac6d8dc-e966–11e2–9f11–00144feabdc0.html#axzz2fP71DZ3F). In Ukraine, the leader of the Meritocratic Party told me that part of his mission is to improve the quality of political leaders by disqualifying criminals from politics (interview with Igor Shevchenko, World Economic Forum [summer] meeting, Dalian, China, Sept. 2011).

165. Li, *Cultural Foundations of Learning*, p. 38.

166. Interview with Chu Fumei, vice-mayor of Qufu, 21 June 2014 (Qufu is known as the home of Confucian culture and the city has been selected by the central government as a special economic and cultural zone). In the Han dynasty, the overemphasis on filial piety as a prerequisite for office caused the explosion of faked filial behavior to the point of self-destruction. Étienne Balázs, *Chinese Civilization and Bureaucracy: Variations on a Theme*, trans. H. M. Wright; ed. Arthur F. Wright (New Haven, Conn.: Yale University Press, 1967). But the idea today is more to deselect those who have clearly violated the minimal conditions of filial piety (e.g., if parents are asked about the virtue of their child during the candidate selection process and the parents have bad things to say, the candidate is deselected), not to reward public officials for exceptional filial behavior.

167. Zhou Qi, "Political Systems, Rights, and Values" [Dialogue with Andrew J.

Nathan], in *Debating China: The U.S.–China Relationship in Ten Conversations*, ed. Nina Hachigan (Oxford: Oxford University Press, 2014), pp. 59–60. Such points are often made in informal conversations with Chinese intellectuals with full access to information about the facts of the case(s), but they are rarely articulated in public both because it is politically sensitive to openly argue with imprisoned dissidents and because fellow intellectuals find it distasteful to criticize dissidents who cannot defend themselves while they are in jail. One important reason that the views of dissidents do not resonate much with Chinese intellectuals is that dissidents often make highly controversial totalizing critiques of Chinese culture and CCP history all the while idealizing electoral democracies in the West. That said, many independent Chinese intellectuals think dissidents should be allowed to express their views, particularly if there is no attempt to organize an alternative to one-party rule.

168. Tsinghua students in the party sometimes serve poor rural communities for a year after they graduate. Even if a mixture of motives may be in play (e.g., being seen to be good can help career prospects), the fact that they are willing to help disadvantaged people under uncomfortable conditions is a good thing, and being exposed to poverty and hardship can help to increase understanding and sympathy for the plight of the disadvantaged.

169. Chris Buckley, "China to Loosen Its One-Child Policy," *New York Times*, 15 Nov. 2013.

170. Xi Jinping interview in 2000, translated by Carsten Boyer Thøgersen and Susanne Posborg (http://nias.ku.dk/news/interview-2000-china%E2%80%99s-vice-president-xi-jinping-translated-western-language-first-time). In March 2014, in the midst of one of Beijing's notorious pollution alerts, President Xi made an "impromptu" visit to a local neighborhood in Beijing and talked to locals without wearing a pollution mask, a clear symbol of his willingness to experience personal harm in order to show solidarity with suffering locals.

171. See Bruce J. Dickson, "Who Wants to Be a Communist? Career Incentives and Mobilized Loyalty in China," *China Quarterly* 217 (Mar. 2014). But once they join, the process designed to improve their other-regarding outlook may not be entirely ineffective: Dickson also found that CCP members are more likely to hold higher standards of citizenship than non–party members, and are more likely to demonstrate their citizenship by donating time and money to various causes and by voting in local People's Congress elections. It is noteworthy that private entrepreneurs prefer to hire party members, all else being equal, because many employers reportedly see party membership as indicating that an individual has already passed a screening process and will be a more dependable employee (ibid.).

172. Cited in Chan, "Political Meritocracy and Meritorious Rule," 46.

173. Ibid., pp. 47–48.

174. Ibid., p. 53n61. See also Chan, *Confucian Perfectionism*, ch. 4.

175. One might add that including senior journalists as the group of selectors makes less sense in mainland China if the aim is to empower selectors with personal knowledge of the moral character of candidates: unlike in Hong Kong, journalists in

mainland China rarely have prolonged interaction with political officials in different settings.

176. Even the moral character of children can be assessed by such means: the Cyrus Tang Compassionate Heart Scholarship is given to Chinese middle and high school students who demonstrate commitment to virtues such as filial piety and willingness to help others, and the scholarship recipients (one per class) are selected through anonymous voting by fellow students in each class (http://www.tangfoundation.org/index.php?option=com_content&view=article&id=20&Itemid=39&site=CTF&sub=2).

177. The Singaporean Army works relatively well as a meritocratic institution because peer ratings are given the most weight in promotion decisions, based (at least partly) on moral character. (In 1918, the U.S. Army first implemented a rigorous peer-rating system designed to favor advancement by merit rather than by prejudice, family influence, or political string-pulling; see Kett, *Merit*, pp. 8–9.) In politics, however, the Singapore government relies on the "helicopter" system, borrowed from Shell Corporation, which gives most weight to the assessments of superiors. Interview with George Yeo at the Institute of Policy Studies, Singapore, 5 Sept. 2013.

178. To screen out fear of retaliation, assessments of moral character should be done anonymously.

179. Cary Huang, "Party Polls 370 Members on Choice of Top Leaders," *South China Morning Posts*, 8 June 2012. The practice of peer decision making at the top is more comprehensive in the sense that there is no clear distinction between assessments of intellectual ability, social skills, and moral character (or virtue). In this chapter, I am arguing that peer ratings should be used as the main mode of assessment for *moral character*; ideally, assessments of intellectual ability and social skills should rely on other modes of assessment (see sections 2 and 3), and the decision to promote or not should be based on a sum of the distinctive modes of assessment for each dimension.

180. He Baogang, "An Empirical Theory of Hybrid Legitimacy System in China," paper presented at workshop on "East Asian Perspectives on Political Legitimacy," University of Hong Kong, 18–19 Aug. 2011.

181. See section 3. For a fictitious (and hugely popular) book by a former public official that recounts (and satirizes) the culture of loyalty to superiors, see Wang Xiaofang, *The Civil Servant's Notebook*, trans. Eric Abrahamsen (Melbourne: Viking, 2012).

182. To counteract unnecessary attachment to the status quo by national leaders, the government established the China Executive Leadership Academy in Pudong (Shanghai), which promotes innovation in managerial thinking and research to enable the party to meet the changing governance requirements of the market transition and economic globalization while preserving the party's rule. Gregory T. Chin, "Innovation and Preservation: Remaking China's National Leadership Training System," *China Quarterly* 205 (Mar. 2011): 18–39. But such institutions won't be sufficient without reform of the evaluation process for the promotion of cadres.

183. One way of dealing with this problem—implemented in imperial China, but not in today's political system—is to penalize superiors who recommend public officials who turn out to be corrupt or ineffective.

184. Again, I have in mind political meritocracies that value leaders with good track records of performance at lower levels of government, which may require the type of social skills exhibited by leaders of large corporations. In democracies, the type of social skills required of stage actors who need to deliver the same speech night after night with equal passion may be more important.

Chapter 3
What's Wrong with Political Meritocracy

1. To be more precise, it would be outlandish from a Confucian perspective to expect that political officials should be deprived of family members, not just for practical reasons but also because morality is learned and practiced within the family and then extended to non–family members. In the Ottoman Empire, however, the sultans took children, selected for their talents and intelligence, from subject Christian families, and those judged most able were trained to be leading administrators (McCarthy, *The Ottoman Turks*, p. 110). The practice was partly justified by the "Platonic" idea that a child stripped of family would become an "enemy to their family and dependents" (Imber, *The Ottoman Empire*, p. 124) and wholly committed to serving the empire, but it didn't always work as planned: "those who became Muslim often kept their language and maybe even their allegiance, some returning to their region of birth as governors, others commanding in their native tongues, and many trying to help family members back in their homeland" (Barkey, *Empire of Difference*, p. 124).

2. Allan Bloom, "Interpretive Essay," in *The Republic of Plato*, trans. Allan Bloom, 2nd ed. (New York: Basic Books, 1991), p. 380. But perhaps Plato's view about appointing rulers without families as a way of combating corruption is not as crazy as it seems. Wang Qishan heads the Central Commission for Discipline Inspection of the Communist Party of China (the party's top anticorruption watchdog; he is also one of the seven members of the ruling Standing Committee of the Politburo), and the fact that Wang does not have any children has been cited as a reason that he has been more serious about cracking down on corruption than other political leaders who often have wealthy children. Wu Di, "Zhongguo fanfu ke yi lao yong yi" [Dealing with Corruption in China Once and for All], *Lianhe zaobao*, 28 Oct. 2013.

3. Michael Young, "Introduction to the Transaction Edition," in *The Rise of the Meritocracy* (New Brunswick, N.J.: Transaction, 1994), p. xvi. Young does not distinguish clearly between economic meritocracy (people should be rewarded according to their productive capabilities) and political meritocracy (the political system should aim to select and promote leaders with superior ability and virtue). My book is a defense of political meritocracy, not economic meritocracy.

4. I do not mean to imply that there are no other problems associated with political meritocracy. For example, it could be argued that Chinese-style political meri-

tocracy is supported by a high-pressure, ultracompetitive educational system that makes people, especially secondary-school students preparing for university entrance examinations, extremely unhappy. But this kind of educational system is also characteristic of some democratic political systems, such as that in South Korea, so the "blame" cannot be put on political meritocracy per se. Moreover, it is possible (and, arguably, desirable) to reform the educational system in China so that it allows for a more diverse expression of human qualities without undermining political meritocracy.

5. A recent issue of the French periodical *Books* reviews all the counterarguments against democracy and suggests that none of them undermine the argument for democracy that bad rulers can be changed by the people at election time. See the introduction to "Pourquoi Voter?" [Why Vote?], *Books* 31 (Apr. 2012): 24, 42.

6. See Gong Ting and Wu Muluan, "Wo guo 2000–2009 nian fubai anli yanjiu baogao: Jiyu 2800 yu ge baodao anli de fenxi" [Research Report on China's Corruption Cases between 2000 and 2009: An Empirical Analysis of 2800 Cases], *Shehuixue yanjiu* 4 (2012): 204–220; Qianwei Wu, "Reorientation and Prospect of China's Combat against Corruption," *Crime, Law and Social Change* 49, no. 2 (Mar. 2008): 86–88; Andrew Wedeman, "Win, Lose, or Draw? China's Quarter Century War on Corruption," *Crime, Law and Social Change* 49, no. 1 (Feb. 2008): 7–26; Melanie Manion, *Corruption by Design: Building Clean Government in Mainland China and Hong Kong* (Cambridge, Mass.: Harvard University Press, 2004), ch. 3. In any case, official statistics are unreliable and it is difficult to determine the extent of corruption with any precision.

7. "Xi Jinping's Anti-Corruption Crusade," *Riskadvisory*, 5 Mar. 2013 (http://news.riskadvisory.net/index.php/2013/03/xi-jinpings-anti-corruption-crusade/). Such worries have been expressed by political leaders in the past: for example, the former president Hu Jintao warned that corruption "could prove fatal to the party, and even cause the collapse of the party and the fall of the state," and his predecessor Jiang Zemin said that "corruption is the cancer in the body of the party and the state. If we let it be, our party, our political power and our socialist modernization cause will be doomed" (cited in Ren Jianming and Du Zhizhou, "Institutionalized Corruption: Power Overconcentration of the First-in-Command in China," *Crime, Law and Social Change* 49, no. 1 [Feb. 2008]: 47). But the campaign against corruption since President Xi assumed power seems to be much more systematic than previous campaigns (Andrew Browne, "In China, Purge Precedes Economic Rebirth," *Wall Street Journal*, 9 Dec. 2014). According to one political observer who is not normally prone to upbeat takes on Chinese politics, "what is strikingly different about the current campaign is the apparent lack of political opportunism. Where previous leaders employed anticorruption as just another strategy to decapitate political opponents, there's no such pattern under Xi" (Russell Leigh Moses, "Why China's Current Anti-Corruption Campaign Is Different," http://blogs.wsj.com/chinarealtime/2013/05/30/why-chinas-current-anti-corruption-campaign-is-different/?mod=WSJBlog&mod=chinablog). Another difference is that more higher-level leaders are being taken down, including (for the first

time) a recently retired Politburo Standing Committee member, Zhou Yongkang; in the past, lower-ranking officials were more likely to be punished for corruption by the center, whereas occupants of executive posts such as vice-mayors and vice-governors were more likely to be removed for mistakes or accidents. Liang Qiao, "For Harmony and How Not to Get Promoted: The Downgraded Chinese Regional Leaders," *Journal of Chinese Political Science* 19 (2013): 206–207. I can testify from personal experience that the anticorruption campaign is reaching down to all levels of society: for the first time, my department at Tsinghua University canceled the annual talent show of teachers and students in an effort to eliminate all activities that could be (mis)perceived as a misuse of funds. This example also points to a common complaint against the current anticorruption campaign: that it has gone too far in a "Legalist" direction, targeting not just corrupt officials and activities that lead to corruption but also morally legitimate social gatherings that are important for forging social bonds and providing work motivation for public officials, thus hurting the productivity of officials and needlessly tarnishing the public's view of the government and the party. Gao Yu and Wang Heyan, "How the Hammer Falls as China Nails Corruption," *CaixinOnline*, 24 July 2014 (http://english.caixin.com/2014-07-24/100708615.html).

8. http://www.transparency.org/cpi2012/results. Moreover, it can be argued that corruption in China is less harmful than corruption in India. David Pilling writes, summarizing his interview with Jagdish Bhagwati: "A crucial difference between the two countries is the type of corruption they have. India's is classic 'rent-seeking,' where people jostle to grab a cut of existing wealth. 'The Chinese have what I [Bhagwati] call profit-sharing corruption': the Communist Party puts a straw in the milkshake so 'they have an interest in having the milkshake grow larger.'" David Pilling, "Lunch with the FT: Jagdish Bhagwati," *Financial Times*, 17 Apr. 2014. Moreover, there may be less "petty corruption" (payoffs to police, customs officers, etc.) in China than in India and Indonesia. Yan Sun and Michael Johnson also argue that China's closed political system means that there is less corruption at the top: "In India accessible elites and economic pressures growing out of scarcity sustain corruption and weaken accountability, in political and bureaucratic arenas at all levels. Closed political and autonomous elites, along with vigorous economic growth, may shield the top levels of China's regime from the worst corruption pressures, shifting the emphasis to political and bureaucratic processes at lower levels." Yan Sun and Michael Johnston, "Does Democracy Check Corruption? Insights from China and India," *Comparative Politics* 42, no. 1 (Oct. 2009): 15.

9. One reason is that political corruption under President Suharto was largely limited to Suharto's family. Democratization opened the way to "hundreds of little Suhartos" (cited in Eric X. Li, "Saints or Thieves, Corruption and the Chinese Dilemma," http://www.scmp.com/comment/insight-opinion/article/1296158/no-how-book-west-can-curb-corruption-china). A high-ranking Golkar official links corruption more directly with democracy: "In Indonesia, democracy is identical to money politics. . . . If there is no money, people will not vote for us" (Norimitsu Onishi, "Lawmakers Sow Disillusion in Indonesia," *New York Times*, 16 Oct. 2010). The chief jus-

tice of the Constitutional Court has recently been arrested, which is a reminder that institutions independent of political rulers cannot safeguard against corruption if they themselves are corrupt ("Top Drama," *Sunday Post* [Jakarta], 6 Oct. 2013).

10. William Overholt, "Is Xi Jinping's Fight against Corruption for Real? A China File Conversation," 26 June 2013 (http://www.chinafile.com/xi-jinping-s-fight-against-corruption-real). Indicators of clean government suggest that people in Taiwan doubt the probity of their public officials, especially elected politicians and political appointees, leading Yu et al. to conclude that the democratic transformation has damaged government integrity. Chilik Yu, Chun-Ming Chen, Lung-Teng Hu, and Wen-Jong Huang, "Evolving Perceptions of Government Integrity and Changing Anticorruption Measures in Taiwan," in *Preventing Corruption in Asia: Institutional Design and Policy Capacity*, ed. Ting Gong and Stephen K. Ma (London: Routledge, 2009), pp. 189–205.

11. Sun and Johnston, "Does Democracy Check Corruption?" pp. 2, 15–16.

12. Randall Peerenboom, *China Modernizes: Threat to the West or Model for the Rest?* (Oxford: Oxford University Press, 2008).

13. Bin Dong and Benno Torgler, "Causes of Corruption: Evidence from China," *China Economic Review* 26 (2013): 152–169. Another study, however, found that higher levels of education and wealth can worsen local corruption if fiscal decentralization increases the size of government without adequate anticorruption mechanisms. Pan Chunyang, He Lixin, and Yuan Congshuai, "Caizheng fenquan yu guanyuan fubai: Jiyu 1999–2007 nian zhongguo shengji mianban shuju de shizheng yanjiu" [Fiscal Decentralization and the Corruption of Cadres: An Empirical Study Based on China's Provincial Data from 1997 to 2007], *Dangdai caijing* 3, no. 316 (2011): 38–46.

14. The claim here is that increased GDP per capita tends to minimize corruption, not eliminate it. I regret to report that the political (democratic) system of my hometown, Montreal, is probably at least as corrupt as city-level politics in (relatively poor) Chinese cities: in July 2013, Mayor Michael Applebaum, who ran on a promise to tackle corruption, was arrested on corruption-related charges (http://www.theglobeandmail.com/news/national/montreal-mayor-michael-applebaum-arrested/article12595439/).

15. Another reason to worry is the impact corruption has on the economy. Although corruption has been justified on the grounds that it can act as a lubricant to motivate the bureaucracy to get things done and facilitate commercial exchanges, recent research shows that counties with a higher degree of anticorruption measures tend to have higher income as measured by county-level per capita GDP (Yinping Wu and Jiangnan Zu, "Corruption, Anti-corruption, and Inter-county Income Disparity in China," *Social Science Journal* 48 [2011]: 435–448), and that years of office selling in Heilongjiang hindered economic development (Jiangnan Zhu, "Why Are Offices for Sale in China? A Case Study of the Office-Selling Chain in Heilongjiang," *Asian Survey* 48, no. 4 [July/Aug. 2008]: 575–576). High levels of corruption also negatively affect government expenditure, and hence negatively affect spending

for social welfare (Guo Jie, Yang Jie, and Cheng Xu, "Diqu fubai zhili yu zhengfu zhichu guimo: Jiyu shengji mianban shuju de kongjian jiliang fenxi" [The Regulation of Local Corruption and the Scale of Government: A Spatial Economic Analysis Based on Provincial Panel Data], *Jingji shehui tizhi bijiao* 1 [2013]: 196–204). Cheng Li and Ryan McElveen predict that in the future a decline in official corruption will help the economy because tax dollars previously used to fund unsanctioned purchases can be returned to public coffers and spent on improved infrastructure and public services. Moreover, Xi's anticorruption campaign will increase his political capital, thus allowing him to implement deeper economic reforms that will induce greater confidence in China's economy (Li and McElveen, "Debunking Misconceptions about Xi's Anti-Corruption Campaign," *China–U.S. Focus*, 17 July 2014).

16. Yan Sun, *Corruption and Market in Contemporary China* (Ithaca, N.Y.: Cornell University Press, 2004).

17. For a more positive evaluation of Bo Xilai and his legacy, see Yuezhi Zhao, "The Struggle for Socialism in China: The Bo Xilai Saga and Beyond," *Monthly Review* 64, no. 5 (Oct. 2012): 1–17.

18. The *Financial Times* also published a long exposé on "The Family Fortunes of Beijing's New Few" (11 July 2012), including a detailed chart of the business interests of China's most powerful leaders and their wealthy relatives, but for some reason the government has not "punished" the FT by blocking its website.

19. To be more precise, in a two-party democratic system a ruling political party that is perceived to be corrupt may worry about being voted out of power, but the same party will have another opportunity to gain power the following election (especially if the voters come to realize that the alternative party is just as corrupt). In a political meritocracy, the whole political system is threatened by corruption and if it collapses, the ruling party is less likely to have another opportunity to gain power.

20. Yao Zhongqiu, "Tian ren zhi ji de zhi dao: Guangchuan Dongzi 'Tian ren san ce' yi shu" [The Way of Governing the Relationship between Heaven and Man: Explanatory Comments on Dong Zhongshu's "Three Answers to Governance between Heaven and Man"], *Zhengzhi sixiang shi* 3, no. 11 (2012): 1–33.

21. The seventeenth-century Confucian critic Huang Zongxi proposed to institutionalize criticism of the emperor by means of an annual session that would compel the emperor to respond to the policy questions of the rector of the highest educational institution in the land. Huang's suggestion was too radical for his day, but the contemporary Confucian thinker Jiang Qing has proposed reviving a similar proposal in contemporary China (see chapter 1, note 137). For a discussion of a Southern Song treatise on the *Zhou Li* that argued for placing constitutional limits on both ministerial tyranny and monarchical autocracy, see Jaeyoon Song, "The Zhou Li and Constitutionalism: A Southern Song Political Theory," *Journal of Chinese Philosophy* 36, no. 3 (Sept. 2009): 424–438. For a proposal to revive ancient remonstrating institutions and independent academies as checks on government power, see Baogang He, "Confucian Deliberation: The Persistence of Authoritarian Deliberation in China," paper presented at the "International Conference on Confucianism, Democracy, and Con-

stitutionalism: Global and East Asian Perspectives," National Taiwan University, 14–15 June 2013.

22. See the discussion in chapter 2, section 2.

23. Miyazaki, *China's Examination Hell*, p. 78.

24. Cited in Kuhn, *The Age of Confucian Rule*, p. 44.

25. For proposals on modern-day versions of the court historian and the censor, both inspired by institutions designed to curb the power of the ruler in Choson dynasty Korea, see Hahm Chaihark, "Constitutionalism, Confucian Civic Virtue, and Ritual Propriety," and Jongryn Mo, "The Challenge of Accountability: Implications of the Censorate," both in *Confucianism for the Modern World*, ed. Daniel A. Bell and Hahm Chaibong (Cambridge: Cambridge University Press, 2003).

26. For an argument that emperors often exercised de facto political power in a wide range of social, economic, and political affairs with generally bad consequences for human dignity, see Liu Zehua, "Wangquanzhuyi: Zhongguo sixiang wenhua de lishi dingwei" [Monarchism: A Historical Orientation of Chinese Intellectual Culture], *Tianjin shehui kexue* 3 (1998): 59–62 (for an English translation, see Yuri Pines, unpublished manuscript). In the case of Emperor Wanli, however, he "realize[d] that he was less the Ruler of All Men than a prisoner of the Forbidden City. His power was basically negative" (Huang, *1587, a Year of No Significance*, p. 93). But Wanli's "negative" power had terrible consequences: he withdrew from active duty, and his passive resistance contributed to the collapse of the whole political system.

27. Fukuyama, *The Origins of Political Order*, pp. 313–314. For another example, see Orville Shell and John Delury, *Wealth and Power: China's Long March to the Twenty-First Century* (London: Little, Brown, 2013), p. 64.

28. Pines, *The Everlasting Empire*, p. 170.

29. Hon S. Chan and Jie Gao, "Old Wine in New Bottles: A County-Level Case Study of Anti-Corruption Reform in the People's Republic of China," *Crime, Law and Social Change* 49, no. 2 (Mar. 2008): 115–116.

30. James T. Areddy, "China's Cadres Balk at Showing the Money," *Wall Street Journal*, 1 Aug. 2013, p. A4.

31. For some evidence that online anticorruption campaigns weaken trust in government (helping to explain the government's aversion to such campaigns), see Cheng Tongshun and Zhang Wenjun, "Wangluo fanfu tisheng zhengzhi xinren de luoji pipan" [Criticism of the Argument That Online Anti-Corruption Campaigns Strengthen Trust in Government], *Lilun yu gaige* 4 (2013).

32. That said, it is possible, as Francis Fukuyama puts it in the second volume of his magnum opus on political order, that the Chinese political system could "produce a charismatic leader who exploited populist passions and built a personal following that upset all of the consensual understandings that have characterized post-Mao leadership." Fukuyama, *Political Order and Political Decay: From the Industrial Revolution to the Globalization of Democracy* (New York: Farrar, Straus and Giroux, 2014), pp. 383–384. If Xi Jinping contrives to hold on to the presidency after two terms in the

Standing Committee of the Politburo—a highly unlikely event, in my view—then I will retract my claim that the traditional one bad emperor problem has been solved.

33. Eric X. Li, "The Life of the Party: The Post-Democratic Future Begins in China," *Foreign Affairs* 92, no. 1 (Jan./Feb. 2013).

34. According to a Pew survey on Chinese attitudes in 2012, half of the respondents said corrupt officials are a major problem, up from 39 percent in 2008 (http://www.pewglobal.org/2012/10/16/growing-concerns-in-china-about-inequality-corruption/). Thirty-two percent also say this about corrupt businesspeople, also up 11 points from 2008.

35. Qin Ailing, "Zhongjiwei biange" [Reform of the Central Commission for Discipline Inspection], *Nanfeng chuang* 2, nos. 13–26 (2014): 46–48; Zheng Yongnian, "Fighting Corruption and China's Second Political Revolution," *United Morning News*, 12 Aug. 2014; Eric X. Li, "Party of the Century: How China Is Reorganizing for the Future," *Foreign Affairs*, 10 Jan. 2014 (http://www.foreignaffairs.com/articles/140645/eric-x-li/party-of-the-century).

36. Huang Jing, "Touxi Zhongguo fubai" [Analyzing China's Corruption] (http://www.21ccom.net/articles/zgyj/xzmj/article_2010050790 88.html).

37. Keane, *The Life and Death of Democracy*, p. xxvii.

38. The Xi Jinping administration has cracked down on independent whistleblowers and has opened an official website for people to report abuses of power (see http://www.ccdi.gov.cn). To be fair, there is a need to prevent false accusations without proper investigations, but better laws to protect whistleblowers would do more good than harm (Yang Tao, "Baohu jubaoren, hexin zai yu guifan gong quanli" [Protect Whistleblowers, the Key Lies in Regulating Public Power], *Beijing qingnian bao*, 17 Apr. 2014).

39. Jun Ma and Xing Ni, "Toward a Clean Government in China: Does the Budget Reform Provide a Hope?" *Crime, Law and Social Change* 49, no. 2 (Mar. 2008): 135–136.

40. "Disclosing Officials' Assets," *China Daily*, 13 Dec. 2012, p. 8.

41. The city-state of ancient Venice, governed by 2 percent of the population, minimized "family corruption" by performing an audit at the end of a ruler's tenure, and if a financial discrepancy was discovered the ruler's children were penalized. Such measures are not in the cards in China now—if only because of an informal understanding over the past couple of decades that the talented children of political families would go into politics and the rest into business; hence such families are likely to fight to the death measures forcing disclosure of family assets. But when political families realize that extravagant wealth accumulation by family members threatens the legitimacy of the whole regime, as happened in Suharto's Indonesia, family asset disclosure may be considered in the future. Another problem is that family members often move wealth abroad and it is difficult for the Chinese government to keep track of such wealth, but—an encouraging sign—China's so-called naked officials, those who have moved their spouses, children, and assets overseas while they

remain at home, will not be considered for promotion (Yimou Lee, "China Cracks Cozy Offshore Code of Perks," *New York Times*, 28 Jan. 2014). In another encouraging sign, China and Australia are now cooperating to track down and seize the possessions of Chinese citizens who live in Australia and are suspected of fraud ("China Media Welcomes Foreign Anti-Corruption Cooperation," BBC News, 21 Oct. 2014).

42. For a discussion of the Hong Kong model and what can be learned from it, see Melanie Manion, *Corruption by Design*, esp. chs. 2 and 6.

43. Stanley Lubman, "What China Needs to Do to Really Put Clamps on Corruption," *China Real Time Report*, 2 Apr. 2013. The government seems to be moving along these lines: at the Third Plenum, it proposed establishing local-level judicial agencies with sources of funding independent of local governments. Li Da, "San zhong quan hui gaige neirong baoguang" [An Exposure of the Contents of the Reform of the Third Plenum], *Xin jiyuan zhoukan*, 30 Sept. 2013.

44. Yan Sun, "Cadre Recruitment and Corruption: What Goes Wrong?" *Crime, Law and Social Change* 49, no. 1 (Feb. 2008): 61–79.

45. Huang, *1587, a Year of No Significance*, p. 76. In modern China, candidates would first need to pass local-level exams to determine basic intellectual ability and appointments could be made by lot depending on the number of positions available. Not only would this process eliminate corruption (and sexism, *guanxi*, and nepotism) from the process, but also the "losers" would not feel as resentful, given that chance would decide the outcome. Promotion to higher levels would then depend on performance.

46. But there are limits to transparency: when the British government published the salaries of civil servants, it led to such an uproar that the government reverted to the earlier practice of secrecy (*Ethos* 12 [June 2013]: 13).

47. Gong and Wu, "Wo guo 2000–2009 nian fubai anli yanjiu baogao" [A Research Report on China's Corruption Cases between 2000–2009].

48. Francesco Sisci, "Xi Cuts CEO Cloth for Bruising Battle," *Sinograph*, 2 July 2013.

49. Zheng Yongnian, "Fighting Corruption and China's Second Political Revolution," *United Morning News*, 12 Aug. 2014.

50. Kilkon Ko and Cuifen Weng, "Structural Changes in Chinese Corruption," *China Quarterly* 211 (Sept. 2012): 718–740. Chinese-style corruption does not always (or even usually) take the form of direct cash payments. I was told of one practice at a fancy Cantonese restaurant in Beijing. Government officials are invited by business executives for dinner. The dinner is ridiculously overpriced (about ten times what it should cost), and the restaurant passes "gifts" (e.g. very expensive tea sets) to the payer, and these "gifts" are then passed to the government official. Hence, the functional equivalent of a bribe has been passed to the official, but with plausible deniability on all sides.

51. The legal barrier between wealth and power began to break down in the Ming dynasty: merchants were allowed to take public service exams, and transference of merchant wealth into educational resources for a classical education for their sons

became de rigueur for merchants hoping to enter the literati via exams and affinal relationships. But wealth alone did not suffice until the mid to late Qing, when lower degrees were sold to pay for military campaigns and many who had failed their exams could thereby purchase local degrees and cash in on that for local appointments. Upper *juren* (provincial) and *jinshi* (capital) degrees, however, remained immune to this commercialization of the degree market. (This note draws on an email sent by Benjamin Elman.)

52. Zhang Lu, "Shichang zhuangui yu fubai moshi de bianqian" [Market Transition and the Changing Forms of Corruption], *Wenhua zongheng*, June 2013, p. 54.

53. Dong and Torgler, "Causes of Corruption," p. 165.

54. For some hopeful signs, see "Will a New Round of Reforms Shake Up State Firms?" *Week in China* (HSBC weekly newsletter), 25 July 2014.

55. Ko and Wong, "Structural Changes in Chinese Corruption," p. 737.

56. As Eric X. Li notes, "Seventy-seven percent of Americans say elected officials are influenced by financial contributors vs. 19 percent say they are led by the best interests of the country (Gallup); 50 percent of Americans say elections are for sale vs. 37 percent believe they are won by the best candidates (Gallup); 70 percent of Americans say the political system is controlled by special interests and not responsive to the country's real needs (Newsweek poll); and 93 percent of Americans say politicians do special favors for campaign contributors (ABC News and Washington Post Poll)." Li, "Saints or Thieves."

57. Zhang, "Shichang zhuangui yu fubai moshi de bianqian," p. 54.

58. Li Yongzhong of the China Academy of Supervision and Discipline Inspection has proposed that amnesty be granted to officials who come clean. Zhang Weiying of the Guanghua School of Management agrees since, if it works, an amnesty might rescue the party.

59. Michelle FlorCruz, "China's High-Ranking Officials and Businessmen Salaries Still Too High for Critics," *International Business Times*, 29 Apr. 2013.

60. Li, "Saints or Thieves"; Huang, *1587, a Year of No Significance*, pp. 13, 89, 90.

61. I leave aside the cynical view—often expressed in informal conversations with journalists and political critics—that the government deliberately keeps salaries low to discourage rebellion in the bureaucracy. The logic is that low salaries force public officials to turn to corruption, and rebels within the bureaucracy can be purged on the grounds of immorality if need be. I do not know of any evidence to support such cynical speculations either in imperial China or now.

62. Cited in Wolfgang Drechsler, "Wang Anshi and the Origins of Modern Public Management in Song Dynasty China," *Public Money and Management* 33, no. 4 (Sept. 2013): 353–360.

63. This section draws on Wong, "Political Meritocracy in Singapore."

64. Jeffrey Chua, Larry Kamener, and Michael Shanahan, "The Making of a Talent Magnet: Lessons from Singapore's Public Service," Boston Consulting Group, May 2012, p. 7. The authors add that a "competitive level of pay in itself isn't sufficient to motivate great performance. So the public service relies on *highly variable* pay—

worth up to 45 percent of total compensation at senior management levels—to reward employees whose actions lead to desired outcomes. Variable pay hinges on both the overall economic situation of the country and on the individual's performance." In my experience working at a public university (the National University of Singapore) in the early 1990s, however, only the overall economic situation of the country counted: my salary varied in accordance with the growth rate of Singapore, not my academic output.

65. Cited in Wong, "Political Meritocracy in Singapore," pp. 293–294.

66. Tan, "Meritocracy and Political Liberalization in Singapore," p. 316.

67. Cited in Wong, "Political Meritocracy in Singapore," p. 294.

68. See "Cong guanfeng zhengzhi dao zhili nengli xiandaihua: Fang Qinghua daxue gonggong guanli xueyuan yuanzhang, jiaoshou Xue Lan" [From Bureaucratic Control to Modernized Governance Capability: Interview with Tsinghua University Dean and Professor Xue Lan], *Renmin luntan wang*, 5 May 2014 (http://politics.rmlt.com.cn/2014/0505/265090.shtml). Another problem that leads to corruption—easier to rectify, perhaps—is that different salaries are paid for the same position. Tang Zhijun, Xiang Guocheng, Shen Ying, "Jinsheng jinbiaosai yu difang zhengfu guanyuan fubai wenti de yanjiu" [Research on the Competitive Promotion and the Problem of Corruption of Local Officials], *Shanghai jingji yanjiu* 4 (2013): 13.

69. Liu Xin, "Rang gongwuyuan de gongzi huigui shichang" [Let the Salaries of Public Servants Be Set by the Market], *21 Shiji jingji baodao*, 20 Jan. 2014, p. 6.

70. That said, there is an advantage to payments in kind: the total compensation is less transparent, and hence public officials are less likely to envy others who may make more in hidden wealth. So perhaps the challenge is to strive for certain forms of payments in kind that are not viewed as corrupt. In the business world, there are also limits to transparency: stock market reports issued every three months made the markets more volatile than reports issued once a year.

71. Without paying attention to the other factors that cause corruption, increasing salaries of public servants can be ineffective and even counterproductive: see Ting Gong and Alfred M. Wu, "Does Increased Civil Service Pay Deter Corruption? Evidence from China," *Review of Public Personnel Administration* 32 (2012): 192–204; and Luis A. Sosa, "Wages and Other Determinants of Corruption," *Review of Development Economics* 8, no. 4 (Nov. 2004): 597–605.

72. Russell Hardin, "Morals for Public Officials," in *Moral Leadership*, p. 115.

73. Ting Gong and Jianming Ren, "Hard Rules and Soft Constraints: Regulating Conflict of Interest in China," *Journal of Contemporary China* 22, no. 79 (2013): 17.

74. Clinton Rossiter, *The American Presidency*, 2nd ed. (New York: Time Inc., 1963), p. 65 (cited in Sabl, *Ruling Passions*, pp. 51–52).

75. Zhang Shai, "Qiangli kongzhi yu jingshen yueshu: Zhengzhi lunli jiaodu de zhongguo fangfu kunjing yu fangfu lujing" [Controlling by Power and Restraining by Spirit: The Predicament of Preventing Corruption in China and the Way of Preventing Corruption Considered from the Perspective of Political Ethics], *Lunli yu gaige* 3 (2013): 37–40.

76. Kwame Anthony Appiah, *The Honor Code: How Moral Revolutions Happen* (New York: Norton, 2010), p. 209.

77. Ibid., ch. 2. The analogy with corruption is not perfect: it is easier to observe (and hence crack down on) footbinding than corruption.

78. "President Xi Promises to Shake Off GDP Obsession in Promoting Officials" (http://news.xinhuanet.com/English/china/2013–06/29/c_132497892.htm).

79. Such politically sensitive claims are made by mainland Chinese scholars in academic publications (see, e.g., Zhang, "Qiangli kongzhi yu jingshen yueshu" [Controlling by Power and Restraining by Spirit], pp. 39–40), but they are rarely articulated in the more popular media.

80. One famous example is Liu Shaoqi's 1939 text "How to Be a Good Communist," with its emphasis on self-cultivation (for an English translation, see http://www.marxists.org/reference/archive/liu-shaoqi/1939/how-to-be/). The "Maoist" self-criticism sessions being revived by Xi Jinping similarly owe more to Confucianism than to Marxism (Yu Zeyuan, "Xi Jinping dudao guanyuan xianghu jieduan" [Xi Jinping Supervises Mutual Self-Criticism Sessions], *Lianhe zaobao*, 9 Sept. 2013).

81. See, e.g., Chen Lai, *Kongfuzi yu xiandai shijie* [Confucius and the Modern World] (Beijing: Peking University Press, 2011); and Jiang, *A Confucian Constitutional Order*. Even Singapore, notorious for its "Legalist" reliance on high salaries and harsh punishments to curb corrupt behavior, recognizes the need for moral education in Confucian classics (Ye Xingqiang, "Yong 'Dizigui' jiao hao nide haizi" [Use "Dizigui" to Educate Your Children in Ethical Behavior], *Lianhe zaobao*, 3 Sept. 2013).

82. Benjamin Kang Lim and Ben Blanchard, "Xi Jinping Hopes Traditional Faiths Can Fill Moral Void in China: Sources," *Reuters*, 29 Sept. 2013; "Xi Jinping canjia Anhui daibiaotuan shenyi shi qiangdiao: Zuofeng jianshi yongyuan zai lu shang" [Xi Jinping Stresses to Anhui Delegates: Building a New Way of Doing Things Is Continuous Work], 9 Mar. 2014 (http://news.xinhuanet.com/politics/2014–03/09/c_119680052.htm).

83. The argument here is not that replacing communism with Confucianism is sufficient to eliminate corruption; rather, my point is that ethical training can be helpful in curtailing corruption (if it is combined with other means) and Confucian ethics has more to contribute in that respect than the Marxist tradition. One study has shown that ethical training in Baltic countries can have an effect in curbing corruption of civil servants, though it needs to be combined with punishment for corrupt officials (Lars Johannsen and Karin Hilmer Pedersen, "How to Combat Corruption: Assessing Anti-Corruption Measures from a Civil Servant's Perspective," *Administrative Culture* 13, no. 2 [2012]: 130–146). In the case of Indonesia, ethical traditions may influence the extent of corruption: the predominantly Hindu island of Bali is alleged to be less corrupt than other parts of the country and an important reason may be related to the Hindu idea of karma: sins in this life influence the form of reincarnation in the next life (in contrast, other religions such as Islam and Catholicism provide various means for cleansing oneself of sins in this life).

84. Quoted in Wong, "Political Meritocracy in Singapore," pp. 299–300.

85. This case is discussed in ibid., pp. 300–302.

86. Tan, "Meritocracy and Political Liberalization in Singapore."

87. Young, *The Rise of the Meritocracy*, p. 97.

88. Lee Hsien Loong, "To Listen, Labour and Lead: Building a Better Singapore Together," *Ethos* 12 (June 2013): 11.

89. Maurice Bernard, *La méritocratie française: Les élites française. Essai critique* (Paris: L'Harmattan, 2010), vol. 1, p. 112.

90. Marie-Laure Delorme, *Les allées du pouvoir* (Paris: Seuil, 2011), p. 11.

91. Ibid., p. 116.

92. Ibid., p. 281. However, a recent exposé (bitter but entertaining) by an ENA graduate denounces the system as rewarding ultracompetitive careerists and conformists who learn little about ethics and how to solve practical administrative problems (Olivier Saby, *Promotion Ubu roi: Mes 27 mois sur les bancs de l'ENA* [Paris: Flammarion, 2012]). For a more positive account of the practical training at the ENA, see Jean-Benoît Nadeau and Julie Barlow, *Sixty Million Frenchmen Can't Be Wrong (Why We Love France but Not the French)* (Naperville, Ill.: Sourcebooks, 2003), pp. 194–195.

93. Delorme, *Les allées du pouvoir*, pp. 120, 265, 272. See also Bernard, *La méritocratie française*, vol. 1, p. 110. And those who do come from less privileged backgrounds often experience culture shock and suffer from various forms of social discrimination at the ENA: see Jules Naudet, *Entrer dans l'élite: Parcours de réussite en France, aux États-Unis et en Inde* [Entering the Elite: Paths to Success in France, the United States and India] (Paris: Presses Universitaires de France, 2012), pp. 201–202.

94. Steven Erlanger, "Top French Schools, Asked to Diversify, Fear for Standards," *New York Times*, 30 June 2010.

95. Quoted in Delorme, *Les allées du pouvoir*, p. 265 (my translations unless indicated otherwise).

96. Similar arguments have been made about the likely consequences of class-based political elitism in the United States: elites live lives separate from the rest and thus have trouble making good decisions even when they want to. Ignorant of the challenges that the poor and the middle class face and separated from the consequence of their actions, elites are susceptible to making policies that seem reasonable but which on-the-ground experience would expose as ineffectual. For example, the evacuation of New Orleans before Hurricane Katrina did not succeed because many New Orleanians had nowhere to go, no money to get there, and no cars to escape—facts that should have been known to political leaders (http://www.theamericanconservative.com/articles/tyranny-of-merit/).

97. In the United Kingdom, leaders are also chosen from a very narrow class of people: see Ferdinand Mount, *The New Few, or A Very British Oligarchy: Power and Inequality in Britain Now* (New York: Simon and Schuster, 2012).

98. In the United States, the voting behavior of political representatives tends to mirror their class allegiances: see Larry M. Bartels, *Unequal Democracy: The Political*

Economy of the New Gilded Age (Princeton, N.J.: Princeton University Press, 2008). See also the discussion in chapter 1, section 2.

99. Delorme, *Les allées du pouvoir*, p. 278.

100. Cited in ibid., p. 14.

101. At least partly as a result of the declining political importance of the ENA, the number of yearly ENA applicants has dropped from a high of about fifteen thousand in the early 1990s to less than one thousand (Nadeau and Barlow, *Sixty Million Frenchmen Can't Be Wrong*, pp. 202–203).

102. See Hong Yiting, "Baorong de jingyingzhuyi?" [Inclusive Elitism?], *Lianhe zaobao*, 29 Sept. 2013; and "Setting Course for a More Equal Society," *Straits Times*, 19 Aug. 2013.

103. The net worth of China's wealthy political elite (not counting the wealth of family members) has far surpassed that of the United States: the collective net worth of the richest seventy members of China's legislature rose to $89.8 billion in 2011, compared to the $7.5 billion net worth of all 660 top officials in the three major branches of the U.S. government (http://www.businessweek.com/articles/2012-03-01/the-chinese-communist-partys-capitalist-elite).

104. The proportion of workers and farmers has decreased in society at large, but the decrease of workers and farmers in the party, particularly at the higher echelons of political power, has been much steeper: for example, the proportion of workers and farmers in the National People's Congress fell by about two-thirds between 1975 and 2003, even though workers and farmers still constitute more than half of the population. Wang Shaoguang, "Is the Way of the Humane Authority a Good Thing? An Assessment of Confucian Constitutionalism," in Jiang, *A Confucian Constitutional Order*, pp. 150–151.

105. Needless to say, such problems are not unique to China: in the United States, South Korea, and Singapore, for example, wealthy parents spend exorbitant sums on tutors and prep courses and draw on social connections to give their children an edge in the competition for prestigious schools and universities.

106. In China, the situation is almost the reverse: students from relatively wealthy cities with prestigious universities (such as Beijing and Shanghai) can be admitted to the universities in their "home" cities with fewer points on the national examinations than candidates from outside. In response, leading Chinese universities have implemented proposals to admit more students from poor, rural regions with lower scores on national university examinations, but vested interests block more substantial reform (Wang Hongyi, "Fudan University Works to Attract Rural Students," *China Daily*, 24 Feb. 2014).

107. In France, some elite universities rejected changes to their admissions procedures to take in more students from disadvantaged backgrounds (Ben Hall, "France's Famed Meritocracy Endangered by Grandes Écoles," *Financial Times*, 9/10 Jan. 2010), though Sciences Po has famously stood out with its efforts to admit more students from disadvantaged backgrounds (Cecilia Gabizon and Raphael Gibour, "Sciences Po: De plus en plus de lycéens venus de ZEP" [Sciences Po: More and More

Students from Secondary Schools in Disadvantaged Regions], *Le Figaro*, 25 July 2012).

108. In the case of public service examinations, however, there may be explicit discrimination against minority groups such as the Muslim, Turkic-speaking Uighurs (Andrew Jacobs, "Uighurs in China Say Bias Is Growing," *New York Times*, 7 Oct. 2013).

109. Jinghan Zeng, "Institutionalization of the Authoritarian Leadership in China: A Power Succession System with Chinese Characteristics?" *Contemporary Politics* 20, no. 3 (2014): 304.

110. One possibility is to reserve spots on the Central Committee and the Politburo for members of religious minorities. But the CCP would have to abandon official atheism (an idea that comes from an imported Marxist Western ideology; Confucians, in contrast, do not have much to say about the afterlife, but they do not dismiss it as a possibility). Another possibility would be to establish a House of Cultural Continuity composed of leaders of diverse religions with a long historical presence in China (including Confucianism, Tibetan Buddhism, Islam, and Christianity) as proposed by Jiang Qing (see his book *A Confucian Constitutional Order*). In principle, it would not be too difficult to reform the Chinese People's Political Consultative Conference (CPPCC) into this kind of institution, but the CPPCC would need to have more formal power in the political system to be viewed as more legitimate by the groups represented in the institution.

111. For an argument that dealing with poverty requires understanding of the daily decisions facing the poor, see Abhijit Banerjee and Esther Duflo, *Poor Economics: A Radical Rethinking of the Way to Fight Global Poverty* (New York: Public Affairs, 2012). Note that there are other forms of disadvantage besides material poverty (such as being deprived of key family relations), and the deliberations about what it means to be disadvantaged also need to include substantial input from disadvantaged sectors of the population. See Jonathan Wolff and Avner de-Shalit, *Disadvantage* (Oxford: Oxford University Press, 2007).

112. A second-best option would be to send candidates from privileged backgrounds on leadership tracks for extended periods of training in disadvantaged parts of the country (or abroad) to sensitize them to the needs of the disadvantaged (see chapter 2, section 4). Of course, the period would need to be finite (say, one year), in contrast to the Cultural Revolution, when youths from cities were sent to poor rural areas without hope of ever returning.

113. Michael Young's (satirical) argument for meritocracy involves weakening family structures in order to equalize opportunities in the meritocratic race to the top (Young, *The Rise of Meritocracy*, ch. 1). From a profamily standpoint, the state can implement measures such as high inheritance tax rates (as in Japan) that serve to equalize opportunities for future generations without substantially weakening family structures.

114. A Marxist may respond that the very existence of such an elite wouldn't matter as much in a condition of relative economic equality, but it would still be impor-

tant for the elite to be able and public spirited in order to implement effective policies in both domestic and foreign affairs.

115. Bernard, *La méritocratie française*, vol. 2, pp. 12, 102, 104, 105, 108–110.

116. Zhu, "Why Are Offices for Sale in China?" p. 577. See also chapter 2, section 3.

117. Pines, "Between Merit and Pedigree," p. 191.

118. Email sent by Yuri Pines, 13 Oct. 2013.

119. Mill's argument that we need freedom of speech to expose wrongdoing and put forward new and better ideas for policy making was also articulated by traditional Confucian thinkers (e.g., in the *Analects* 13.15, Confucius says that the following sentence—"if a ruler's policies are not good and no one opposes them"—can lead to the ruin of a country). Such sayings were not mere theory: in the Tang and the Northern Song, perhaps the most vibrant dynasties in Chinese imperial history, there was substantial space for political criticism; in Confucian-influenced Korea during the Choson dynasty, the ruler's advisors were encouraged to drink alcohol before meetings so they'd have more courage to raise critical points. In early 2013, contemporary Confucian thinkers (courageously) signed a petition supported with quotations from earlier thinkers criticizing the crackdown on the liberal weekly *Southern Weekend* (http://www.confucius2000.com/admin/list.asp?id=5519). That said, there may still be key differences between Confucian and liberal approaches to freedom of speech: for example, Confucians might argue for a paternalistic approach to freedom of the press that would justify both freedom to criticize mistakes and state funding for media that report on issues likely to be neglected by market-funded media, such as coverage of the Special Olympics meant to increase sensitivity toward disabled people in society at large (see the preface to the new edition of my book *China's New Confucianism*). There may also be a Confucian case for state-subsidized news media that attempt to convey and justify state policy in as balanced a manner as possible, so long as there is also room for privately funded media outlets.

120. John Stuart Mill, "On Liberty," in *Three Essays* (Oxford: Oxford University Press, 1975), pp. 83, 88, 89.

121. This proposal may sound radical in the Chinese government—why would the government, which is concerned with political stability, agree to freedom of speech simply in order to open political opportunities for a few outliers?—but there is already substantial freedom of speech helpful for identifying some potential leaders outside the official track. According to the first large-scale, multiple-source analysis of China's censorship program, the censors allow a great deal of substantive criticism of the state and its policies, and censorship appears to be aimed at collective action by silencing comments that represent, reinforce, or spur social mobilization, regardless of content. Gary King, Jennifer Pan, and Margaret E. Roberts, "How Censorship Allows Government Criticism but Silences Collective Expression," *American Political Science Review* 107, no. 10 (May 2013): 326–343. Nonetheless, I can testify from my own experience that many censored works do not aim for any collective action (even this book—a defense of the overall system!—is likely to be censored in its Chinese

translation). Moreover, the issue of how to assess new and different forms of merit may require some social mobilization to show that the new forms of assessing merit have desirable social impacts. And there may be some naturally cautious types who prefer to keep quiet simply because the seemingly arbitrary boundaries of the censorship regime induce an element of fear, however irrational. Thus, a relaxation of censorship and clarification of the boundaries would allow the government to identify more innovative people and social groups from diverse walks of life to put forward ideas in a constructive way and show that they have desirable social impact. Such voices need not threaten political stability because they will rely on moral power above all else and the government can still prohibit speech aimed at toppling the regime (see also chapter 4, section 3).

122. This is not to deny that there is some de facto experimentation at the state level in federal systems such as the United States (e.g., regarding legalization of marijuana, gay marriage, and health care reform), but local experiments are not driven by a conscious desire to experiment by the central-level (federal) government and they cannot be generalized to the whole country by central-level decisions that contravene constitutionally assigned state powers.

123. Systematic experimentation was institutionalized for the first time under Deng's rule, but experimentation below the national level was also carried out in imperial China (see concluding thoughts).

124. Ann Florini, Hairong Lai, and Yeling Tan, *China Experiments: From Local Innovation to National Reform* (Washington, D.C.: Brookings Institution Press, 2012), pp. 4–5.

125. Ibid., p. 158. See also Baogang He and Mark E. Warren, "Authoritarian Deliberation: The Deliberative Turn in Chinese Political Development," *Perspectives on Politics* 9, no. 2 (June 2011): 269–289; Ma Jun, "Accountability without Elections," in *China 3.0*, ed. Mark Leonard (London: European Council on Foreign Relations, 2012); and concluding thoughts, section 2.

126. The government is experimenting with new ways of assessing merit—see chapter 2, section 3, and concluding thoughts, section 2—but the system is still far too rigid. As it stands, the same bureaucratic hierarchies are used in all public institutions, no matter how different their functions and character (monks in temples, academics in universities, and government officials are all ranked according to the same official categories!). And within the government, it may be possible and desirable to experiment with different tracks for civil servants and political officials.

127. Jean-Marc Coicaud, "Legitimacy, across Borders and over Time," in *Fault Lines of International Legitimacy*, ed. Hilary Charlesworth and Jean-Marc Coicaud (Cambridge: Cambridge University Press, 2010), p. 17.

128. From a normative viewpoint, it is also worth asking if the people are morally justified in thinking that the government is morally justified. In the case of closed regimes, such as North Korea, that seem to rely almost exclusively on propaganda and coercion, we have good reasons for thinking that apparent support for the regime may not be justified, and we can safely predict that the regime would collapse if the coun-

try opened up and the people were made aware of (desirable) political alternatives in the rest of the world. In the case of China, however, the government is relatively open to the rest of the world (notwithstanding censorship), millions of Chinese study and travel abroad and return to China without changed political beliefs, and reliable opinion polls consistently show support for the regime (see below); hence I will not pursue the possibility that Chinese suffer from a collective form of "false consciousness." What I can say with confidence is that many Chinese academics are educated abroad and/or have full access to information through various means; they are no more "brainwashed" than American academics, and probably less so than "average" Americans exposed to (manipulated by?) mainstream media in the United States.

129. Philippe C. Schmitter, "What Is Political Legitimacy and How Can It Be Acquired? Lessons from a Deviant Case," in *Reviving Legitimacy: Lessons for and from China*, ed. Deng Zhenglai and Sujian Guo (Lanham, Md.: Lexington Books, 2011), p. 27.

130. Why did East Asian countries with a Confucian heritage (other than China) adopt "Western-style" democracy in the form of one person, one vote and a multiparty competitive system? I will not pursue this question in this book, other than to note that military, economic, and moral pressure from the United States played a role. In the case of China, such pressure matters less because the country has the economic and military clout as well as the cultural confidence to resist foreign interference and affirm its own political model.

131. Wang, "Is the Way of the Humane Authority a Good Thing?" pp. 142–143.

132. Ibid., p. 144.

133. Shi Tianjian, "China: Democratic Values Supporting an Authoritarian System," in *How East Asians View Democracy*, p. 210. It is important, however, to distinguish between support for particular politicians and the current character of political institutions, on the one hand, and support for the underlying constitutional system, on the other. In Taiwan, for example, fragile regime legitimacy coexists with strong support for electoral democracy as a mechanism to choose political leaders (Min-Hua Huang, "Polarized Politics, Regime Evaluation and Democratic Legitimacy in Taiwan," paper presented at workshop on "East Asian Perspectives on Political Legitimacy," University of Hong Kong, 18–19 Aug. 2011). Similarly, in the United States a majority of people oppose the current character of the U.S. House of Representatives but (I would surmise) an even larger majority support the constitutional system. In China, by contrast, there may be strong support for the central government but weaker support for the constitutional system as a whole. In that basic sense, the constitutional systems in Taiwan and the United States are more legitimate, and hence more stable, than the Chinese system.

134. Tom Phillips, "Migrant Workers Clash with Police in China's Industrial Heartland," *The Telegraph*, 27 June 2012.

135. "180,000 Protests in 2010: China's Spending on Internal Policing Outstrips Defense Budget," *Bloomberg News*, 6 Mar. 2011.

136. Tony Saich, "Chinese Governance Seen through the People's Eyes," *East Asia Forum*, 24 July 2011.

137. He, "An Empirical Theory of Hybrid Legitimacy System in China."

138. Tianjian Shi and Lu Jie, "Cultural Impacts on People's Understanding of Democracy," paper presented at the 2010 American Political Science Association Annual Meeting, Washington, D.C., 1–5 Sept., p. 10. See also Tianjian Shi, *The Cultural Logic of Politics in Mainland China and Taiwan* (New York: Cambridge University Press, 2014), ch. 7. It is not just "ordinary Chinese" who hold this view. In spring 2011, I taught an "Introduction to Political Philosophy" course at Tsinghua University with about thirty-five students who are supposed to be members of the educated elite. Halfway through the course—after I had taught J. S. Mill and Rawls—I asked the students if the best definition of democracy should be "government for the people, by the people, or of the people." A large majority chose "government for the people," and "by the people" came in last place.

139. Doh Chull Shin argues (based on the findings of the Asian Barometer Survey) that the majority of East Asians in other states with a Confucian legacy also tend to be attached to "paternalistic meritocracy," prioritize economic well-being over freedom, and define democracy in substantive (rather than procedural) terms. Doh, *Confucianism and Democratization in East Asia*, ch. 9. Also based on empirical findings, Yun-han Chu, Yu-tzung Chang, and Wen-Chin Wu show that citizens in East Asian states with a Confucian heritage believe that the integrity of political officials, law-abiding government, and fair treatment of the people are sufficient to legitimize the regime without the standard fixtures of liberal democracies that emphasize input legitimacy in terms of popular accountability and electoral procedures ("Sources of Regime Legitimacy in Confucian Societies," paper presented at the conference on "Confucianism, Democracy, and Constitutionalism: Global and East Asian Perspectives," National Taiwan University, 14–15 June 2013). The idea that electoral democracy is the foundation of political legitimacy has been questioned in the Western political context as well. Bo Rothstein argues that there is scant evidence for the claim that electoral democracy underpins legitimacy even in the successful and stable Nordic democracies. Instead of input legitimacy, "the main sources of political legitimacy are situated on the output side of the political system and have to do with the quality of government. It is the absence of corruption, discrimination, and similar violations of the principle of impartiality in exercising political power that serves to create political legitimacy" (Rothstein, "Creating Political Legitimacy: Electoral Government Versus Quality of Government," *American Behavioral Scientist* 53 [2009]: 325).

140. Shi, "China: Democratic Values Supporting an Authoritarian System," p. 216.

141. Quoted in John Makeham, *Lost Soul: "Confucianism" in Contemporary Chinese Academic Discourse* (Cambridge, Mass.: Harvard University Asia Center, 2008), p. 262. See also Tang Wenming, "Gu jin zhengjiao hejie zhi zhengzhao yu qianjing—xiaoyi guojia bowuguan men qian kongzi xiang de li yu yi" [The Prospect and Mean-

ing of Reconciling Politics and Education in the Past and the Present—A Brief Analysis of the Erecting and the Removal of the Confucius Statue in Front of the National Museum], *Rujia youbao,* 10 June 2011.

142. See Cui Zhiyuan, "Partial Intimations of the Coming Whole: The Chongqing Experiment in Light of the Theories of Henry George, James Meade, and Antonio Gramsci," *Modern China* 37, no. 6 (2011): 646–660.

143. Allen Carlson, "Reimagining the Frontier: Patterns of Sinicization and the Emergence of New Thinking about China's Territorial Periphery," paper presented at the Civilizations and Sinicization Workshop, Beijing University, 25–26 Mar. 2011, pp. 3–4.

144. Quoted in Orville Shell, "China: Humiliation and the Olympics," *New York Review of Books*, 14 Aug. 2008.

145. On the importance of "humiliation" as a motivating force in Chinese politics since the mid-nineteenth century, see Schell and Delury, *Wealth and Power.*

146. Zheng Wang, *Never Forget National Humiliation: Historical Memory in Chinese Politics and Foreign Relations* (New York: Columbia University Press, 2012).

147. Cited in Robert L. Kuhn, *How China's Leaders Think: The Inside Story of China's Past, Current and Future Leaders* (Singapore: John Wiley & Sons, 2011), p. 4.

148. It's also worth asking if there is a nonresentful form of nationalism, given that nationalism often emphasizes the greatness of one's nation by way of comparison with others. But there are differences: less resentful forms of nationalism do not emphasize stories of suffering at the hands of other nations, and nations can take pride in characteristics—say, a language—that are not meant to be better than characteristics in other nations (simply different). And to the extent the nation is viewed as "great," its people can take pride in contributions to human civilization that others can enjoy, just as foreign visitors can enjoy national treasures displayed in national museums, and the main point is not to keep score in national competitions about greatness.

149. Tang Wenming, "Cong Rujia zhengjiu minzuzhuyi" [Rescuing Nationalism by Confucianism], *Wenhua zongheng* 5 (Oct. 2011) (http://www.21bcr.com/a/zhuan__ti/bitan_rujiayuminzuzhuyi/2011/1027/3196.html).

150. The analogy is imperfect and in reality one cannot leave aside moral concerns. The Thatcher government did not suffer immediate economic costs because its war with Argentina was not widely perceived as unjust by other economically dominant powers. But if China launches a war that is widely perceived to be unjust by other dominant economic powers, the economic costs will be so high as to potentially undermine the regime, even in the short term.

151. Again, there are precedents in Chinese history. The Manchu emperor Qianlong gained the support of the Han Chinese and more legitimacy for the empire by commissioning a book (*Qinding shengchao xunjie zhuchen lu* [Records of the Royal Officials Who Sacrificed Themselves for the Previous Dynasty]) that documents a list of morally admirable generals and politicians who fervently opposed Qianlong's forefathers in wars during the late Ming dynasty.

152. On the distinction between "hard" and "soft" nationalism, see my comment: http://www.csmonitor.com/Commentary/Global-Viewpoint/2013/0204/Soft-nationalism-is-good-for-China.

153. Jyrki Kallio, "Tradition in Chinese Politics," in *FIFA Report* (Helsinki: Finnish Institute of International Affairs, 2011), p. 1.

154. See Jiang, *A Confucian Constitutional Order*. Jiang is careful to point out, however, that Confucianism's embrace of nationalism is a short-term response to a historical situation (the threat faced by Chinese culture); the Confucian ideal of *wangdao* (the way of the humane authority) is meant to be a universal ideal, not tied to any particular nation (Jiang Qing, *Xinxi leida*, 21 Apr. 2011, http://info.whb.cn/xxld/view/10080). See also Kang Xiaoguang, *Dangdai Zhongguo dalu: Wenhua minzuzhuyi yundong yanjiu* [Contemporary Mainland China: Research on the Movement of Cultural Nationalism] (Singapore: World Scientific Publishing Co., 2008); and Kang's article "Rujia xianzheng lun gang" [A Sketch of the Theory of Confucian Constitutionalism] on this Confucian website: http://www.21ccom.net/articles/zgyj/xzmj/article_2011053036449.html.

155. Also, there may be legitimate worries that the official promotion of Confucianism, even desirable interpretations of Confucianism that leave much room for respect for (if not celebration of) minority views, will increase tensions with restive minorities because Confucianism will be (mis)perceived as an exclusively Han project rather than an effort to promote universal (Confucian) values. One way of dealing with this problem is to promote desirable interpretations of Confucian values without the Confucian label.

156. http://sinosphere.blogs.nytimes.com/2013/10/18/full-text-of-the-oxford-consensus-2013/ (I have modified the translation on this website).

157. Baogang Guo, *China's Quest for Political Legitimacy: The New Equity-Enhancing Politics* (Lanham, Md.: Lexington Books, 2010), pp. 7–12. In contrast, the idea that the government has a moral obligation to alleviate poverty has fairly recent roots in the West: Samuel Fleischacker traces the development of this view from the eighteenth century on (Fleischacker, *A Short History of Distributive Justice* [Cambridge, Mass.: Harvard University Press, 2005]). Although earlier thinkers such as Aristotle and Machiavelli favored regimes that minimized conflict between rich and poor, their concern was political stability, not the alleviation of poverty.

158. Here and elsewhere, I have modified the translations in *The Analects of Confucius: A Philosophical Translation*, trans. Roger T. Ames and Henry Rosemont Jr. (New York: Ballantine Books, 1998).

159. Tianjian Shi and Lu Jie claim that the aim of the *minben* doctrine (the Confucian idea that the government should promote the welfare of the people) is to "keep the rulers in power" (Shi and Lu, "The Shadow of Confucianism," *Journal of Democracy* 21, no. 4 [Oct. 2010]: 125), but such an interpretation owes more to Legalist ideas about government (and perhaps is meant to be an interpretation of the motivation of political leaders) than to Confucian ethics. Confucians emphasize that the moral aim of government is to benefit the people, not rulers (see chapter 2, section 4).

160. Here and elsewhere, I have modified the translations in *Mencius*, vol. 1–2, trans. D. C. Lau (Hong Kong: Chinese University Press, 1984).

161. Yanqi Tong, "Morality, Benevolence, and Responsibility: Regime Legitimacy in China from Past to Present," in *Reviving Legitimacy: Lessons for and from China*, ed. Deng Zhenglai and Sujian Guo (Lanham, Md.: Lexington Books, 2011), p. 200.

162. R. Bin Wong, "Confucian Agendas for Material and Ideological Control in Modern China," in *Culture and State in Chinese History*, ed. Theodore Huters, R. Bin Wong, and Pauline Yu (Stanford, Calif.: Stanford University Press, 1997), p. 307.

163. Tong, "Morality, Benevolence, and Responsibility," p. 204.

164. The "right to food" is not anachronistic here because it is a right in the modern sense of a legally enforceable norm.

165. To be fair, Mao embarked on similar market-oriented reforms in the 1950s and in 1961–1963, but they were smaller in scale and less open to the outside world.

166. http://www.globalissues.org/article/4/poverty-around-the-world#WorldBanksPovertyEstimatesRevised.

167. As suggested earlier in this chapter, if perceptions are manufactured due to censorship and propaganda, then we can question whether support for the state is morally justified. But social media has led to a much more open society and it is harder to cover up disasters now than in the recent past.

168. Wang Shaoguang, "Why Is State Effectiveness Essential for Democracy? Asian Examples," in *Contemporary Chinese Political Thought: Debates and Perspectives*, ed. Fred Dallmayr and Zhao Tingyang (Lexington: University Press of Kentucky, 2012). Wang argues that since an effective state is a prerequisite for democracy, such institutionalized participation should not be accompanied by the enfeeblement of state power.

169. From a normative point of view, Confucianism would also justify more popular participation once economic needs are met. According to the early Confucians, the first task of government is the elimination of poverty, but after that it must turn to the education of the people, meaning the provision of the conditions for the ethical and intellectual development of the people. Given the Confucian premise that human self-realization involves serving the community, it follows that as many people as possible should be given the opportunity to realize that goal. In practice, it would mean more opportunities to participate in politics in a public-spirited way. At higher levels of economic development, in other words, it becomes harder to justify exclusion of the people from politics (see Sungmoon Kim, "To Become a Confucian Democratic Citizen: Against Meritocratic Elitism," *British Journal of Political Science* 43, no. 3 [July 2013]: 579–599). Still, it doesn't follow that Confucians would seek to justify the right to equal political participation in the form of one person, one vote. Even in an ideal society as portrayed in the *Record of Rites*, there will still be a distinction between exemplary persons (*junzi*) who seek justice and petty persons (*xiao ren*) who narrowly pursue their own self-interest, and the political system should still be designed with the aim of selecting and promoting *junzi*. In fact, the political reality may be even worse than Confucians anticipated. As discussed in chapter 1 (section 1),

most people suffer from cognitive and emotional biases that get in the way of the pursuit of self-interest, even in rich, industrialized societies like the United States. So it's enough of a challenge to become a *xiao ren*, never mind striving to be a *junzi*!

170. Doh, *Confucianism and Democratization in East Asia*, p. 322.

171. Shi and Lu, "Cultural Impacts on People's Understanding of Democracy," p. 10.

172. Shi, *The Cultural Logic of Politics in Mainland China and Taiwan*, ch. 4. Government manipulation may be part of the reason for the growing attachment to Confucian political values, but China's recent economic rise is perhaps even more important: on the one hand, with economic might comes cultural pride; on the other hand, modernization leads to worries about excessive individualism that needs to be countered (in the minds of many Chinese intellectuals and educators) by traditional ethics that value social responsibility. So the revival of "Confucianism" might have happened even without government encouragement.

173. See the introduction and Han Fangming, "Cong zui re men 'zhengzhi kepupian' kan guoji zhengzhi yingxiao" [Looking at the Selling of Politics from the Perspective of a Popular "Political Cartoon"], *Lianhe zaobao*, 22 Oct. 2013.

174. Ho-fung Hung, *Protest with Chinese Characteristics: Demonstrations, Riots, and Petitions in the Mid-Qing Dynasty* (New York: Columbia University Press, 2011).

175. Ho-fung Hung, "Confucianism and Political Dissent in China," *East Asia Forum*, 26 July 2011, http://www.eastasiaforum.org/2011/07/26/confucianism-and-political-dissent-in-china/. See also Du Lun, "'Ren xue hefaxing sixiang' gaiyao jiqi xianshi yiyi" [Outline of the Practical Meaning of "The Theory of a Legitimate Humane Government"], in *Rujia de dangdai shiming* [The Contemporary Mission of Confucianism] (Beijing: Jiuzhou Press, 2010), p. 315.

176. The problem is "deep" because it can fatally undermine a regime if politically ambitious people feel totally shut out from the system and resort to overthrow of the system as the only alternative. Consider the case of Mao Zedong, clearly a talented and ambitious person who wanted to do something big for his country even as a young man. Before he led the CCP, Mao worked as an assistant to Peking University librarian Li Dazhao (an early Chinese communist) between 1918 and 1919 (Stuart Schram, *Mao Tse-Tung* [London: Simon & Schuster, 1966], pp. 48–49). At the university, Mao was widely snubbed due to his rural Hunanese accent and lowly position, and he developed a lifelong aversion to intellectuals working within a system that did not recognize and reward his political potential. No doubt other factors were at play, but history could have taken a different turn if Mao had been identified as a potential leader by reformist Confucian and liberal intellectuals at Peking University.

177. See chapter 2, section 2.

178. A recent headline in a Chinese-language newspaper in Singapore emphasizes this point: "Wei min fuwu bu dang" [To Serve the Public without Entering the Party], *Lianhe zaobao*, 21 Aug. 2013.

179. Such programs are more likely to be effective in a society with a relatively paternalistic political culture (such as China). Even then, however, the programs

must generate true emotions. Two of the most widely watched shows in China—the yearly celebration of the Spring Festival (*Chunwan*) and the weekly talent search (*Zhongguo mengxiang xiu*)—combine humor and touching stories to show the social value of representatives of various social groups.

180. To repeat, political leaders are supposed to be above average in terms of intellectual ability, social skills, and virtue, but they need not be at the top of the scale on any one dimension (see chapter 2, end).

181. A cynic inspired by the thought of Michel Foucault may want to add that there are many sources of power in society—in families, schools, workplaces, hospitals, prisons, etc.—and if ambitious people can realize their power-hungry desires in other social spheres, they may worry less about making it to the top of the political power pyramid.

Chapter 4
Three Models of Democratic Meritocracy

1. The myth, according to Plato, should persuade not just the people, but the rulers themselves. He recognizes that it would be a challenge for the Guardians to persuade themselves in the first generation, but "it might succeed with the second and later generations" (*The Republic*, trans. Desmond Lee [Harmondsworth: Penguin, 1974], 415d). One wonders whether Kim Jong-un, the young Supreme Leader of North Korea, believes that he has inherited the quasi-divine qualities of his grandfather or is motivated purely by cynicism.

2. Aristotle, *The Politics*, trans. Ernest Barker (London: Oxford University Press, 1958), 1294b.

3. But see Yves Sintomer, *Petite histore de l'expérimentation démocratique: Tirage au sort et politique d'Athènes à nos jours* [A Short History of Democratic Experimentation: Selection by Lot from Athens to the Present] (Paris: La Découverte, 2011). Sintomer argues that modern methods of statistical sampling allow for a truly representative sample of the population to rule if selected by lot (in contrast to ancient Athens); hence, contemporary democracies can and should be further democratized by systematic use of lots for selecting political officials. But Sintomer does not go so far as to argue that political leaders should be selected by lottery rather than by vote; at most, randomly selected officials can advise democratically elected leaders. John P. McCormick argues for a political institution at the top that combines lottery and election ("Contain the Wealthy and Patrol the Magistrates: Restoring Elite Accountability to Popular Government," *American Political Science Review* 100, no. 2 [May 2006]: 147–163), though his proposals may not be realistic (see chapter 1, section 2). Wang Shaoguang argues for the use of lots in the Chinese context, but he does not directly say that central-level political leaders should be selected by such means (Wang Shaoguang, *Minzhu si jiang* [Four Lectures about Democracy] [Beijing: Sanlian shudian, 2008]).

4. I do not mean to imply that voter ignorance directly explains Hitler's rise to

power—Sheri Berman argues that it was facilitated by weak political institutionalization and an active civil society that provided a critical training ground for Nazi cadres (Sheri Berman, "Civil Society and the Collapse of the Weimar Republic," *World Politics* 49, no. 3 [1997]: 401–429)—but electoral democracy allowed Hitler's rise, which arguably could have been prevented by meritocratic mechanisms such as exams meant to test voters' competence.

5. See chapter 1, section 1.

6. Caplan, *The Myth of the Rational Voter.*

7. Brennan, *The Ethics of Voting.*

8. John Stuart Mill, *Three Essays* (Oxford: Oxford University Press, 1975), pp. 277, 276.

9. Ibid., pp. 282, 286. Mill also argued for the idea that civil servants entrusted with the task of drafting legislation should be selected by meritocratic means such as examinations. In modern parliamentary systems (and, to a lesser extent, U.S.-style presidential systems), meritocratically selected civil servants are supposed to implement the decisions of democratically elected politicians, but they are not supposed to exercise their own moral judgment in a wide array of political affairs. In practice, however, civil servants supposedly bound by rules of strict neutrality and impartiality often exercise political power. More pertinently, defenders of political meritocracy such as J. S. Mill would object to the idea that democracy should always trump meritocracy: meritocratic considerations should also influence the selection of political decision makers (see my introduction to *The East Asian Challenge for Democracy*).

10. Lee Kuan Yew floated his proposal in an interview with Fareed Zakaria, "Culture Is Destiny: A Conversation with Lee Kuan Yew," *Foreign Affairs* 73, no. 2 (Mar./Apr. 1994): 109–126. On disenchantment with Singapore-style meritocracy, see the articles by Wong and Tan in *The East Asian Challenge for Democracy.*

11. Mill, *Three Essays*, p. 285.

12. Richard Arneson, "Democratic Rights at National and Workplace Levels," in *The Idea of Democracy*, ed. David Copp, Jean Hampton, and John Roemer (Cambridge: Cambridge University Press, 1993), p. 137.

13. One possibility—not likely to be rejected by the voters themselves—is to ask voters whether they are well informed about a topic, and if they answer "yes," their vote can be weighted more than ordinary votes. But this procedure would reward those who hold irrational or overconfident views of their own abilities and penalize the (minority of?) realistic voters (one is reminded of the joke that 80 percent of people think they are above average).

14. In Thailand, supporters of the relatively educated and affluent "yellow shirts" have floated the idea of extra votes for educated people, but the measure has been opposed, not surprisingly, but the more populist "red shirts."

15. Caplan, *The Myth of the Rational Voter*, pp. 197–198.

16. One possibility, put forward by Elena Ziliotti, would be to test voters on party platforms that cover more ground. This proposal can be institutionalized in ways respectful of underlying democratic values (http://www.huffingtonpost.com/daniel-a

-bell/voter-test-europe-china_b_4776362.html) but it still faces the problem that voters are not likely to agree to proposals that qualify their right to an equal vote. Another practical issue is that not all parties publish platforms (as in Israel) and it might be a challenge to get them to do so, especially if they are already a popular party.

17. Mill, *Three Essays*, p. 286.

18. Sun Yat-sen, *Prescriptions for Saving China: Selected Writings of Sun Yat-sen*, ed. Julie Lee Wei, Ramon H. Myers, and Donald G. Gillin; trans. Julie Lee Wei, E-su Zen, and Linda Chao (Stanford, Calif.: Hoover Institution Press, 1994), pp. 49–50 (I have modified the translation).

19. The same problems would affect a modified version of Sun's proposal—asking politicians to take exams *before* running for office—because popular leaders might not be willing to take exams set by an independent branch of government and citizens might object to a system that excluded popular leaders who did not take the exams. Similar problems would affect any proposal to impose qualifications on those running for office, such as a record of public experience: the most popular leaders might not fall into the relevant category and hence those elected might lack democratic legitimacy in a system that is supposed to be democratic.

20. See Olivia Leboyer, *Élite et libéralisme* (Paris: CNRS Editions, 2012), p. 203.

21. Friedrich A. von Hayek, *Law, Legislation, and Liberty*, vol. 3, *The Political Order of a Free People* (Chicago: University of Chicago Press, 1981), pp. 111, 113.

22. See chapter 1.

23. See, e.g., Jeremy Waldron, "The Core of the Case against Judicial Review," *Yale Law Journal* 115 (2006): 1346–1406.

24. See John Darnton, "Labor Peers into the Lords' Future," *International Herald Tribune*, 22 Apr. 1996.

25. See John F. Burns, "Cracks in British Governing Coalition as House of Lords Overhaul Falls Apart," *International Herald Tribune*, 6 Aug. 2012.

26. Martin Wolf, "Why Reform of House of Lords Is a Botch," *Financial Times*, 1 Mar. 2012. For a similar argument on behalf of the (appointed) Canadian senate, see Mel Cappe, "In Defense of an Appointed Senate," *Globe and Mail*, 17 June 2003.

27. See chapter 1.

28. See chapter 3, section 3. For discussion of a more recent political survey, see Shi Yan, "Diaocha Zhongguoren yan zhong de minzhu" [A Survey of the Way Chinese People Look at Democracy], *Nanfang zhoumo*, 2 May 2013.

29. This section draws on my introduction to Jiang, *A Confucian Constitutional Order*.

30. See the critical comments by Joseph Chan, Bai Tongdong, and Li Chenyang in Jiang, *A Confucian Constitutional Order*.

31. Rawls made famous systematic argumentation on behalf of such a strategy for seeking consensus in politics, but the strategy itself is older. For example, the drafters of the 1948 UN Universal Declaration of Human Rights (including the Confucian philosopher P. C. Chang) allowed for disagreement about foundations as a way of seeking consensus on human rights.

32. Jiang's proposal also includes an argument for distributing some seats on the basis of functional constituencies, like the practice in Hong Kong's Legislative Council (Legco); for a critique of functional constituencies, see chapter 1, section 4.

33. Doh, *Confucianism and Democratization in East Asia*, pp. 119–123; and Doh, "How East Asians View Democracy: A Confucian Perspective," in *The East Asian Challenge for Democracy*. These political surveys, however, pose a stark choice between democratic elections and meritocratic selection; had the respondents been asked to choose, say, between a pure democratic system with all political leaders chosen by competitive elections and a hybrid system with central-level leaders selected and promoted on the basis of their ability and virtue and lower-level leaders chosen by competitive elections, there might have been more support for the latter.

34. It is worth asking why the right to an equal vote has come to be seen as the modern political equivalent of a sacred religious practice. Partly, there are cultural reasons: in countries with a Christian heritage, the idea that we are equal in the eyes of God has come to mean that we are equal in the eyes of government, which translates into one person, one vote. But the same thing has happened in countries with predominantly non-Christian cultures, so the Christian context can't be the main explanation. A key factor, in my view, is that the process of voting is psychologically empowering—as I vote, I feel that the act means that I have a say in deciding who exercises power in my political community—however irrational it may be to hold this belief (see chapter 1 for more detailed discussion). And few want to be *disempowered* once one person, one vote has been institutionalized: those "downgraded" will be viewed as "losers" and will object to the change. Such considerations do not apply in a country such as China without elections to choose top leaders, where people generally support political meritocracy, and where the government generally performs well compared to democratic regimes at similar levels of economic development. But if China moves toward electoral democracy at the top, political preferences in favor of one person, one vote will probably change rapidly regardless of whether they ought to.

35. In one extreme case, Perry Link wrote a letter to the *New York Times* claiming that Jiang Qing's constitutional proposal "would be nothing more than new clothes for today's authoritarianism. There is nothing in it that the Politburo Standing Committee in Beijing would not like, except, perhaps for the headache of trying to implement such an awkward plan and defend it before public opinion" ("How to Govern China," *New York Times*, 13 July 2012). This response is way off base—it is true that liberal-minded political critics in mainland China often object to Jiang's arguments against democracy, but Jiang's proposals cannot even be published or discussed in mainland China's leading media outlets because his proposals are such a radical challenge to the political status quo (disclosure: Link responded to a *New York Times* oped I coauthored with Jiang Qing).

36. See Berggruen and Gardels, *Intelligent Governance for the 21st Century*, ch. 5; and the essays by Bai and Chan in *The East Asian Challenge for Democracy*.

37. Conversely, it can be argued that political meritocracy works least well in small communities. At the local level, political leaders are often expected to show

more empathetic and direct concern with the personal plight of ordinary citizens: for example, a taxi driver in Singapore told me that he appreciated the fact that a representative for the (opposition) Workers' Party came to his father's funeral and that's why he voted for the Workers' Party in the 2011 election (the ruling PAP lost the district, and George Yeo, perhaps the most talented leader of his generation, lost his seat in parliament). Consequently, political leaders in Singapore will need to spend more time shaking hands and talking to people in coffeeshops if they are to retain power, and they will have less time to study and learn about key issues affecting the whole country and the rest of the world. (In a large country like China, there is, needless to say, no expectation that Xi Jinping and other top party leaders will attend the funerals of ordinary citizens.) Besides the fact that Singapore's attempt to graft a political meritocracy onto a Westminster-style parliamentary system may not be sustainable, Singapore's tiny size is another reason to doubt the long-term prospects of political meritocracy in that country.

38. See Bai, "A Confucian Version of the Hybrid Regime," pp. 61–62. The Chinese thinker Kang Youwei, who surveyed and compared constitutional systems from around the world in the early twentieth century, also argued that a participatory form of democracy works best in small communities such as Switzerland, whereas a more centralized form of political rule is more appropriate in a big country like China. Zhang Yongle, *Jiu bang xin zao, 1911–1917* [The Remaking of an Old Country, 1911–1917] (Beijing: Beijing daxue chubanshe, 2011), p. 118.

39. In contrast, the U.S. founding father James Madison famously argued that large republics are superior to small political communities on the grounds that they will be led by representatives "whose wisdom may best discern the true interest of their country" and because diverse factions reduce the likelihood that any one faction can systematically dominate the political process and oppress other groups (http://www.constitution.org/fed/federa10.htm; for discussion, see Cass R. Sunstein, "The Enlarged Republic—Then and Now," *New York Review of Books*, 26 Mar. 2009, http://www.nybooks.com/articles/archives/2009/mar/26/the-enlarged-republicthen-and-now/). Had Madison been witness to today's United States, he would likely have been disappointed by the quality of political leaders as well as the relative ease with which well-funded factions ensure that the political system systematically works in their interest (see chapter 1, sections 1 and 2).

40. Media report mentioned in Yawei Liu et al., *China Elections and Governance Review* 1, no. 1 (Feb. 2009).

41. See Ethan Leib and He Baogang, eds., *The Search for Deliberative Democracy in China* (New York: Palgrave Macmillan, 2010).

42. See concluding thoughts, section 2, for more detailed discussion.

43. Lack of support for national-level electoral democracy can be inferred from widespread support for "guardianship discourse" in mainland China. One study showed that the majority of farmers who participate in village elections do not support direct elections even at the township level. Gunter Schubert, "Village Elections, Citizenship and Regime Legitimacy in Contemporary Rural China," in *Regime Legiti-*

macy in Contemporary China: Institutional Change and Stability, ed. Thomas Heberer and Gunter Schubert (London: Routledge, 2009), p. 67. One survey of seven hundred local officials who had attended a provincial training program in 2004 found that 67 percent of the cadres supported popular elections for village leaders, 41 percent for county heads, 13 percent for provincial governors, and just 9 percent for China's president. John L. Thornton, "The Prospects for Democracy in China," *Foreign Affairs* 87, no. 1 (Jan./Feb. 2008): 20. In Hong Kong, limited experience with electoral democracy has helped to generate widespread demand for one person, one vote at the level of Hong Kong's Special Administrative Region, but the demand for electoral democracy does not seem to go much beyond that.

44. The main purpose of village elections is to clean out incompetent and corrupt cadres, not to challenge the political system with CCP as the ruling party (see Kevin J. O'Brien and Lianjiang Li, "Accommodating 'Democracy' in a One-Party State: Introducing Village Elections in China," *China Quarterly* 162 [June 2000]: 488–489), but it's worth asking why local elections have not led to a feeling of empowerment that could have the (unintended by party leaders) consequence of widespread demand for electoral democracy at higher levels. At the local level (in China and elsewhere), politics is easily captured by small groups—party branches (in the case of China), clans, capitalists, religious organizations, and criminal gangs—which makes it easier to "fix" outcomes, hence limiting genuine political competition and the psychological feeling of empowerment generated by the act of voting in truly competitive elections. Robert A. Pastor and Qingshan Tan, "The Meaning of China's Village Elections," *China Quarterly* 162 (June 2000): 509; see also Kevin J. O'Brien and Rongbin Han, "Path to Democracy? Assessing Village Elections in China," *Journal of Contemporary China* 18, no. 60 (June 2009): esp. 368–369; and K. S. Louie, "Village Self-Governance and Democracy in China: An Evaluation," *Democratization* 8, no. 4 (Winter 2001): 147–148. On the other hand, local-level democracy may generate a particular kind of empowerment that is not easily felt at higher levels of government: (1) the farmers who objected to the idea of direct township elections explained that they did not know the township government personnel (i.e., they only care about voting for people they know), and (2) local-level voters derive feelings of dignity not just through elections, but also through being treated on a personal level as respected citizens by responsive cadres (Schubert, "Village Elections, Citizenship and Regime Legitimacy in Contemporary Rural China," pp. 67, 69). Empowerment that is the result of face-to-face interaction is not possible to generate at higher levels of government, a fact that serves to limit the desire to extend elections from the local to higher levels.

45. I don't think it's too controversial to assert that it would not be wise for a young academic striving to get a job and tenure in a political science department of a major Western university to argue that (1) meaningful (and desirable) political reform is possible without electoral democracy at higher levels of government, and (2) China has (at least partly) enacted such reforms over the past couple of decades. That said, philosophers and legal theorists who more directly assess normative issues seem to take seriously such arguments: see, e.g., Stephen C. Angle, "Decent Democratic Central-

ism," *Political Theory* 33, no. 4 (Aug. 2005): 518–546; Andrew Stark, "Charting a Democratic Future in China," *Dissent*, Summer 2012, pp. 18–24; Larry Cata Backer, "From Constitution to Constitutionalism: A Global Framework for Legitimate Power Systems," *Penn State Law Review* 113, no. 3 (2008): esp. 173–174; and Backer, "A Constitutional Court for China within the Chinese Communist Party: Scientific Development and a Reconsideration of the Institutional Role of the CCP," *Suffolk University Law Review* 43, no. 3 (2010): 593–624. Such views are also expressed by political thinkers who need not fear retaliation by guardians of disciplinary orthodoxy: see, e.g., Berggruen and Gardels, *Intelligent Governance for the 21st Century*; John Naisbitt and Doris Naisbitt, *China's Megatrends: The 8 Pillars of a New Society* (New York: Harper Business, 2010), esp. pillar 2; Eric X. Li, "The Life of the Party"; Zhang Weiwei, "China's New Political Discourse," *New Perspectives Quarterly*, Fall 2012, http://onlinelibrary.wiley.com/doi/10.1111/j.1540-5842.2012.01340.x/pdf; and Martin Jacques, "How Will China Change the Political Map?" Transatlantic Academy, Mar. 2013, pp. 1–6.

46. See chapters 2 and 3, as well as concluding thoughts.

47. See Hu Angang, "Is China More Democratic Than the U.S.?" *Huffington Post*, 12 May 2014.

48. See James Fallows, "Obama Explained," *The Atlantic*, Mar. 2012.

49. This is not to say that CCP leaders have a direct incentive to take into account the interests of the unborn and people living outside the state. My argument is that they are less constrained than democratically elected leaders who worry about the results of the next election, but CCP leaders may face their own constraints, such as the need to consider the interests of their "factions" and political protégés. To overcome these constraints, the political selection and recruitment mechanism should be designed to reward those who adopt longer-term outlooks that consider the interests of all those affected by the policies (for example, giving extra points to local officials who consider the environmental consequences of economic growth, as Li Yuanchao tried to do when he was party secretary of Jiangsu province). At the highest level of government, perhaps an institution or a spot on the Standing Committee of the Politburo should be allocated for political leaders whose main responsibility is to argue for the interests of the unborn, ancestors, and people living outside the state, and even animals (for an argument that the interests of animals should be represented in the political process, see Donaldson and Kymlicka, *Zoopolis*). For further discussion, see chapters 2 and 3.

50. J. A. Chandler, "Civil Service in the United States," in *The Civil Service in Liberal Democracies: An Introductory Survey*, ed. J. E. Kindom (London: Routledge, 1990), p. 166.

51. In the United States, only 3 percent of university graduates view the civil service as their top career choice, compared to 76.4 percent in mainland China (Cary Huang, "Deleted Xinhua Report Gives Rare Insight into China Corruption," *South China Morning Post*, 30 Nov. 2014). A recent conversation with a young recipient of a Rhodes scholarship (perhaps the most prestigious scholarship in the American educa-

tional system, designed to choose future leaders) is revealing. She expressed interest in international affairs, and I suggested that she can join the U.S. State Department, but she said that she had been warned that it is hard for people of ambition and talent to succeed in that setting.

52. At a panel of CEOs of leading corporations at the annual meeting of the World Economic Forum in Davos, 2012, the panelists argued that more talent finds its way to the political top in China than in any other country.

53. Again, democracy refers here to the idea that political leaders should be chosen by the people. Values and practices meant to improve the policy-making process often labeled as "democratic," such as public consultation and deliberative polling, can and should be used by meritocratically selected leaders to improve the policy-making process. Moreover, democratic procedures such as voting and competition between candidates can be employed as mechanisms for evaluating public officials being considered for promotion (see concluding thoughts, sections 1 and 2), but in a vertical democratic meritocracy, the further up the chain of political command, the less influence the public has on the promotion process.

54. See He, "An Empirical Theory of Hybrid Legitimacy System in China"; and Hsiao-wen Lee, "Public Opinion in China," Policy Paper series, China Studies Center, University of Sydney, Oct. 2012.

55. Cheng Li, "The End of the CCP's Resilient Authoritarianism: A Tripartite Assessment of Shifting Power in China," *China Quarterly* 211 (Sept. 2012): 595–623; Wang Hui, "Helmut Schmidt: 'I Would Not Sell Democracy to the Chinese'—Part I," *World Post*, 1 Apr. 2014.

56. Of course, the CCP could call an election when it's popular, and it may win the election and perhaps subsequent elections: as Dan Slater and Joseph Wong show by drawing on the cases of Taiwan, South Korea, and Indonesia, ruling parties can concede democratization and continue to thrive if they concede from positions of strength (Slater and Wong, "The Strength to Concede: Ruling Parties and Democratization in Developmental Asia," *Perspectives on Politics* 11, no. 3 [Sept. 2013]: 717–733). But my point is that the *meritocratic* political system will be wrecked: the ruling party can't be assured of victory in future elections and it will have to change from an organization that grooms leaders over decades and plans for the long term to a party that devotes most of its time and resources to appealing to the desires of the electorate and devising strategies for winning the next election. Another possibility is that the CCP could adopt a "Russian-style" democracy, with civil liberties curtailed and the mainstream media heavily stacked in favor of the ruling party, but even going this route would force the CCP to substantially cut back on its long-term focus in favor of concern with the next electoral cycle.

57. I use scare quotes both because (1) one person, one vote has spread to non-Western countries, and (2) the idea that multiparty competition is a necessary condition of a functioning democracy is a relatively recent phenomenon in the West. The founding fathers of the United States endorsed the idea that political leaders should be chosen by means of the voting process but they intended the government to be nonpar-

tisan: George Washington famously warned of the "baneful effects of the spirit of party" in his Farewell Address of 1792 (http://en.wikisource.org/wiki/Washington%27s_Farewell_Address#20). Democratic theorists such as Jean-Jacques Rousseau and John Stuart Mill argued against political parties on the grounds that they cause divisiveness and undermine commitment to the common good. In Western countries, however, a consensus emerged in the post–World War II era that democracy involves both one person, one vote and multiparty competition, with the exception that efforts have been made to outlaw parties that threaten the whole democratic system (such as the Nazis in Germany). Nonpartisan democracies are possible in states with small populations such as Nauru (http://www.dfat.gov.au/geo/nauru/nauru_brief.html), territorial governments such as American Samoa and Nunavut, and municipal governments such as Toronto, but democracy in large national states today includes both one person, one vote and multiparty competition.

58. The film has been criticized for neglecting the role of political organizing and mobilizing by the "No" side (Larry Rohter, "One Prism on the Undoing of Pinochet: Oscar-Nominated 'No' Stirring Debate in Chile," *New York Times*, 8 Feb. 2013), and I do not mean to imply that lighthearted marketing techniques were sufficient for victory.

59. See, e.g., Minxin Pei in http://www.theatlantic.com/international/archive/2012/07/now-online-china-and-democracy-debate-with-minxin-pei-and-eric-li/260102/.

60. As it stands, the government is overly concerned about its legitimacy and takes measures that needlessly undermine its support. For example, my then-colleague and friend Shi Tianjian (who was also a professor at Duke University) and I were both disturbed by the document named Charter 2008 that engaged in a polemical critique of CCP history and called for competitive electoral democracy in China. Tianjian suggested that I write up my thoughts and have it circulated within the party (he said it would be more effective if the critique came from a foreigner). I wrote a sharp critique of the Charter and argued that the government should not intervene and instead let independent intellectuals openly debate and criticize the Charter. Tianjian said we should keep the memo private and he asked a well-connected friend to have it distributed within the higher echelons of the party. Unfortunately, we never received a response (I can tell this story because Tianjian passed away at a tragically young age in 2010, so I do not have to worry about retaliation against him). A few months later the government arrested Liu Xiaobo, a key person behind the manifesto, and sentenced him to an unusually harsh eleven-year jail term (Liu was subsequently awarded the Nobel Peace Prize). I decided not to publicly release my critique of the Charter because I do not want to criticize the ideas of somebody who cannot defend himself while he is in jail (once he is released and has freedom of political speech, I'll be happy to do so). It's worth asking what would have been the reaction of a political meritocracy with more democratic legitimacy of the sort provided by a referendum in favor of the China model. For one thing, the government would not have to worry as much about a document calling for electoral democracy at the top because it could

show that the political system has majority support. In a more open political environment, independent intellectuals could criticize such documents, and calls for electoral democracy would not gain much support in the court of public opinion. Of course, the line must be drawn at the point that social forces seek to mobilize political support for a multiparty competitive system and electoral democracy at the top: the government should specify clear penalties for such actions (supporters of the Charter 2008 claim that the Chinese constitution allows for electoral democracy at the top; if that's the case, the constitution needs to be changed).

61. From personal experience I can vouch that the debates prior to the referenda on Quebec independence in 1980 and 1995 were both deeper and broader than the political debates prior to regular provincial elections. Needless to say, such referenda need to be carried out in a relatively free atmosphere with time for deliberation (in contrast to, say, the referendum on Crimean independence on 16 March 2014, which was carried out on a few days' notice under the watchful eyes of Russian troops).

62. There is a paradox in the sense that the need for a referendum endorsing the political system becomes more acute as the system comes under greater political challenge. So the government would have to choose a propitious moment for calling such a referendum, perhaps just as it's enjoying a high level of support (and shortly before an expected drop in support).

63. "Uganda Backs Multi-Party Return," BBC News, 1 Aug. 2005.

64. What if the CCP does not respect the terms of the referendum within this period? Social critics could make their case and the government would lose whatever legitimacy it had gained via the referendum (the government could also imprison or silence its critics, thus further undermining its legitimacy). The assumption is that the concern for legitimacy (and hence, political stability) would provide a strong incentive for the CCP to respect the terms of the referendum. And the people hold the ultimate trump card in the sense that they can rebel against the government, as they did in imperial Chinese history when rulers appeared to have lost the "mandate of heaven." Such rebellions are costly and bloody, but they can also do some good if they overthrow a thoroughly unjust government: as Yuri Pines puts it, "Rebellions can be interpreted as a peculiar (and very costly) readjustment system, a kind of bloody popular 'election,' which determined what family would rule for another dynastic cycle, corrected certain wrongs, allowed the influx of new blood into the government apparatus, and thus contributed toward the improvement of the empire's functioning" (Pines, *The Everlasting Empire*, p. 161).

65. A liberal democrat might reply that it's unfair to bind future generations to a vote held by their parents. But such an objection owes much to an individualistic view of the self and may not resonate as deeply in a culture with a family-oriented view of the self as tightly bound to ancestors and descendants. Just to give one concrete example of how these different views of the self affect social behavior and expectations: in the West, it is widely understood that a child becomes independent at the age of eighteen or so, and ties with parents become optional from then on; in China, the ties

that bind parents and children are meant to generate a lifetime of obligations and responsibilities and there is no "age of maturity" at which point they become optional.

Concluding Thoughts

1. See Minglu Chen and David S. G. Goodman, "The China Model: One Country, Six Authors," *Journal of Contemporary China* 21, no. 73 (Jan. 2011): 171.

2. To be more precise, such accounts of the China model are more common in the foreign press and academic publications. Within mainland China, accounts of the China model are generally more positive (and more nuanced): see Pan Wei, ed., *Zhongguo moshi: Jiedu renmin gongheguo de 60 nian* [China Model: Explaining Sixty Years of the People's Republic] (Beijing: Zhongyang bianyi chubanshe, 2009).

3. Suisheng Zhao, "The China Model: Can It Replace the Western Model of Modernization?" *Journal of Contemporary China* 19, no. 65 (June 2010): 420–422.

4. Barry Naughton, "China's Distinctive System: Can It Be a Model for Others?" *Journal of Contemporary China* 19, no. 65 (June 2010): 445.

5. Qiu Feng has argued that there are other possible standards for evaluating China's political progress (or regress) within a framework of vertical democratic meritocracy, such as meritocracy at the top, democracy in the middle, and meritocracy at the bottom. Local communities can draw on traditional forms of elite selection without divisive and expensive elections, whereas there may be a good case for competitive elections at the level of cities ("Comment on Political Meritocracy and Democracy" [in Chinese], Unirule Institute of Economics, Beijing, 9 June 2014). Other possibilities include a model with meritocracy at the top, democracy in the middle, and experimentation at the bottom. I leave aside such possibilities for both theoretical and political reasons (the best case for democracy can be made at the local level, traditional forms of elite selection at the local level in China have more often than not been destroyed by political upheaval in the twentieth century, and the costs of changing the current China model are likely to outweigh the benefits).

6. Jaeyoon Song, "Redefining Good Government: Shifting Paradigms in Song Dynasty (960–1279) Discourse on Fengjian," *T'oung Pao* 97 (2011): 338. See also Bol, *Neo-Confucianism in History*.

7. This paragraph draws on Louie, "Village Self-Governance and Democracy in China," pp. 136–141.

8. O'Brien and Han, "Path to Democracy?" pp. 359–360.

9. Jude Howell, "Prospects for Village Self-Governance in China," *Journal of Peasant Studies* 55, no. 3 (1998): 87–93.

10. Victor Cunrui Xiong, *Emperor Yang of the Sui Dynasty: His Life, Times, and Legacy* (Albany: State University of New York Press, 2006).

11. Sebastian Heilmann, "From Local Experiments to National Policy: The Origins of China's Distinctive Policy Process," *China Journal* 59 (Jan. 2008): 10. My discussion of the second plank draws from this article. See also Heilmann, "Policy Mak-

ing through Experimentation: The Formation of a Distinctive Policy Process," in *Mao's Invisible Hand: The Political Foundations of Adaptive Governance in China,* ed. Sebastian Heilmann and Elizabeth Perry (Cambridge, Mass.: Harvard University Asia Center, 2011).

12. Sebastian Heilmann, "Policy Experimentation in China's Economic Rise," *Studies in Comparative International Development* 43 (2008): 23.

13. The special economic zones have historical precedents and also show the Chinese government's creative adaptation and reinterpretation of the past: the zones are similar to the treaty cities from the colonial period in the sense that "both are demarcated areas where different rules apply, with a concentration of activity as a result. The greatest difference is that the Chinese themselves set the conditions in the post-1978 economic zones, rather than governments in Paris, London, Berlin, or Moscow" (Michiel Hulshof and Daan Roggeveen, *How the City Moved to Mr. Sun: China's New Megacities* [Amsterdam: SUN, 2011], p. 92).

14. Wu Hao and Wen Tianli, "Zhongguo difang zhengce shiyanshi gaige de youshi yu juxianxing" [The Advantages and Limitations of China's Experimental Reforms with Local Policy], *Shehui kexue zhanxian* 10 (2012): 37–45. For an argument that experimental approach to risk detection has advantages compared to the practice in Western countries, where most policies have been imposed universally and simultaneously, see Jingyi Zhang, "Practice-Based Risk Detection," mimeo, Shanghai Jiaotong University, 2012. For a favorable comparison of China's approach to experimental reform with India's more rigid model, see Zheng Yongnian, "Zhongguo tizhi changxin jingyan de xianshi qishi" [The Real Inspiration of China's System of Creative Experimentation], *Lianhe zaobao,* 3 Sept. 2013.

15. Florini, Lai, and Tan, *China Experiments,* p. 5.

16. Heilmann, "Policy Experimentation in China's Economic Rise," pp. 8–9.

17. Daniel A. Bell, "What China Can Teach Europe," *New York Times,* 8 Jan. 2012.

18. Florini, Lai, and Tan, *China Experiments,* p. 6; Micklethwait and Wooldridge, *The Fourth Revolution,* p. 158.

19. Tom Miller and Warren Lu, "Better Governance through Kung-Fu," *Gavekal Dragonomics China Research,* 14 Feb. 2014, p. 3.

20. Gabriel Wildau, "Small Chinese Cities Steer Away from GDP as Measure of Success," *Financial Times,* 13 Aug. 2014.

21. In addition, Bo Rothstein argues that China's relative success at delivering high growth and public services (compared to other countries with similarly low rankings on rule of law and corruption indexes) can be explained by a cadre organization that relies on public officials committed to implementing policy doctrine from above but with the ability and discretion to use different tools and skills depending on local circumstances. Rothstein, "The Chinese Paradox of High Growth and Low Quality of Government: The Cadre Organization meets Max Weber," forthcoming in *Governance.*

22. Heilmann, "Policy Experimentation in China's Economic Rise," p. 5 (citing D. F. Pile on India).

23. To be more precise, Chinese scholars have written more extensively on the CCP experience with experimentation both before the revolution and in the reform era (see Zheng Wenhuan, "Difang shidian yu guojia zhengce: Yi xin nongbao wei li" [Local Experimentation and National Policy: Using the Rural Pension Policy as an Example], *Zhongguo xingzheng guanli* 2 [2013]: 16–20; and the footnotes to Heilmann's article "From Local Experiments to National Policy"), but English-language research on Chinese governance has tended to focus more on village elections. This scholarly bias can be explained by the following factors: (1) the Chinese government encourages foreign researchers to monitor and write about elections; (2) it is easier to produce quantifiable academic output by researching elections; and (3) foreign researchers have an ideological bias in favor of the view that only electoral democracy counts as substantial political reform.

24. See also Xiangdong Gu, Louise T. Higgins, Lixiang Weng, and Xiaoye Holt, "Civil Service Leadership Selection in China: Historical Evolution and Current Status," *Journal of Chinese Human Resource Management* 3, no. 1 (2012): 67–78.

25. Frank N. Pieke, *The Good Communist: Elite Training and State Building in Today's China* (Cambridge: Cambridge University Press, 2009), p. 1.

26. In the 1980s, party membership was not viewed as particularly prestigious and many students at leading universities shied away from it, but today there is a rigorous process for admission to party membership and membership is actively sought by most high-performing students. For a more detailed account of the CCP's strategy for recruiting new members and the application process for college students, see Dickson, "Who Wants to Be a Communist?"

27. In 2013, there were more than 1.19 million exam takers, with an average success rate of 1 out of 57 (He Hui, "You geng duo gongping jihui 'Guokao re' cai hui jiangwen" [The "Fever over National Public Service Examinations" Will Cool Down Only with More Equal Opportunities], *Huanqiu shibao*, 25 Nov. 2013). In 2014, however, there was a substantial drop-off in the number of test takers, allegedly due to cuts in benefits such as low-cost healthcare and housing and the high-profile anticorruption crackdown, which has choked off the flow of gray income (Patti Waldmeir, "A Game Change in Public Service," *Financial Times*, 16 Apr. 2014; Gao Bo, "Civil Service Exam Hit Amid Graft Crackdown," *China Daily*, 25–26 Oct. 2014). It may not be a bad thing if recent changes filter out test-takers with more materialistic motivation, though the problem of low salaries for public officials still needs to be resolved (see chapter 3, section 1).

28. Prior to the establishment of examinations, cadres were recruited via the national assignment of jobs for university and polytechnic graduates, the placement of army soldiers transferred to civilian work, and recommendation from workers, farmers, and other social groups. Su Yutang, ed. *Guojia gongwuyuan zhidu jianghua* [The Discourse on the State Civil Service System] (Beijing: Labor and Personnel Publishing House, 1989), p. 109.

29. Xiaowei Zhang, *Elite Dualism and Leadership Selection in China* (London: Routledge/Curzon, 2004), esp. chs. 5–6.

30. Xiao and Li, "China's Meritocratic Examinations and the Ideal of Virtuous Talents," pp. 348–349. A report titled "Advance along the Road of Socialism with Chinese Characteristics," delivered to the Thirteenth National Congress of the CCP on 25 Oct. 1987 by Zhao Ziyang, proposed dividing public officials into political officials and professional public servants (*People's Republic of China Yearbook* [Beijing: PRC Yearbook Ltd; Hong Kong: N.C.N. Limited, 1988/89]), but this recommendation was not implemented. The aim of Zhao's report was to establish a more "Western-style" meritocratic civil service, but had the recommendation for a strict division between civil servants and political officials been implemented, the result might have been less meritocracy in the political system because political officials might not have had to go through the examination system that was established in the early 1990s.

31. Zheng Yongnian and Chen Gang, "Intra-Party Democracy in Practice: Balloting for City Leaders in Jiangsu," in *China: Development and Governance*, ed. Wang Gungwu and Zheng Yongnian (Singapore: World Scientific, 2013), pp. 22–23. See also Pieke, *The Good Communist*, ch. 6; and for an early account of the organization of China's administrative sector, see Yan Huai, *Zhonggong zhengzhi jiegou yu minzhuhua lungang* [The CCP's Political Structure and an Outline for China's Democratization] (Taipei: Mainland Commission of Taiwan's Executive Council, 1991).

32. Eighty percent of the survey work for the CCP is carried out by Horizons, China's largest private polling company (interview with Yuan Yue, CEO of Horizons, Beijing, 7 Mar. 2014). Horizons uses scientific methods to canvass the views of the public and relevant stakeholders that bear on the assessment of candidates being considered for promotion (e.g., ex-cons are interviewed in order to assess the performance of prison wardens).

33. Provisional Regulation on the Promotion and Demotion of State Public Servants, art. 7 (in John P. Burns et al., eds., "Provisional Chinese Public Service Regulations," in *Chinese Law and Government* (New York: M. E. Sharpe, 1990), p. 10.

34. Li, "The Life of the Party." See also Zhang Weiwei, "Meritocracy Versus Democracy," *New York Times*, 10–11 Nov. 2012. The point here is not that experience makes for smarter or more virtuous leaders: President Obama seems to be at the top of the scale in both categories. But experience helps the political leader avoid beginner's mistakes, provides a kind of background knowledge that improves the political judgment necessary for sound decision making (especially in response to new and unexpected crises that require quick decisions), and tests for the social skills necessary for effective persuasion of people and the implementation of political proposals (see chapter 2, section 3). It is highly unlikely that a loner such as Obama—with a disdain for politics that alienates both his ideological foes and members of his own party, negatively affecting his capacity to manage issues at home and abroad (see Carl Hulse, Jeremy W. Peters, and Michael D. Shear, "Obama Is Seen as Frustrating His Own Party," *New York Times*, 18 Aug. 2014)—could have made it through a Chinese-

style meritocratic process that requires a high level of social skills. It could be argued that the former Chinese president Hu Jintao similarly lacked social skills, but the Chinese leadership is collective and depends less on the qualities of one leader (i.e., the political system won't be paralyzed if any one leader falls short on one of the attributes necessary for effective leadership).

35. Reasons include: (1) the lack of transparency of the selection and promotion process, and (2) an ideological bias (especially by foreign scholars) that views talk of meritocracy as a mere façade for continued authoritarian rule, hence not "real" political reform.

36. Zheng and Chen, "Intra-Party Democracy in Practice," p. 22.

37. Wu Ji and Wei Yunheng, "Take Away the 'Iron Armchair,' and Bring Up Good Cadres—Report on the Reform of the Personnel System for Cadres in Liaoning Province," *Liaowang* 24 (11 June 1990): 104.

38. Cited in Kuhn, *How China's Leaders Think*, p. 479.

39. O'Brien and Han, "Path to Democracy?" p. 367.

40. Ibid., pp. 367–376. See also Liu Mingxing, *Zhongguo nongcun caizheng tizhi gaige yu jiceng zhili jiegou bianqian* [China's Rural Fiscal System Reform and Structural Change of Local Governance] (Beijing: People's Daily Press, 2013), ch. 6.

41. Louie, "Village Self-Governance and Democracy in China," pp. 147–148.

42. Xin Sun, Travis J. Warner, Dali L. Yang, and Mingxing Liu, "Patterns of Authority and Governance in Rural China: Who's in Charge? Why?" *Journal of Contemporary China* 22, no. 83 (2013): 733–754.

43. Shuna Wang and Yang Yao, "Grassroots Democracy and Local Governance: Evidence from Rural China," *World Development* 35, no. 10 (2007): 1637–1638, 1647.

44. Lily L. Tsai, *Accountability without Democracy: Solidary Groups and Public Goods Provision in Rural China* (Cambridge: Cambridge University Press, 2007), p. 253.

45. Howell, "Prospects for Village Self-Governance in China," p. 107; O'Brien and Han, "Path to Democracy?" p. 375.

46. I do not mean to imply that decision making by deliberative polling should be carried out at higher levels of government where political experience matters more than at local levels and decisions often need to be made either more slowly, involving years of political persuasion, or more rapidly, in response to national and global crises. Plus, leaders at higher levels of government in political meritocracies derive substantial legitimacy by being viewed as having performed well on ultracompetitive tests and trials over the course of several decades, which is not true of local-level leaders.

47. He and Warren, "Authoritarian Deliberation," p. 277.

48. Xia Ming, "Innovations in China's Local Governance," in *China: Development and Governance*.

49. Heilmann, "From Local Experiments to National Policy," p. 28.

50. Ibid., p. 27.

51. For example, the municipality of Chengdu aims to reduce the income gap between urban and rural residents by improving the surrounding countryside rather

than encouraging large-scale migration to the city, but such policies are not likely to work in Chongqing's harsh terrain or the arid parts of northern China.

52. To promote controversial political reforms, however, provincial elites need to rely on a close factional relationship with the general secretary who acts as their patron. Wen-Hsuan Tsai and Nicola Dean, "Experimentation under Hierarchy in Local Conditions: Cases of Political Reform in Guangdong and Sichuan, China," *China Quarterly* 218 (June 2014): 356.

53. Shell and Delury, *Wealth and Power*, p. 65.

54. O'Brien and Li, "Accommodating 'Democracy' in a One-Party State," p. 467.

55. I use scare quotes because although such experiments include democratic practices such as elections, online consultation, and opinion polling, they are constrained by meritocratic selection procedures such as nomination by the party. As Zheng Yongnian and Chen Gang comment, "The Party's long-term goal is still meritocracy rather than democracy" (Zheng and Chen, "Intra-Party Democracy in Practice," p. 21). One might add that "intraparty democracy" is not meant to undermine the status of the CCP as the ruling party. Hu Wei, "Minzhu zhengzhi fazhan de Zhongguo daolu: Dangnei minzhu moshi de xuanze" [China's Road to Democratic Political Development: Choosing the Model of Intraparty Democracy], *Kexue shehuizhuyi* 1 (2010): 14–23).

56. Kuhn, *How China's Leaders Think*, pp. xix, 483. Li was promoted to head of the Organization Department in 2007, and as the senior leader responsible for party and government promotions he himself had more power to replicate experiments in the assessment of cadres. On the growing importance of online consultation in the policy-making process, see Steven J. Balla and Zhou Liao, "Online Consultation Citizen Feedback in Chinese Policymaking," *Journal of Current Chinese Affairs* 3 (2013): 101–120.

57. For official websites, see http://www.eco-city.gov.cn/ (Chinese government, in Chinese) and http://www.tianjinecocity.gov.sg/ (Singapore government, in English).

58. Ho Ai Li, "Growing Pains for Tianjin Eco-City, *Straits Times*, 13 Oct. 2013.

59. In 2009, I had breakfast with a government official from Tianjin at the World Economic Forum meeting in Dalian. He was severely critical of Dalian and explained to me that Tianjin could host a similar meeting at lower cost. As it turns out, both cities upgraded their infrastructure and it was decided to alternate World Economic Forum (summer) meetings between Dalian and Tianjin on a yearly basis.

60. Hong Kong's legal and political structure is a British legacy, but the Chinese government agreed to sustain the Hong Kong way of life for fifty years (until 2047), so in that sense Hong Kong can be viewed as an experiment.

61. http://www.rfa.org/english/news/tibet/allowed-06262013180033.html.

62. See Zhang Yongle, "Zhongguo de xianneng zhengzhi ji qi minzhu zhengdangxing" [China's Political Meritocracy and Its Democratic Legitimacy], comment presented at workshop on democracy and meritocracy, Sungkyunkwan University, Seoul, 30 May 2014; and Xiao Jianzhong, "Lingdao ganbu xuanba yu xieshang minzhu" [Cadre Selection and Deliberative Democracy], *Guancha yu sikao* 4 (2014):

33–34. This paragraph also draws on discussions with two Chinese public officials who prefer to remain anonymous.

63. Let me speculate: there might have been more continuity in efforts to standardize the promotion evaluation process by means of voting and examinations had Li Yuanchao been promoted to the Standing Committee of the Politburo rather than the less powerful post of vice-president. Still, it is worth noting that change of leadership at the top takes place every ten years in China and there is more continuity than in electoral democracies that change ruling parties every few years, so the shifts in policy are typically less drastic (and arbitrary) than in electoral democracies.

64. Heilmann, "Policy Experimentation in China's Economic Rise," p. 19.

65. Such an independent commission could also recommend experimentation in hitherto taboo areas that relatively cautious political leaders may be reluctant to push forward. For example, the commission could recommend an experiment that eliminates barriers against same-sex marriage in a part of the country—say, Shanghai—that is relatively tolerant of the public expression of homosexuality. The success of the experiment would depend not just on the public reaction, but also on the results of social scientific studies, the experience of other countries, and lessons from China's own history. If the expert commission concludes that same-sex marriage helps the people involved without substantially undermining family and social harmony, the commission could publicize the results and political leaders would have the moral authority to extend the experiments to other parts of the country. That said, not all sensitive experiments can be carried out and evaluated in a fully transparent way. For example, an experiment in ideological reform might generate too much opposition from high-level political leaders and retired cadres, and hence might need to be carried out away from public view in the initial period, with the hope that key political leaders could be brought on board once the experiment had proven popular in a particular locale without generating too much political opposition.

66. For additional suggestions meant to improve the scaling up of local experiments, see Zheng Yongnian, "Zhongguo ruhe yingde xin yi bo kaifang zhengce" [How Can China Succeed at the Next Wave of Open Policies?], *Lianhe zaobao*, 12 Nov. 2013; and Florini, Lai, and Tan, *China Experiments*, pp. 177–179.

67. Articles in the leading media outlets of English-speaking countries (more like comments masquerading as news reports) routinely point to the political rise of princelings as a way of "proving" that the Chinese political system is not meritocratic (see, e.g., Edward Wong, "Family Ties and Hobnobbing Trump Merit at China Helm," *New York Times*, 17 Nov. 2012). The problem with such reports is not that they are false but rather that they are biased in the sense that they draw broader political conclusions from isolated examples. When they do draw on social scientific research, they make use of negative articles in English-speaking journals and ignore the more balanced or positive accounts of actually existing political meritocracy in English and Chinese academic journals. And some books about Chinese politics written by journalists—see, e.g., Richard McGregor, *The Party: The Secret World of China's Communist Rulers* (London: Penguin, 2010)—make hardly any use of English-language

academic articles on Chinese politics and no use at all of Chinese-language academic articles; if academics can draw on newspaper articles, why can't journalists draw on academic articles? When leading media outlets publish comments largely in favor of actually existing meritocracy, they may be followed by critiques (for example, Eric X. Li's article "The Life of the Party: The Post-Democratic Future Begins in China," in the Jan./Feb. 2013 issue of *Foreign Affairs*, is followed by Huang Yasheng's rebuttal titled "Democratize or Die: Why China's Communists Face Reform or Revolution"; it is highly unusual for *Foreign Affairs* to publish a rebuttal to an article in the same issue). These complaints aside, I am grateful to leading media outlets that have published my own contributions on the topic (and for the friendship of many journalists).

68. Even in a fully meritocratic system, however, there might still be a disproportionately large number of political leaders from families with political backgrounds. The reason is that such backgrounds help provide opportunities to learn the social skills necessary for persuading others and for effectively implementing policy proposals (see chapter 2, section 3). For example, Singapore's prime minister Lee Hsien Loong probably dined and conversed with high-level political leaders at a young age by virtue of the fact that he is the son of Singapore's founding father Lee Kuan Yew. As a result, he would have learned how best to engage with such leaders without feeling overly self-conscious, and thus is more likely to have developed the social skills required of a political leader than others with similar levels of intelligence and virtue but without such illustrious family backgrounds.

69. In 1982, Chen Yun appointed Li Rui, a former secretary of Mao Zedong, as head of a bureau "dealing with cadres which should be run by outstanding young people" (*Dang de zuzhi gongzuo wenxian xuanbian* [Collection on the Party's Organizational Work], ed. Central Organization Department [Beijing: CCP School Publishing House, 1986], p. 232). This "Young Cadres Bureau," mainly composed of the children of high-ranking cadres, was considered a reformist and heretical wing within the conservative bastion of the Central Organization Department at the time.

70. See the Provisional Regulation on the Avoidance System of the State Administrative Personnel, in General Office of the State Council of the People's Republic of China, ed., *Guowuyuan gongbao* [Bulletin of the State Council], Beijing, no. 5 (1991): 162–163.

71. I say "blatant" because one of the (unintended?) consequences of the regulations preventing political nepotism is that relatives of political officials often went into business and drew on informal political connections to enrich themselves.

72. Joseph Fewsmith, "Inner-Party Democracy: Development and Limitations," *China Leadership Monitor*, no. 31, p. 9 (http://www.cerium.ca/IMG/pdf/Fewsmith_Inner-party_democracy.pdf).

73. Pieke, *The Good Communist*, pp. 161–162.

74. China has exported its model of special economic zones (SEZs) to Nigeria, Ethiopia, and Mauritius: "These African SEZs represent a Chinese development plan, initiated by the Chinese government, executed by Chinese companies and

planned by Chinese urbanists—but on African soil." Michiel Hulshof and Daan Roggeveen, "Lekki, the Next African Shenzhen?" *Chengshi Zhongguo: Zhongguoshi zaocheng zai Feizhou* 63, no. 3 (2014): 88. Such SEZs can be sustained even with political changes in democratic contexts so long as all sides benefit economically, but it is more difficult to sustain more ambitious experiments in political reform without stable meritocracies: for example, the president of Madagascar was intrigued by Paul Romer's idea of a charter city (an economic zone founded on the land of a poor country but governed with the legal and political system of a rich country) but the plan ended when he was ousted in a coup (Adam Davidson, "Who Wants to Buy Honduras?" *New York Times*, 8 May 2012).

75. Small countries can still experiment with new forms of government—political experimentation was common in the city-states of ancient Greece, including the famous democratic reforms that Athens pursued between the sixth and third centuries BCE (Rebecca Newberger Goldstein, *Plato at the Googleplex: Why Philosophy Won't Go Away* [New York: Pantheon Books, 2014], p. 152)—but experimentation in smaller political units under the control of a relatively powerful central government assumes the context of a large country.

76. As a method of revolutionary transformation, experimentation was exported to Vietnam: the 1953–1956 land reform in North Vietnam was designed by a team of experienced cadres and initiated by small-scale "experimental waves," including the initial establishment of "experimental points" and "typical models" before scaling up reforms in a phased manner, depending on the success of the experimental units and local circumstances. Vietnamese policy makers have again made use of the experimental point methodology since the 1980s for the purpose of promoting economic reform (Heilmann, "From Local Experiments to National Policy," p. 12). Vietnam also relies on the experimental method to pursue political reform and may offer lessons to China in this respect (John Ruwitch, "Vietnam Political Reform Experiments Move Up a Notch," *Reuters*, 29 Sept. 2010).

77. In a large-scale survey of civil servants, only 11.6 percent of respondents in the United States agreed that civil servants should pass civil service examinations, as against more than 80 percent in six East Asian countries saying there is a need to do so, "probably due to the influence of the Confucian examination model from the past." Poocharoen and Brillantes, "Meritocracy in the Asia Pacific," p. 150.

78. Such efforts are already taking place on an ad hoc basis—for example, government officials from countries in Asia, Africa, and Latin America undergo training at the China National School of Administration, and African government employees are given scholarships for training at Chinese universities (Michiel Hulshof and Daan Roggeveen, "Black in China: The New Soft Power Approach," *Chengshi Zhongguo* 63, no. 3 [2014]: 104)—but there is a need for more systematic efforts to promote political meritocracy outside of China.

79. Pan Wei, "Western System Versus Chinese System," University of Nottingham, China Policy Institute, Briefing Series, no. 61, July 2010.

80. The view that the CCP is really "Communist" may be more prevalent in the

United States, where politicians routinely use the word *Communist* to demonize the Chinese political system. A name change that drops the word *Communist* may therefore increase China's soft power abroad (or at least reduce fear of its political system).

81. The CCP is "Leninist" in the sense that the party is vertically organized and is supreme over the state apparatus (Steve Tsang, "Consultative Leninism: China's New Political Framework," *Journal of Contemporary China* 18, no. 62 (2009): 865–880), but it lacks the other key features of a Leninist party—the idea that class conflict is the motor of history, leadership by the proletariat, a commitment to the ideal of communism at home, and support for the revolutionary overthrow of capitalist regimes abroad. And the days of Leninist-style political mobilization are long gone because the party must be more sensitive to public opinion; the CCP can mobilize around causes (such as efforts to combat corruption) if there is already substantial social demand, but it can no longer mobilize people around harebrained schemes (such as the Great Leap Forward) that radically conflict with what people need and want (and with what independent scholars and scientists regard as sensible policy). Moreover, republics had a constitutional right to withdraw from the union in Soviet-style Leninism; regions in China, no matter how autonomous, do not have a right to withdraw from the country. Last but not least, the key features of the China model—democracy at the bottom, experimentation in the middle, and meritocracy at the top—were not key features of the Soviet political system.

82. On the differences between the CCP and political parties in the West, see Zheng Yongnian, *The Chinese Communist Party as Organizational Emperor: Culture, Reproduction and Transformation* (London: Routledge, 2010), pp. 16–17.

83. On the frequent use of the term *democracy* (*minzhu*) in official Chinese political discourse, see Bo Zhiyue, *China's Elite Politics: Governance and Democratization* (Hackensack, N.J.: World Scientific, 2010), p. 390. By "democratic characteristics" I mean not just local-level electoral democracy and "intraparty democracy," but also the National People's Congress. See Pu Xingzu, "Yi renda minzhu wei zhongdian jixu tuijin Zhongguo minzhu zhengzhi de fazhan" [Continuously Carrying Forward the Development of Democracy Politics in China by Focusing on the National People's Congress], *Fudan xuebao (shehui kexue)* 5 (2005): 129–134.

84. B. L. McCormick, "China's Leninist Parliament and Public Sphere: A Comparative Analysis," in *China after Socialism: In the Footsteps of Eastern Europe or East Asia?*, ed. B. L. McCormick and J. Unger (Armonk, N.Y.: M. E. Sharpe, 1996), pp. 29–53.

85. It's worth asking why the CCP persists in using an obsolete name to describe itself. One reason is that it fears losing legitimacy if it changes its name, but improving the China model in practice should take care of that problem. Another reason is that revolutionary heroes who fought for the establishment of a great country are attached to the old name. This book is dedicated to my Chinese parents-in-law, who met in North Korea during the Korean War. My father-in-law first joined the CCP at the age of fifteen and fought in three wars with the CCP. Although he never rose high in the ranks and suffered much during political campaigns (including a year in soli-

tary confinement during the Cultural Revolution), he never lost faith in the leadership of the CCP. My father-in-law is open-minded and intellectually curious, but I do not think he could tolerate a change in the name of the CCP. As a filial son-in-law, I do not want him to be upset. Hence, my own view is that the CCP should not change its name until the generation of revolutionary heroes, sadly, departs from this world.

SELECTED BIBLIOGRAPHY

Albritton, Robert B., and Thawilwadee Bureekul. "Developing Democracy under a New Constitution in Thailand." In *How East Asians View Democracy*, ed. Yun-Han Chu, Larry Diamond, Andrew J. Nathan, and Doh Chull Shin. New York: Columbia University Press, 2008.

Angle, Stephen C. "Decent Democratic Centralism." *Political Theory* 33, no. 4 (Aug. 2005).

Appiah, Kwame Anthony. *The Honor Code: How Moral Revolutions Happen*. New York: Norton, 2010.

Aristotle. *The Politics*, trans. Ernest Barker. London: Oxford University Press, 1958.

Arkless, David. "The Secret to Asia's Long-Term Prosperity? Improving Roles for Women at Work." *Global Asia* 6, no. 3 (Fall 2011).

Arneson, Richard. "Democratic Rights at National and Workplace Levels." In *The Idea of Democracy*, ed. David Copp, Jean Hampton, and John Roemer. Cambridge: Cambridge University Press, 1993.

Backer, Larry Cata. "A Constitutional Court for China within the Chinese Communist Party: Scientific Development and a Reconsideration of the Institutional Role of the CCP." *Suffolk University Law Review* 43, no. 3 (2010).

———. "From Constitution to Constitutionalism: A Global Framework for Legitimate Power Systems." *Penn State Law Review* 113, no. 3 (2008).

Bai, Tongdong. *China: The Political Philosophy of the Middle Kingdom*. London: Zed Books, 2012.

———. "A Confucian Version of Hybrid Regime: How Does It Work, and Why Is It Superior?" In *The East Asian Challenge for Democracy*, ed. Daniel A. Bell and Chenyang Li. New York: Cambridge University Press, 2013.

Bakewell, Sarah. *How to Live or A Life of Montaigne in One Question and Twenty Attempts at an Answer*. New York: Other Press, 2010.

Balázs, Étienne. *Chinese Civilization and Bureaucracy: Variations on a Theme*, trans. H. M. Wright; ed. Arthur F. Wright. New Haven, Conn.: Yale University Press, 1967.

Balla, Steven J., and Zhou Liao. "Online Consultation and Citizen Feedback in Chinese Policymaking." *Journal of Current Chinese Affairs* 3 (2013).

Banerjee, Abhijit, and Esther Duflo. *Poor Economics: A Radical Rethinking of the Way to Fight Global Poverty*. New York: Public Affairs, 2012.

Barkey, Karen. *Empire of Difference: The Ottomans in Comparative Perspective*. Cambridge: Cambridge University Press, 2008.

Bartels, Larry M. *Unequal Democracy: The Political Economy of the New Gilded Age* Princeton, N.J.: Princeton University Press, 2008.

Bauer, Joanne, and Daniel A. Bell, eds. *The East Asian Challenge for Human Rights*. New York: Cambridge University Press, 1999.

Bell, Daniel. "The Old War: After Ideology, Corruption." *New Republic*, 23 and 30 Aug. 1993.

———. "On Meritocracy and Equality." *National Affairs* 29 (Fall 1972).

Bellah, Robert, Richard Madsen, William Sullivan, and Ann Swidler. *Habits of the Heart*. Berkeley: University of California Press, 1985.

Benko, Cathy, and Bill Pelster. "How Women Decide." *Harvard Business Review*, Sept. 2013.

Bergère, Marie-Claire. *Chine: Le nouveau capitalisme d'État*. Paris: Fayard, 2013.

Berggruen, Nicolas, and Nathan Gardels. *Intelligent Governance for the 21st Century: A Middle Way between West and East*. Cambridge: Polity Press, 2012.

———. "Political Meritocracy and Direct Democracy: A Hybrid Experiment in California." In *The East Asian Challenge for Democracy*, ed. Daniel A. Bell and Chenyang Li. New York: Cambridge University Press, 2013.

Berman, Sheri. "Civil Society and the Collapse of the Weimar Republic." *World Politics* 49, no. 3 (1997).

Bernard, Maurice. *La méritocratie française: Les élites française. Essai critique*, 2 vols. Paris: L'Harmattan, 2010.

Bialystok, E., F.I.M. Craik, M. A. Binns, L. Ossher, and M. Freedman. "Effects of Bilingualism on the Age of Onset and Progression of MCI and AD: Evidence from Executive Function Tests." *Neuropsychology* 28, no. 2 (2014).

Bloom, Allan. "Interpretive Essay." In *The Republic of Plato*, trans. Allan Bloom. 2nd ed. New York: Basic Books, 1991.

Bo, Zhiyue. *China's Elite Politics: Governance and Democratization*. Hackensack, N.J.: World Scientific, 2010.

Bol, Peter K. *Neo-Confucianism in History*. Cambridge, Mass.: Harvard University Asia Center, 2008.

Brennan, Jason. *The Ethics of Voting*. Princeton, N.J.: Princeton University Press, 2011.

———. "Political Liberty: Who Needs It?" *Social Philosophy and Policy* 29, no. 1 (2012).

———. "The Right to a Competent Electorate." *Philosophical Quarterly* 61, no. 245 (2011).

Brunell, Thomas L. "Ideological Representation and Competitive Congressional Elections." *Electoral Studies* 28, no. 3 (Sept. 2009).

Bulman, David J. "Promotion-Based Incentives for Growth: Evidence from the County Level in Jiangsu and Anhui." Paper presented at the Association for Asian Studies Annual Conference, San Diego, Mar. 2013.

Burns, John P. "The CCP's Nomenklatura System as a Leadership Selection System: An Evaluation." In *The Chinese Communist Party in Reform*, ed. Kjeld Erik Brodsgaard and Zheng Yongnian. London: Routledge, 2006.

Burns, John P., and Wang Xiaoqi. "Civil Service Reform in China: Impacts on Civil Servants' Behavior." *China Quarterly* 201 (Mar. 2010).

Burns, John P., et al., eds. "Provisional Chinese Public Service Regulations." In *Chinese Law and Government*. New York: M. E. Sharpe, 1990.

Caplan, Bryan. *The Myth of the Rational Voter: Why Democracies Choose Bad Policies*. Princeton, N.J.: Princeton University Press, 2007.

Carlson, Allen. "Reimagining the Frontier: Patters of Sinicization and the Emergence of New Thinking about China's Territorial Periphery." Paper presented at the Civilizations and Sinicization Workshop, Beijing University, 25–26 Mar. 2011.

Carr, Nicholas. *The Shallows: What the Internet Is Doing to Our Brains*. New York: Norton, 2011.

Castiglione, Baldassare. *The Book of the Courtier*, trans. Sir Thomas Hoby, introduction by Walter Raleigh. London: David Nutt, 1900 [orig. pub. 1561].

CCP Central Committee et al. *Zhongyang jiguan jiqi zhishu jigou 2013 niandu kaoshi luyong gongwuyuan gonggong kemu kaoshi dagang* [2013 National Public Service Examination Syllabus for Central-Level Organs and Direct Subordinate Organizations]. http://bm.scs.gov.cn/2013/UserControl/download/2013zkjz.rar.

Chaffee, John W. *The Thorny Gates of Learning in Sung China*, new ed. Albany: State University of New York Press, 1995.

Chaihark, Hahm. "Constitutionalism, Confucian Civic Virtue, and Ritual Propriety." In *Confucianism for the Modern World*, ed. Daniel A. Bell and Hahm Chaibong. Cambridge: Cambridge University Press, 2003.

Chan, Hon S., and Jie Gao. "Old Wine in New Bottles: A County-Level Case Study of Anti-Corruption Reform in the People's Republic of China." *Crime, Law and Social Change* 49, no. 2 (Mar. 2008).

Chan, Joseph. *Confucian Perfectionism: A Political Philosophy for Modern Times*. Princeton, N.J.: Princeton University Press, 2014.

———. "Political Meritocracy and Meritorious Rule: A Confucian Perspective." In *The East Asian Challenge for Democracy*, ed. Daniel A. Bell and Chenyang Li. New York: Cambridge University Press, 2013.

Chandler, J. A. "Civil Service in the United States." In *The Civil Service in Liberal Democracies: An Introductory Survey*, ed. J. E. Kindom. London: Routledge, 1990.

Chen, Albert H. Y. "Mediation, Litigation, and Justice: Confucian Reflections in a Modern Liberal Society." In *Confucianism for the Modern World*, ed. Daniel A. Bell and Hahm Chaibong. Cambridge: Cambridge University Press, 2003.

Chen, Guoping. "Mingdai guanyuan kaohe zhidu shulun" [On the Assessment System of Public Officials in the Ming Dynasty], *Zhongguo zhengfayuan xuebao* 1 (1993).

Chen, Lai. *Kongfuzi yu xiandai shijie* [Confucius and the Modern World]. Beijing: Peking University Press, 2011.

Chen, Minglu, and David S. G. Goodman. "The China Model: One Country, Six Authors." *Journal of Contemporary China* 21, no. 73 (Jan. 2011).

Cheng, Chung-ying, et al. Special issue: "Legalist Philosophy of Han Fei." *Journal of Chinese Philosophy* 8, no. 1 (Mar. 2013).
Cheng, Tongshun, and Zhang Wenjun. "Wangluo fanfu tisheng zhengzhi xinren de luoji pipan" [Criticism of the Argument That Online Anti-Corruption Campaigns Strengthen Trust in Government]. *Lilun yu gaige* 4 (2013).
Ch'ien, Mu [Qian Mu]. *Traditional Government in Imperial China: A Critical Analysis*, trans. Chu-tu Hsueh and George O. Totten. Hong Kong: Chinese University Press, 1982.
Chin, Gregory T. "Innovation and Preservation: Remaking China's National Leadership Training System." *China Quarterly* 205 (Mar. 2011).
Cho, Il Yun. "Democratic Instability: Democratic Consolidation, National Identity and Security Dynamics in East Asia." *Foreign Policy Analysis* 8, no. 2 (Apr. 2012).
Christiano, Thomas. "An Instrumental Argument for a Human Right to Democracy." *Philosophy and Public Affairs* 39, no. 2 (2011).
Chu, Hsi. *Learning to Be a Sage*, trans. Daniel K. Gardner. Berkeley: University of California Press, 1990.
Chu, Yun-han, Yu-tzung Chang, and Wen-Chin Wu. "Sources of Regime Legitimacy in Confucian Societies." Paper presented at the conference on "Confucianism, Democracy, and Constitutionalism: Global and East Asian Perspectives," National Taiwan University, 14–15 June 2013.
Chua, Jeffrey, Larry Kamener, and Michael Shanahan. "The Making of a Talent Magnet: Lessons from Singapore's Public Service." Boston Consulting Group, May 2012.
Coicaud, Jean-Marc. "Legitimacy, across Borders and over Time." In *Fault Lines of International Legitimacy*, ed. Hilary Charlesworth and Jean-Marc Coicaud. Cambridge: Cambridge University Press, 2010.
Collier, Paul. *Wars, Guns, and Votes: Democracy in Dangerous Places*. London: Vintage, 2010).
Collins, Harry, and Robert Evans. *Rethinking Expertise*. Chicago: University of Chicago Press, 2009.
Confucius. *The Analects of Confucius: A Philosophical Translation*, trans. Roger T. Ames and Henry Rosemont Jr. New York: Ballantine Books, 1998.
Correll, Shelly J. "Minimizing the Motherhood Penalty: What Works, What Doesn't and Why?" Paper presented at conference on "Gender & Work: Challenging Conventional Wisdom," Harvard Business School, 28 Feb.–1 Mar. 2013. http://www.hbs.edu/faculty/conferences/2013-w50-research-symposium/Documents/correll.pdf.
Cui, Zhiyuan. "Partial Intimations of the Coming Whole: The Chongqing Experiment in Light of the Theories of Henry George, James Meade, and Antonio Gramsci." *Modern China* 37, no. 6 (2011).
Cummins, Denise D. *Good Thinking: Seven Powerful Ideas That Influence the Way We Think*. Cambridge: Cambridge University Press, 2012.
Delman, Jørgen. "China's 'Radicalism at the Center': Regime Legitimation through

Climate Politics and Climate Governance." *Journal of Chinese Political Science* 16, no. 2 (June 2011).

Delorme, Marie-Laure. *Les allées du pouvoir*. Paris: Seuil, 2011.

De Weerdt, Hilde. *Competition over Content: Negotiating Standards for the Civil Service Examinations in Imperial China (1127–1279)*. Cambridge, Mass.: Harvard University Asia Center, 2007.

Dickson, Bruce J. "Who Wants to Be a Communist? Career Incentives and Mobilized Loyalty in China." *China Quarterly* 217 (Mar. 2014).

Dobbs, David. "Appendix: A Geek Manifesto for America." In Mark Henderson, *The Geek Manifesto: Why Science Matters*. London: Corgi Books, 2012.

Dodson, Bill. *China Fast Forward: The Technologies, Green Industries and Innovations Driving the Mainland's Future*. Singapore: John Wiley & Sons, 2012.

Doh, Chull Shin. *Confucianism and Democratization in East Asia*. Cambridge: Cambridge University Press, 2011.

———. "How East Asians View Democracy: A Confucian Perspective." In *The East Asian Challenge for Democracy*, ed. Daniel A. Bell and Chenyang Li. New York: Cambridge University Press, 2013.

Donaldson, Sue, and Will Kymlicka. *Zoopolis: A Political Theory of Animal Rights*. Oxford: Oxford University Press, 2011.

Dong, Bin, and Benno Torgler. "Causes of Corruption: Evidence from China." *China Economic Review* 26 (2013).

Doshi, Tilak, and Peter Coclanis. "The Economic Architect: Goh Keng Swee." In *Lee's Lieutenants: Singapore's Old Guard*, ed. Peng Er Lam and Kevin Tan. St. Leonards, N.S.W.: Allen & Unwin, 1999.

Drechsler, Wolfgang. "Wang Anshi and the Origins of Modern Public Management in Song Dynasty China." *Public Money and Management* 33, no. 4 (Sept. 2013).

Du, Lun. "'Renxue hefaxing sixiang' gaiyao jiqi xianshi yiyi" [Outline and the Practical Meaning of "The Theory of a Legitimate Humane Government"]. Paper presented at "The Fifth Congress of the International Confucian Association, Beijing, 23–26 Sept. 2009. In *Guoji ruxue yanjiu*, China (2010).

Elman, Benjamin A. *Civil Examinations and Meritocracy in Late Imperial China*. Cambridge, Mass.: Harvard University Press, 2013.

———. *A Cultural History of Civil Examinations in Late Imperial China*. Berkeley: University of California Press, 2000.

———. "A Society in Motion: Unexpected Consequences of Political Meritocracy in Late Imperial China, 1400–1900." In *The East Asian Challenge for Democracy*, ed. Daniel A. Bell and Chenyang Li. New York: Cambridge University Press, 2013.

Fan, Ruiping. "Confucian Meritocracy for Contemporary China." In *The East Asian Challenge for Democracy*, ed. Daniel A. Bell and Chenyang Li. New York: Cambridge University Press, 2013.

Fewsmith, Joseph. "Inner-Party Democracy: Development and Limitations." *China Leadership Monitor*, no. 31 (Winter 2010). http://media.hoover.org/sites/default/files/documents/CLM31JF.pdf.

Flaum, Sander A., and Jonathon A. Flaum, with Mechele Flaum. *The 100-Mile Walk: A Father and a Son Find the Essence of Leadership*. New York: American Management Association, 2006.

Fleischacker, Samuel. *A Short History of Distributive Justice*. Cambridge, Mass.: Harvard University Press, 2005.

Florini, Ann, Hairong Lai, and Yeling Tan. *China Experiments: From Local Innovation to National Reform*. Washington, D.C.: Brookings Institution Press, 2012.

Frenkiel, Émilie. *Parler politique en Chine: Les intellectuels chinois pour ou contre la démocratie* [Talking about Politics in China: Chinese Intellectuals for or against Democracy]. Paris: Presses Universitaires de France, 2014.

Fu, Zhengyuan. *Autocratic Tradition and Chinese Politics*. Cambridge: Cambridge University Press, 1993.

Fukuyama, Francis. *The Origins of Political Order: From Prehuman Times to the French Revolution*. New York: Farrar, Straus, and Giroux, 2011.

———. *Political Order and Political Decay: From the Industrial Revolution to the Globalization of Democracy*. New York: Farrar, Straus, and Giroux, 2014.

Gallagher, Kelly Sims, and Qi Ye. "Climate and Clean Energy." In *Debating China: The U.S.–China Relationship in Ten Conversations*. Oxford: Oxford University Press, 2014.

Galvany, Albert. "Sly Mouths and Silver Tongues: The Dynamics of Psychological Persuasion in Ancient China." *Extrême-Orient, Extrême-Occident* 34 (2012).

Gan, Chunsong. *Chonghui Wangdao: Rujia yu shijie zhixu* [A Return to the Way of the Humane Authority: Confucianism and the World Order]. Shanghai: Huadong shifan daxue chubanshe, 2012.

Gao, Minzheng. "Zhongguoshi minzhu ye shi ge hao dongxi—You 'Minzhu shi ge hao dongxi' yinfa de ji dian sikao" [Chinese-Style Democracy Is Also a Good Thing—A Few Thoughts Sparked by "Democracy Is a Good Thing"]. *Tansuo yu zhengming* 11 (2013).

General Office of the State Council of the People's Republic of China, ed. *Guowuyuan gongbao* [Bulletin of the State Council], Beijing, no. 5 (1991).

Gilens, Martin, and Benjamin I. Page. "Testing Theories of American Politics: Elites, Interest Groups, and Average Citizens." *Perspectives on Politics* 12, no. 3 (Sept. 2014).

Goffee, Robert, and Gareth Jones. "Why Should Anyone Be Led by You?" In *On Leadership*. Boston: Harvard Business Review Press, 2011.

Goldin, Claudia, and Laurence F. Katz. *The Race between Education and Technology*. Cambridge, Mass.: Harvard University Press, 2010.

Goldin, Paul R., ed. *Dao Companion to the Philosophy of Han Fei*. Dordrecht: Springer, 2013.

Goldstein, Rebecca Newberger. *Plato at the Googleplex: Why Philosophy Won't Go Away*. New York: Pantheon Books, 2014.

Goleman, Daniel. "What Makes a Leader?" In *On Leadership*. Boston: Harvard Business Review Press, 2011.

Goleman, Daniel, Richard Boyatzis, and Annie McKee. *Primal Leadership: Realizing the Power of Emotional Intelligence*. Boston: Harvard Business School Press, 2002.

Gong, Ting, and Jianming Ren. "Hard Rules and Soft Constraints: Regulating Conflict of Interest in China." *Journal of Contemporary China* 22, no. 79 (2013).

Gong, Ting, and Alfred M. Wu. "Does Increased Civil Service Pay Deter Corruption? Evidence from China." *Review of Public Personnel Administration* 32 (2012).

Gong, Ting, and Wu Muluan. "Wo guo 2000–2009 nian fubai anli yanjiu baogao: Jiyu 2800 yu ge baodao anli de fenxi" [Research Report on China's Corruption Cases between 2000 and 2009: An Empirical Analysis of 2800 Cases]. *Shehuixue yanjiu* 4 (2012).

Graffin, Dennis. "Reinventing China: Pseudobureaucracy in the Early Southern Dynasties." In *State and Society in Early Medieval China*, ed. Albert Dien. Stanford, Calif.: Stanford University Press, 1990.

Grant, Adam M., Francesca Gino, and David A. Hoffman. "The Hidden Advantages of Quiet Bosses." *Harvard Business Review*, Dec. 2010.

Green, Jeffrey Edward. *The Eyes of the People: Democracy in an Age of Spectatorship*. Oxford: Oxford University Press, 2011.

Greenspan, Alan. *The Map and the Territory: Risk, Human Nature, and the Future of Forecasting*. New York: Penguin, 2013.

Grossman, I., M. Karasawa, S. Izumi, J. Na, M. Varnum, S. Kitayama, and R. Nisbett. "Aging and Wisdom: Culture Matters." *Psychological Science* 23, no. 10 (2012).

Groysberg, Boris. *Chasing Stars: The Myth of Talent and the Portability of Performance*. Princeton, N.J.: Princeton University Press, 2010.

Groysberg, Boris, and Katherine Connolly. "Great Leaders Who Make the Mix Work." *Harvard Business Review*, Sept. 2013.

Gu, Xiangdong, Louise T. Higgins, Lixiang Weng, and Xiaoye Holt. "Civil Service Leadership Selection in China: Historical Evolution and Current Status." *Journal of Chinese Human Resource Management* 3, no. 1 (2012).

Guo, Baogang. *China's Quest for Political Legitimacy: The New Equity-Enhancing Politics*. Lanham, Md.: Lexington Books, 2010.

Guo, Jie, Yang Jie, and Cheng Xu. "Diqu fubai zhili yu zhengfu zhichu guimo: Jiyu shengji mianban shuju de kongjian jiliang fenxi" [The Regulation of Local Corruption and the Scale of Government: A Spatial Economic Analysis Based on Provincial Panel Data]. *Jingji shehui tizhi bijiao* 1 (2013).

Gürpinar, Doğan. *Ottoman Imperial Diplomacy: A Political, Social and Cultural History*. London: I. B. Tauris, 2014.

Gutmann, Amy, and Dennis Thompson. *Democracy and Disagreement*. Cambridge, Mass.: Harvard University Press, 1998.

Hacker, Jacob S., and Paul Pierson. *Winner-Take-All Politics: How Washington Made the Rich Richer—and Turned Its Back on the Middle Class*. New York: Simon and Schuster, 2010.

Hall, Stephen S. *Wisdom: From Philosophy to Neuroscience*. New York: Vintage Books, 2010.

Han, Fook Kwang, Warren Fernandez, and Sumiko Tan. *Lee Kuan Yew: The Man and His Ideas*. Singapore: Times Editions, 1998.

Hardin, Russell. "Morals for Public Officials." In *Moral Leadership: The Theory and Practice of Power, Judgment and Policy*. San Francisco: John Wiley & Sons, 2006.

Hayek, Friedrich A. von. *Law, Legislation, and Liberty*, vol. 3, *The Political Order of a Free People*. Chicago: University of Chicago Press, 1981.

Hayes, Christopher. *Twilight of the Elites: America after Meritocracy*. New York: Crown, 2012.

He, Baogang. "Confucian Deliberation: The Persistence of Authoritarian Deliberation in China." Paper presented at the "International Conference on Confucianism, Democracy, and Constitutionalism: Global and East Asian Perspectives," National Taiwan University, 14–15 June 2013.

———. "An Empirical Theory of Hybrid Legitimacy System in China." Paper presented at workshop on "East Asian Perspectives on Political Legitimacy," University of Hong Kong, 18–19 Aug. 2011.

He, Baogang, and Mark E. Warren. "Authoritarian Deliberation: The Deliberative Turn in Chinese Political Development." *Perspectives on Politics* 9, no. 2 (June 2011).

Hegel, G.W.F. *Elements of the Philosophy of Right*, trans. H. B. Nisbet. Cambridge: Cambridge University Press, 1991.

Heilmann, Sebastian. "From Local Experiments to National Policy: The Origins of China's Distinctive Policy Process." *China Journal* 59 (Jan. 2008).

———. "Policy Experimentation in China's Economic Rise." *Studies in Comparative International Development* 43 (2008).

———. "Policy Making through Experimentation: The Formation of a Distinctive Policy Process." In *Mao's Invisible Hand: The Political Foundations of Adaptive Governance in China*, ed. Sebastian Heilmann and Elizabeth Perry. Cambridge, Mass.: Harvard University Asia Center, 2011.

Henderson, Mark. *The Geek Manifesto: Why Science Matters*. London: Corgi Books, 2012.

Henrich, Joseph, Steven J. Heine, and Ara Norenzayan. "The Weirdest People in the World?" *Behavioral and Brain Sciences* 33 (2010).

Herbert, Penelope A. *Examine the Honest, Appraise the Able: Contemporary Assessments of Civil Service Selection in Early T'ang China*. Canberra: Faculty of Asian Studies, Australian National University Press, 1988.

Horowitz, Michael C., and Philip E. Tetlock. "Trending Upward: How the Intelligence Community Can Better See into the Future." *Foreign Policy*, 6 Sept. 2012.

Hou, Zanhua. "Lun zhuanbian jingji fazhan fangshi de zhengzhi dongli—Ji yu difang zhengfu dongli queshi de shijiao" [An Analysis of the Political Motivation for the Transformation of Economic Development—From the Perspective of the Lack of Motivation in the Local Government], *Yunnan shehui kexue* 4 (2012).

Howell, Jude. "Prospects for Village Self-Governance in China." *Journal of Peasant Studies* 55, no. 3 (1998).

Hu, Shuli. "Changing Realities for Asian Women Leaders." *Global Asia* 6, no. 3 (Fall 2011).

Hu, Wei. "Minzhu zhengzhi fazhan de Zhongguo daolu: Dangnei minzhu moshi de xuanze" [China's Road to Democratic Political Development: Choosing the Model of Intraparty Democracy]. *Kexue shehuizhuyi* 1 (2010).

Huang, Min-Hua. "Polarized Politics, Regime Evaluation and Democratic Legitimacy in Taiwan." Paper presented at workshop on "East Asian Perspectives on Political Legitimacy," University of Hong Kong, 18–19 Aug. 2011.

Huang, Ray. *1587, a Year of No Significance: The Ming Dynasty in Decline*. New Haven, Conn.: Yale University Press, 1981.

Huang, Yasheng. "Democratize or Die: Why China's Communists Face Reform or Revolution." *Foreign Affairs* 92, no. 1 (Jan./Feb. 2013).

Huang, Zongxi. *Waiting for the Dawn: A Plan for the Prince*, trans. Wm. Theodore de Bary. New York: Columbia University Press, 1993.

Hulshof, Michiel, and Daan Roggeveen. "Black in China: The New Soft Power Approach." *Chengshi Zhongguo* 63, no. 3 (2014).

———. *How the City Moved to Mr. Sun: China's New Megacities*. Amsterdam: SUN, 2011.

———. "Lekki, the Next African Shenzhen?" *Chengshi Zhongguo: Zhongguoshi zaocheng zai Feizhou* 63, no. 3 (2014).

Hung, Ho-fung. "Confucianism and Political Dissent in China." *East Asia Forum*, 26 July 2011.

———. *Protest with Chinese Characteristics: Demonstrations, Riots, and Petitions in the Mid-Qing Dynasty*. New York: Columbia University Press, 2011.

Huntington, Samuel P. *Political Order in Changing Societies*, new ed. New Haven, Conn.: Yale University Press, 2006.

Ignatieff, Michael. *Fire and Ashes: Success and Failure in Politics*. Cambridge, Mass.: Harvard University Press, 2013.

Imber, Colin. *The Ottoman Empire*, 2nd ed. Houndmills: Palgrave Macmillan, 2009.

Ip, Po-Keung. "Harmony as Happiness? Social Harmony in Two Chinese Societies." *Social Indicators Research*, 117, no. 3 (2014).

Jacques, Martin. "How China Will Change the Global Political Map." Transatlantic Academy, Mar. 2013.

Jiang, Qing. *A Confucian Constitutional Order: How China's Ancient Past Can Shape Its Political Future*, ed. Daniel A. Bell and Fan Ruiping; trans. Edmund Ryden. Princeton, N.J.: Princeton University Press, 2012.

———. "Xianneng zhengzhi de zhidu jiagou: "Rujiao xianzheng" dui minzhuxianzheng de chaoyue yu xina" [The System and Structure of Political Meritocracy: How Confucian Constitutionalism Transcends and Learns from Democratic Politics]. Paper presented at conference "Quanguo zhengzhi ruxue he xiandai shijie taolun" [Political Confucianism and Its Contemporary Significance in China and the World], Tsinghua University, 27–28 Oct. 2012.

Johannsen, Lars, and Karin Hilmer Pedersen. "How to Combat Corruption: Assessing

Anti-Corruption Measures from a Civil Servant's Perspective." *Administrative Culture* 13, no. 2 (2012).

Joppke, Christian. "The Evolution of Alien Rights in the United States, Germany, and the European Union." In *Citizenship Today*, ed. T. Alexander Aleinikoff and Douglas Klusmeyer. Washington, D.C.: Carnegie Endowment for International Peace, 2001.

Kahn, Paul W. *Putting Liberalism in Its Place*. Princeton, N.J.: Princeton University Press, 2005.

Kahneman, Daniel. *Thinking, Fast and Slow*. London: Penguin, 2011.

Kallio, Jyrki. "Tradition in Chinese Politics." In *FIFA Report*. Helsinki: Finnish Institute of International Affairs, 2011.

Kane, John, and Haig Patapan. *The Democratic Leader: How Democracy Defines, Empowers, and Limits Its Leaders*. New York: Oxford University Press, 2012.

Kang, Xiaoguang. *Dangdai Zhongguo dalu: Wenhua minzuzhuyi yundong yanjiu* [Contemporary Mainland China: Research on the Movement of Cultural Nationalism]. Singapore: World Scientific Publishing Co., 2008.

Kant, Immanuel. "Perpetual Peace." In *Kant: Political Writings*, ed. Hans Reiss; trans. H. B. Nisbet. Cambridge: Cambridge University Press, 1991.

Keane, John. *The Life and Death of Democracy*. London: Simon and Schuster, 2009.

Kelly, Jamie Terence. *Framing Democracy: A Behavioral Approach to Democratic Theory*. Princeton, N.J.: Princeton University Press, 2012.

Kett, Joseph F. *Merit: The History of a Founding Ideal from the American Revolution to the 21st Century*. Ithaca, N.Y.: Cornell University Press, 2013.

Keyssar, Alexander. *The Right to Vote: The Contested History of Democracy in the United States*. New York: Basic Books, 2009.

Kidd, David Comer, and Emanuele Castano. "Reading Literary Fiction Improves Theory of Mind." *Science*, 18 Oct. 2013.

Kim, Dae Jung. "Is Culture Destiny? The Myth of Asian's Anti-Democratic Values." *Foreign Affairs* 73, no. 6 (Nov./Dec. 1994).

Kim, Sungmoon. "To Become a Confucian Democratic Citizen: Against Meritocratic Elitism." *British Journal of Political Science* 43, no. 3 (July 2013).

King, Gary, Jennifer Pan, and Margaret E. Roberts. "How Censorship Allows Government Criticism but Silences Collective Expression." *American Political Science Review* 107, no. 10 (May 2013).

Ko, Kilkon, and Cuifen Weng. "Structural Changes in Chinese Corruption." *China Quarterly* 211 (Sept. 2012).

Kuhn, Dieter. *The Age of Confucian Rule: The Song Transformation of China*. Cambridge, Mass.: Harvard University Press, 2009.

Kuhn, Robert L. *How China's Leaders Think: The Inside Story of China's Past, Current and Future Leaders*. Singapore: John Wiley & Sons, 2011.

Kupchan, Charles A. "The Democratic Malaise." *Foreign Affairs* 91, no. 1 (Jan./Feb. 2012).

Kwok, Kian-Woon. "The Social Architect: Goh Keng Swee." In *Lee's Lieutenants: Sin-*

gapore's Old Guard, ed. Peng Er Lam and Kevin Tan. St. Leonards, N.S.W.: Allen & Unwin, 1999.

Lam, Peng Er. "The Voters Speak: Voices, Choices and Implications." In *Voting in Change: Politics of Singapore's 2011 General Election*, ed. Kevin Y. L. Tan and Terence Lee. Singapore: Ethos Books, 2011.

Landry, Pierre F. *Decentralized Authoritarianism in China: The Communist Party's Control of Local Elites in the Post-Mao Era*. Cambridge: Cambridge University Press, 2008.

Laqueur, Walter. "The Weimar Union: Europe, Back to the 30s." *New Republic*, 2 Aug. 2012.

Leboyer, Olivia. *Élite et libéralisme*. Paris: CNRS Éditions, 2012.

Lee, Edwin. *Singapore: The Unexpected Nation*. Singapore: ISEAS, 2008.

Lee, Hsiao-wen. "Public Opinion in China." Policy Paper Series, no. 1, China Studies Center, University of Sydney, Oct. 2012.

Lee, Hsien Loong. "To Listen, Labour and Lead: Building a Better Singapore Together." *Ethos* 12 (June 2013).

Lee, Kuan Yew. *From Third World to First: The Singapore Story, 1965–2000*. New York: Harper, 2000.

Lee, Kuan Yew, and Fareed Zakaria. "Culture Is Destiny: A Conversation with Lee Kuan Yew." *Foreign Affairs* 73, no. 2 (Mar./Apr. 1994).

Leib, Ethan, and He Baogang, eds. *The Search for Deliberative Democracy in China*. New York: Palgrave Macmillan, 2010.

Levine, Ari. *Divided by a Common Language: Factional Conflict in Late Northern Song China*. Honolulu: University of Hawai'i Press, 2008.

Lewis, Michael. *The Big Short*. London: Penguin, 2010.

———. *Boomerang: The Biggest Bust*. London: Penguin, 2011.

Li, Cheng. "The End of the CCP's Resilient Authoritarianism: A Tripartite Assessment of Shifting Power in China." *China Quarterly* 211 (Sept. 2012).

Li, Eric X. "The Life of the Party: The Post-Democratic Future Begins in China." *Foreign Affairs* 92, no. 1 (Jan./Feb. 2013).

———. "Party of the Century: How China Is Reorganizing for the Future." *Foreign Affairs*, 10 Jan. 2014.

Li, Hongbin, and Li-An Zhou. "Political Turnover and Economic Performance: The Incentive Role of Personnel Control in China." *Journal of Public Economics* 89 (2005).

Li, Jin. *Cultural Foundations of Learning: East and West*. Cambridge: Cambridge University Press, 2012.

Li, Yonggang, and Guan Yue. "Difang guanyuan jingzheng de zhengzhi jinbiaosai moxing ji qi youhua" [The Model for Competitive Promotion of Local Officials and Its Optimization]. *Jiangsu xingzheng xueyuanbao* 2, no. 56 (2011).

Liu, Haifeng. "Influence of China's Imperial Examinations on Japan, Korea, and Vietnam." *Frontiers of Philosophy in China* 2, no. 4 (Oct. 2007).

———. "Kejuzhi dui xifang kaoshi zhidu yingxiang xintan" [A New Exploration of the

Influence of the Imperial Examination System on Western Examination Systems]. *Zhongguo shehui kexue* 5 (2001).

Liu, Haifeng. "Kejuzhi yu xianneng zhiguo chuantong" [The Imperial Examination System and the Tradition of Building a Meritocratic State]. Paper presented at conference "Quanguo zhengzhi ruxue he xiandai shijie taolun" [Political Confucianism and Its Contemporary Significance in China and the World], Tsinghua University, 27–28 Oct. 2012.

Liu, Mingxing. *Zhongguo nongcun caizheng tizhi gaige yu jiceng zhili jiegou bianqian* [China's Rural Fiscal System Reform and Structural Change of Local Governance]. Beijing: People's Daily Press, 2013.

Liu, Yawei, et al. *China Elections and Governance Review* 1, no. 1 (Feb. 2009). http://www.cartercenter.org/resources/pdfs/peace/china/CEG-review-issue1.pdf.

Liu, Zehua. "Wangquanzhuyi: Zhongguo sixiang wenhua de lishi dingwei" [Monarchism: A Historical Orientation of Chinese Intellectual Culture]. *Tianjin shehui kexue* 3 (1998).

Louie, K. S. "Village Self-Governance and Democracy in China: An Evaluation." *Democratization* 8, no. 4 (Winter 2001).

Loveband, Anne. "Positioning the Product: Indonesian Migrant Women Workers in Contemporary Taiwan." Working Papers Series, no. 43, City University of Hong Kong, Apr. 2003.

Lui, Adam Yuen-Chung. "Syllabus of the Provincial Examination (Hsiang-shih) under the Early Ch'ing (1644–1795)." *Modern Asian Studies* (Cambridge University Press) 8, no. 3 (1974).

Ma, Jun. "Accountability without Elections." In *China* 3.0, ed. Mark Leonard. London: European Council on Foreign Relations, 2012. http://ecfr.eu/page/-/ECFR66_CHINA_30_final.pdf.

Ma, Jun, and Xing Ni. "Toward a Clean Government in China: Does the Budget Reform Provide a Hope?" *Crime, Law and Social Change* 49, no. 2 (Mar. 2008).

Ma, Liang. "Guanyuan jinsheng jili yu zhengfu jixiao mubiao shezhi: Zhongguo shengji mianban shuju de shizheng yanjiu" [Promotion Incentives of Government Officials and Government Performance Target-Setting: An Empirical Analysis of Provincial Panel Data in China]. *Gonggong guanli xuebao* 10, no. 2 (Apr. 2013).

Ma, Ling. "Daiyizhi dui minzhu de fenjie: Minzhu xuanju, minzhu juece he minzhu jiandu" [An Analysis of Representative Democracy: Democratic Elections, Democratic Decision-Making, and Democratic Supervision]. *Zhanlue yu guanli* 5, no. 6 (2012).

Macedo, Stephen. "Meritocratic Democracy: Learning from the American Constitution." In *The East Asian Challenge for Democracy*, ed. Daniel A. Bell and Chenyang Li. New York: Cambridge University Press, 2013.

Makeham, John. *Lost Soul: "Confucianism" in Contemporary Chinese Academic Discourse*. Cambridge, Mass.: Harvard University Asia Center, 2008.

Manion, Melanie. *Corruption by Design: Building Clean Government in Mainland China and Hong Kong*. Cambridge, Mass.: Harvard University Press, 2004.

Mann, Michael. *The Dark Side of Democracy: Explaining Ethnic Cleansing*. Cambridge: Cambridge University Press, 2005.

Mbiti, John. "'Ancestors' (Ancestral Spirits) as Aspects of African Ontology and Genealogy." Paper presented at the Chinese/African Philosophy Colloquium, Shanghai Jiaotong University, 10–12 May 2013.

McCarthy, Justin. *The Ottoman Turks*. London: Longman, 1997.

McCormick, B. L. "China's Leninist Parliament and Public Sphere: A Comparative Analysis." In *China after Socialism: In the Footsteps of Eastern Europe or East Asia?*, ed. B. L. McCormick and J. Unger. Armonk, N.Y.: M. E. Sharpe, 1996.

McCormick, John P. "Contain the Wealthy and Patrol the Magistrates: Restoring Elite Accountability to Popular Government." *American Political Science Review* 100, no. 2 (May 2006).

———. *Machiavellian Democracy*. Cambridge: Cambridge University Press, 2011.

McGregor, Richard. *The Party: The Secret World of China's Communist Rulers*. London: Penguin, 2010.

Mei, Ciqi. "Bringing the Politics Back In: Political Incentives and Policy Distortion in China." Ph.D dissertation, University of Maryland, College Park, 2009.

Mencius. *Mencius*, vols. 1–2, trans. D. C. Lau. Hong Kong: Chinese University Press, 1984.

Micklethwait, John, and Adrian Wooldridge. *The Fourth Revolution: The Global Race to Reinvent the State*. New York: Penguin, 2014.

Mill, John Stuart. "Considerations on Representative Government" [orig. pub. 1861]. In *Collected Works of John Stuart Mill*, ed. J. M. Robson. Toronto: University of Toronto Press, 1977.

———. "On Liberty." In *Three Essays*. Oxford: Oxford University Press, 1975.

Miller, Richard. "How Does Political Equality Matter? Mencius Meets Walt Whitman." Paper presented at the "Philosophy and Public Policy" Colloquium, Wuhan University, 22–23 Mar. 2014.

Miller, Tom, and Warren Lu. "Better Governance through Kung-Fu." *Gavekal Dragonomics China Research*, 14 Feb. 2014.

Miyazaki, Ichisada. *China's Examination Hell: The Civil Service Examinations of Imperial China*, trans. Conrad Schirokauer. New Haven, Conn.: Yale University Press, 1976.

Mo, Jongryn. "The Challenge of Accountability: Implications of the Censorate." In *Confucianism for the Modern World*, ed. Daniel A. Bell and Hahm Chaibong. Cambridge: Cambridge University Press, 2003.

Mount, Ferdinand. *The New Few, or A Very British Oligarchy: Power and Inequality in Britain Now*. New York: Simon and Schuster, 2012.

Mulgan, Tim. *Ethics for a Broken World: Imagining Philosophy after Catastrophe*. Montreal: McGill–Queen's University Press, 2011.

Mutz, Diana. *Hearing the Other Side: Deliberative versus Participatory Democracy*. Cambridge: Cambridge University Press, 2006.

Nadeau, Jean-Benoît, and Julie Barlow. *Sixty Million Frenchmen Can't Be Wrong (Why We Love France but Not the French)*. Naperville, Ill.: Sourcebooks, 2003.

Nair, Chandran. *Consumptionomics: Asia's Role in Reshaping Capitalism and Saving the Planet*. Oxford: Infinite Ideas Limited, 2011.

Naisbitt, John, and Doris Naisbitt. *China's Megatrends: The 8 Pillars of a New Society*. New York: Harper Business, 2010.

Naudet, Jules. *Entrer dans l'élite: Parcours de réussite en France, aux États-Unis et en Inde* [Entering the Elite: Paths to Success in France, the United States, and India]. Paris: Presses Universitaires de France, 2012.

Naughton, Barry. "China's Distinctive System: Can It Be a Model for Others?" *Journal of Contemporary China* 19, no. 65 (June 2010).

Nisbett, Richard E. *Intelligence and How to Get It: Why Schools and Cultures Count*. New York: Norton, 2009.

Noah, Timothy. *The Great Divergence: America's Growing Inequality Crisis and What We Can Do about It*. New York: Bloomsbury Press, 2012.

Noblo, Michael A., et al. "Who Wants to Deliberate—and Why?" Faculty Research Working Paper Series, Kennedy School, Harvard University, Sept. 2009.

Nussbaum, Martha C. *Not for Profit: Why Democracy Needs the Humanities*. Princeton, N.J.: Princeton University Press, 2010.

O'Brien, Kevin J., and Rongbin Han. "Path to Democracy? Assessing Village Elections in China." *Journal of Contemporary China* 18, no. 60 (June 2009).

O'Brien, Kevin J., and Lianjiang Li. "Accommodating 'Democracy' in a One-Party State: Introducing Village Elections in China." *China Quarterly* 162 (June 2000).

Ober, Josiah. "Democracy's Wisdom: An Aristotelian Middle Way for Collective Judgment." *American Political Science Review* 107, no. 1 (Feb. 2013).

———. *Political Dissent in Democratic Athens: Intellectual Critics of Popular Rule*. Princeton, N.J.: Princeton University Press, 1998.

Organization Department of the CCP Central Committee, ed. *Dang de zuzhi gongzuo wenxian xuanbian* [Collection on the Party's Organizational Work]. Beijing: CCP School Publishing House, 1986.

Ouyang, Jing. "'Guanxi' ruhe, yuanhe yingxiang jiceng guanyuan jinsheng" [How Personal Relations Influence the Promotion of Grassroots Officials in a Differentiated Model Association]. *Gansu xingzheng xueyuan xuebao* 1 (2012).

Pan, Chunyang, He Lixin, and Yuan Congshuai. "Caizheng fenquan yu guanyuan fubai: Jiyu 1999–2007 nian zhongguo shengji mianban shuju de shizheng yanjiu" [Fiscal Decentralization and the Corruption of Cadres: An Empirical Study Based on China's Provincial Data from 1997 to 2007]. *Dangdai caijing* 3, no. 316 (2011).

Pan, Wei. "Western System Versus Chinese System." University of Nottingham, China Policy Institute, Briefing Series, no. 61, July 2010.

———, ed. *Zhongguo moshi: Jiedu renmin gongheguo de 60 nian* [China Model: Explaining Sixty Years of the People's Republic]. Beijing: Zhongyang bianyi chubanshe, 2009.

Pastor, Robert A., and Qingshan Tan. "The Meaning of China's Village Elections." *China Quarterly* 162 (June 2000).

Peerenboom, Randall. *China Modernizes: Threat to the West or Model for the Rest?* Oxford: Oxford University Press, 2008.

Pettit, Philip. "Meritocratic Representation." In *The East Asian Challenge for Democracy: Political Meritocracy in Comparative Perspective*, ed. Daniel A. Bell and Chenyang Li. New York: Cambridge University Press, 2013.

Pieke, Frank N. *The Good Communist: Elite Training and State Building in Today's China*. Cambridge: Cambridge University Press, 2009.

Piketty, Thomas. *Capital in the Twenty-First Century*, trans. Arthur Goldhammer. Cambridge, Mass.: Belknap Press, 2014.

Pines, Yuri. "Between Merit and Pedigree: Evolution of the Concept of 'Elevating the Worthy' in Pre-imperial China." In *The East Asian Challenge for Democracy*, ed. Daniel A. Bell and Chenyang Li. New York: Cambridge University Press, 2013.

———. *The Everlasting Empire: The Political Culture of Ancient China and Its Imperial Legacy*. Princeton, N.J.: Princeton University Press, 2012.

Plato. *The Republic*, trans. Desmond Lee. Harmondsworth: Penguin, 1974.

Poocharoen, Ora-orn, and Alex Brillantes. "Meritocracy in Asia Pacific: Status, Issues, and Challenges." *Review of Public Personnel Administration* 33 (Apr. 2013).

Powell, Jonathan. *The New Machiavelli: How to Wield Power in the Modern World*. London: Vintage Books, 2010.

Pu, Xingzu. "Yi renda minzhu wei zhongdian jixu tuijin Zhongguo minzhu zhengzhi de fazhan" [Continuously Carrying Forward the Development of Democracy Politics in China by Focusing on the National People's Congress]. *Fudan xuebao (shehui kexue)* 5 (2005).

Qian, Mu. *Guoshi xinlun* [New Studies of Chinese History]. Taipei: Dongda Publishing, 2004.

Qiao, Kunyuan. "Wo guo guanyuan jinsheng jinbiaosai jizhi de zai kaocha: Lai zi sheng, shi liang ji zhengfu de zhengju" [A Reexamination of the Mechanism for Competitive Promotion in China: Evidence from Provincial and Municipal Governments]. *Caijing yanjiu* 39, no. 4 (Apr. 2013).

Qiao, Liang. "For Harmony and How Not to Get Promoted: The Downgraded Chinese Regional Leaders." *Journal of Chinese Political Science* 19 (2013).

Qin, Ailing. "Zhongjiwei biange" [Reform of the Central Commission for Discipline Inspection]. *Nanfeng chuang* 4 (13–26 Feb. 2014).

Quah, Jon S. T. *Combating Corruption Singapore-Style: Lessons for Other Asian Countries*. Maryland Series in Contemporary Asian Studies, no. 2. Baltimore: School of Law, University of Maryland, 2007.

Ramo, Joshua Cooper. *The Age of the Unthinkable: Why the New World Disorder Constantly Surprises Us*. New York: Back Bay Books, 2009.

Rawls, John. *A Theory of Justice*. Oxford: Clarendon Press, 1972.

Rejali, Darius. *Torture and Democracy*. Princeton, N.J.: Princeton University Press, 2007.

Ren, Jianming, and Du Zhizhou. "Institutionalized Corruption: Power Overconcentration of the First-in-Command in China." *Crime, Law and Social Change* 49, no. 1 (Feb. 2008).

Ren, Jiantao. "Jiazhi yinni yu zhishi niuqu: Liu meiguo zhengzhixue boshi dui minzhu de juchi" [Hidden Values and Distortion of Knowledge: The Rejection of Democracy by Chinese Scholars Who Have Received Ph.D.s in Political Science in the United States]. *Zhanlue yu guanli* 1 (2012).

Rhode, Deborah L. "Introduction." In *Moral Leadership: The Theory and Practice of Power, Judgment and Policy*. San Francisco: John Wiley & Sons, 2006.

Risse, Mathias. "Arguing for Majority Rule." *Journal of Political Philosophy* 12, no. 1 (2004).

———. *On Global Justice*. Princeton, N.J.: Princeton University Press, 2012.

———. "The Virtuous Group—Foundations for the 'Argument from the Wisdom of the Multitude.'" *Canadian Journal of Philosophy* 31, no. 1 (Mar. 2001).

Rossiter, Clinton. *The American Presidency*, 2nd ed. New York: Time Inc., 1963.

Rothstein, Bo. "Creating Political Legitimacy: Electoral Government Versus Quality of Government." *American Behavioral Scientist* 53 (2009).

Runciman, David. *The Confidence Trap: A History of Democracy in Crisis from World War I to the Present*. Princeton, N.J.: Princeton University Press, 2013.

Sabl, Andrew. *Ruling Passions: Political Offices and Democratic Ethics*. Princeton, N.J.: Princeton University Press, 2002.

Saby, Olivier. *Promotion Ubu roi: Mes 27 mois sur les bancs de l'ENA*. Paris: Flammarion, 2012.

Sagar, Rahul. "Presaging the Moderns: Demosthenes' Critique of Popular Government." *Journal of Politics* 71, no. 4 (Oct. 2009).

Saint Gregory the Great. *The Book of Pastoral Rule*, trans. George E. Demacopoulos. Crestwood, N.Y.: St. Vladimir's Seminary Press, 2007.

Schak, David C. "The Development of Civility in Taiwan." *Pacific Affairs* 82, no. 3 (Fall 2009).

Schmitter, Philippe C. "Reflections on Political Meritocracy: Its Manipulation and Transformation." In *The East Asian Challenge for Democracy*, ed. Daniel A. Bell and Chenyang Li. New York: Cambridge University Press, 2013.

———. "What Is Political Legitimacy and How Can It Be Acquired? Lessons from a Deviant Case." In *Reviving Legitimacy: Lessons for and from China*, ed. Deng Zhenglai and Sujian Guo. Lanham, Md.: Lexington Books, 2011.

Schneider, Henrique. "Legalism: Chinese-Style Constitutionalism?" *Journal of Chinese Philosophy* 38, no. 1 (Mar. 2011).

Schram, Stuart. *Mao Tse-Tung*. London: Simon & Schuster, 1966.

Schubert, Gunter. "Village Elections, Citizenship and Regime Legitimacy in Contemporary Rural China." In *Regime Legitimacy in Contemporary China: Institutional Change and Stability*, ed. Thomas Heberer and Gunter Schubert. London: Routledge, 2009.

Schwab, Klaus, Lee Howell, et al. *Global Risks 2012*, 7th ed. Geneva: World Economic Forum, 2012.

Sen, Amartya. *Democracy as Freedom*. New York: Anchor, 1999.

Shell, Orville. "China: Humiliation and the Olympics." *New York Review of Books*, 14 Aug. 2008.

Shell, Orville, and John Delury. *Wealth and Power: China's Long March to the Twenty-First Century*. London: Little, Brown, 2013.

Sheng, Hong. *Jingjixue jingshen* [The Spirit of Economics]. Guangzhou: Guangdong Jingji, 1999.

Shi, Tianjian. "China: Democratic Values Supporting an Authoritarian System." In *How East Asians View Democracy*, ed. Yun-Han Chu, Larry Diamond, Andrew J. Nathan, and Doh Chull Shin. New York: Columbia University Press, 2008.

———. *The Cultural Logic of Politics in Mainland China and Taiwan*. New York: Cambridge University Press, 2015.

Shi, Tianjian, and Lu Jie. "Cultural Impacts on People's Understanding of Democracy." Paper presented at the 2010 American Political Science Association Annual Meeting, Washington, D.C., 1–5 Sept.

———. "The Shadow of Confucianism." *Journal of Democracy* 21, no. 4 (Oct. 2010).

Shih, Victor, Christopher Adolf, and Mingxing Liu. "Getting Ahead in the Communist Party: Explaining the Advancements of Central Committee Members in China." *American Political Science Review* 106 (Feb. 2012).

Shu, Hede, Yu Minzhong, et al. *Qinding Shengchao Xunjie Zhuchen Lu* [Records of the Royal Officials Who Sacrificed Themselves for the Previous Dynasty]. Shanghai: Shanghai guji chubanshe, 1987.

Shue, Vivienne. "China: Transition Postponed?" *Problems of Communism* 41, nos. 1–2 (Jan.–Apr. 1992).

Sintomer, Yves. *Petite histoire de l'expérimentation démocratique: Tirage au sort et politique d'Athènes à nos jours* [A Short History of Democratic Experimentation: Selection by Lot from Athens to the Present]. Paris: La Découverte, 2011.

Slater, Dan, and Joseph Wong. "The Strength to Concede: Ruling Parties and Democratization in Developmental Asia." *Perspectives on Politics* 11, no. 3 (Sept. 2013).

Slingerland, Edward. *Trying Not to Try: The Art and Science of Spontaneity*. New York: Crown, 2014.

Smith, Richard J. *The I Ching: A Biography*. Princeton, N.J.: Princeton University Press, 2012.

Song, Jaeyoon. "Redefining Good Government: Shifting Paradigms in Song Dynasty (960–1279) Discourse on Fengjian." *T'oung Pao* 97 (2011).

———. "The Zhou Li and Constitutionalism: A Southern Song Political Theory." *Journal of Chinese Philosophy* 36, no. 3 (Sept. 2009).

Sosa, Luis A. "Wages and Other Determinants of Corruption." *Review of Development Economics* 8, no. 4 (Nov. 2004).

Spence, Jonathan D. *Return to Dragon Mountain: Memories of a Late Qing Man*. New York: Penguin, 2007.

Stark, Andrew. "Charting a Democratic Future in China." *Dissent*, Summer 2012.

Stone, Richard. "Climate Talks Still at Impasse, China Buffs Its Green Reputation." *Science*, 15 Oct. 2010.

Su, Yutang, ed. *Guojia gongwuyuan zhidu jianghua* [The Discourse on the State Civil Service System]. Beijing: Labor and Personnel Publishing House, 1989.

Sun, Xin, Travis J. Warner, Dali L. Yang, and Mingxing Liu. "Patterns of Authority and Governance in Rural China: Who's in Charge? Why?" *Journal of Contemporary China* 22, no. 83 (Sept. 2013).

Sun, Yan. "Cadre Recruitment and Corruption: What Goes Wrong?" *Crime, Law and Social Change* 49, no. 1 (Mar. 2008).

———. *Corruption and Market in Contemporary China*. Ithaca, N.Y.: Cornell University Press, 2004.

Sun, Yan, and Michael Johnston. "Does Democracy Check Corruption? Insights from China and India." *Comparative Politics* 42, no. 1 (Oct. 2009).

Sun, Yat-sen. *Prescriptions for Saving China: Selected Writings of Sun Yat-sen*, ed. Julie Lee Wei, Ramon H. Myers, and Donald G. Gillin; trans. Julie Lee Wei, E-su Zen, and Linda Chao. Stanford, Calif.: Hoover Institution Press, 1994.

Sunstein, Cass R. "The Enlarged Republic—Then and Now." *New York Review of Books*, 26 Mar. 2009.

Tan, Eugene K. B. "Re-engaging Chineseness: Political, Economic and Cultural Imperatives of Nation-Building in Singapore." *China Quarterly* 175 (Sept. 2003).

Tan, Fuxian. "Xin xingshi xia jiaqiang ganbu de de kaohe pingjia wenti yanjiu" [Research on Strengthening Moral Evaluation in the Selection of Cadres under New Conditions]. *Xiandai rencai* 6 (2010).

Tan, Kenneth Paul. "Meritocracy and Political Liberalization in Singapore." In *The East Asian Challenge for Democracy*, ed. Daniel A. Bell and Chenyang Li. New York: Cambridge University Press, 2013.

Tan, Kevin Y. L., and Lam Peng Er, eds. *Managing Political Change in Singapore: The Elected Presidency*. London: Routledge, 1997.

Tan, Kevin Y. L., and Terence Lee, eds. *Voting in Change: Politics of Singapore's 2011 General Election*. Singapore: Ethos Books, 2011.

Tan, Sek-loong. "Realizing Political Meritocracy: Lessons from Business." Paper prepared for the Center for International and Comparative Political Philosophy, Tsinghua University, 20 July 2011.

Tang, Wenming. "Cong Rujia zhengjiu minzuzhuyi" [Rescuing Nationalism by Confucianism]. *Wenhua zongheng* 5 (Oct. 2011).

Tang, Zhijun, Xiang Guocheng, and Shen Ying. "Jinsheng jinbiaosai yu difang zhengfu guanyuan fubai wenti de yanjiu" [Research on the Competitive Promotion and the Problem of Corruption of Local Officials]. *Shanghai Jingji Yanjiu* 4 (2013).

Tao, Ran, Lu Xi, Su Fubing, and Wang Hui. "Diqu jingzheng geju yanbian xia de zhongguo zhuangui: Caizheng jili he fazhan moshi fansi" [China's Transition under Evolving Patterns of Regional Competition: Reflections on Financial Incentives and China's Development Model]. *Jingji yanjiu* 7 (2009).

Tetlock, Philip E. *Expert Political Judgment: How Good Is It? How Can We Know?* Princeton, N.J.: Princeton University Press, 2005.

Thomas, M. E. "Confessions of a Sociopath." *Psychology Today*, May/June 2011.

Thomas, Paul. *Performance Measurement, Reporting, Obstacles and Accountability: Recent Trends and Future Directions*. Canberra: ANU E Press, 2006.

Thornton, John L. "The Prospects for Democracy in China." *Foreign Affairs* 87, no. 1 (Jan./Feb. 2008).

Tichy, Noel M., and Stratford Sherman. *Control Your Destiny or Someone Else Will*. New York: Random House, 1994.

Tong, Yanqi. "Morality, Benevolence, and Responsibility: Regime Legitimacy in China from Past to Present." In *Reviving Legitimacy: Lessons for and from China*, ed. Deng Zhenglai and Sujian Guo. Lanham, Md.: Lexington Books, 2011.

Tsai, Lily L. *Accountability without Democracy: Solidary Groups and Public Goods Provision in Rural China*. Cambridge: Cambridge University Press, 2007.

Tsai, Wen-Hsuan, and Nicola Dean. "Experimentation under Hierarchy in Local Conditions: Cases of Political Reform in Guangdong and Sichuan, China." *China Quarterly* 218 (June 2014).

Tsang, Steve. "Consultative Leninism: China's New Political Framework." *Journal of Contemporary China* 18, no. 62 (2009).

UN General Assembly. "The Universal Declaration of Human Rights." 1948. http://www.un.org/en/documents/udhr/.

Vaillant, George E. *Triumphs of Experience: The Men of the Harvard Grant Study*. Cambridge, Mass.: Harvard University Press, 2012.

Waal, Frans de. *The Bonobo and the Atheist: In Search of Humanism among the Primates*. New York: Norton, 2013.

Waldron, Jeremy. "The Core of the Case against Judicial Review." *Yale Law Journal* 115 (2006).

Wang, Alex. "The Search for Sustainable Legitimacy: Environmental Law and Bureaucracy in China," *Harvard Environmental Law Review* 37 (2013).

Wang, Guoliang. "Rujia xianneng zhengzhi sixiang yu Zhongguo xianneng tuiju zhidu de fazhan" [The Political Theory of Confucian Meritocracy and the Development of a Meritocratic Recommendation System in China]. *Wenshizhe* 3, no. 336 (2013).

Wang, Shaoguang. "Is the Way of the Humane Authority a Good Thing? An Assessment of Confucian Constitutionalism." In Jiang Qing, *A Confucian Constitutional Order: How China's Ancient Past Can Shape Its Political Future*, ed. Daniel A. Bell and Ruiping Fan. Princeton, N.J.: Princeton University Press, 2013.

———. *Minzhu si jiang* [Four Lectures about Democracy]. Beijing: Sanlian shudian, 2008.

———. "Why Is State Effectiveness Essential for Democracy? Asian Examples." In *Contemporary Chinese Political Thought: Debates and Perspectives*, ed. Fred Dallmayr and Zhao Tingyang. Lexington: University Press of Kentucky, 2012.

Wang, Shuna, and Yang Yao. "Grassroots Democracy and Local Governance: Evidence from Rural China." *World Development* 35, no. 10 (2007).

Wang, Tao. "Recharging China's Electric Vehicle Policy." Carnegie–Tsinghua Center for Global Policy, 2013. http://carnegieendowment.org/files/china_electric_vehicles.pdf.

Wang, Xiaofang. *The Civil Servant's Notebook*, trans. Eric Abrahamsen. Melbourne: Viking, 2012.

Wang, Zheng. *Never Forget National Humiliation: Historical Memory in Chinese Politics and Foreign Relations*. New York: Columbia University Press, 2012.

Wedeman, Andrew. "Win, Lose, or Draw? China's Quarter Century War on Corruption." *Crime, Law and Social Change* 49, no. 1 (Feb. 2008).

Wei, Xiaohong, and Li Qingyuan. "The Confucian Value of Harmony and Its Influence on Chinese Social Interaction." *Cross-Cultural Communication* 9 (2013).

Whyte, Martin King. "Soaring Income Gaps: China in Comparative Perspective." *Daedalus* 143, no. 2 (Spring 2014).

Wilkinson, Richard G. *The Impact of Inequality: How to Make Sick Societies Healthier*. New York: New Press, 2005.

Wilkinson, Richard G., and Kate Pickett. *The Spirit Level: Why Equal Societies Almost Always Do Better*. London: Allen Lane, 2009.

Wilson, A. N. *Hitler*. New York: Basic Books, 2012.

Wiredu, Kwasi. "Democracy by Consensus: Some Conceptual Considerations." *Philosophical Papers* 30, no. 3 (Nov. 2001).

Wolff, Jonathan, and Avner de-Shalit. *Disadvantage*. Oxford: Oxford University Press, 2007.

Wong, Benjamin. "Political Meritocracy in Singapore: Lessons from the PAP Government." In *The East Asian Challenge for Democracy*, ed. Daniel A. Bell and Chenyang Li. New York: Cambridge University Press, 2013.

Wong, Benjamin, and Xunming Huang. "Political Legitimacy in Singapore." *Politics and Policy* 38, no. 3 (2010).

Wong, R. Bin. "Confucian Agendas for Material and Ideological Control in Modern China." In *Culture and State in Chinese History*, ed. Theodore Huters, R. Bin Wong, and Pauline Yu. Stanford, Calif.: Stanford University Press, 1997.

Woodside, Alexander. *Lost Modernities: China, Vietnam, Korea, and the Hazards of World History*. Cambridge, Mass.: Harvard University Press, 2006.

Wu, Hao, and Wen Tianli. "Zhongguo difang zhengce shiyanshi gaige de youshi yu juxianxing" [The Advantages and Limitations of China's Experimental Reforms with Local Policy]. *Shehui kexue zhanxian* 10 (2012).

Wu, Ji, and Wei Yunheng. "Take Away the 'Iron Armchair,' and Bring Up Good Cadres—Report on the Reform of the Personnel System for Cadres in Liaoning Province." *Liaowang* 24 (11 June 1990).

Wu, Jingzi. *The Scholars*, trans. Yang Xianyi and Gladys Yang. New York: Columbia University Press, 1992.

Wu, Qianwei. "Reorientation and Prospect of China's Combat against Corruption." *Crime, Law and Social Change* 49, no. 2 (Mar. 2008).

Wu, Yinping, and Jiangnan Zu. "Corruption, Anti-corruption, and Inter-county Income Disparity in China." *Social Science Journal* 48 (2011).

Wurster, Stefan. "Comparing Ecological Sustainability in Autocracies and Democracies." *Contemporary Politics* 19, no. 1 (2013).

Xia, Ming. "Innovations in China's Local Governance." In *China: Development and Governance*, ed. Wang Gungwu and Zheng Yongnian. Singapore: World Scientific, 2013.

Xiao, Hong, and Chenyang Li. "China's Meritocratic Examinations and the Ideal of Virtuous Talents." In *The East Asian Challenge for Democracy*, ed. Daniel A. Bell and Chenyang Li. New York: Cambridge University Press, 2013.

Xiao, Jianzhong. "Lingdao ganbu xuanba yu xieshang minzhu" [Cadre Selection and Deliberative Democracy]. *Guancha yu sikao* 4 (2014).

Xinhua News Agency, ed. *People's Republic of China Yearbook*. Beijing: PRC Yearbook Ltd.; Hong Kong: N.C.N. Limited, 1988/89.

Xiong, Victor Cunrui. *Emperor Yang of the Sui Dynasty: His Life, Times, and Legacy*. Albany: State University of New York Press, 2006.

Yan, Cang. "Xinjiapo moshi de xingcheng yu chixu" [The Formation and Continuance of the Singapore Model]. *Wenhua zongheng*, Apr. 2013.

Yan, Huai. *Zhonggong zhengzhi jiegou yu minzhuhua lungang* [The CCP's Political Structure and an Outline for China's Democratization]. Taipei: Mainland Commission of Taiwan's Executive Council, 1991.

Yao, Zhongqiu. "Tian ren zhi ji de zhi dao: Guangchuan Dongzi 'Tian ren san ce' yi shu" [The Way of Governing the Relationship between Heaven and Man: Explanatory Comments on Dong Zhongshu's "Three Answers to Governance between Heaven and Man"]. *Zhengzhi sixiang shi* 3, no. 11 (2012).

Young, Michael. "Introduction to the Transaction Edition." In *The Rise of the Meritocracy*. New Brunswick, N.J.: Transaction, 1994.

———. *The Rise of the Meritocracy*. London: Thames and Hudson, 1958.

Yu, Chilik, Chun-Ming Chen, Lung-Teng Hu, and Wen-Jong Huang. "Evolving Perceptions of Government Integrity and Changing Anticorruption Measures in Taiwan." In *Preventing Corruption in Asia: Institutional Design and Policy Capacity*, ed. Ting Gong and Stephen K. Ma. London: Routledge, 2009.

Yu, Chongsheng. "Cha'e xuanju: Zhongguoshi minzhu de yingran zhi lu" [Multi-Candidate Elections: A Necessary Way for Chinese-Style Democracy]. *Tansuo yu zhengming* 5, no. 271 (2012).

Yu, Keping. *Democracy Is a Good Thing*. Washington, D.C.: Brookings Institution Press, 2009.

Zakaria, Fareed. "Can America Be Fixed? The New Crisis of Democracy." *Foreign Affairs* 92, no. 1 (Jan./Feb. 2013).

Zeng, Jinghan. "Institutionalization of the Authoritarian Leadership in China: A

Power Succession System with Chinese Characteristics?" *Contemporary Politics* 20, no. 3 (2014).

———. "What Matters Most in Selecting Top Chinese Leaders." *Journal of Chinese Political Science* 18 (2013).

Zhang, Jingyi. "Practice-Based Risk Detection." Mimeo, Shanghai Jiaotong University, 2012.

Zhang, Joy Y., and Michael Barr. *Green Politics in China: Environmental Governance and State–Society Relations*. London: Pluto Press, 2013.

Zhang, Lawrence Lok Cheung. "Power for a Price: Office Purchase, Elite Families, and Status Maintenance in Qing China." Ph.D. dissertation, Harvard University, 2010.

Zhang, Lu. "Shichang zhuangui yu fubai moshi de bianqian" [Market Transition and the Changing Forms of Corruption]. *Wenhua zongheng*, June 2013.

Zhang, Shai. "Qiangli kongzhi yu jingshen yueshu: Zhengzhi lunli jiaodu de zhongguo fangfu kunjing yu fangfu lujing" [Controlling by Power and Restraining by Spirit: The Predicament of Preventing Corruption in China and the Way of Preventing Corruption Considered from the Perspective of Political Ethics]. *Lilun yu gaige* 3 (2013).

Zhang, Weiwei. "China's New Political Discourse." *New Perspectives Quarterly*, Fall 2012.

Zhang, Xiaowei. *Elite Dualism and Leadership Selection in China*. London: Routledge/Curzon, 2004.

Zhang, Yongle. *Jiu bang xin zao, 1911–1917* [The Remaking of an Old Country, 1911–1917]. Beijing: Beijing daxue chubanshe, 2011.

———. "Zhongguo de xianneng zhengzhi ji qi minzhu zhengdangxing" [China's Political Meritocracy and Its Democratic Legitimacy]. Comment presented at workshop on democracy and meritocracy, Sungkyunkwan University, Seoul, 30 May 2014.

Zhao, Suisheng. "The China Model: Can It Replace the Western Model of Modernization?" *Journal of Contemporary China* 19, no. 65 (June 2010).

Zhao, Yuezhi. "The Struggle for Socialism in China: The Bo Xilai Saga and Beyond." *Monthly Review* 64, no. 5 (Oct. 2012).

Zheng, Wenhuan. "Difang shidian yu guojia zhengce: Yi xin nongbao wei li" [Local Experimentation and National Policy: Using the Rural Pension Policy as an Example]. *Zhongguo xingzheng guanli* 2 (2013).

Zheng, Yongnian. *The Chinese Communist Party as Organizational Emperor: Culture, Reproduction and Transformation*. London: Routledge, 2010.

Zheng, Yongnian, and Chen Gang. "Intra-Party Democracy in Practice: Balloting for City Leaders in Jiangsu." In *China: Development and Governance*, ed. Wang Gungwu and Zheng Yongnian. Singapore: World Scientific, 2013.

Zhou, Li'an. "Zhongguo difang guanyuan de jinsheng jinbiaosai moshi yanjiu" [Research on Model of Competitive Promotion of Local Chinese Officials]. *Jingji yanjiu* 7 (2007).

Zhou, Qi. "Political Systems, Rights, and Values" [Dialogue with Andrew J. Nathan]. In *Debating China: The U.S.–China Relationship in Ten Conversations*, ed. Nina Hachigan. Oxford: Oxford University Press, 2014.

Zhu, Jiangnan. "Why Are Offices for Sale in China? A Case Study of the Office-Selling Chain in Heilongjiang." *Asian Survey* 48, no. 4 (July/Aug. 2008).

INDEX